Sources of
The Making of the West

PEOPLES AND CULTURES

Volume I: To 1750

Sources of
THE MAKING OF THE WEST

PEOPLES AND CULTURES

Sixth Edition

Volume I: To 1750

KATHARINE J. LUALDI
Southern Maine Community College

bedford/st.martin's
Macmillan Learning

Boston | New York

For Bedford/St. Martin's
Vice President, Editorial, Macmillan Learning Humanities: Edwin Hill
Senior Program Director for History: Michael Rosenberg
Senior Program Manager for History: William J. Lombardo
History Marketing Manager: Melissa Rodriguez
Director of Content Development, Humanities: Jane Knetzger
Developmental Editor: Evelyn Denham
Content Project Manager: Lidia MacDonald-Carr
Senior Workflow Project Manager: Jennifer Wetzel
Production Coordinator: Brianna Lester
Senior Media Project Manager: Michelle Camisa
Media Editor: Tess Fletcher
Manager of Publishing Services: Andrea Cava
Project Management: Lumina Datamatics, Inc.
Composition: Lumina Datamatics, Inc.
Photo Permission Manager: Jennifer MacMillan
Photo Researcher: Bruce Carson
Text Permissions Researcher: Arthur Johnson, Lumina Datamatics, Inc.
Text Permissions Manager: Kalina Ingham
Director of Design, Content Management: Diana Blume
Cover Design: William Boardman
Cover Art: *The Feast of Saint George* (oil on panel), Cleve, Maerten van (1527–81) / Private
    Collection / Photo © Christie's Images / Bridgeman Images
Printing and Binding: LSC Communications

Manufactured in the United States of America.

1 2 3 4 5 6 7   23 22 21 20 19 18

For information, write: Bedford/St. Martin's, 75 Arlington Street, Boston, MA 02116

ISBN 978-1-319-15451-6

Acknowledgments
Text acknowledgments and copyrights appear at the back of the book on pages A-1–A-5, which constitute an extension of the copyright page. Art acknowledgments and copyrights appear on the same page as the art selections they cover.

Preface

Designed to accompany *The Making of the West* and *The Making of the West, Value Edition, Sources of The Making of the West* is intended to help instructors bring the history of Western civilization to life for their students. This thoroughly revised collection parallels the major topics and themes covered in each chapter of *The Making of the West* and offers instructors many opportunities to promote classroom discussion of primary documents and to help students develop essential historical thinking skills. By engaging with primary sources, students will come to see that the study of history is not fixed but is an ongoing process of evaluation and interpretation.

Guided by the textbook's integrated narrative that weaves together social, cultural, political, and economic history, each chapter brings together a variety of source types illuminating historical experience from many perspectives. This edition has been revised to include visual sources as well as a new comparative source feature in every chapter, "Sources in Conversation." I have included more than thirty new sources that both broaden and deepen coverage. With new documents covering perspectives from Eastern Europe and the Middle East, a new emphasis on geographic and quantitative sources, and new selections by essential authors from Cicero and Dante to Wollstonecraft and Fanon, this edition provides sources for instructors to consider the history of the West from within and without.

To assist students with their journey into the past, each chapter opens with a summary that situates the sources within the broader historical context and addresses their relationship to one another and to the main themes in the corresponding chapter of *The Making of the West*, Sixth Edition. An explanatory headnote accompanies each source to provide fundamental context on the author or creator and the source while highlighting its historical significance. Revised and expanded discussion questions guide students through evaluating the sources, considering questions of context and audience, and engaging with scholarly arguments. Each chapter concludes with a set of comparative questions intended to encourage students both to see how sources can inform and challenge each other and to prompt them to make historical connections. These editorial features intentionally strengthen the coherence of each chapter as a unit while allowing instructors to choose sources and questions that best suit their specific goals and methods. Within each chapter, the documents also were selected based on their accessibility, depth in content, and appeal to students. For this reason, when necessary, I have carefully edited documents to speak to specific themes without impairing the documents' overall sense and tone. I have also included documents of varying lengths to increase their utility for both short class exercises and outside writing assignments.

Of course, asking the right questions and finding the right answers is at the heart of "doing" history. For this reason, *Sources of The Making of the West*, Sixth Edition, begins with an introduction on how to interpret written and visual primary sources that leads students step-by-step through the process of historical analysis. A brief overview of what this process entails is followed by an extended discussion of the process at work in the analysis of two sources drawn specifically from this collection. I adopted this approach for the Introduction to help students move easily from abstract concepts to concrete examples. As a result, the Introduction does not rely on telling students what to do but rather on showing them how to do it for themselves based on the raw data of history.

New to This Edition

In response to instructors' comments and recommendations, as well as new scholarship, I have made several changes for the sixth edition. This edition contains over thirty new written and visual sources that complement the thematic and chronological framework of the textbook and highlight the intellectual, emotional, and visual landscapes of many different peoples and places. These sources have been selected to reflect an expanded understanding of the West that allows us to consider key cultural, social, political, economic, and intellectual developments in a new light and within broader contexts. To that end, each chapter contains both visual sources and a "Sources in Conversation" comparative source set. These paired sources deepen the interpretive possibilities of the individual sources while providing students more opportunities to develop their historical thinking skills. The digital version of this collection, available in LaunchPad, goes even further with assignable auto-graded multiple-choice questions to accompany each source.

In this edition, I have incorporated a wider variety of source types, including more quantitative and visual sources, while focusing on themes that carry across historical time periods. Students will examine historical responses to inequality by analyzing records of an ancient Greek auction of confiscated slaves, excerpts from the city of Norwich Poor Rolls of 1570, and graphs that capture the current distribution of global wealth. They will engage with different conceptions of world geography, ranging from the thirteenth-century Hereford map to the nineteenth-century Imperial Federation map of the British Empire. I ask students to consider how communities define themselves through new sources, including a Greek Janiform flask, a Levantine Torah niche, and a popular eighteenth-century ceramic motif, as well as excerpts from Cicero's *In Defense of Archias*, Hume's *Of National Characters*, and Fanon's *The Wretched of the Earth*. Other new sources ground history in the lives of everyday people, including a Roman household shrine, a medieval Labors of the Month sculpture, a portrait of a family at tea, and a firsthand account of Soviet collectivization. Finally, I invite students to reflect on how we remember and memorialize history with Picasso's *Guernica*, photographer Nick Ut's memory of capturing a famous Vietnam photo, and Bosnian artist Aida Sehovic's interactive memorial to the Serebrenica genocide.

Acknowledgments

Many people deserve thanks for helping to bring this sixth edition to fruition. First among them are the authors of *The Making of the West*: Lynn Hunt, Thomas R. Martin, Barbara H. Rosenwein, and Bonnie G. Smith. Many thanks as well to reviewers of the previous edition who provided valuable insights and suggestions: Jean Berger, University of Wisconsin, Fox Valley; Edwin Bezzina, Grenfell Campus Memorial University; Dorothea Browder, Western Kentucky University; Eric Cimino, Molloy College; Courtney Doucette, Rutgers University; Valeria L. Garver, Northern Illinois University; Michael McGregor, Northern Virginia Community College; Jennifer M. Morris, College of Mount St. Joseph; Jason E. St. Pierre, University of Massachusetts, Lowell; Sarah L. Sullivan, McHenry County College; Paul Teverow, Missouri Southern State University; Leigh Ann Whaley, Acadia University; David K. White, McHenry County College; and Corinne Wieben, University of Northern Colorado.

I would also like to thank Anne Thayer, Jeannine Uzzi, Nancy Artz, and Helen Evans for their expertise and editorial assistance with sources as well as the team at Bedford/St. Martin's: Michael Rosenberg, Bill Lombardo, Leah Strauss, Evelyn Denham, Belinda Huang, Emily Brower, and Lidia MacDonald-Carr.

Contents

Introduction: Working with Historical Sources

The long history of Western civilization encompasses a broad range of places and cultures. Textbooks provide an essential chronological and thematic framework for understanding the formation of the West as a cultural and geographical entity. Yet the process of historical inquiry extends beyond textbook narratives into the thoughts, words, images, and experiences of people living at the time. Primary sources expose this world so that you can observe, analyze, and interpret the past as it unfolds before you. History is thus not a static collection of facts and dates. Rather, it is an ongoing attempt to make sense of the past and its relationship to the present through the lens of both written and visual primary sources.

Sources of The Making of the West, Sixth Edition, provides this lens for you, with a wide range of engaging sources—from Egyptian tomb art to an engraving of a London coffee-house to firsthand accounts of student revolts. When combined, the sources reflect historians' growing appreciation of the need to examine Western civilization from different conceptual angles—political, social, cultural, and economic—and geographic viewpoints. The composite picture that emerges reveals a variety of historical experiences shaping each era from both within and outside Europe's borders. Furthermore, the documents here demonstrate that the most historically significant of these experiences are not always those of people in formal positions of power. Men and women from all walks of life have also influenced the course of Western history.

The sources in this reader were selected with an eye toward their ability not only to capture the multifaceted dimensions of the past but also to ignite your intellectual curiosity. Each written and visual source is a unique product of human endeavor and as such is often colored by the personal concerns, biases, and objectives of the author or creator. Among the most exciting challenges facing you is to sift through these nuances to discover what they reveal about the source and its broader historical context.

Interpreting Written Sources

Understanding a written document and its connection to larger historical issues depends on knowing which questions to ask and how to find the answers. The following six questions will guide you through this process of discovery. Like a detective, you will begin by piecing together basic facts and then move on to more complex levels of analysis, which usually requires reading any given source more than once. You should keep these questions in mind every time you read a document, no matter how long or how short, to help you uncover its meaning and significance. As you practice actively reading these texts and thinking critically about them, you will improve your ability to read and think like a historian. Soon enough, you will be asking your own questions and conducting your own historical analysis.

1. Who wrote this document, when, and where?

The "doing" of history depends on historical records, the existence of which in turn depends on the individuals who composed them in a particular time and place and with specific goals in mind. Therefore, before you can begin to understand a document and its significance, you need to determine who wrote it and when and where it was written. Ultimately, this information will shape your interpretation because the language of documents often reflects the author's social and/or political status as well as the norms of the society in which the author lived.

2. What type of document is this?

Because all genres have their own defining characteristics, identifying the type of document at hand is vital to elucidating its purpose and meaning. For example, in content and organization, an account of a saint's life looks very different from an imperial edict, which in turn looks very different from a trial record. Each document type follows certain rules of composition that shape what authors say and how they say it.

3. Who is the intended audience of the document?

The type of source often goes hand in hand with the intended audience. For example, popular songs in the vernacular are designed to reach people across the socioeconomic spectrum, whereas papal bulls written in Latin are directed to a tiny, educated, and predominantly male elite. Moreover, an author often crafts the style and content of a document to appeal to a particular audience and to enhance the effectiveness of his or her message.

4. What are the main points of this document?

All primary sources contain stories, whether in numbers, words, and/or images. Before you can begin to analyze their meanings, you need to have a good command of a document's main points. For this reason, while reading, you should mark words, phrases, and passages that strike you as particularly important to create visual and mental markers that will help you navigate the document. Don't worry about mastering all of the details; you can work through them later once you have sketched out the basic content.

5. Why was this document written?

The simplicity of this question masks the complexity of the possible answers. Historical records are never created in a vacuum; they were produced for a reason, whether public or private, pragmatic or fanciful. Some sources will state outright why they were created, whereas others will not. Yet, with or without direct cues, you should look for less obvious signs of the author's intent and rhetorical strategies as reflected in word choice, for example, or the way in which a point is communicated.

6. What does this document reveal about the particular society and period in question?

This question strikes at the heart of historical analysis and interpretation. In its use of language, its structure, and its biases and assumptions, every source opens a window into its author and time period. Teasing out its deeper significance will allow you to assess the value of a source and to articulate what it adds to our understanding of the historical context in which it is embedded. Thus, as you begin to analyze a source fully, your own interpretive voice will assume center stage.

As you work through each of these questions, you will progress from identifying the basic content of a document to inferring its broader meanings. At its very heart, the study of primary sources centers on the interplay between "facts" and interpretation. To help you engage in this interplay, let us take a concrete example of a historical document. Read it carefully, guided by the questions outlined above. In this way, you will gain insight into this particular text while training yourself in interpreting written primary sources in general.

1. Legislating Tolerance

Henry IV, *Edict of Nantes* (1598)

The promulgation of the Edict of Nantes in 1598 by King Henry IV (r. 1589–1610) marked the end of the French Wars of Religion by recognizing French Protestants as a legally protected religious minority. Drawing largely on earlier edicts of pacification, the Edict of Nantes was composed of ninety-two general articles, fifty-six secret articles, and two royal warrants. The two series of articles represented the edict proper and were registered by the highest courts of law in the realm (parlements). The following excerpts from the general articles reveal the triumph of political concerns over religious conformity on the one hand and the limitations of religious tolerance in early modern France on the other.

Henry, by the grace of God, King of France, and Navarre, to all present, and to come, greeting. Among the infinite mercies that it has pleased God to bestow upon us, that most signal and remarkable is, his having given us power and strength not to yield to the dreadful troubles, confusions, and disorders, which were found at our coming to this kingdom, divided into so many parties and factions, that the most legitimate was almost the least, enabling us with constancy in such manner to oppose the storm, as in the end to surmount it, now reaching a part of safety and repose for this state. . . . For the general difference among our

---

Modernized English text adapted from Edmund Everard, *The Great Pressures and Grievances of the Protestants in France* (London, 1681), 1–5, 10, 14, 16.

good subjects, and the particular evils of the soundest parts of the state, we judged might be easily cured, after the principal cause (the continuation of civil war) was taken away. In which having, by the blessing of God, well and happily succeeded, all hostility and wars through the kingdom being now ceased, we hope that we will succeed equally well in other matters remaining to be settled, and that by this means we shall arrive at the establishment of a good peace, with tranquility and rest. . . . Among our said affairs . . . one of the principal has been the complaints we have received from many of our Catholic provinces and cities, that the exercise of the Catholic religion was not universally re-established, as is provided by edicts or statutes heretofore made for the pacification of the troubles arising from religion; as well as the supplications and remonstrances which have been made to us by our subjects of the Reformed religion, regarding both the non-fulfillment of what has been granted by the said former laws, and that which they desired to be added for the exercise of their religion, the liberty of their consciences and the security of their persons and fortunes; presuming to have just reasons for desiring some enlargement of articles, as not being without great apprehensions, because their ruin has been the principal pretext and original foundation of the late wars, troubles, and commotions. Now not to burden us with too much business at once, as also that the fury of war was not compatible with the establishment of laws, however good they might be, we have hitherto deferred from time to time giving remedy herein. But now that it has pleased God to give us a beginning of enjoying some rest, we think we cannot employ ourself better than to apply to that which may tend to the glory and service of His holy name, and to provide that He may be adored and prayed unto by all our subjects: and if it has not yet pleased Him to permit it to be in one and the same form of religion, that it may at the least be with one and the same intention, and with such rules that may prevent among them all troubles and tumults. . . . For this cause, we have upon the whole judged it necessary to give to all our said subjects one general law, clear, pure, and absolute, by which they shall be regulated in all differences which have heretofore risen among them, or may hereafter rise, wherewith the one and other may be contented, being framed according as the time requires: and having had no other regard in this deliberation than solely the zeal we have to the service of God, praying that He would from this time forward render to all our subjects a durable and established peace. . . . We have by this edict or statute perpetual and irrevocable said, declared, and ordained, saying, declaring, and ordaining;

That the memory of all things passed on the one part and the other, since the beginning of the month of March 1585 until our coming to the crown, and also during the other preceding troubles, and the occasion of the same, shall remain extinguished and suppressed, as things that had never been. . . .

We prohibit to all our subjects of whatever state and condition they be, to renew the memory thereof, to attack, resent, injure, or provoke one another by reproaches for what is past, under any pretext or cause whatsoever, by disputing, contesting, quarrelling, reviling, or offending by factious words; but to contain themselves, and live peaceably together as brethren, friends, and fellow-citizens, upon penalty for acting to the contrary, to be punished for breakers of peace, and disturbers of the public quiet.

We ordain, that the Catholic religion shall be restored and re-established in all places, and quarters of this kingdom and country under our obedience, and where the exercise of the same has been interrupted, to be there again, peaceably and freely exercised without any trouble or impediment. . . .

And not to leave any occasion of trouble and difference among our subjects, we have permitted and do permit to those of the Reformed religion, to live and dwell in all the cities and places of this our kingdom and countries under our obedience, without being inquired after, vexed, molested, or compelled to do any thing in religion, contrary to their conscience. . . .

We permit also to those of the said religion to hold, and continue the exercise of the same in all the cities and places under our obedience, where it was by them established and made public at several different times, in the year 1586, and in 1597.

In like manner the said exercise may be established, and re-established in all the cities and places where it has been established or ought to be by the Statute of Pacification, made in the year 1577. . . .

We prohibit most expressly to all those of the said religion, to hold any exercise of it . . . except in places permitted and granted in the present edict. As also not to exercise the said religion in our court, nor in our territories and countries beyond the mountains, nor in our city of Paris, nor within five leagues of the said city. . . .

We prohibit all preachers, readers, and others who speak in public, to use any words, discourse, or propositions tending to excite the people to sedition; and we enjoin them to contain and comport themselves modestly, and to say nothing which shall not be for the instruction and edification of the listeners, and maintaining the peace and tranquility established by us in our said kingdom. . . .

They [French Protestants] shall also be obliged to keep and observe the festivals of the Catholic Church, and shall not on the same days work, sell, or keep open shop, nor likewise the artisans shall not work out of their shops, in their chambers or houses privately on the said festivals, and other days forbidden, of any trade, the noise whereof may be heard outside by those that pass by, or by the neighbors. . . .

We ordain, that there shall not be made any difference or distinction upon the account of the said religion, in receiving scholars to be instructed in the universities, colleges, or schools, nor of the sick or poor into hospitals, sick houses or public almshouses. . . .

We will and ordain, that all those of the Reformed religion, and others who have followed their party, of whatever state, quality or condition they be, shall be obliged and constrained by all due and reasonable ways, and under the penalties contained in the said edict or statute relating thereunto, to pay tithes to the curates, and other ecclesiastics, and to all others to whom they shall appertain. . . .

To the end to re-unite so much the better the minds and good will of our subjects, as is our intention, and to take away all complaints for the future; we declare all those who make or shall make profession of the said Reformed religion, to be capable of holding and exercising all estates, dignities, offices, and public charges whatsoever. . . .

We declare all sentences, judgments, procedures, seizures, sales, and decrees made and given against those of the Reformed religion, as well living as dead, from the death of the deceased King Henry the Second our most honored Lord and father in law, upon the occasion of the said religion, tumults and troubles since happening, as also the execution of the same judgments and decrees, from henceforward canceled, revoked, and annulled. . . .

Those also of the said religion shall depart and desist henceforward from all practices, negotiations, and intelligences, as well within or without our kingdom; and the said assemblies and councils established within the provinces, shall readily separate, and also all the leagues and associations made or to be made under any pretext, to the prejudice of our present edict, shall be cancelled and annulled, . . . prohibiting most expressly to all our subjects to make henceforth any assessments or levies of money, fortifications, enrollments of men, congregations and assemblies of other than such as are permitted by our present edict, and without arms. . . .

We give in command to the people of our said courts of parlement, chambers of our courts, and courts of our aids, bailiffs, chief-justices, provosts and other of our justices and officers to whom it appertains, and to their lieutenants, that they cause to be read, published, and registered this present edict and ordinance in their courts and jurisdictions, and the same keep punctually, and the contents of the same to cause to be enjoined and used fully and peaceably to all those to whom it shall belong, ceasing and making to cease all troubles and obstructions to the contrary, for such is our pleasure: and in witness hereof we have signed these presents with our own hand; and to the end to make it a thing firm and stable for ever, we have caused to put and endorse our seal to the same. Given at *Nantes* in the month of April in the year of Grace 1598, and of our reign the ninth.

Signed

HENRY

1. Who wrote this document, when, and where?

Many documents will not answer these questions directly; therefore, you will have to look elsewhere for clues. In this case, however, the internal evidence is clear. The author is Henry IV, king of France and Navarre, who issued the document in the French town of Nantes in 1598. Aside from the appearance of his name in the edict, there are other, less explicit markers of his identity. He uses the first-person plural ("we") when referring to himself, a grammatical choice that both signals and accentuates his royal stature.

2. What type of document is this?

In this source, you do not have to look far for an answer to this question. Henry IV describes the document as an "edict," "statute," or "law." These words reveal the public and official nature of the document, echoing their use in our own society today. Even if you do not know exactly what an edict, statute, or law meant in late sixteenth-century terms, the document itself points the way: "we [Henry IV] have upon the whole, judged it necessary to give to all our subjects one general law, clear, pure, and absolute. . . ." Now you know that the document is a body of law issued by King Henry IV in 1598, which helps to explain its formality as well as the predominance of legal language.

3. Who is the intended audience of the document?

The formal and legalistic language of the edict suggests that Henry IV's immediate audience is not the general public but rather some form of political and/or legal body.

The final paragraph supports this conclusion. Here Henry IV commands the "people of our said courts of parlement, chambers of our courts, and courts of our aids, bailiffs, chief-justices, provosts, and other of our justices and officers . . ." to read and publish the edict. Reading between the lines, you can detect a mixture of power and dependency in Henry IV's tone. Look carefully at his verb choices throughout the edict: *prohibit, ordain, will, declare, command.* Each of these verbs casts Henry IV as the leader and the audience as his followers. This strategy was essential because the edict would be nothing but empty words without the courts' compliance. Imagine for a moment that Henry IV was not the king of France but rather a soldier writing a letter to his wife or a merchant preparing a contract. In either case, the language chosen would have changed to suit the genre and audience. Thus, identifying the relationship between author and audience can help you to understand what the document both does and does not say.

4. What are the main points of this document?

To answer this question, you should start with the preamble, for it explains why the edict was issued in the first place: to replace the "frightful troubles, confusions, and disorders" in France with "one general law . . . by which they [our subjects] might be regulated in all differences which have heretofore risen among them, or may hereafter rise. . . ." But what differences specifically? Even with no knowledge of the circumstances surrounding the formulation of the edict, you should notice the numerous references to "the Catholic religion" and "the Reformed religion." With this in mind, read the preamble again. Here we learn that Henry IV had received complaints from Catholic provinces and cities and from Protestants ("our subjects of the Reformed religion") regarding the exercise of their respective religions. Furthermore, as the text continues, since "it has pleased God to give us a beginning of enjoying some rest, we think we cannot employ ourself better than to apply to that which may tend to the glory and service of His holy name, and to provide that He may be adored and prayed unto by all our said subjects, and if it has not yet pleased Him to permit it to be in one and the same form of religion, that it may be at the least with one and the same intention, and with such rules that may prevent among them all troubles and tumults. . . ." Now the details of the document fall into place. Each of the articles addresses specific "rules" governing the legal rights and obligations of French Catholics and Protestants, ranging from where they can worship to where they can work.

5. Why was this document written?

As we have already seen, Henry IV relied on the written word to convey information and, at the same time, to express his "power" and "strength." The legalistic and formal nature of the edict aided him in this effort. Yet, as Henry IV knew all too well, the gap between law and action could be large indeed. Thus, Henry IV compiled the edict not simply to tell people what to do but to persuade them to do it by delineating the terms of religious coexistence point by point and presenting them as the best safeguard against the return of confusion and disorder. He thereby hoped to restore peace to a country that had been divided by civil war for the previous thirty-six years.

6. What does this document reveal about the particular society and period in question?

Historians have mined the Edict of Nantes for insight into various facets of Henry IV's reign and Protestant–Catholic relations at the time. Do not be daunted by such complexity; you should focus instead on what you see as particularly predominant and revealing themes. One of the most striking in the Edict of Nantes is the central place of religion in late sixteenth-century society. Our contemporary notion of the separation of church and state had no place in the world of Henry IV and his subjects. As he proclaims in the opening lines, he was king "by the Grace of God" who had given him "virtue" and "strength." Furthermore, you might stop to consider why religious differences were the subject of royal legislation in the first place. Note Henry IV's statement that "if it has not yet pleased Him [God] to permit [Christian worship in France] to be in one and the same form of religion, that it may at the least be with one and the same intention. . . ." What does this suggest about sixteenth-century attitudes toward religious difference and tolerance? You cannot answer this question simply by reading the document in black-and-white terms; you need to look beyond the words and between the lines to draw out the document's broader meanings.

Interpreting Visual Sources

Historians do not rely on written records alone to reconstruct the past; they also turn to nonwritten sources, which are equally varied and rich. Nonwritten sources range from archaeological and material sources to sculpture, paintings, and photographs. This book includes a range of visual representations to enliven your view of history while enhancing your interpretive skills. Interpreting a visual document is very much like interpreting a nonvisual one — you begin with six questions similar to the ones you have already applied to a written source and move from ascertaining the "facts" of the document to a more complex analysis of the visual document's historical meanings and value.

1. Who created this image, when, and where?

Just as with written sources, identifying the artist or creator of an image and when and where it was produced will provide a foundation for your interpretation. Some visual sources, such as a painting or political cartoon signed by the artist, are more forthcoming in this regard. But if the artist is not known (and even if he or she is), there are other paths of inquiry to pursue. Did someone commission the production of the image? What was the historical context in which the image was produced? Piecing together what you know on these two fronts will allow you to draw some basic conclusions about the image.

2. What type of image is this?

The nature of a visual source shapes its form and content because every visual genre has its own conventions. Take a map as an example. At the most basic level, maps are composites of images created to convey topographical and geographical information about a particular place, whether a town, a region, or a continent. Think about how you use maps in your own life. Sometimes they can be fanciful in their designs, but typically they have a practical function — to enable the viewer to get from one place to another or at the very least to get a sense of an area's spatial characteristics. A formal portrait, by contrast, would conform to a different set of conventions and, of equal significance, a different set of viewer expectations and uses.

3. Who are the intended viewers of the image?

As with written sources, identifying the relationship between the image's creator and audience is essential to illuminate fully what the artist is trying to convey. Was the image intended for the general public, such as a photograph published in a newspaper? Or was the intended audience more private? Whether public, private, or somewhere in between, the creator's target audience shapes his or her choice of subject matter, format, and style, which in turn should shape your interpretation of its meaning and significance.

4. What is the central message of the image?

Images convey messages just as powerfully as the written word. The challenge is to learn how to "read" pictorial representations accurately. Since artists use images, color, and space to communicate with their audiences, you must train your eyes to look for visual rather than verbal cues. A good place to start is to note the image's main features, followed by a closer examination of its specific details and their interrelationship.

5. Why was this image produced?

Images are produced for a range of reasons — to convey information, to entertain, or to persuade, to name just a few. Understanding the motivations underlying an image's creation is key to unraveling its meaning (or at least what it was supposed to mean) to people at the time. For example, the impressionist painters of the nineteenth century did not paint simply to paint — their style and subject matter intentionally challenged contemporary artistic norms and conventions. Without knowing this, you cannot appreciate the broader context and impact of impressionist art.

6. What does this image reveal about the society and time period in which it was created?

Answering the first five questions will guide your answer here. Identifying the artist, the type of image, and when, where, and for whom it was produced allows you to step beyond a literal reading of the image into the historical setting in which it was produced. Although the meaning of an image can transcend its historical context, its point of origin and intended audience cannot. Therein rests an image's broader value as a window onto the past, for it is a product of human activity in a specific time and place, just like written documents.

Guided by these six questions, you can evaluate visual sources on their own terms and analyze the ways in which they speak to the broader historical context. Once again, let's take an example.

2. Illustrating an Indigenous Perspective

Lienzo de Tlaxcala (c. 1560)

Like Bernal Díaz del Castillo, the peoples of central Mexico had a stake in recording the momentous events unfolding around them, for they had long believed that remembering the past was essential to their cultural survival. Traditionally, local peoples used pictoriographic representations to record legends, myths, and historical events. After the Spaniards' arrival, indigenous artists borrowed from this tradition to produce their own accounts of the conquest, including the image below. It is one of a series contained in the Lienzo de Tlaxcala, *painted on cloth in the mid-sixteenth century. Apparently, the* Lienzo *was created for the Spanish viceroy to commemorate the alliance of the Tlaxcalans with the Spaniards. The Tlaxcalans were enemies of the Aztecs and after initial resistance to the Spanish invasion decided to join their forces. This particular image depicts two related events. The first is the meeting between the Aztec leader Moctezuma and Hernán Cortés in Tenochtitlán in August 1519. Cortés is accompanied by Doña Marina, his translator and cultural mediator; Moctezuma appears with warriors at his side. Rather than showing Moctezuma in his traditional garb, the artist dressed him in the manner of the Tlaxcalans. Both sit in European-style chairs, a nod to European artistic influence, and a Tlaxcalan headdress is suspended in*

The British Library, London, UK / Bridgeman Images

the air between them. Game and fowl offered to the Spaniards are portrayed at the bottom.
Within a week of this meeting, Cortés imprisoned Moctezuma in his own palaces with the
Tlaxcalans' help. Moctezuma the prisoner appears in the upper right of the image as an old,
weak ruler whose sun has set.

1. Who created this image, when, and where?

In this case, you will have to rely on the headnote to answer these questions. The image was
created by an unknown Tlaxcalan artist in the mid-sixteenth century as part of a pictorial
series, the *Lienzo de Tlaxcala,* depicting the Spanish conquest of Aztec Mexico. Although
the image commemorates events that took place in 1519, it was produced decades later,
when Spanish imperial control was firmly entrenched. Thus, the image represents a visual
point of contact between Spanish and indigenous traditions in the age of European global
expansion. Although knowing the identity of the artist would be ideal, the fact that he was
Tlaxcalan is of greater value. The Tlaxcalans had allied themselves with the Spanish and
considered the *Lienzo* a way of highlighting their role in the Aztecs' defeat.

2. What type of image is this?

On the one hand, this image fits into a long pictorial tradition among the peoples of central Mexico. Before the conquest, they had no alphabetic script. Instead, they drew on a
rich repertoire of images and symbols to preserve legends, myths, and historical events.
These images and symbols, which included the stylized warriors shown here, were typically painted into books made of deerskin or a plant-based paper. On the other hand,
the image also reveals clear European influences, most noticeably in the type of chair
in which both Cortés and Moctezuma sit. Looking at the image again with these dual
influences in mind, think about how the pictorial markers allowed both indigenous and
Spanish viewers to see something recognizable in an event that marked the destruction of
one world and the creation of another.

3. Who are the intended viewers of the image?

As the headnote reveals, the image's creator had a specific audience in mind, a Spanish colonial administrator. You should take this fact into account as you think about the
image's meaning and significance. Just because a Tlaxcalan artist created the image does
not necessarily mean that it represents an unadulterated native point of view. And just
because the image documents two historical events does not necessarily mean that the
"facts" are objectively presented.

4. What is the central message of the image?

There are many visual components of this image, each of which you should consider
individually and then as part of the picture as a whole. As you already know, the artist
combined indigenous and European representational traditions. What does this suggest

about the image's message? The merging of these two traditions represents the alliance the Tlaxcalans forged with the Spanish. Looking closer, think about how the two leaders, Cortés and Moctezuma, are represented. Cortés is accompanied by his translator, Doña Marina, a Nahua woman. Originally a slave, she had been given to Cortés after his defeat of the Maya at Potonchan. She became a crucial interpreter and cultural mediator for Cortés in the world of the Mexica. Language appears here as a source of his power as well as his alliance with the Tlaxcalans. Although the Spanish contingent was relatively small, thousands of Tlaxcalan and other native warriors entered Tenochtitlán with them, a show of force not lost on local residents. The artist captures this fact by clothing Moctezuma in Tlaxcalan dress — he had once ruled over them, but now he was to be ruled. Soon after this meeting, Moctezuma was imprisoned in his own palaces. The artist captures this event in the upper right, where Moctezuma is shown as a prisoner.

5. Why was this image produced?

Examining this image reveals the complexity of this question, regardless of the nature of the source. At first glance, the answer is easy: the image was created to commemorate specific events. Yet given what you know about the setting in which the image was produced, the "why" takes on a deeper meaning. The image does not simply record events; it sets a scene in which multiple meanings are embedded — the chairs, Doña Marina, the warriors — that suggest how the Spanish conquest transformed native culture. The image thus served a dual function — to inform the Spanish of the Tlaxcalans' role in the conquest while affirming Spanish dominance over them.

6. What does this image reveal about the society and time period in which it was created?

Answering this question requires you to step beyond a literal meaning of the image into the historical setting in which it was produced. Here you will uncover multiple layers of the image's broader significance. Consider the artist, for example, and his audience. What does the fact that a native artist created the image for a Spanish audience suggest about the nature of Spanish colonization? Clearly, the Spaniards did not make their presence felt as a colonial power simply by seizing land and treasure; they also reshaped indigenous people's understanding of themselves in both the past and the present. That the Tlaxcalans expressed this understanding visually in a historical document lent an air of permanence and legitimacy to Spanish colonization and, equally important, to the Tlaxcalans' contributions to it.

Conclusion

Through your analysis of historical sources, you will not only learn details about the world in which the sources were created but also become an active contributor to our understanding of these details' broader significance. Written documents and visual and material sources don't just "tell" historians what happened; they require historians to step into their own imaginations as they strive to understand the past. In this regard, historians' approach to primary sources is exactly that which is described here. They determine the basics of the source — who created it, when, and where — as a springboard for increasingly complex levels of analysis. Each level builds upon the other, just like rungs on a ladder. If you take the time to climb each rung in sequence, you will be able to master the content of a source and to use it to make your own historical arguments. The written and visual primary sources included in *Sources of The Making of the West*, Sixth Edition, will allow you to participate firsthand in the process of historical inquiry by exploring the people, places, and sights of the past and how they shaped their own world and continue to shape ours today.

Early Western Civilization
4000–1000 B.C.E.

T he roots of Western culture cut across distant lands and ancient societies. The six
documents in this chapter expose the fundamental features of these early civilizations
as they developed between the twentieth and tenth centuries B.C.E. The evidence reveals
that, on the one hand, peoples then living in the Near East, Africa, and the Mediterranean
developed their own distinctive beliefs, mythologies, customs, and sense of identity. On
the other, they shared many attributes, such as large urban populations, the use of writing, devotion to religion, and economies based on trade and agriculture. This unique
mixture of cross-cultural similarities and differences forged the path for the future.

1. Defining Humanity

Epic of Gilgamesh (c. 2000 B.C.E.)

*Invented by the Sumerians in Mesopotamia around 3500 B.C.E., writing was one of the
most important products of civilization. People could now record and preserve traditions
and beliefs without having to rely exclusively on memory and the spoken word. In this way,
writing helped to shape a community's sense of belonging from one generation to the next.
Originally written on twelve clay tablets, the poem* Epic of Gilgamesh *is one of the oldest
recorded stories in the world. The hero is Gilgamesh, the legendary king of the Sumerian
city-state of Uruk. His desire to gain immortality drives the plot of the story. The epic's first
tablet, excerpted below, sets the tale into motion. It describes Gilgamesh as part god and
part man, who heaped abuse on his subjects. Distressed, they beseech the gods to create
a match for Gilgamesh's stormy heart. The mother of the gods, Aruru, responds by creating Enkidu, a man of nature who personifies the time before civilization. He ultimately
befriends Gilgamesh after being convinced to leave the wilderness and journey to Uruk.
Over the course of their ensuing adventures together, Enkidu teaches Gilgamesh about his
own humanity in life and in death.*

From *The Epic of Gilgamesh*, trans. N. K. Sandars (Baltimore: Penguin Classics, 1972), 61–66.

Enkidu, and now you have become like a god. Why do you want to run wild with the beasts in the hills? Come with me. I will take you to strong-walled Uruk, to the blessed temple of Ishtar and of Anu, of love and of heaven: there Gilgamesh lives, who is very strong, and like a wild bull he lords it over men."

When she had spoken Enkidu was pleased; he longed for a comrade, for one who would understand his heart. "Come, woman, and take me to that holy temple, to the house of Anu and of Ishtar, and to the place where Gilgamesh lords it over the people. I will challenge him boldly, I will cry out aloud in Uruk, 'I am the strongest here, I have come to change the old order, I am he who was born in the hills, I am he who is strongest of all.'"

She said, "Let us go, and let him see your face. I know very well where Gilgamesh is in great Uruk. O Enkidu, there all the people are dressed in their gorgeous robes, every day is holiday, the young men and the girls are wonderful to see. How sweet they smell! All the great ones are roused from their beds. O Enkidu, you who love life, I will show you Gilgamesh, a man of many moods; you shall look at him well in his radiant manhood. His body is perfect in strength and maturity; he never rests by night or day. He is stronger than you, so leave your boasting. Shamash the glorious sun has given favors to Gilgamesh, and Anu of the heavens, and Enlil, and Ea the wise has given him deep understanding. I tell you, even before you have left the wilderness, Gilgamesh will know in his dreams that you are coming."

DISCUSSION QUESTIONS

1. How does the poem describe Gilgamesh and Enkidu before their first meeting? What do they look like physically? What is the source of their strength?

2. Why does Enkidu need to be tamed? What does he gain in the process? What does he lose?

3. What does the creation of Enkidu suggest about how Mesopotamians understood the relationship between the gods and humans?

4. Based on this excerpt, in what ways do Gilgamesh and Enkidu embody the broader shift in patterns of life in the region at the time?

2. Establishing Law and Justice

King Hammurabi, *The Code of Hammurabi*

(Early Eighteenth Century b.c.e.)

The law code promulgated by King Hammurabi (r. c. 1792–1750 b.c.e.) of Babylon elucidates the inner workings of Mesopotamian society, the cradle of the world's first civilization. The copy of the code excerpted here is inscribed on a stone pillar, crowned by a sculptural relief

From James B. Pritchard, ed., *Ancient Near Eastern Texts Relating to the Old Testament*, 3rd ed. with supplement (Princeton, NJ: Princeton University Press, 1969), 166–168, 170–172, 175–176, 178.

depicting the god of justice commissioning Hammurabi to write the laws. This image embodies the Mesopotamian belief that kings were divinely appointed and thereby responsible for imparting justice and promoting their subjects' well-being. As a messenger of the divine will, King Hammurabi influenced both the public and the private lives of his people. As the following selection reveals, he was especially concerned with protecting property rights and a social hierarchy that positioned slaves at the bottom and free persons at the top. By codifying laws in writing, Hammurabi helped set an enduring precedent in the Western tradition.

The Prologue
(v)

When Marduk[1] commissioned me to guide the people aright, to direct the land,
I established law and justice in the language of the land,
thereby promoting the welfare of the people.
At that time (I decreed):

The Laws

3: If a man[2] came forward with false testimony in a case, and has not proved the word which he spoke, if that case was a case involving life, that man shall be put to death.

15: If a man has helped either a male slave of the state or a female slave of the state or a male slave of a private citizen or a female slave of a private citizen to escape through the city-gate, he shall be put to death.

16: If a man has harbored in his house either a fugitive male or female slave belonging to the state or to a private citizen and has not brought him forth at the summons of the police, that householder shall be put to death.

17: If a man caught a fugitive male or female slave in the open and has taken him to his owner, the owner of the slave shall pay him two shekels[3] of silver.

18: If that slave has not named his owner, he shall take him to the palace in order that his record may be investigated, and they shall return him to his owner.

19: If he has kept that slave in his house (and) later the slave has been found in his possession, that man shall be put to death.

42: If a man rented a field for cultivation, but has not produced grain in the field, they shall prove that he did no work on the field and he shall give grain to the owner of the field on the basis of those adjoining it.

43: If he did not cultivate the field, but has neglected (it), he shall give grain to the owner of the field on the basis of those adjoining it; furthermore, the field which he neglected he shall break up with mattocks, harrow and return to the owner of the field.

---

[1] The god of Babylon and in Hammurabi's time the god of the Babylonian Empire.
[2] The word *awēlum*, used here, is literally "man," but in the legal literature it seems to be used in at least three senses: (1) sometimes to indicate a man of the higher class, a noble; (2) sometimes a free man of any class, high or low; and (3) occasionally a man of any class, from king to slave.
[3] A weight of about 8 gr.

49: When a man borrowed money from a merchant and pledged to the merchant a field prepared for grain or sesame, if he said to him, "Cultivate the field, then harvest (and) take the grain or sesame that is produced," if the tenant has produced grain or sesame in the field, the owner of the field at harvest-time shall himself take the grain or sesame that was produced in the field and he shall give to the merchant grain for his money, which he borrowed from the merchant, together with its interest, and also for the cost of cultivation.

50: If he pledged a field planted with <grain> or a field planted with sesame, the owner of the field shall himself take the grain or sesame that was produced in the field and he shall pay back the money with its interest to the merchant.

51: If he does not have the money to pay back, <grain or> sesame at their market value in accordance with the ratio fixed by the king[4] he shall give to the merchant for his money, which he borrowed from the merchant, together with its interest.

55: If a man, upon opening his canal for irrigation, became so lazy that he has let the water ravage a field adjoining his, he shall measure out grain on the basis of those adjoining his.

57: If a shepherd has not come to an agreement with the owner of a field to pasture sheep on the grass, but has pastured sheep on the field without the consent of the owner of the field, when the owner of the field harvests his field, the shepherd who pastured the sheep on the field without the consent of the owner of the field shall give in addition twenty *kur* of grain per eighteen *iku* to the owner of the field.

104: If a merchant lent grain, wool, oil, or any goods at all to a trader to retail, the trader shall write down the value and pay (it) back to the merchant, with the trader obtaining a sealed receipt for the money which he pays to the merchant.

128: If a man acquired a wife, but did not draw up the contracts for her, that woman is no wife.

129: If the wife of a man has been caught while lying with another man, they shall bind them and throw them into the water. If the husband[5] of the woman wishes to spare his wife, then the king in turn may spare his subject.[6]

131: If a man's wife was accused by her husband, but she was not caught while lying with another man, she shall make affirmation by god and return to her house.

132: If the finger was pointed at the wife of a man because of another man, but she has not been caught while lying with the other man, she shall throw herself into the river[7] for the sake of her husband.

133: If a man was taken captive, but there was sufficient to live on in his house, his wife [shall not leave her house, but she shall take care of her person by not] entering [the house of another].[8]

---

[4]In ancient Mesopotamia the ratio between silver (the money of the time) and various commodities was fixed by the state, showing that price control is not such a modern institution after all.
[5]Lit., "owner, master."
[6]Lit., "his slave."
[7]I.e. submit to the water ordeal, with the river as divine judge.
[8]I.e. in order to live there as another man's wife.

134: If the man was taken captive and there was not sufficient to live on in his house, his wife may enter the house of another, with that woman incurring no blame at all.

138: If a man wishes to divorce his wife who did not bear him children, he shall give her money to the full amount of her marriage-price and he shall also make good to her the dowry which she brought from her father's house and then he may divorce her.

139: If there was no marriage-price, he shall give her one mina[9] of silver as the divorce-settlement.

140: If he is a peasant, he shall give her one-third mina of silver.

141: If a man's wife, who was living in the house of the man, has made up her mind to leave in order that she may engage in business, thus neglecting her house (and) humiliating her husband, they shall prove it against her; and if her husband has then decided on her divorce, he may divorce her, with nothing to be given her as her divorce-settlement upon her departure. If her husband has not decided on her divorce, her husband may marry another woman, with the former woman living in the house of her husband like a maidservant.

142: If a woman so hated her husband that she has declared, "You may not have me," her record shall be investigated at her city council, and if she was careful and was not at fault, even though her husband has been going out and disparaging her greatly, that woman, without incurring any blame at all, may take her dowry and go off to her father's house.

143: If she was not careful, but was a gadabout, thus neglecting her house (and) humiliating her husband, they shall throw that woman into the water.

150: If a man, upon presenting a field, orchard, house, or goods to his wife, left a sealed document with her, her children may not enter a claim against her after (the death of) her husband, since the mother may give her inheritance to that son of hers whom she likes, (but) she may not give (it) to an outsider.

195: If a son has struck his father, they shall cut off his hand.

196: If a man has destroyed the eye of a member of the aristocracy, they shall destroy his eye.

197: If he has broken a(nother) man's bone, they shall break his bone.

198: If he has destroyed the eye of a commoner or broken the bone of a commoner, he shall pay one mina of silver.

199: If he has destroyed the eye of a man's slave or broken the bone of a man's slave, he shall pay one-half his value.

200: If a man has knocked out a tooth of a man of his own rank, they shall knock out his tooth.

201: If he has knocked out a commoner's tooth, he shall pay one-third mina of silver.

202: If a man has struck the cheek of a man who is superior to him, he shall be beaten sixty (times) with an oxtail whip in the assembly.

---

[9]mina: A weight of about 500 gr. divided into about 60 shekels.

203: If a member of the aristocracy has struck the cheek of a(nother) member of the aristocracy who is of the same rank as himself, he shall pay one mina of silver.

204: If a commoner has struck the cheek of a(nother) commoner, he shall pay ten shekels of silver.

205: If a man's slave has struck the cheek of a member of the aristocracy, they shall cut off his ear.

215: If a physician performed a major operation on a man with a bronze lancet and has saved the man's life, or he opened up the eye-socket of a man with a bronze lancet and has saved the man's eye, he shall receive ten shekels of silver.

216: If it was a member of the commonalty, he shall receive five shekels.

217: If it was a man's slave, the owner of the slave shall give two shekels of silver to the physician.

218: If a physician performed a major operation on a man with a bronze lancet and has caused the man's death, or he opened up the eye-socket of a man and has destroyed the man's eye, they shall cut off his hand.

219: If a physican performed a major operation on a commoner's slave with a bronze lancet and has caused (his) death, he shall make good slave for slave.

228: If a builder constructed a house for a man and finished (it) for him, he shall give him two shekels of silver per *sar*[10] of house as his remuneration.

229: If a builder constructed a house for a man, but did not make his work strong, with the result that the house which he built collapsed and so has caused the death of the owner of the house, that builder shall be put to death.

230: If it has caused the death of a son of the owner of the house, they shall put the son of that builder to death.

231: If it has caused the death of a slave of the owner of the house, he shall give slave for slave to the owner of the house.

232: If it has destroyed goods, he shall make good whatever it destroyed; also, because he did not make the house strong which he built and it collapsed, he shall reconstruct the house which collapsed at his own expense.

233: If a builder constructed a house for a man and has not done his work properly so that a wall has become unsafe, that builder shall strengthen that wall at his own expense.

The Epilogue

The laws of justice, which Hammurabi, the efficient king, set up,
and by which he caused the land to take the right way and have good government.
I, Hammurabi, the perfect king,
was not careless (or) neglectful of the black-headed (people),[11]
whom Enlil[12] had presented to me,
(and) whose shepherding Marduk had committed to me;
I sought out peaceful regions for them;

---

[10]A measure equal to about 42 1/5 square yards.
[11]**black-headed (people):** Sumerian expression for men in general. [Ed.]
[12]**Enlil:** The storm-god and most powerful Sumerian god. [Ed.]

I overcame grievous difficulties;
I caused light to rise on them . . .
In my bosom I carried the peoples of the land of Sumer and Akkad;
they prospered under my protection;
I always governed them in peace;
I sheltered them in my wisdom.
In order that the strong might not oppress the weak,
that justice might be dealt the orphan (and) the widow,
in Babylon, the city whose head Anum[13] and Enlil raised aloft,
in Esagila, the temple whose foundations stand firm like heaven and earth,
I wrote my precious words on my stela,
and in the presence of the statue of me, the king of justice,
I set (it) up in order to administer the law of the land,
to prescribe the ordinances of the land,
to give justice to the oppressed.

DISCUSSION QUESTIONS

1. What do the Prologue and Epilogue indicate about the status of Mesopotamian rulers?
2. What do these laws reveal about the social and economic structures of Mesopotamian society? What role does social rank play?
3. What does the code reveal in particular about women's position in Mesopotamian society?
4. Based on these laws, in what ways was the individual responsible for maintaining the welfare of the community as a whole?

3. Praising the One God

Hymn to the Aten (Fourteenth Century B.C.E.)

In the fourth and third millennia B.C.E., Egypt emerged as a great civilization to rival that of Mesopotamia. Guided by a succession of powerful kings, Egypt became a prosperous, unified country despite intermittent periods of turmoil and disarray. Among the reasons for Egypt's rise as a large-scale state was a deeply held belief in the gods as a model for central authority and stability. Egyptians considered their kings, ultimately known as pharaohs, to be divinity in human form; as such, they had a particular responsibility to pay tribute to the traditional gods. The New Kingdom pharaoh Akhenaten (r. 1372–1355 B.C.E.) sought to reform this tradition. Instead of honoring the older state and local gods, he ordered that all worship center on the god Aten, who represented the sun. The "Hymn to the Aten" points

From Miriam Lichtheim, *Ancient Egyptian Literature: Volume II: The New Kingdom* (Berkeley: University of California Press, 1976), 91–92.

[13]**Anum:** The sky-god and king of the Sumerian gods. [Ed.]

to Akhenaten's special relationship with Aten as his "son"; it was most likely composed by his scribes to reflect basic royal doctrine. Although Egyptians had long revered Aten as a manifestation of the sun god Re, their religion remained fundamentally polytheistic. By contrast, through hymns such as this one, Akhenaten elevated Aten to new heights of importance as the sole god. His religion never received popular support and consequently did not survive Akhenaten's death; even so, it reveals both the profound religiosity of the Egyptian people and also their inherent conservatism.

Adoration of *Re-Harakhti-who-rejoices-in-lightland In-his-name-Shu-who-is-Aten*, who gives life forever, by the King who lives by Maat,[1] the Lord of the Two Lands: *Neferkheprure, Sole-one-of-Re*; the Son of Re who lives by Maat, the Lord of crowns: *Akhenaten*, great in his lifetime, given life forever.[2]

Splendid you rise, O living Aten, eternal lord!
You are radiant, beauteous, mighty,
Your love is great, immense.
Your rays light up all faces,
Your bright hue gives life to hearts,
When you fill the Two Lands with your love.
August God who fashioned himself,
Who made very land, created what is in it,
All peoples, herds, and flocks,
All trees that grow from soil;
They live when you dawn for them,
You are mother and father of all that you made.

When you dawn their eyes observe you,
As your rays light the whole earth;
Every heart acclaims your sight,
When you are risen as their lord.
When you set in sky's western lightland,
They lie down as if to die,
Their heads covered, their noses stopped,
Until you dawn in sky's eastern lightland.
Their arms adore your *ka*,[3]
As you nourish the hearts by your beauty;
One lives when you cast your rays,
Every land is in festivity.

---

[1]**Maat**: The divine principle of order and justice. Egyptians believed that their rulers were responsible for providing Maat for the gods. [Ed.]
[2]As originally composed, the hymn was recited by the king, hence this introduction. In the final portion of the hymn, the king speaks in the first person. . . .
[3]**ka**: In ancient Egyptian religion, *ka* was a primary aspect of the soul of a human being or of a god. [Ed.]

Singers, musicians, shout with joy,
In the court of the *benben*-shrine,[4]
And in all temples in Akhet-Aten,
The place of truth in which you rejoice.
Foods are offered in their midst,
Your holy son performs your praises,
O Aten living in his risings,
And all your creatures leap before you.
Your august son exults in joy,
O Aten living daily content in the sky,
Your offspring, your august son, Sole one of Re;[5]
Your Son of Re does not cease to extol his beauty,[6]
Neferkheprure, Sole-one-of-Re.

I am your son who serves you, who exalts your name,
Your power, your strength, are firm in my heart;
You are the living Aten whose image endures,
You have made the far sky to shine in it,
To observe all that you made.
You are One yet a million lives are in you,
To make them live <you give> the breath of life to their noses;
By the sight of your rays all flowers exist,
What lives and sprouts from the soil grows when you shine.
Drinking deep of your sight all flocks frisk,
The birds in the nest fly up in joy;
Their folded wings unfold in praise
Of the living Aten, their maker.

DISCUSSION QUESTIONS

1. Describe Aten as he is presented in this hymn. What are his attributes?

2. How do these attributes reflect Egyptian beliefs about the role of the gods in the every-day world?

3. What does this hymn suggest about the relationship between Aten and Akhenaten? Why do you think the pharaoh wanted to celebrate this relationship?

4. Some scholars argue that the cult of Aten represents an early form of monotheism. Is there any evidence in this hymn to support this argument?

---

[4]A sanctuary of Aten at El Amarna, which seems to have been named after the sanctuary of Re at Heliopolis that bore this name.
[5]The epithet which forms part of Akhenaten's throne name.
[6]One expects "your beauty."

4. Writing in Life and the Afterlife

SOURCES IN CONVERSATION | *Agricultural Scenes, Tomb of Nakhut* (c. 1400–1390 b.c.e.) and *Egyptian Scribal Exercise Book* (Twelfth Century b.c.e.)

After a period of turmoil, the successors of the Middle Kingdom rulers transformed Egypt into an imperial power. Key to their success was a legion of professional scribes who oversaw governmental affairs. To ensure they were fit for service, a new literary genre known as "school texts" emerged for the use of teachers and scribes in training. The book excerpted here was compiled precisely for this purpose. In it, a high-ranking scribe, frustrated by his apprentice's poor performance, contrasts the prestige and comfort of the scribal profession to other forms of employment across all segments of Egyptian society. While this book attests to scribes' special status as masters of the technology of writing, the tomb of Nakhut, a wealthy scribe, affirms that they could leave their mark in other ways. Located in Thebes on the west bank of the Nile, Nakhut's tomb includes a series of wall paintings on a variety of subjects, including everyday activities that Nakhut hoped to continue in the afterlife. In the top left, Nakhut and his wife, Tawy, identified as "his beloved, the chantress of Amun [the king of the gods]," stand before copious offerings of food, ointments, and oils to be dedicated to specific deities.

Artokoloro Quint Lox Limited / Alamy Stock Photo

From Miriam Lichtheim, *Ancient Egyptian Literature: Volume II: The New Kingdom* (Berkeley: University of California Press, 1976), 168–72.

And, like in the exercise book, the scribe's position is contrasted with that of other Egyptians: Nakhut is portrayed overseeing men plowing, sowing, winnowing, and felling trees and women gathering flax. In the early twentieth century, a team under the direction of the Metropolitan Museum of Art in New York completed a series of full-scale facsimiles of the wall paintings, including the one reproduced here.

Title

(1,1) [Beginning of the instruction in letter writing made by the royal scribe and chief overseer of the cattle of Amen-Re, King of Gods, Nebmare-nakht] for his apprentice, the scribe Wenemdiamun.

The Idle Scribe Is Worthless

The royal scribe and chief overseer of the cattle of Amen-Re, King of Gods, Nebmarenakht, speaks to the scribe Wenemdiamun, as follows. You are busy coming and going, and don't think of writing. You resist listening to me; (3,5) you neglect my teachings.

You are worse than the goose of the shore, that is busy with mischief. It spends the summer destroying the dates, the winter destroying the seed-grain. It spends the balance of the year in pursuit of the cultivators. It does not let seed be cast to the ground without snatching it in its fall. One cannot catch it by snaring. One does not offer it in the temple. The evil, sharp-eyed bird that does no work!

You are worse than the desert antelope that lives by running. It spends no day in plowing. Never at all does it tread on the threshing-floor. It lives on the oxen's labor, without entering among them. But though I spend the day telling you "Write," it seems like a plague to you. Writing is very (4,1) pleasant! ———.

All Occupations Are Bad Except That of the Scribe

See for yourself with your own eye. The occupations lie before you.

The washerman's day is going up, going down. All his limbs are weak, [from] whitening his neighbors' clothes every day, from washing their linen.

The maker of pots is smeared with soil, like one whose relations have died. His hands, (4,5) his feet are full of clay; he is like one who lives in the bog.

The cobbler mingles with vats. His odor is penetrating. His hands are red with madder, like one who is smeared with blood. He looks behind him for the kite, like one whose flesh is exposed.

The watchman[1] prepares garlands and polishes vase-stands. He spends a night of toil just as one on whom the sun shines.

The merchants travel downstream and upstream. They are as busy as can be, carrying goods from one town to another. They supply him who has wants. But the tax collectors carry off the gold, that most precious of metals.

---

[1]This word is obscure, but the context suggests a man who guards and cleans the temple at night and makes it ready for the morning service. [Ed.]

The ships' crews from every house (of commerce), they receive their loads. (5,1) They depart from Egypt for Syria, and each man's god is with him. (But) not one of them says: "We shall see Egypt again!"

The carpenter who is in the shipyard carries the timber and stacks it. If he gives today the output of yesterday, woe to his limbs! The shipwright stands behind him to tell him evil things.

His outworker who is in the fields, his is the toughest of all the jobs. He spends the day loaded (5,5) with his tools, tied to his tool-box. When he returns home at night, he is loaded with the tool-box and the timbers, his drinking mug, and his whetstones.

The scribe, he alone, records the output of all of them. Take note of it!

The Misfortunes of the Peasant

Let me also expound to you the situation of the peasant, that other tough occupation. [Comes] the inundation and soaks him, he attends to his equipment. By day he cuts his farming tools; (6,1) by night he twists rope. Even his midday hour he spends on farm labor. He equips himself to go to the field as if he were a warrior. The dried field lies before him; he goes out to get his team. When he has been after the herdsman for many days, he gets his team and comes back with it. He makes for it a place in the field. (6,5) Comes dawn, he goes to make a start and does not find it in its place. He spends three days searching for it; he finds it in the bog. He finds no hides on them; the jackals have chewed them. He comes out, his garment in his hand, to beg for himself a team.

When he reaches his field he finds [it] broken up. He spends time cultivating, and the snake is after him. It finishes off the seed as it is cast to the ground. He does not see a green blade. He does three plowings with borrowed grain. His wife (7,1) has gone down to the merchants and found nothing for barter. Now the scribe lands on the shore. He surveys the harvest. Attendants are behind him with staffs, Nubians with clubs. One says (to him): "Give grain." "There is none." He is beaten savagely. He is bound, thrown in the well, submerged head down. His wife is bound in his presence. His children are in fetters. His neighbors (7,5) abandon them and flee. When it's over, there's no grain.

If you have any sense, be a scribe. If you have learned about the peasant, you will not be able to be one. Take note of it!

Be a Scribe

The scribe of the army and commander[2] of the cattle of the house of Amun, Nebmare-nakht, speaks to the scribe Wenemdiamun, as follows. Be a scribe! Your body will be sleek; your hand will be soft. You will not flicker like a flame, like one whose body is feeble. For there is not the bone of a man in you. You are tall and thin. If you lifted a load to carry it, you would stagger, your legs would tremble. You are lacking in strength; (8,1) you are weak in all your limbs; you are poor in body.

Set your sight on being a scribe; a fine profession that suits you. You call for one; a thousand answer you. You stride freely on the road. You will not be like a hired ox. You are in front of others.

---

[2]A joking alteration of the teacher's title.

I spend the day instructing you. You do not listen! Your heart is like an [empty] room. My teachings are not in it. Take their [meaning] to yourself!

The marsh thicket is before you each day, as a nestling is after its mother. You follow the path of (8,5) pleasure; you make friends with revellers. You have made your home in the brewery, as one who thirsts for beer. You sit in the parlor with an idler.[3] You hold the writings in contempt. You visit the whore. Do not do these things! What are they for? They are of no use. Take note of it!

The Scribe Does Not Suffer Like the Soldier

Furthermore. Look, I instruct you to make you sound; to make you hold the palette freely. To make you become one whom the king trusts; to make you gain entrance to treasury and granary. To make you receive the ship-load at the gate of the granary. To make you issue the offerings on feast days. You are dressed in fine clothes; you own horses. Your boat is on (9,1) the river; you are supplied with attendants. You stride about inspecting. A mansion is built in your town. You have a powerful office, given you by the king. Male and female slaves are about you. Those who are in the fields grasp your hand, on plots that you have made. Look, I make you into a staff of life! Put the writings in your heart, and you will be protected from all kinds of toil. You will become a worthy official.

Do you not recall the (fate of) the unskilled man? His name is not known. He is ever burdened [like an ass carrying] in front of the scribe who knows what he is about.

Come, [let me tell] you the woes of (9,5) the soldier, and how many are his superiors: the general, the troop-commander, the officer who leads, the standard-bearer, the lieutenant, the scribe, the commander of fifty, and the garrison-captain. They go in and out in the halls of the palace, saying: "Get laborers!" He is awakened at any hour. One is after him as (after) a donkey. He toils until the Aten sets in his darkness of night. He is hungry, his belly hurts; he is dead while yet alive. When he receives the grain-ration, having been released from duty, it is not good for grinding.

He is called up for Syria. He may not rest. There are no clothes, no sandals. The weapons of war are assembled at the fortress of Sile. (10,1) His march is uphill through mountains. He drinks water every third day; it is smelly and tastes of salt. His body is ravaged by illness. The enemy comes, surrounds him with missiles, and life recedes from him. He is told: "Quick, forward, valiant soldier! Win for yourself a good name!" He does not know what he is about. His body is weak, his legs fail him. When victory is won, the captives are handed over to his majesty, to be taken to Egypt. The foreign woman faints on the march; she hangs herself [on] (10,5) the soldier's neck. His knapsack drops, another grabs it while he is burdened with the woman. His wife and children are in their village; he dies and does not reach it. If he comes out alive, he is worn out from marching. Be he at large, be he detained, the soldier suffers. If he leaps and joins the deserters, all his people are imprisoned. He dies on the edge of the desert, and there is none to perpetuate his name. He suffers in death as in life. A big sack is brought for him; he does not know his resting place.

Be a scribe, and be spared from soldiering! You call and one says: "Here I am." You are safe from torments. Every man seeks to raise himself up. Take note of it!

---

[3]Lit., "He whose back is turned to his job."

DISCUSSION QUESTIONS

1. What do these sources reveal about Egyptian religious beliefs at the time?

2. What sets the scribe apart from the other trades and professions according to the exercise book and the scene from Nakhut's tomb?

3. What do the exercise book and tomb scene reveal about the structure of both the Egyptian economy and Egyptian society in the New Kingdom?

4. According to scholars, Egyptian women enjoyed a certain measure of gender equality. Does the portrayal of women in Nakhut's tomb scene and in the exercise book support this assertion? Why or why not?

5. Allying for Peace

The "Eternal Treaty" between the Egyptians and Hittites

(c. 1259 b.c.e.)

Even after the emergence of great civilizations in Mesopotamia and Egypt, new societies took root in the Mediterranean. The Hittites were the most ambitious of these newcomers. By around 1750 b.c.e., they had forged a powerful and wealthy kingdom in Anatolia. Their success depended largely on an aggressive campaign of territorial expansion, a strategy that brought them into direct military conflict with New Kingdom Egypt. Since neither was able to gain the upper hand, and with new threats brewing, the Egyptian pharaoh Ramses II (r. 1304–1237 b.c.e.) and the Hittite king Hattusilis III (r. 1267–1237 b.c.e.) agreed to make peace. Both Egyptian and Hittite versions of their agreement survive. Although their content is largely the same, the Hittite version (excerpted below) may be a closer rendition of the formally agreed on text. In it, Ramses and Hattusilis forged an "eternal" alliance aimed at protecting their rule both at home and abroad. As a result, the two countries remained close allies until the Hittite Empire collapsed in the late twelfth and early eleventh centuries b.c.e. A copy of the treaty appears above the entrance to the Security Council Chamber of the United Nations, a nod to the treaty's emphasis on the power of diplomacy as an instrument of peace.

Title

Treaty of Rea-mashesha mai Amana, the great king, the king of the land of Egypt, the valiant, with Hattusilis, the king of the Hatti land, his brother, for establishing [good] peace [and] good brotherhood [worthy of] great [king]ship between them forever.

Preamble

These are the words of Rea-mashesha mai Amana, the great king of the land of Egypt, the valiant of all lands, . . . (spoken) to Hattusilis, the great king, the king of the Hatti land, the valiant. . . .

From James B. Pritchard, ed., *Ancient Near Eastern Texts Relating to the Old Testament*, 3rd ed. with supplement (Princeton, NJ: Princeton University Press, 1969), 202–3.

Relations up to the Conclusion of the Treaty

Now I have established good brotherhood (and) good peace between us forever. In order to establish good peace (and) good brotherhood in [the relationship] of the land of Egypt with the Hatti land forever (I speak) thus: Behold, as for the relationship between the land of Egypt and the Hatti land, since eternity the god does not permit the making of hostility between them because of a treaty (valid) forever. Behold, Rea-mashesha mai Amana, the great king, the king of the land of Egypt, in order to bring about the relationship that the Sun-god[1] and the Storm-god[2] have effected for the land of Egypt with the Hatti land finds himself in a relationship valid since eternity which [does not permi]t the making of hostility between [them] until all and everlasting time.

The Present Treaty

Rea-mashesha mai Amana, the great king, the king of the land of Egypt, has entered into a treaty (written) upon a silver tablet with Hattusilis, the great king, the king of the Hatti land, [his] brother, [from] this [da]y on to establish good peace (and) good brotherhood be[tween us] forever. He is a brother [to me] and I am a brother to him and at peace with him forever. And as for us, our brotherhood and our peace is being brought about and it will be better than the brotherhood and the peace which existed formerly for the land of Egypt with the Hatti land.

Future Relations of the Two Countries

Behold, Rea-mashesha mai Amana, the king of the land of Egypt, is a good peace (and) in good brotherhood with [Hattusilis], the great king, the king of the Hatti land.

Behold the sons of Rea-mashesha mai Amana, the king of the land of Egypt, are in peace with (and) brothers of the sons of Hattusilis, the great king, the king of the Hatti land, forever. They are in the same relationship of brotherhood and peace as we.

And as for (the relationship of) the land of Egypt with the Hatti land, they are at peace and brothers like us forever.

Mutual Renunciation of Aggression

Rea-mashesha mai Amana, the great king, the king of the land of Egypt, shall not trespass into the Hatti land to take anything therefrom in the future. And Hattusilis, the great king, the king of the Hatti land, shall not trespass into the land of Egypt to take anything therefrom in the future.

Behold, the holy ordinance (valid) forever which the Sun-god and the Storm-god had brought about for the land of Egypt with the Hatti land (calls for) peace and brotherhood so as not to make hostility between them. Behold, Rea-mashesha mai Amana, the great king, the king of the land of Egypt, has seized hold of it in order to bring about well-being from this day on. Behold, the land of Egypt (in its relation) with the Hatti land—they are at peace and brothers forever.

---

[1] Rea (Re), the chief god of the Egyptians.
[2] The chief god of the Hittites.

Defensive Alliance

If an enemy from abroad comes against the Hatti land, and Hattusilis, the great king, the king of the Hatti land, sends to me saying: "Come to me to help me against him," Rea-mashesha mai Amana, the great king, the king of the land of Egypt, shall send his foot soldiers (and) his charioteers and they shall slay [his enemy and] take revenge upon him for the sake of the Hatti land.

And if Hattusilis, the great king, the king of the Hatti land, is angry with servants belonging to him (and if) they have failed against him and sends to Rea-mashesha mai Amana, the great king, the king of the land of Egypt, on their account—lo! Rea-mashesha mai Amana shall send his foot soldiers (and) his charioteers and they shall destroy all those with whom he is angry.

If an enemy from abroad comes against the land of Egypt and Rea-mashesha mai Amana, the king of the land of Egypt, your brother, sends to Hattusilis, the king of the Hatti land, his brother, saying: "Come here to help me against him"—lo! Hattusilis, the king of the Hatti land, shall send his foot soldiers (and) his charioteers and shall slay my enemies.

And if Rea-mashesha ma[i Amana, the king of] the land of Egypt, is angry with servants belonging to him (and if) they have committed sin again[st him and I send] to Hattusilis, the king of the Hatti land, my brother, on his account—lo! Hattusilis, [the king of the Hatti land,] my brother, shall send his foot soldiers (and) his charioteers and they shall destroy all those with whom he is angry.

Succession to the Throne

Behold, the son of Hattusilis, the king of the Hatti land, shall be made king of the Hatti land in place of Hattusilis, his father, after the many years of Hattusilis, the king of the Hatti land. If the noblemen of the Hatti land commit sin against him—lo! [Rea-mashesha mai Amana, the king of Egypt, shall send foot soldiers] (and) charioteers to take revenge upon them [for the sake of the Hatti land. And after they have reestablished order] in the country of the king of the Hatti land, [they shall return] to the country [of Egypt].

[Corresponding provision concerning Egypt lost in a gap.]

Extradition of Fugitives

[If a nobleman flees from the Hatti land and i]f one (such) man comes [to Rea-mashesha mai Amana, the great king, the king of the land of Egypt,] in order to enter his services . . . [Rea-mashesha mai Amana, the great king, the king of the land of Egypt, shall seize them and] shall have them brought back to the king of the Hatti land.

[several badly broken lines]

[If a nobleman] flees [from Rea-mashesha mai Amana, the king of the land of Egypt, and if one (such) man] comes to the [Hatti] land, [Ha]ttusilis, [the great king, the king of the Hatti land, shall seize him and] shall have him brought back to R[ea-mashesha mai] Amana, the great king, the king of Egypt, his brother.

If one man flees from the [Hatti land or] two men, [or three men and come to] Rea-mashesha mai [Amana, the great king, the king of the land of Egyp]t, [Rea-mashesha] mai Amana, the great king, [the king of the land of Egypt, shall seize them and have them brought back t]o Hattusilis, his brother. [Rea-mashesha mai Amana and Hattusilis are verily] brothers; hence [let them not *exact punishment for*] their sins, [let them not] tear out [their eyes; let them not *take revenge upon*] their people [. . . together with] their [wives and wi]th their children.

If [one man flees from Egypt] or two men or three men [and come to Hattusilis, the great king, the king of the Hatti land, Hattusilis, the great king], the king of the Hatti land, his brother, shall seize them and have them brought [back to Rea-mashesha mai Amana, the great king, the king of] the land of Egypt. [Hattusilis, the king of the Hatti land], and Rea-mashesha, the great king, the k[ing of the land of Egypt, are verily brothers; hence let them not *exact punishment for* their sins,] [. . .] let them not tear out their eyes; [let them not *take revenge upon* their people . . . together with] their wives (and) with their children.[3]

DISCUSSION QUESTIONS

1. What are the central terms of the alliance? What does each ruler want to guard against, and why?
2. What do these terms suggest about the nature of Egyptian and Hittite rule? What was the basis of Ramses II's and Hattusilis III's power?
3. How does religion come into play in the treaty? What gods does it invoke, and why?

COMPARATIVE QUESTIONS

1. Using evidence from all six sources, compare and contrast social, political, and religious life in ancient Mesopotamia, Egypt, and the Mediterranean.
2. How do deities function in the different societies? Why are some rulers portrayed as gods or godlike? How would this affect their governance? In what ways did Akhenaten both build upon and depart from these precedents in his worship of Aten?
3. What qualities and characteristics are associated with women in the *Epic of Gilgamesh*, Hammurabi's code, and the agricultural scenes from Nakhut's tomb? What do these sources say about gender attitudes in these societies?
4. How do these documents portray the relationship between humans and the natural world? In what ways did this relationship change with the rise of trade and agriculture?

---

[3]After some fragmentary lines the text breaks off altogether. With the end of the treaty the list of the gods who were invoked as witnesses is missing.

Empires in the Near East and the Reemergence of Civilization in Greece

1000–500 B.C.E.

Although dire economic conditions and foreign invasions caused havoc across the Near East and the Mediterranean from 1200 to 1000 B.C.E., by the eighth century B.C.E., local economies and societies were well on their way to recovery. The documents in this chapter allow us to chart the course of renewal in both regions, beginning with the Persian Empire. Between the sixth and fifth centuries, Persian rulers enhanced the traditional Near Eastern model of monarchical government, with its emphasis on a king's divine right to rule, by conquering new territories and enriching their treasury. The second document reveals that a new religion — Judaism — took shape against this backdrop. With its exclusive worship of a single God, Judaism forever changed the religious landscape of Western civilization. The third, fourth, and fifth documents turn from the Near East to the Mediterranean, illuminating important facets of Greek society at the time, which soon became a target of Persia's imperial ambitions. As these documents demonstrate, Greeks shaped a sense of their own distinctive identity through innovative social, political, and cultural forms, ranging from city-states based on the concept of citizenship to epic poetry celebrating the individual's quest for excellence. At the same time, however, the last document reveals that Greeks shared a fundamental similarity with their Near Eastern neighbors: the acceptance of slavery as an essential element in public and private life.

1. Empires and Divine Right

Inscription Honoring Cyrus, King of Persia (c. 557–530 B.C.E.)

The Persian king Cyrus founded the third in a series of powerful kingdoms that emerged from the shadows of the Dark Age in the Near East. Following the example of his Babylonian and Assyrian counterparts, Cyrus embraced imperial monarchy as a model of government while striving to expand his wealth and territorial holdings. The inscription that follows, etched originally on a clay barrel, describes a pivotal event in Cyrus's reign — his conquest of Babylon in 539 B.C.E. Like the Epic of Gilgamesh, *it begins with a tale of woe. The ruler of Babylon was tormenting its inhabitants and dishonoring the gods. Upon hearing the people's complaints, Marduk, the king of the gods, decided to take action. In its account of the ensuing events, the inscription glorifies Cyrus's success while exposing its foundations — the king's military might, cultural tolerance, and the belief in his divine right to rule. Following his lead, his successors built an even more formidable empire that threatened everything in its path, including the Greek city-states.*

... He [Marduk] scanned and looked (through) all the countries, searching for a righteous ruler willing to lead him. . . . (Then) he pronounced the name of Cyrus, king of Anshan, [Persia] declared him . . . the ruler of all the world. He made the Guti country and all the Manda-hordes bow in submission to his (i.e., Cyrus') feet. And he (Cyrus) did always endeavor to treat according to justice the black-headed whom he (Marduk) has made him conquer. Marduk, the great lord, a protector of his people/worshipers, beheld with pleasure his (i.e., Cyrus') good deeds and his upright mind (lit.: heart) (and therefore) ordered him to march against his city Babylon. He made him set out on the road to Babylon going at his side like a real friend. His widespread troops — their number, like that of the water of a river, could not be established — strolled along, their weapons packed away. Without any battle, he made him enter his town Babylon, sparing Babylon any calamity. He delivered into his (i.e., Cyrus') hands Nabonidus, the king who did not worship him (i.e., Marduk). All the inhabitants of Babylon as well as of the entire country of Sumer and Akkad, princes and governors (included), bowed to him (Cyrus) and kissed his feet, jubilant that he (had received) the kingship, and with shining faces. Happily they greeted him as a master through whose help they had come (again) to life from death (and) had all been spared damage and disaster, and they worshiped his (very) name.

I am Cyrus, king of the world, great king, legitimate king, king of Babylon, king of Sumer and Akkad, king of the four rims (of the earth), son of Cambyses, great king, king of Anshan, grandson of Cyrus, great king, king of Anshan, descendant of Teipes, great king, king of Anshan, of a family (which) always (exercised) kingship; whose rule Bel and Nebo love, whom they want as king to please their hearts.

When I entered Babylon as a friend and (when) I established the seat of the government in the palace of the ruler under jubilation and rejoicing, Marduk, the great lord, [induced] the magnanimous inhabitants of Babylon [to love me], and I was daily endeavoring to worship him. My numerous troops walked around in Babylon in peace, I did not allow anybody to terrorize (any place) of the [country of Sumer] and Akkad. I strove for peace in Babylon and in all his (other) sacred cities. As to the inhabitants of Babylon, [who] against the will of the gods [had/were . . . , I abolished] the corvé (lit.: yoke) which was against their (social) standing. I brought relief to their dilapidated housing, putting (thus) an end to their (main) complaints. Marduk, the great lord, was well pleased with

From James B. Pritchard, ed., *Ancient Near Eastern Texts Relating to the Old Testament*, 3rd ed. with supplement (Princeton, NJ: Princeton University Press, 1969), 315–16.

my deeds and sent friendly blessings to myself, Cyrus, the king who worships him, to Cambyses, my son, the offspring of [my] loins, as well as to all my troops, and we all [praised] his great [godhead] joyously, standing before him in peace.

All the kings of the entire world from the Upper to the Lower Sea, those who are seated in throne rooms, (those who) live in other [types of buildings as well as] all the kings of the West land living in tents, brought their heavy tributes and kissed my feet in Babylon. (As to the region) from . . . as far as Ashur and Susa, Agade, Eshnunna, the towns Zamban, Me-Turnu, Der as well as the region of the Gutians, I returned to (these) sacred cities on the other side of the Tigris, the sanctuaries of which have been ruins for a long time, the images which (used) to live therein and established for them permanent sanctuaries. I (also) gathered all their (former) inhabitants and returned (to them) their habitations. Furthermore, I re-settled upon the command of Marduk, the great lord, all the gods of Sumer and Akkad whom Nabonidus has brought into Babylon to the anger of the lord of the gods, unharmed, in their (former) chapels, the places which make them happy.

May all the gods whom I have re-settled in their sacred cities ask daily Bel and Nebo for a long life for me and may they recommend me (to him); to Marduk, my lord, they may say this: "Cyrus, the king who worships you, and Cambyses, his son, . . ." . . . all of them I settled in a peaceful place . . . ducks and doves, . . . I endeavored to fortify/repair their dwelling places.

DISCUSSION QUESTIONS

1. According to the inscription, why did Cyrus conquer Babylon? What does this reveal about the relationship between political and religious beliefs at the time?

2. How did the residents of the city and the neighboring regions respond to the Persian conquest, and why?

3. What specific examples does the inscription provide of Cyrus's religious tolerance?

4. What might have been the purpose of this inscription, and who was its intended audience?

2. Monotheism and Mosaic Law

The Book of Exodus, Chapters 19–20

(c. Tenth–Sixth Centuries B.C.E.)

The Hebrews were among the many peoples caught up in the web of King Cyrus's empire. Upon conquering Babylon, he allowed them to return to Canaan and freely practice their religion after years in exile. The region had long been central to the Hebrews' identity. They believed that centuries earlier, their god, Yahweh, had chosen them to be his special agents in the world. The relationship between Yahweh and the Hebrews was definitively forged when Yahweh led them out of slavery in Egypt into this "promised land" and gave them laws

---

From *The Jerusalem Bible: Reader's Edition* (New York: Doubleday, 1966), 80–86.

*by which to live. The Book of Exodus includes the best known of these laws, the Ten Com-
mandments, which God revealed to the Hebrew leader Moses on Mount Sinai. The biblical
story casts him in much the same role as that of Hammurabi in his code — both are agents
of divine justice and protection. Although the Hebrews did not deny the existence of other
gods, their covenant with Yahweh was a crucial stage in the development of monotheism.
In gradually accepting Yahweh as the only God, the Hebrews created a new religion that
transformed the course of religious history in Western civilization.*

III. The Covenant at Sinai

A. The Covenant and the Decalogue

The Israelites Come to Sinai   19 Three months after they came out of the land of Egypt . . .
on that day the sons of Israel came to the wilderness of Sinai.[1] From Rephidim they set out
again; and when they reached the wilderness of Sinai, there in the wilderness they pitched
their camp; there facing the mountain Israel pitched camp.

Yahweh Promises a Covenant   Moses then went up to God, and Yahweh called to him
from the mountain, saying, "Say this to the House of Jacob, declare this to the sons of
Israel, 'You yourselves have seen what I did with the Egyptians, how I carried you on eagle's
wings and brought you to myself. From this you know that now, if you obey my voice and
hold fast to my covenant, you of all the nations shall be my very own for all the earth is
mine. I will count you a kingdom of priests, a consecrated nation.' Those are the words you
are to speak to the sons of Israel." So Moses went and summoned the elders of the people,
putting before them all that Yahweh had bidden him. Then all the people answered as one,
"All that Yahweh has said, we will do." And Moses took the people's reply back to Yahweh.

Preparing for the Covenant   Yahweh said to Moses, "I am coming to you in a dense
cloud so that the people may hear when I speak to you and may trust you always." And
Moses took the people's reply back to Yahweh.

   Yahweh said to Moses, "Go to the people and tell them to prepare themselves today
and tomorrow. Let them wash their clothing and hold themselves in readiness for the third
day, because on the third day Yahweh will descend on the mountain of Sinai in the sight of
all the people. You will mark out the limits of the mountain and say, 'Take care not to go
up the mountain or to touch the foot of it. Whoever touches the mountain will be put to
death. No one must lay a hand on him: he must be stoned or shot down by arrow, whether
man or beast; he must not remain alive.' When the ram's horn sounds a long blast, they are
to go up the mountain."

   So Moses came down from the mountain to the people and bade them prepare themselves; and they washed their clothing. Then he said to the people, "Be ready for the third
day; do not go near any woman."

---

[1]According to tradition, Mount Sinai was at Jebel Musa in the southern region of the Sinai
peninsula.

The Theophany on Sinai   Now at daybreak on the third day there were peals of thunder on the mountain and lightning flashes, a dense cloud, and a loud trumpet blast, and inside the camp all the people trembled. Then Moses led the people out of the camp to meet God; and they stood at the bottom of the mountain. The mountain of Sinai was entirely wrapped in smoke, because Yahweh had descended on it in the form of fire. Like smoke from a furnace the smoke went up, and the whole mountain shook violently. Louder and louder grew the sound of the trumpet. Moses spoke, and God answered him with peals of thunder. Yahweh came down on the mountain of Sinai, on the mountain top, and Yahweh called Moses to the top of the mountain; and Moses went up. Yahweh said to Moses, "Go down and warn the people not to pass beyond their bounds to come and look on Yahweh, or many of them will lose their lives. The priests, the men who do approach Yahweh, even these must purify themselves, or Yahweh will break out against them." Moses answered Yahweh, "The people cannot come up the mountain of Sinai because you warned us yourself when you said, 'Mark out the limits of the mountain and declare it sacred.'" "Go down," said Yahweh to him, "and come up again bringing Aaron with you. But do not allow the priests or the people to pass beyond their bounds to come up to Yahweh, or he will break out against them." So Moses went down to the people and spoke to them. . . .

The Decalogue   20 Then God spoke all these words. He said, "I am Yahweh your God who brought you out of the land of Egypt, out of the house of slavery.

"You shall have no gods except me.

"You shall not make yourself a carved image or any likeness of anything in heaven or on earth beneath or in the waters under the earth; you shall not bow down to them or serve them. For I, Yahweh your God, am a jealous God and I punish the father's fault in the sons, the grandsons, and the great-grandsons of those who hate me; but I show kindness to thousands of those who love me and keep my commandments.

"You shall not utter the name of Yahweh your God to misuse it,[2] for Yahweh will not leave unpunished the man who utters his name to misuse it.

"Remember the Sabbath day and keep it holy. For six days you shall labor and do all your work, but the seventh day is a Sabbath for Yahweh your God. You shall do no work that day, neither you nor your son nor your daughter nor your servants, men or women, nor your animals nor the stranger who lives with you. For in six days Yahweh made the heavens and the earth and the sea and all that these hold, but on the seventh day he rested; that is why Yahweh has blessed the Sabbath day and made it sacred.

"Honor your father and your mother so that you may have a long life in the land that Yahweh your God has given to you.

"You shall not kill.

"You shall not commit adultery.

"You shall not steal.

"You shall not bear false witness against your neighbor.

"You shall not covet your neighbor's house. You shall not covet your neighbor's wife, or his servant, man or woman, or his ox, or his donkey, or anything that is his."

---

[2]Either in a false oath or irreverently.

All the people shook with fear at the peals of thunder and the lightning flashes, the sound of the trumpet, and the smoking mountain; and they kept their distance. "Speak to us yourself" they said to Moses "and we will listen; but do not let God speak to us, or we shall die." Moses answered the people, "Do not be afraid; God has come to test you, so that your fear of him, being always in your mind, may keep you from sinning." So the people kept their distance while Moses approached the dark cloud where God was.

DISCUSSION QUESTIONS

1. What does God mean by his "covenant," and what is its significance for the Hebrew people?
2. What are the core moral and religious features of God's covenant as described in the Ten Commandments?
3. How do these features set the Hebrews apart from other peoples in the region at the time?

3. Concepts of Civilization

Homer, *The Odyssey* (Eighth Century B.C.E.)

Economic and political turmoil engulfed Greece during what scholars have dubbed the Dark Age, but this period also set the stage for the remaking of Greek civilization. Greece's geography encouraged continued contact with other peoples, thereby allowing for economic, cultural, and political recovery and innovation. In the process, Greeks fashioned a new sense of identity centered on the values of both individual excellence (arête in Greek) and shared community values, such as hospitality. Drawing on long-standing oral tradition, the Greek poet Homer celebrated these values in his epic poem The Odyssey. Composed in the eighth century B.C.E., the poem recounts the adventures of Odysseus, who sets sail for his home off the west coast of Greece after having fought in the Trojan War. (Homer told the tale of this war in The Iliad, his other epic poem.) Odysseus's homecoming proves to be no easy feat; he faces one peril after another during his ten-year journey back to Ithaca. The excerpt below from Book 9 describes his visit to the "land of the Cyclops," a civilization described in sharp contrast to the ideal of Greek society.

From there we sailed on, our spirits now at a low ebb,
And reached the land of the high and mighty Cyclops,
lawless brutes, who trust so to the everlasting gods
they never plant with their own hands or plow the soil.
Unsown, unplowed, the earth teems with all they need,

From "Book 9: In the One-Eyed Giant's Cave" from *The Odyssey* by Homer, trans. Robert Fagles (New York: Penguin Group, 1996), 214–17.

wheat, barley and vines, swelled by the rains of Zeus[1]
to yield a big full-bodied wine from clustered grapes.
They have no meeting place for council, no laws either,
no, up on the mountain peaks they live in arching caverns —
each a law to himself, ruling his wives and children,
not a care in the world for any neighbor...

When young Dawn with her rose-red fingers shone once more
I called a muster briskly, commanding all the hands,
'The rest of you stay here, my friends-in-arms.
I'll go across with my own ship and crew
and probe the natives living over there.
What *are* they — violent, savage, lawless?
or friendly to strangers, god-fearing men?'

With that I boarded ship and told the crew
to embark at once and cast off cables quickly.
They swung aboard, they sat to the oars in ranks
and in rhythm churned the water white with stroke on stroke.
But as soon as we reached the coast I mentioned — no long trip —
We spied a cavern just at the shore, gaping above the surf,
towering, overgrown with laurel...
Here was a giant's lair, in fact, who always pastured
his sheepflocks far afield and never mixed with others.
A grim loner, dead set in his own lawless ways.
Here was a piece of work, by god, a monster
built like no mortal who ever supped on bread,
no, like a shaggy peak, I'd say — a man-mountain
rearing head and shoulders above the world.

DISCUSSION QUESTIONS

1. How does Odysseus describe the land of the Cyclops and its inhabitants?

2. What does this description suggest about Odysseus's understanding of the nature of Greek society and how it compares to other societies?

3. How do the Cyclops relate to their natural environment? How does this differ from Odysseus's assumptions about the ideal relationship between the natural environment and human society?

---

[1]Zeus: The supreme god of Olympus; known as the father of gods and men. [Ed.]

4. Two Visions of the City-State

SOURCES IN CONVERSATION | Tyrtaeus of Sparta and Solon of Athens, *Poems* (Seventh–Sixth Centuries B.C.E.)

Among the most remarkable products of Greece's recovery from its Dark Age was the creation of a new social and political entity, the city-state. These poems elucidate the values shaping two of these communities, Sparta and Athens. The author of the first, Tyrtaeus of Sparta (originally from Athens, according to some ancient sources), was active when Sparta launched the Second Messenian War in the mid-sixth century B.C.E. His poem reveals the preeminent importance of military glory to the Spartans' communal identity. The author of the second work, the Athenian statesman Solon, emphasizes shared justice as the ideal basis of society. Democratic reforms instituted in Athens in the late sixth century B.C.E. transformed his vision into reality. Both poems are written in the elegiac meter, a style often used at the time to instruct the public.

Tyrtaeus

It is a beautiful thing when a good man falls
    and dies fighting for his country.
The worst pain is leaving one's city and fertile
    fields for the life of a beggar,
wandering with mother, old father, little
    children, and wedded wife.
The man beaten by need and odious poverty
    is detested everywhere he goes,
a disgrace to his family and noble appearance, trailed
    by every dishonor and evil.
If no one takes care of the wanderer or gives him
    honor, respect, or pity,
we must fight to the death for our land and children, giving
    no thought to lengthening life.
Fight in a stubborn, close array, my boys!
    Never waver or retreat!
Feel your anger swell. There is no place
    in combat for love of life.
Older soldiers, whose knees are not so light,
    need you to stand and protect them.
An aging warrior cut down in the vanguard of battle
    disgraces the young. His head

From *Early Greek Lyric Poetry*, trans. David Mulroy (Ann Arbor: University of Michigan Press, 1992), 48–49, 68–69.

is white, his beard is grey, and now he is spilling
    his powerful spirit in dust,
naked, clutching his bloody groin: a sight
    for shame and anger. But youthful
warriors always look good, until the blossom
    withers. Men gape
at them in life and women sigh, and dying
    in combat they are handsome still.
Now is the time for a man to stand, planting
    his feet and biting his lip.

Solon

Our city will never perish by decree of Zeus
    or whim of the immortals; such
is the great-hearted protector, child of thunder, who holds
    her hands over us: Athena.
But by thoughtless devotion to money, the citizens are willing
    to destroy our great city.
Our leaders' minds are unjust; soon they will suffer
    The pangs of great arrogance.
They cannot control their greed and enjoy the cheerful
    feast at hand in peace . . .[1]
    Their wealth depends on crime. . . .
    They seize and steal at random
without regard for the holy, the public good,
    or the sacred foundations of Justice,
who is silent but knows present and past, and comes
    for full retribution in time.
The deadly infection spreads throughout the city,
    rushing it into slavery,
which wakens internal strife and war that kills
    so many beautiful youths.
Malicious conspiracies easily ruin a city,
    though the people love it dearly.
These are the evils stalking the people: many
    impoverished leave for foreign
soil, bound and sold in chains of disgrace. . . .
The public evil visits every home;
    undeterred by courtyard gates,
it leaps the high hedge and finds its man,
    though he runs to his bedroom to hide.

---

[1]The ellipses here and below indicate at least one missing line in the original Greek text. [Ed.]

My heart bids me to teach the Athenians that lawless
    behavior is the bane of a city,
but respect for law spreads order and beauty;
    it shackles the legs of the unjust,
smooths and moderates, diminishes arrogance and withers
    delusion's burgeoning blossoms;
it straightens crooked judgments, humbles pride,
    halts partisanship and the anger
born of faction. Everything righteous and wise
    depends on respect for the law.

DISCUSSION QUESTIONS

1. What does Tyrtaeus reveal about the values and modes of conduct that Spartan warriors were expected to embody?
2. How does Tyrtaeus describe warriors who do not live up to these expectations? What do his criticisms reveal about Spartan culture?
3. Why does Solon think Athenian citizens pose a threat to the polis?
4. What message does Solon seek to convey to Athenian citizens in this poem?

5. Representations of Difference

Greek Janiform Flask (c. 520–510 B.C.E.)

Archaeological evidence provides an especially rich source on the development of ancient Greeks' collective identity. Geography afforded the Greeks the opportunity to interact with peoples of many different ethnicities. These included dark-skinned Africans whom the Greeks (and later the Romans) generically classified as "Ethiopian." Echoing ancient commentators, Greek artists captured what they considered to be key physical differences between themselves and Ethiopians, creating a yardstick by which Greeks measured not only people of other ethnicities but also themselves. Standing less than five inches in height, the flask pictured below offers a glimpse into Greeks' understanding of racial contrast. Designed to hold perfume or oil, these small flasks were often used when bathing. This flask juxtaposes a dark-skinned African woman and a Greek woman, and it achieves an extraordinary level of detail given the flask's small size. Scholars have argued against imposing modern notions of race onto our interpretation of this flask and others like it, opting instead to focus on what they can tell us about ancient understanding of difference.

Well, so long as the maximum number of workmen was employed in them, no one ever wanted a job; in fact, there were always more jobs than the labourers could deal with. And even at the present day no owner of slaves employed in the mines reduces the number of his men; on the contrary, every master obtains as many more as he can. The fact is, I imagine, that when there are few diggers and searchers, the amount of metal recovered is small, and when there are many, the total of ore discovered is multiplied. Hence of all the industries with which I am acquainted this is the only one in which expansion of business excites no jealousy.

Further than this, every farmer can tell just how many yoke of oxen are enough for the farm and how many labourers. To put more on the land than the requisite number is counted loss. In mining undertakings, on the contrary, everyone tells you that he is short of labour. Mining, in fact, is quite different from other industries. An increase in the number of coppersmiths, for example, produces a fall in the price of copper work, and the coppersmiths retire from business. The same thing happens in the iron trade. Again, when corn and wine are abundant, the crops are cheap, and the profit derived from growing them disappears, so that many give up farming and set up as merchants or shopkeepers or moneylenders. But an increase in the amount of the silver ore discovered and of the metal won is accompanied by an increase in the number of persons who take up this industry. Neither is silver like furniture, of which a man never buys more when once he has got enough for his house. No one ever yet possessed so much silver as to want no more; if a man finds himself with a huge amount of it, he takes as much pleasure in burying the surplus as in using it.

Mark too that, whenever states are prosperous, silver is in strong demand. The men will spend money on fine arms and good horses and magnificent houses and establishments, and the women go in for expensive clothes and gold jewelry. If, on the other hand, the body politic is diseased owing to failure of the harvest or to war, the land goes out of cultivation and there is a much more insistent demand for cash to pay for food and mercenaries.

If anyone says that gold is quite as useful as silver, I am not going to contradict him; but I know this, that when gold is plentiful, silver rises and gold falls in value.

With these facts before us, we need not hesitate to bring as much labour as we can get into the mines and carry on work in them, feeling confident that the ore will never give out and that silver will never lose its value. . . .

To make myself clearer on the subject . . . I will now explain how the mines may be worked with the greatest advantage to the state. Not that I expect to surprise you by what I am going to say, as if I had found the solution of a difficult problem. For, some things that I shall mention are still to be seen by anyone at the present day, and as for conditions in the past, our fathers have told us that they were similar. But what may well excite surprise is that the state, being aware that many private individuals are making money out of her, does not imitate them. Those of us who have given thought to the matter have heard long ago, I imagine, that Nicias son of Niceratus, once owned a thousand men in the mines, and let them out to Sosias the Thracian, on condition that Sosias paid him an *obol*[1] a day per man net and filled all vacancies as they occurred. Hipponicus, again, had six hundred

---

[1]*obol*: An ancient Greek coin worth one-sixth of a drachma. [Ed.]

slaves let out on the same terms and received a rent of a *mina* a day net. Philemonides had three hundred, and received half a *mina*.[2] There were others too, owning numbers in proportion, I presume, to their capital. But why dwell on the past? At this day there are many men in the mines let out in this way. Were my proposals adopted, the only innovation would be, that just as private individuals have built up a permanent income by becoming slave owners, so the state would become possessed of public slaves, until there were three for every citizen. Whether my plan is workable, let anyone who chooses judge for himself by examining it in detail.

So let us take first the cost of the men. Clearly the treasury is in a better position to provide the money than private individuals. Moreover the Council can easily issue a notice inviting all and sundry to bring slaves, and can buy those that are brought to it. When once they are purchased, why should there be more hesitation about hiring from the treasury than from a private person, the terms offered being the same? At any rate men hire consecrated lands and houses, and farm taxes under the state.

The treasury can insure the slaves purchased by requiring some of the lessees to become guarantors, as it does in the case of the tax-farmers.[3] In fact a tax-farmer can swindle the state more easily than a lessee of slaves. For how are you to detect the export of public money? Money looks the same whether it is private property or belongs to the state. But how is a man to steal slaves when they are branded with the public mark and it is a penal offence to sell or export them?

So far, then, it appears to be possible for the state to acquire and to keep men. But, one may ask, when labour is abundant, how will a sufficient number of persons be found to hire it? Well, if anyone feels doubtful about that, let him comfort himself with the thought that many men in the business will hire the state slaves as additional hands, since they have abundance of capital, and that among those now working in the mines many are growing old. Moreover there are many others, both Athenians and foreigners, who have neither will nor strength to work with their own hands, but would be glad to make a living by becoming managers.

DISCUSSION QUESTIONS

1. Why does Xenophon think the Athenian government should adopt his proposal? What does he think the government has to gain?

2. What role do slaves play in his plan? How does he describe them and their value to the state and to private citizens?

3. The Greeks are credited with creating a unique political model in the ancient world based on the concept of citizenship and shared governance. Does Xenophon's proposal offer any insights as to why Greek slavery expanded at the same time?

---

[2]*mina*: An ancient unit of weight and value equal to 100 drachma. [Ed.]

[3]**tax-farmers**: Tax-farmers were independent bidders in an annual, state-run auction for the contract to collect taxes. In exchange for the contract, tax-farmers had to pay a guaranteed set amount to the state while keeping something additional above that amount as their profit. [Ed.]

COMPARATIVE QUESTIONS

1. Based on these documents, what similarities and differences do you see between Near Eastern and Greek social and political organization?

2. According to scholars, in this period Greeks came to see themselves as a people set apart by linguistic, cultural, and ethnic differences. What do the last four documents reveal about how Greeks conceived of their identity? What would you describe as some of the key attributes Greeks ascribed to themselves?

3. According to Solon, what should be the basis of society, and why? In appealing to the Athenian government to adopt his proposal for the state-owned mines, in what ways does Xenophon build on Solon's ideal while revealing its paradoxes?

4. What role does the divine play in the accounts of the conquest of Babylon and the Hebrews' flight from Egypt? What does this suggest about the place of religion in the Near East at the time?

CHAPTER 3

The Greek Golden Age
c. 500–c. 400 B.C.E.

In the fifth century, Greece enjoyed a period of extraordinary prosperity and achievement, with Athens leading the way. Its economy was booming and its culture flourishing. At the same time, its male citizens developed the first democracy in history, and under their guidance, Athens became the leader of the Greek world. The first five documents attest to the dynamic nature of Greek politics, art, philosophy, and science. They also reveal that, even as innovation fueled Greece's rise to glory, the pull of traditional beliefs and practices remained strong. Such beliefs were especially influential in establishing expected behavior for both women and men. As the last two selections demonstrate, a woman's status was inextricably linked to her roles as wife and mother. To put either in jeopardy threatened the very foundations of Greek society.

1. The Golden Age of Athens
Thucydides, *The Funeral Oration of Pericles* (429 B.C.E.)

The most renowned Athenian politician in his day, Pericles (c. 495–429 B.C.E.) contributed greatly to the brilliance of Athens's Golden Age. Not only did he help to build the city-state's empire abroad, but he also devoted much of his career to strengthening democracy at home. In his History of the Peloponnesian War, *Thucydides brings Pericles to life in a description of a speech he delivered to honor those who had died during the first year of fighting. The Peloponnesian War pitted Athens against its authoritarian rival, Sparta, from 431 to 404 B.C.E., ending ultimately with Athens's defeat. While some scholars have questioned the authenticity of the speech's content, nonetheless it vividly memorializes a time when Athens was still brimming with confidence in the greatness of its people and government.*

In the same winter the Athenians gave a funeral at the public cost to those who had first fallen in this war. It was a custom of their ancestors . . .

Modernized English text adapted from Thucydides, *The History of the Peloponnesian Wars*, trans. Richard Crawley (New York: E. P. Dutton & Co., 1910) II, 34–46.

Pericles . . . was chosen to pronounce their eulogy. When the proper time arrived, he advanced from the sepulchre to an elevated platform in order to be heard by as many of the crowd as possible, and spoke as follows: . . .

I shall begin with our ancestors: it is both just and proper that they should have the honour of the first mention on an occasion like the present. They dwelt in the country without break in the succession from generation to generation, and by their valour handed it down free to the present time. And if our more remote ancestors deserve praise, much more do our own fathers, who added to their inheritance the empire which we now possess. . . . But what was the road by which we reached our position, what the form of government under which our greatness grew, what the national habits out of which it sprang; these are questions which I may try to solve before I proceed to my praise of these men; since I think this to be a subject upon which on the present occasion a speaker may properly dwell, and to which the whole assembly, whether citizens or foreigners, may listen with advantage.

Our constitution does not copy the laws of neighbouring states; we are rather a pattern to others than imitators ourselves. Its administration favours the many instead of the few; this is why it is called a democracy. If we look to the laws, they afford equal justice to all in their private differences; if no social standing, advancement in public life falls to reputation for capacity, class considerations not being allowed to interfere with merit; nor again does poverty bar the way, if a man is able to serve the state, he is not hindered by the obscurity of his condition. The freedom which we enjoy in our government extends also to our ordinary life. There, far from exercising a jealous surveillance over each other, we do not feel called upon to be angry with our neighbour for doing what he likes, or even to indulge in those injurious looks which cannot fail to be offensive, although they inflict no positive penalty. But all this ease in our private relations does not make us lawless as citizens. Against this fear is our chief safeguard, teaching us to obey the magistrates and the laws, particularly such as regard the protection of the injured, whether they are actually on the statute book, or belong to that code which, although unwritten, yet cannot be broken without acknowledged disgrace.

Further, we provide plenty of means for the mind to refresh itself from business. We celebrate games and sacrifices all the year round, and the elegance of our private establishments forms a daily source of pleasure and helps to banish melancholy; while the magnitude of our city draws the produce of the world into our harbour, so that to the Athenian the fruits of other countries are as familiar a luxury as those of his own.

If we turn to our military policy, there also we differ from our antagonists. We throw open our city to the world, and never by alien acts exclude foreigners from any opportunity of learning or observing, although the eyes of an enemy may occasionally profit by our liberality; trusting less in system and policy than to the native spirit of our citizens; while in education, where our rivals from their very cradles by a painful discipline seek after manliness, at Athens we live exactly as we please, and yet are just as ready to encounter every legitimate danger. In proof of this it may be noticed that the Lacedaemonians[1] do not invade our country alone, but bring with them all their confederates; while we Athenians advance unsupported into the territory of a neighbour, and fighting upon a foreign soil usually vanquish with ease men who are defending their homes. . . .

---

[1]**Lacedaemonians:** Spartans. [Ed.]

Nor are these the only points in which our city is worthy of admiration. We cultivate refinement without extravagance and knowledge without effeminacy; wealth we employ more for use than for show, and place the real disgrace of poverty not in owning to the fact but in declining the struggle against it. Our public men have, besides politics, their private affairs to attend to, and our ordinary citizens, though occupied with the pursuits of industry, are still fair judges of public matters; for, unlike any other nation, regarding him who takes no part in these duties not as unambitious but as useless, we Athenians can reliably assess policy even if few of us are originators, and, instead of looking on discussion as a stumbling-block in the way of action, we think it an indispensable preliminary to any wise action at all. Again, in our enterprises we present the singular spectacle of daring and deliberation, each carried to its highest point, and both united in the same persons; although usually decision is the fruit of ignorance, hesitation of reflection. But the palm of courage will surely be adjudged most justly to those, who best know the difference between hardship and pleasure and yet are never tempted to shrink from danger. . . .

Indeed if I have dwelt at some length upon the character of Athens, it has been to show that our stake in the struggle is not the same as theirs who have no such blessings to lose, and also that the merit of the men over whom I am now speaking might by definite proofs be established. Their praise is now in a great measure complete; for the Athens that I have celebrated is only what the heroism of these and their like have made her, men whose fame, unlike that of most Hellenes,[2] will be found to be only commensurate with their deeds. And if a test of worth be wanted, it is to be found in their closing scene, and this not only in cases in which it set the final seal upon their merit, but also in those in which it gave the first hint of their having any. For there is justice in the claim that steadfastness in his country's battles should be as a cloak to cover a man's other imperfections; since the good action has blotted out the bad, and his merit as a citizen more than outweighed his demerits as an individual. . . . Thus choosing to die resisting, rather than to live submitting, they fled only from dishonour, but met danger face to face, and after one brief moment, while at the summit of their fortune, escaped, not from their fear, but from their glory.

So died these men as became Athenians. You, their survivors, must determine to have as unfaltering a resolution in the field, though you may pray that it may have a happier issue. And not contented with ideas derived only from words of the advantages which are bound up with the defense of your country, though these would furnish a valuable text to a speaker even before an audience so alive to them as the present, you must yourselves realize the power of Athens, and feed your eyes upon her from day to day, till love of her fills your hearts; and then, when all her greatness shall break upon you, you must reflect that it was by courage, sense of duty, and a keen feeling of honour in action that men were enabled to win all this, and that no personal failure in an enterprise could make them consent to deprive their country of their valour, but they laid it at her feet as the most glorious contribution that they could offer. . . .

Turning to the sons or brothers of the dead, I see an arduous struggle before you. When a man is gone, all tend to praise him, and should your merit be ever so transcendent, you will still find it difficult not merely to overtake, but even to approach their renown. The living have envy to contend with, while those who are no longer in our path are honoured with a goodwill into which rivalry does not enter. On the other

---

[2]**Hellenes:** Greeks. [Ed.]

hand, if I must say anything on the subject of female excellence to those of you who will now be in widowhood, it will be all comprised in this brief exhortation. Great will be your glory in not falling short of your natural character; and greatest will be hers who is least talked of among the men, whether for good or for bad.

My task is now finished. I have performed it to the best of my ability, and in word, at least, the requirements of the law are now satisfied. If deeds be in question, those who are here interred have received part of their honours already, and for the rest, their children will be brought up till manhood at the public expense: the state thus offers a valuable prize, as the garland of victory in this race of valour, for the reward both of those who have fallen and their survivors. And where the rewards for merit are greatest, there are found the best citizens.

And now that you have brought to a close your lamentations for your relatives, you may depart.

DISCUSSION QUESTIONS

1. According to Pericles, what sets Athens apart from its neighbors and adversaries?

2. As described here, what are the guiding principles of Athenian democracy?

3. How does Pericles characterize his fellow Athenians and their contributions to the city's glory, and what obligations does he believe they have to the state?

4. What does Pericles' short admonition to widows suggest about his conception of gender roles within Athenian society and its relationship to his understanding of democracy?

2. Movement in Stone

SOURCES IN CONVERSATION | Myron of Eleutherae, *Discus Thrower* (c. 450 b.c.e.) and *Atalanta* (c. 300–200 b.c.e.)

According to Thucydides, Athenians were innovators, not emulators. Although this statement applies to many facets of the Greek Golden Age, it is perhaps nowhere more visible than in its art. Greek sculptors abandoned the stiffness characteristic of earlier statues and replaced it with a new style of human movement. The Discus Thrower *by Myron (c. 480–440 b.c.e.) is among the most renowned examples of this type of statuary. Originally sculpted in bronze, the* Discus Thrower *is known today only through later Roman copies. The figure is presented in arrested motion as he swings his arm back, about to fling the discus. A favorite sport in ancient Greece, discus throwing was part of the Olympic pentathlon competition. Barred from the men's competition, women had their own Olympic festival in which unmarried women could compete. The marble statue of Atalanta by an unknown artist demonstrates that Greek sculptors' innovations were not limited to the depiction of male athletes. This statue has a complicated history: it is an early eighteenth-century copy based on a lost original Greek statue from the third century b.c.e. The head and body are Roman,*

Gianni Dagli Orti / REX / Shutterstock

Musée du Louvre, Paris, France / SEF / Art Resource, NY

and the restorer may also have used fragments of a statue of Diana to compose the figure. In Greek mythology, Atalanta was renowned as a swift and fierce huntress who agreed to marry only if her suitors could outrun her in a race; anyone who lost would die. Here she is depicted setting off on a race against a suitor, intent on victory.

DISCUSSION QUESTIONS

1. Why do you think the two artists chose these poses rather than upright ones? How did this choice contribute to the statues' sense of motion?

2. How are the bodies and faces of these two athletes portrayed? What differences do you see, and do these differences add anything to the statues' overall visual effect?

3. What evidence do these statues provide to support scholars' assertion that a newfound confidence in human potential for beauty and perfection characterized the Greek Golden Age?

3. The Emergence of Philosophy

Plato, *The Apology of Socrates* (399 B.C.E.)

Political and artistic innovation were not the only distinctive features of fifth-century Athens. Socrates (469–399 B.C.E.) was a famous philosopher of the day, and his views on ethics and morality challenged conventional values while steering Greek philosophy in new directions. Unlike the Sophists, Socrates offered no classes and did not write his ideas down. He relied instead on conversation and critical questioning to draw people into his way of thinking. In this document, we hear Socrates speaking for himself before a jury as described by his pupil Plato. At the time, Socrates was on trial for impiety, and he spoke to convince his fellow citizens of his innocence while urging them to examine the basis of a just life. In the process, despite his ultimate conviction, he articulated key elements of his philosophy that would exert an enduring influence on Western thought.

How you, O Athenians, have been affected by my accusers, I cannot tell; but I know that they almost made me forget who I was — so persuasively did they speak; and yet they have hardly uttered a word of truth. But of the many falsehoods told by them, there was one which quite amazed me; — I mean when they said that you should be upon your guard and not allow yourselves to be deceived by the force of my eloquence. To say this, when they were certain to be detected as soon as I opened my lips and proved myself to be anything but a great speaker, did indeed appear to me most shameless — unless by the force of eloquence they mean the force of truth; for if such is their meaning, I admit that I am eloquent. But in how different a way from theirs! Well, as I was saying, they have scarcely spoken the truth at all; but from me you shall hear the whole truth: not, however, delivered after their manner in a set oration duly ornamented with words and phrases. No, by heaven! but I shall use the words and arguments which occur to me at the moment; for I am confident in the justice of my cause. . . .

I will begin at the beginning, and ask what is the accusation which has given rise to the slander of me, and in fact has encouraged Meletus to prefer this charge against me. Well, what do the slanderers say? They shall be my prosecutors, and I will sum up their words in an affidavit: "Socrates is an evil-doer, and a curious person, who searches into things under the earth and in heaven, and he makes the worse appear the better cause; and he teaches the aforesaid doctrines to others." Such is the nature of the accusation: it is just what you have yourselves seen in the comedy of Aristophanes, who has introduced a man whom he calls Socrates, going about and saying that he walks in air, and talking a deal of nonsense concerning matters of which I do not pretend to know either much or little — not that I mean to speak disparagingly of any one who is a student of natural philosophy. I should be very sorry if Meletus could bring so grave a charge against me. But the simple truth is, O Athenians, that I have nothing to do with physical speculations. Very many of those here present are witnesses to the truth of this, and to them I appeal. . . .

From Plato, *The Dialogues of Plato*, vol. 2, 3rd ed., trans. Benjamin Jowett (New York: Macmillan and Co., 1892), 109, 111–16, 121–23.

Men of Athens, this reputation of mine has come of a certain sort of wisdom which I possess. If you ask me what kind of wisdom, I reply, wisdom such as may perhaps be attained by man, for to that extent I am inclined to believe that I am wise; whereas the persons of whom I was speaking have a superhuman wisdom, which I may fail to describe, because I have it not myself; and he who says that I have, speaks falsely, and is taking away my character. And here, O men of Athens, I must beg you not to interrupt me, even if I seem to say something extravagant. For the word which I will speak is not mine. I will refer you to a witness who is worthy of credit; that witness shall be the God of Delphi — he will tell you about my wisdom, if I have any, and of what sort it is. You must have known Chaerephon; he was early a friend of mine, and also a friend of yours, for he shared in the recent exile of the people, and returned with you. Well, Chaerephon, as you know, was very impetuous in all his doings, and he went to Delphi and boldly asked the oracle to tell him whether — as I was saying, I must beg you not to interrupt — he asked the oracle to tell him whether any one was wiser than I was, and the Pythian prophetess answered, that there was no man wiser. Chaerephon is dead himself; but his brother, who is in court, will confirm the truth of what I am saying.

Why do I mention this? Because I am going to explain to you why I have such an evil name. When I heard the answer, I said to myself, What can the god mean? and what is the interpretation of his riddle? for I know that I have no wisdom, small or great. What then can he mean when he says that I am the wisest of men? And yet he is a god, and cannot lie; that would be against his nature. After long consideration, I thought of a method of trying the question. I reflected that if I could only find a man wiser than myself, then I might go to the god with a refutation in my hand. I should say to him, "Here is a man who is wiser than I am; but you said that I was the wisest." Accordingly I went to one who had the reputation of wisdom, and observed him — his name I need not mention; he was a politician whom I selected for examination — and the result was as follows: When I began to talk with him, I could not help thinking that he was not really wise, although he was thought wise by many, and still wiser by himself; and thereupon I tried to explain to him that he thought himself wise, but was not really wise; and the consequence was that he hated me, and his enmity was shared by several who were present and heard me. So I left him, saying to myself, as I went away: Well, although I do not suppose that either of us knows anything really beautiful and good, I am better off than he is, — for he knows nothing, and thinks that he knows; I neither know nor think that I know. In this latter particular, then, I seem to have slightly the advantage of him. Then I went to another who had still higher pretensions to wisdom, and my conclusion was exactly the same. Where-upon I made another enemy of him, and of many others besides him.

Then I went to one man after another, being not unconscious of the enmity which I provoked, and I lamented and feared this: but necessity was laid upon me, — the word of God, I thought, ought to be considered first. And I said to myself, Go I must to all who appear to know, and find out the meaning of the oracle. And I swear to you, Athenians, by the dog I swear! — for I must tell you the truth — the result of my mission was just this: I found that the men most in repute were all but the most foolish; and that others less esteemed were really wiser and better. I will tell you the tale of my wanderings and of the "Herculean" labors, as I may call them, which I endured only to find at last the oracle irrefutable. After the politicians, I went to the poets; tragic, dithyrambic, and all sorts.

And there, I said to myself, you will be instantly detected; now you will find out that you are more ignorant than they are. Accordingly, I took them some of the most elaborate passages in their own writings, and asked what was the meaning of them — thinking that they would teach me something. Will you believe me? I am almost ashamed to confess the truth, but I must say that there is hardly a person present who would not have talked better about their poetry than they did themselves. Then I knew that not by wisdom do poets write poetry, but by a sort of genius and inspiration; they are like diviners or sooth-sayers who also say many fine things, but do not understand the meaning of them. The poets appeared to me to be much in the same case; and I further observed that upon the strength of their poetry they believed themselves to be the wisest of men in other things in which they were not wise. So I departed, conceiving myself to be superior to them for the same reason that I was superior to the politicians.

At last I went to the artisans, for I was conscious that I knew nothing at all, as I may say, and I was sure that they knew many fine things; and here I was not mistaken, for they did know many things of which I was ignorant, and in this they certainly were wiser than I was. But I observed that even the good artisans fell into the same error as the poets; — because they were good workmen they thought that they also knew all sorts of high matters, and this defect in them overshadowed their wisdom; and therefore I asked myself on behalf of the oracle, whether I would like to be as I was, neither having their knowledge nor their ignorance, or like them in both; and I made answer to myself and to the oracle that I was better off as I was.

This inquisition has led to my having many enemies of the worst and most danger-ous kind, and has given occasion also to many calumnies. And I am called wise, for my hearers always imagine that I myself possess the wisdom which I find wanting in others: but the truth is, O men of Athens, that God only is wise; and by his answer he intends to show that the wisdom of men is worth little or nothing; he is not speaking of Socrates, he is only using my name by way of illustration, as if he said, He, O men, is the wisest, who, like Socrates, knows that his wisdom is in truth worth nothing. And so I go about the world, obedient to the god, and search and make enquiry into the wisdom of any one, whether citizen or stranger, who appears to be wise; and if he is not wise, then in vindi-cation of the oracle I show him that he is not wise; and my occupation quite absorbs me, and I have no time to give either to any public matter of interest or to any concern of my own, but I am in utter poverty by reason of my devotion to the god.

There is another thing: — young men of the richer classes, who have not much to do, come about me of their own accord; they like to hear the pretenders examined, and they often imitate me, and proceed to examine others; there are plenty of persons, as they quickly discover, who think that they know something, but really know little or nothing; and then those who are examined by them instead of being angry with them-selves are angry with me: This confounded Socrates, they say; this villainous misleader of youth! — and then if somebody asks them, Why, what evil does he practice or teach? they do not know, and cannot tell; but in order that they may not appear to be at a loss, they repeat the ready-made charges which are used against all philosophers about teaching things up in the clouds and under the earth, and having no gods, and making the worse appear the better cause; for they do not like to confess that their pretense of knowledge has been detected — which is the truth; and as they are numerous and ambitious and energetic, and are drawn up in battle array and have persuasive tongues, they have filled your ears with their loud and inveterate calumnies. And this is the reason why my three accusers, Meletus and Anytus and Lycon, have set upon me; Meletus, who has a quarrel with me on behalf of the poets; Anytus, on behalf of the craftsmen and politicians; Lycon, on behalf of the rhetoricians: and, as I said at the beginning, I cannot expect to get rid of such a mass of calumny all in a moment. And this, O men of Athens, is the truth and the whole truth; I have concealed nothing, I have dissembled nothing. And yet, I know that my plainness of speech makes them hate me, and what is their hatred but a proof that I am speaking the truth? — Hence has arisen the prejudice against me; and this is the reason of it. . . .

Some one will say: And are you not ashamed, Socrates, of a course of life which is likely to bring you to an untimely end? To him I may fairly answer: There you are mistaken: a man who is good for anything ought not to calculate the chance of living or dying; he ought only to consider whether in doing anything he is doing right or wrong — acting the part of a good man or of a bad. . . .

For the fear of death is indeed the pretense of wisdom, and not real wisdom, being a pretense of knowing the unknown; and no one knows whether death, which men in their fear apprehend to be the greatest evil, may not be the greatest good. Is not this ignorance of a disgraceful sort, the ignorance which is the conceit that a man knows what he does not know? And in this respect only I believe myself to differ from men in general, and may perhaps claim to be wiser than they are: — that whereas I know but little of the world below, I do not suppose that I know: but I do know that injustice and disobedience to a better, whether God or man, is evil and dishonorable, and I will never fear or avoid a possible good rather than a certain evil. And therefore if you let me go now, and are not convinced by Anytus, who said that since I had been prosecuted I must be put to death; (or if not that I ought never to have been prosecuted at all); and that if I escape now, your sons will all be utterly ruined by listening to my words — if you say to me, Socrates, this time we will not mind Anytus, and you shall be let off, but upon one condition, that you are not to enquire and speculate in this way any more, and that if you are caught doing so again you shall die; — if this was the condition on which you let me go, I should reply: Men of Athens, I honor and love you; but I shall obey God rather than you, and while I have life and strength I shall never cease from the practice and teaching of philosophy, exhorting any one whom I meet and saying to him after my manner: You, my friend, — a citizen of the great and mighty and wise city of Athens, — are you not ashamed of heaping up the greatest amount of money and honor and reputation, and caring so little about wisdom and truth and the greatest improvement of the soul, which you never regard or heed at all? And if the person with whom I am arguing, says: Yes, but I do care; then I do not leave him or let him go at once; but I proceed to interrogate and examine and cross-examine him, and if I think that he has no virtue in him, but only says that he has, I reproach him with undervaluing the greater, and overvaluing the less. And I shall repeat the same words to every one whom I meet, young and old, citizen and alien, but especially to the citizens, inasmuch as they are my brethren. For know that this is the command of God; and I believe that no greater good has ever happened in the State than my service to the God. For I do nothing but go about persuading you all, old and young alike, not to take thought for your persons or your properties, but first and chiefly to care about the greatest improvement of the soul. I tell you that virtue is not given by money, but that from virtue comes money and every other good of man, public as well as private. This is my teaching, and if this is the doctrine which corrupts the youth, I am a mischievous person. But if any one says that this is not my teaching, he is speaking an untruth. Wherefore, O men of Athens, I say to you, do as Anytus bids or not as Anytus bids, and either acquit me or not; but whichever you do, understand that I shall never alter my ways, not even if I have to die many times.

DISCUSSION QUESTIONS

1. According to Socrates, what accusations have been levied against him, and why?
2. In refuting these accusations, what does Socrates reveal about his fundamental intellectual beliefs and methods?
3. Why do you think many of Socrates' contemporaries found his views so threatening?
4. What impressions do Socrates' words give you of him as a man?

4. The Advance of Science

Hippocrates of Cos, *On the Sacred Disease* (400 B.C.E.)

Science was yet another forum for innovation and change during Greece's Golden Age. Hippocrates of Cos (c. 460–377 B.C.E.) gained fame across the Hellenic world as an exceptional medical teacher and practitioner who helped to transform contemporary theories regarding the cause and treatment of disease. Traditional Greek medicine looked to religion and magic to understand and heal illness. By contrast, Hippocrates emphasized the need to view disease as a physical ailment rooted in the natural world. The text excerpted below, On the Sacred Disease, is one of the earliest of the many treatises attributed to Hippocrates. The "sacred disease" in question is epilepsy. Although scholars cannot prove definitively that Hippocrates wrote the work, they agree that its advocation of rational, observation-based medicine represents a key feature of his scientific legacy.

The Sacred Disease

I am about to discuss the disease called "sacred." It is not, in my opinion, any more divine or more sacred than other diseases, but has a natural cause, and its supposed divine origin is due to men's inexperience, and to their wonder at its peculiar character. Now while men continue to believe in its divine origin because they are at a loss to understand it, they really disprove its divinity by the facile method of healing which they adopt, consisting as it does of purifications and incantations. But if it is to be considered divine just because it is wonderful, there will be not one sacred disease but many, for I will show that other

From *Hippocrates*, vol. 2, trans. W. H. S. Jones (Cambridge, MA: Harvard University Press, 1959), 139, 141, 143, 145, 153, 175, 179, 181, 183.

diseases are no less wonderful and portentous, and yet nobody considers them sacred. For instance, quotidian fevers, tertians, and quartans seem to me to be no less sacred and god-sent than this disease,[1] but nobody wonders at them. Then again one can see men who are mad and delirious from no obvious cause, and committing many strange acts; while in their sleep, to my knowledge, many groan and shriek, others choke, others dart up and rush out of doors, being delirious until they wake, when they become as healthy and rational as they were before, though pale and weak; and this happens not once but many times. Many other instances, of various kinds, could be given, but time does not permit us to speak of each separately.

My own view is that those who first attributed a sacred character to this malady were like the magicians, purifiers, charlatans, and quacks of our own day, men who claim great piety and superior knowledge. Being at a loss, and having no treatment which would help, they concealed and sheltered themselves behind superstition, and called this illness sacred, in order that their utter ignorance might not be manifest. They added a plausible story, and established a method of treatment that secured their own position. They used purifications and incantations; they forbade the use of baths, and of many foods that are unsuitable for sick folk . . . [they forbade] the wearing of black (black is the sign of death); not to lie on or wear goat-skin, not to put foot on foot or hand on hand. . . . These observances they impose because of the divine origin of the disease, claiming superior knowledge and alleging other causes, so that, should the patient recover, the reputation for cleverness may be theirs; but should he die, they may have a sure fund of excuses, with the defense that they are not at all to blame, but the gods. Having given nothing to eat or drink, and not having steeped their patients in baths, no blame can be laid, they say, upon them. So I suppose that no Libyan dwelling in the interior can enjoy good health, since they lie on goat-skins and eat goats' flesh, possessing neither coverlet nor cloak nor footgear that is not from the goat; in fact they possess no cattle save goats. But if to eat or apply these things engenders and increases the disease, while to refrain works a cure, then neither is godhead[2] to blame nor are the purifications beneficial; it is the foods that cure or hurt, and the power of godhead disappears.

Accordingly I hold that those who attempt in this manner to cure these diseases cannot consider them either sacred or divine; for when they are removed by such purifications and by such treatment as this, there is nothing to prevent the production of attacks in men by devices that are similar. If so, something human is to blame, and not godhead. He who by purifications and magic can take away such an affection can also by similar means bring it on, so that by this argument the action of godhead is disproved. By these sayings and devices they claim superior knowledge, and deceive men by prescribing for them purifications and cleansings, most of their talk turning on the intervention of gods and spirits. . . .

The fact is that the cause of this affection, as of the more serious diseases generally, is the brain. . . .

---

[1] Because of the regularity of the attacks of fever, which occur every day (quotidians), every other day (tertians), or with intermissions of two whole days (quartans).

[2] [The Greek word for godhead] does not imply any sort of monotheism. The article is generic, and the phrase therefore means "*a* god" rather than "*the* god."

Men ought to know that from the brain, and from the brain only, arise our pleasures, joys, laughter, and jests, as well as our sorrows, pains, griefs, and tears. Through it, in particular, we think, see, hear, and distinguish the ugly from the beautiful, the bad from the good, the pleasant from the unpleasant, in some cases using custom as a test, in others perceiving them from their utility. It is the same thing which makes us mad or delirious, inspires us with dread and fear, whether by night or by day, brings sleeplessness, inopportune mistakes, aimless anxieties, absent-mindedness, and acts that are contrary to habit. These things that we suffer all come from the brain, when it is not healthy, but becomes abnormally hot, cold, moist, or dry, or suffers any other unnatural affection to which it was not accustomed. . . .

In these ways I hold that the brain is the most powerful organ of the human body, for when it is healthy it is an interpreter to us of the phenomena caused by the air, as it is the air that gives it intelligence. Eyes, ears, tongue, hands, and feet act in accordance with the discernment of the brain; in fact the whole body participates in intelligence in proportion to its participation in air. To consciousness the brain is the messenger. For when a man draws breath into himself, the air first reaches the brain, and so is dispersed through the rest of the body. . . .

. . . As therefore it is the first of the bodily organs to perceive the intelligence coming from the air, so too if any violent change has occurred in the air owing to the seasons, the brain also becomes different from what it was. Therefore I assert that the diseases too that attack it are the most acute, most serious, most fatal, and the hardest for the inexperienced to judge of.

This disease styled sacred comes from the same causes as others, from the things that come to and go from the body, from cold, sun, and from the changing restlessness of winds. . . . Each has a nature and power of its own; none is hopeless or incapable of treatment. Most are cured by the same things as caused them. One thing is food for one thing, and another for another, though occasionally each actually does harm. So the physician must know how, by distinguishing the seasons for individual things, he may assign to one thing nutriment and growth, and to another diminution and harm. For in this disease as in all others it is necessary, not to increase the illness, but to wear it down by applying to each what is most hostile to it, not that to which it is conformable. For what is conformity gives vigor and increase; what is hostile causes weakness and decay. Whoever knows how to cause in men by regimen moist or dry, hot or cold, he can cure this disease also, if he distinguish the seasons for useful treatment, without having recourse to purifications and magic.

DISCUSSION QUESTIONS

1. According to traditional medicine, what was the cause of epilepsy? Why does Hippocrates reject this belief?

2. What course of treatment does Hippocrates think physicians should follow when treating this disease, and why?

3. Many scholars regard Hippocrates as the father of scientific medicine. Do you view his explanation of the causes and treatment of epilepsy as scientific? Why or why not?

5. Human Commodities

Auction of Confiscated Slaves (c. 414 b.c.e.)

Despite momentous changes during Greece's Golden Age, ancient traditions retained their grip on a growing segment of society: slaves. Slavery had been a fact of life in the Greek city-states since their origins but had expanded significantly by the fifth century b.c.e. as free citizens drew sharper boundaries between themselves and slaves. Slaves came from many different sources — they could be captives of war, raised in a private home or on an estate, or kidnap victims — and they were an indispensable source of manpower for families, businesses, and the government. The inscription below records the sale at auction of slaves owned by a metic (a foreign resident), Kephisodoros, who had been condemned of a crime by the state. As punishment, the state confiscated and sold all of his property, including his sixteen slaves. Records of the auctioneers' sale were cut on stone slabs approximately five feet tall and three feet wide and erected in the central market square in Athens, the agora. The first column records the sales tax paid by the buyer, the second column the price for each slave, and the third column their gender and national origin.

Property of Kephisodoros, a metic [living] in the Peira[ieus]

2 dr.[1]	165 dr.	A Thracian[2] woman
1 dr. 3 obols[3]	135 dr.	A Thracian woman
[2] dr.	170 dr.	A Thracian
2 dr. 3 obols	240 dr.	A Syrian
[1] dr. 3 obols	105 dr.	A Carian[4]
2 dr.	161 dr.	An Illyrian[5]
2 dr. 3 obols	220 dr.	A Thracian woman
1 dr. 3 obols	115 dr.	A Thracian
1 dr. 3 obols	144 dr.	A Scythian[6]
1 dr. 3 obols	121 dr.	An Illyrian
2 dr.	153 dr.	A man from Colchis[7]
2 dr.	174 dr.	A Carian child
1 dr.	72 dr.	A little Carian child
[3] dr. 1 obol	301 dr.	A Syrian
[2] dr.	151 dr.	A Melitt[enian (man or woman)][8]
1 dr.	85[..] dr. 1 ob.	A Lydian[9] woman

[1]**dr**: drachma. [Ed.]
[2]**Thracian**: A person from Thrace, a region in northeastern mainland Greece. [Ed.]
[3]**obol**: An ancient Greek coin worth one-sixth of a drachma. [Ed.]
[4]**Carian**: A person from Caria, a territory in southwestern Anatolia bordering the Aegean Sea. [Ed.]
[5]**Illyrian**: A person from Illyria, a region in the western part of the Balkan Peninsula. [Ed.]
[6]**Scythian**: A person from north of the Black Sea or from the Caucasus Mountains. [Ed.]
[7]**Colchis**: A kingdom on the western coast of the Black Sea. [Ed.]
[8]**Melittenian**: A person from Melita, the island of Malta located in the Mediterranean Sea between Sicily and Libya. [Ed.]
[9]**Lydian**: A person from Lydia, a kingdom on the western coast of Asia Minor. [Ed.]

DISCUSSION QUESTIONS

1. What does this record suggest about the value of slaves as a commodity in this period?

2. What do you think may account for the variations in sales tax and sales price paid for each slave?

3. What do the national origins of the slaves listed here suggest about the scope of slavery and the slave trade in the Greek Golden Age?

6. Domestic Boundaries

Euphiletus, *A Husband Speaks in His Own Defense*
(c. 400 B.C.E.)
and
Overhead Views of a House on the North Slope of the Areopagus (Fifth Century B.C.E.)

Although Greek citizenship granted free women a new measure of security and status in society, traditional paternalism remained intact. Defined by their roles as daughters, wives, and widows, women were closely supervised and had limited legal and political rights. The testimony below is that of a man named Euphiletus who was put on trial for murdering his wife's lover. He presented the following arguments in his own defense, as prepared for him by the speechwriter Lysias (c. 440–380 B.C.E.). Although not directly related to Euphiletus's case, the overhead views of a Greek house illuminate the physical geography of the domestic values underlying his defense. Most women spent a significant portion of their lives segregated in their own quarters (gynakeion), usually on the second floor of the house to limit access to the street. Typically, men's quarters (andron) were on the first floor, intended in part to prevent unsupervised meetings between women and men from outside the family. The drawings show the first floor of an excavated house on the north slope of Areopagus, a rocky hill west of the Acropolis in Athens.

I would give a great deal, members of the jury, to find you, as judges of this case, taking the same attitude towards me as you would adopt towards your own behavior in similar circumstances. I am sure that if you felt about others in the same way as you did about yourselves, not one of you would fail to be angered by these deeds, and all of you would consider the punishment a small one for those guilty of such conduct.

Moreover, the same opinion would be found prevailing not only among you, but everywhere throughout Greece. This is the one crime for which, under any government, democratic or exclusive, equal satisfaction is granted to the meanest against the mightiest, so that the least of them receives the same justice as the most exalted. Such is the detestation, members of the jury, in which this outrage is held by all mankind.

From Kathleen Freeman, ed., *The Murder of Herodes and Other Trials from the Athenian Law Courts* (Indianapolis, IN: Hackett Publishing, 1994), 43–52.

Concerning the severity of the penalty, therefore, you are, I imagine, all of the same opinion: not one of you is so easy-going as to believe that those guilty of such great offenses should obtain pardon, or are deserving of a light penalty. What I have to prove, I take it, is just this: that Eratosthenes seduced my wife, and that in corrupting her he brought shame upon my children and outrage upon me, by entering my home; that there was no other enmity between him and me except this; and that I did not commit this act for the sake of money, in order to rise from poverty to wealth, nor for any other advantage except the satisfaction allowed by law.

I shall expound my case to you in full from the beginning, omitting nothing and telling the truth. In this alone lies my salvation, I imagine — if I can explain to you everything that happened.

Members of the jury: when I decided to marry and had brought a wife home, at first my attitude towards her was this: I did not wish to annoy her, but neither was she to have too much of her own way. I watched her as well as I could, and kept an eye on her as was proper. But later, after my child had been born, I came to trust her, and I handed all my possessions over to her, believing that this was the greatest possible proof of affection.

Well, members of the jury, in the beginning she was the best of women. She was a clever housewife, economical and exact in her management of everything. But then, my mother died; and her death has proved to be the source of all my troubles, because it was when my wife went to the funeral that this man Eratosthenes saw her; and as time went on, he was able to seduce her. He kept a look out for our maid who goes to market; and approaching her with his suggestions, he succeeded in corrupting her mistress.

Now first of all, gentlemen, I must explain that I have a small house which is divided into two — the men's quarters and the women's — each having the same space, the women upstairs and the men downstairs.

After the birth of my child, his mother nursed him; but I did not want her to run the risk of going downstairs every time she had to give him a bath, so I myself took over the upper story, and let the women have the ground floor. And so it came about that by this time it was quite customary for my wife often to go downstairs and sleep with the child, so that she could give him the breast and stop him from crying.

This went on for a long while, and I had not the slightest suspicion. On the contrary, I was in such a fool's paradise that I believed my wife to be the chastest woman in all the city.

Time passed, gentlemen. One day, when I had come home unexpectedly from the country, after dinner, the child began crying and complaining. Actually it was the maid who was pinching him on purpose to make him behave so, because — as I found out later — this man was in the house.

Well, I told my wife to go and feed the child, to stop his crying. But at first she refused, pretending that she was so glad to see me back after my long absence. At last I began to get annoyed, and I insisted on her going.

"Oh, yes!" she said. "To leave *you* alone with the maid up here! You mauled her about before, when you were drunk!"

I laughed. She got up, went out, closed the door — pretending that it was a joke — and locked it. As for me, I thought no harm of all this, and I had not the slightest suspicion. I went to sleep, glad to do so after my journey from the country.

Towards morning, she returned and unlocked the door.

I asked her why the doors had been creaking during the night. She explained that the lamp beside the baby had gone out, and that she had then gone to get a light from the neighbors.

I said no more. I thought it really was so. But it did seem to me, members of the jury, that she had done up her face with cosmetics, in spite of the fact that her brother had died only a month before. Still, even so, I said nothing about it. I just went off, without a word.

After this, members of the jury, an interval elapsed, during which my injuries had progressed, leaving me far behind. Then, one day, I was approached by an old hag. She had been sent by a woman — Eratosthenes' previous mistress, as I found out later. This woman, furious because he no longer came to see her as before, had been on the look-out until she had discovered the reason. The old crone, therefore, had come and was lying in wait for me near my house.

"Euphiletus," she said, "please don't think that my approaching you is in any way due to a wish to interfere. The fact is, the man who is wronging you and your wife is an enemy of ours. Now if you catch the woman who does your shopping and works for you, and put her through an examination, you will discover all. The culprit," she added, "is Eratosthenes from Oea. Your wife is not the only one he has seduced — there are plenty of others. It's his profession."

With these words, members of the jury, she went off.

At once I was overwhelmed. Everything rushed into my mind, and I was filled with suspicion. I reflected how I had been locked into the bedroom. I remembered how on that night the middle and outer doors had creaked, a thing that had never happened before; and how I had had the idea that my wife's face was rouged. All these things rushed into my mind, and I was filled with suspicion.

I went back home, and told the servant to come with me to market. I took her instead to the house of one of my friends; and there I informed her that I had discovered all that was going on in my house.

"As for you," I said, "two courses are open to you: either to be flogged and sent to the tread-mill, and never be released from a life of utter misery; or to confess the whole truth and suffer no punishment, but win pardon from me for your wrong-doing. Tell me no lies. Speak the whole truth."

At first she tried denial, and told me that I could do as I pleased — she knew nothing. But when I named Eratosthenes to her face, and said that he was the man who had been visiting my wife, she was dumbfounded, thinking that I had found out everything exactly. And then at last, falling at my feet and exacting a promise from me that no harm should be done to her, she denounced the villain. She described how he had first approached her after the funeral, and then how in the end she had passed the message on, and in course of time my wife had been over-persuaded. She explained the way in which he had contrived to get into the house, and how when I was in the country my wife had gone to a religious service with this man's mother, and everything else that had happened. She recounted it all exactly.

When she had told all, I said:

"See to it that nobody gets to know of this; otherwise the promise I made you will not hold good. And furthermore, I expect you to show me this actually happening. I have no use for words. I want the *fact* to be exhibited, if it really is so."

She agreed to do this.

Four or five days then elapsed, as I shall prove to you by important evidence. But before I do so, I wish to narrate the events of the last day.

I had a friend and relative named Sôstratus. He was coming home from the country after sunset when I met him. I knew that as he had got back so late, he would not find any of his own people at home; so I asked him to dine with me. We went home to my place, and going upstairs to the upper story, we had dinner there. When he felt restored, he went off; and I went to bed.

Then, members of the jury, Eratosthenes made his entry; and the maid wakened me and told me that he was in the house.

I told her to watch the door; and going downstairs, I slipped out noiselessly.

I went to the houses of one man after another. Some I found at home; others, I was told, were out of town. So collecting as many as I could of those who were there, I went back. We procured torches from the shop near by, and entered my house. The door had been left open by arrangement with the maid.

We forced the bedroom door. The first of us to enter saw him still lying beside my wife. Those who followed saw him standing naked on the bed.

I knocked him down, members of the jury, with one blow. I then twisted his hands behind his back and tied them. And then I asked him why he was committing this crime against me, of breaking into my house.

He answered that he admitted his guilt; but he begged and besought me not to kill him — to accept a money-payment instead.

But I replied:

"It is not I who shall be killing you, but the law of the State, which you, in transgressing, have valued less highly than your own pleasures. You have preferred to commit this great crime against my wife and my children, rather than to obey the law and be of decent behavior."

Thus, members of the jury, this man met the fate which the laws prescribe for wrong-doers of his kind. . . .

[To the Clerk of the Court]:

Read the Law.

[The Law of Solon is read, that an adulterer may be put to death by the man who catches him.]

He made no denial, members of the jury. He admitted his guilt, and begged and implored that he should not be put to death, offering to pay compensation. But I would not accept his estimate. I preferred to accord a higher authority to the law of the State, and I took that satisfaction which you, because you thought it the most just, have decreed for those who commit such offenses. . . .

It is my belief, members of the jury, that this punishment was inflicted not in my own interests, but in those of the whole community. Such villains, seeing the rewards which await their crimes, will be less ready to commit offenses against others if they see that you too hold the same opinion of them. Otherwise it would be far better to wipe out the existing laws and make different ones, which will penalize those who keep guard over their own wives, and grant full immunity to those who criminally pursue them. This would be a far more just procedure than to set a trap for citizens by means of the laws, which urge the man who catches an adulterer to do with him whatever he will, and yet allow the injured party to undergo a trial far more perilous than that which faces the law-breaker who seduces other men's wives. Of this, I am an example — I, who now stand in danger of losing life, property, everything, because I have obeyed the laws of the State.

House on the North Slope of the Areopagus: probable functions of rooms

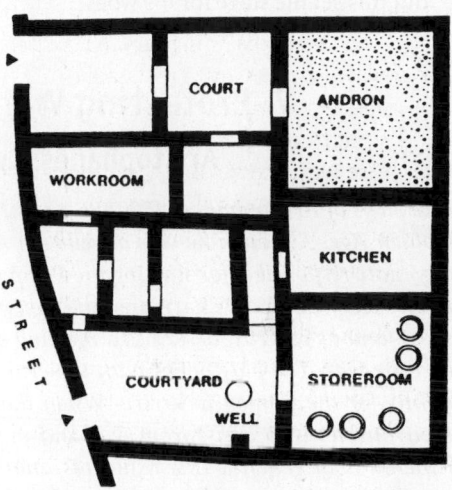

House on the North Slope of the Areopagus: use of rooms by men and by women

Areas used by women are marked +; those used by men are shaded. Entrances to houses from the street are marked with arrows.

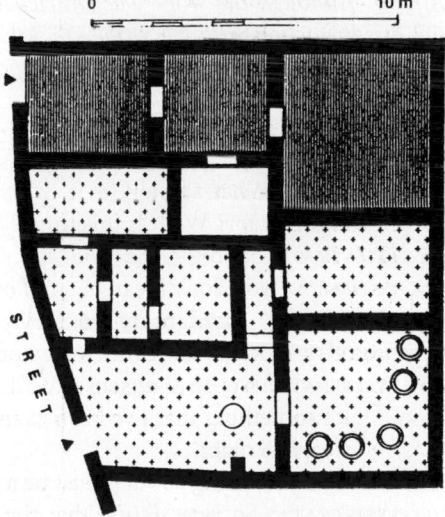

From *Images of Women in Antiquity*, ed. Averil Cameron and Amelie Kuhrt (London: Routledge, 1993), 87.

DISCUSSION QUESTIONS

1. What does Euphiletus's testimony suggest about the roles that both men and women were expected to play in Athenian society in general and within the home in particular?

2. How did these expectations shape the physical geography of domestic space as revealed in the overhead views of a Greek house?

3. According to Euphiletus, why did his wife cross the boundaries of this geography? How did this set the stage for his woes?

7. Protesting War, Performing Satire

Aristophanes, *Lysistrata* (411 B.C.E.)

The plays of Aristophanes (450–386 B.C.E.) are the only comedies to survive from Greece's Golden Age. Although he was a wellborn Athenian, Aristophanes held the leaders of his city-state responsible for starting the Peloponnesian War (431–404) and refusing to make peace. He produced Acharnians, *the first antiwar play, in 425.* Lysistrata, *Aristophanes' most famous comedy, describes a meeting of women who come together to decide how to end the war. The play opens with the group's Athenian leader, Lysistrata, waiting impatiently for the women to arrive. When they do, she suggests a bold strategy to convince their husbands to desist from war and make peace — a sex strike. To force the hand of Athenians in general, Lysistrata has another plan in place. As she tells the gathering, women are about to seize the Acropolis, the geographic, political, and religious center of Athens. Although the work was satiric, Aristophanes' antiwar stance signaled increasing dissatisfaction with conditions in Athens as a result of the war. As the excerpt here reveals, his message in* Lysistrata *is so powerful and timeless that the play is still performed throughout the world.*

CALONICE: What actually *is* it, Lysistrata dear, that you're calling us women together for? What is this thing? What's the size of it?

LYSISTRATA: It's big —

CALONICE: you don't mean big *and meaty*?

LYSISTRATA: — and meaty too, I tell you.

CALONICE: Then how come we're not all here?

LYSISTRATA: Not in *that* sense! We'd have assembled fast enough if it was. No, it's something that I've been examining and tossing about through many a sleepless night.

CALONICE: Tossing about? Must be a dainty little thing.

LYSISTRATA: So very *dainty* that the salvation of all Greece is actually in the hands of her women.

From *The Comedies of Aristophanes, vol. 7: Lysistrata*, ed. and trans. Alan H. Sommerstein (Warminster, England: Arris & Phillips, 1990), 17, 19, 21, 23, 25, 27, 29, 31, 33, 35, 39, 41.

CALONICE: In the hands of her women? Then it's resting on very little!

LYSISTRATA: I tell you that the fortunes of the country depend on us. Either there will be no more Peloponnesians —[1]

CALONICE: Well, that would be splendid, by Zeus, for them to be no more!

LYSISTRATA: — and the Boeotians will all be utterly destroyed —

CALONICE: Oh, please not *all* of them — do make an exception for the eels![2]

LYSISTRATA: I won't utter any words of that kind about Athens, but you can infer my meaning. But if the wives come together here — those from Boeotia, those of the Peloponnesians, and ourselves — won't we'll save Greece.

CALONICE: But what can women achieve that is clever or glorious — we who sit at home all dolled up, wearing saffron gowns and cosmetics and Cimberic[3] straight-liners and riverboat slippers?

LYSISTRATA: Why, that's exactly what I'm counting on to save Greece — our pretty saffron gowns and our perfumes and our riverboat slippers and our rouge and our see-through shifts.

CALONICE: How on earth do you mean?

LYSISTRATA: To make it that none of the men living today will take up the spear against each other —

CALONICE: In that case, by the Two Goddesses,[4] — I'm going to dye a gown with saffron!

LYSISTRATA: — or take up a shield

CALONICE: I'm going to put on a Cimberic!

LYSISTRATA: — or even a little toy sword.

CALONICE: I'm going to buy riverboat slippers!

LYSISTRATA: So shouldn't the women be here now?

CALONICE: Not *now*, in heaven's name — they should have taken wing and been here long ago!

LYSISTRATA: Ah, I tell you, my good friend, you'll see they're thoroughly Athenian — everything they do is too late. Why, there isn't even a single woman here from the Paralia, nor from Salamis.[5]

CALONICE: Oh, as for them, they'll have been working over on their pinnaces well before daylight.

LYSISTRATA: And the Acharnian[6] women too, whom I was expecting and counting on their being first here, they haven't come.

---

[1]**Peloponnesians**: People of Peloponnese, a region forming the southern Greek peninsula. [Ed.]

[2]**exception for the eels**: Eels from Lake Copaïs in Boeotia, a region in south-central Greece, were a culinary delicacy. [Ed.]

[3]**Cimberic**: Negligée. [Ed.]

[4]Reference to Demeter and her daughter Persephone; oaths in their name were used only by women.

[5]**Paralia . . . Salamis**: The Paralia and Salamis were key strategic areas under Athens's jurisdiction. [Ed.]

[6]The district of Acharnae was in the central part of the Athenian polis.

CALONICE: Well, at any rate Theogenes'[7] wife was putting on all sail to come here. [*pointing offstage*] But look, here you are, some of them are arriving now.

LYSISTRATA: [*looking in the other direction*]: And here come some others.

[*Enter Lampito, accompanied by a Theban woman (Ismenia) and a Corinthian woman, and followed by several other Spartan women. Their garments, unlike those of the Athenian women, are open at the side in the Doric fashion.*]

LYSISTRATA: Welcome, Lampito, my very dear Laconian[8] friend! Darling, what beauty you display! What a fine colour, and what a robust frame you've got! You could throttle a bull.

LAMPITO [*in Laconian dialect*]: Yes, indeed, I reckon, by the Two Gods;[9] at any rate I do gymnastics and jump heel-to-buttocks.

CALONICE [*feeling Lampito's breasts*]: *What* a splendid pair of tits you've got!

LAMPITO [*annoyed*]: Really, you're feeling me over like a victim for sacrifice!

LYSISTRATA: And where does this other young lady come from [*indicating Ismenia*]?

LAMPITO: She's come to you, don't you know, by the Two Gods, as a representative of Boeotia.

MYRRHINE [*looking inside Ismenia's revealing costume*]: Yes, she represents Boeotia all right, with that fine lowland region she's got!

CALONICE: *And*, by Zeus, with the mint shoots very neatly plucked out!

LYSISTRATA: And who's the other girl?

LAMPITO: A lady of noble line, by the Two Gods, a Corinthian.

CALONICE: Yes, it's certainly obvious she *does* have noble lines — here and here [*pointing to the Corinthian's belly and buttocks*]!

LAMPITO: Now who has convened this gathering of women?

LYSISTRATA: Here I am; I did.

LAMPITO: Tell us, pray, what you wish of us.

CALONICE: Yes, indeed, dear lady, do tell us what this important business of yours is.

LYSISTRATA: I will tell you now. But before doing so, I will ask you this one small question.

CALONICE: Whatever you like.

LYSISTRATA: Don't you miss the fathers of your children badly, when they're away on campaign? I know that every one of you has a man away from home.

CALONICE: *My* husband, my dear, anyway, has been off on the Thracian Coast for five months, keeping a watch on Eucrates.[10]

---

[7]Theogenes of Acharnae was a merchant and shipowner who had the reputation of a vain boaster pretending to be much richer than he was.

[8]**Laconian:** A term sometimes used to refer to the people of Sparta. [Ed.]

[9]To a Spartan, the "Two Gods" are Castor and Pollux, brothers of Helen and special patrons of Sparta.

[10]**Eucrates:** An Athenian general of questionable loyalty. [Ed.]

MYRRHINE: And *mine*'s been seven solid months at Pylos.[11]

LAMPITO: And *mine*, even when he does ever come home from his active service, right away he's fastened on his shield-band and gone flying off again.

LYSISTRATA: Why, there isn't even a *lover* left us now — not the least glim-
mer of one. Since the Milesians[12] deserted us, I haven't even seen a
six-inch dildo that might have given us some slender comfort. If I were
to find a plan, then, would you be willing to join me in bringing the war
to an end?

CALONICE: By the Two Goddesses, I would, for one, even if I had to pawn this
mantle and drink my purse dry all in one day!

MYRRHINE: And *I* think I'd even be ready to slice myself in two like a flounder
and donate half of my body!

LAMPITO: And I would climb right to the top of Mount Taÿgetum,[13] if I was
going to be able to see peace from there.

LYSISTRATA: I will say it: there's no need for the idea to stay hidden. What we must
do, women, if we mean to compel the men to live in peace, is to abstain —

CALONICE: From what? Tell us.

LYSISTRATA: You'll do it, then?

CALONICE: We'll do it, even if we have to give our lives. [*The others indicate
enthusiastic agreement.*]

LYSISTRATA: Well then: we must abstain from — cock and balls. [*Strong murmurs of dissent; some of the women seem on the point of quitting the meeting.*] Why are you turning your backs on me? Where are you going? I ask
you, why are you pursing your lips and tossing your heads? "Why pales
your colour, why this flow of tears?" Will you do it or will you not? or why
do you hesitate?

CALONICE: I won't do it. Let the war carry on.

MYRRHINE: By Zeus, nor will I. Let the war carry on.

LYSISTRATA: *You* say that, Madam Flounder? Why, a moment ago you were saying you'd be ready to slice off half of your body!

CALONICE: Anything else you want — anything! And if need be, I'm willing
to walk through fire — rather that than cock and balls! There is nothing,
Lysistrata dear, nothing like it!

LYSISTRATA [*turning to another of the women*]: And what about you?

WOMAN: I'd rather go through fire too!

---

[11]A strategic promontory on the west coast of the Peloponnese, seized by the Athenians in 425 and
held ever since by an Athenian garrison.

[12]**Milesians**: Miletus was an important Greek city in Asia Minor. Once an ally of Athens, it revolted
in 412. Apparently it was known for the production of artificial leather penises. [Ed.]

[13]This range forms the western boundary of Laconia. From the plain of Sparta, its highest peak
would have seemed to an ancient Spartan literally impossible to climb.

LYSISTRATA: What an absolute race of nymphomaniacs we are, the lot of us! No wonder the tragedies get written round us: we're nothing but Poseidon and a tub. [*to Lampito*] Look, my dear Laconian friend, if you, just you, join with me, we can still save the situation. Do cast your vote on my side.

LAMPITO: Well, by the Two Gods, it's a hard thing for women to sleep alone without Big Red. But all the same, yes; we do need peace back again.

LYSISTRATA: Oh my darling, you're the only real woman here!

CALONICE: But suppose we abstained as much as you like from . . . what you said — which heaven forbid — would that make peace any more likely to happen?

LYSISTRATA: It very much would, by the Two Goddesses. If we sat there at home in our make-up, and came into their rooms wearing our lawn shifts and nothing else and plucked down below delta-style, and our husbands got all horny and eager for the old spleck-spleck, but we kept away and didn't come to them — they'd make peace fast enough, I know for sure.

CALONICE: But, my dear girl, what if our husbands just ignore us?

LYSISTRATA: In the words of Pherecrates — skin the skinned dog.

CALONICE: Those imitation things are just sheer garbage. And what if they take us and drag us into the bedroom by force?

LYSISTRATA: You should cling to the door.

CALONICE: And if they beat us?

LYSISTRATA: You should submit in the grudgingest way — there's no pleasure in it when it's done by force — and you should vex them generally; and have no fear, they'll tire of it very quickly. For no man is ever going to get any gratification unless it suits the woman that he should.

CALONICE: Well, if that's what you both think, then we agree. [*The others indicate assent.*]

LAMPITO: And *we'll* see to it that *our* menfolk keep the peace with complete honesty and sincerity. But your Athenians — how is one going to persuade that riffraff not to act barmy?

LYSISTRATA: Don't you worry, we'll do our part of the persuading all right.

LAMPITO: Not while your warships still have feet, and while there's that bottomless store of money in the house of your Goddess.[14]

LYSISTRATA: Ah, that's also been thoroughly provided for. We're going to occupy the Acropolis today. The over-age women have instructions to do that: while we get our act together, they're to seize the Acropolis under pretence of making a sacrifice.

LAMPITO: That should be absolutely fine — another good idea of yours.

LYSISTRATA: Well then, Lampito, why don't we bind ourselves together straight away by an oath, so as to make our resolution unbreakable?

---

[14]For over twenty years the financial reserves of the Athenian state had been kept on the Acropolis in the west end of the ancient temple of Athena.

LAMPITO: Present us with the oath, then; we are ready to swear.

. . . .

LYSISTRATA: Let one of you, on behalf of all, repeat the exact words that I say, and the rest will swear to them afterwards in confirmation. No man whatever, neither lover nor husband —

CALONICE: No man whatever, neither lover nor husband —

LYSISTRATA: — shall come near me with his cock up. [*Calonice hesitates.*] Say it.

CALONICE: — shall come near me with his cock up. [*swaying as if about to swoon*] Help, help, Lysistrata, my knees are buckling!

LYSISTRATA: And I will pass my life at home, pure and chaste —

CALONICE [*recovering*]: And I will pass my life at home, pure and chaste —

LYSISTRATA: — in make-up and saffron gown —

CALONICE: — in make-up and saffron gown —

LYSISTRATA: — so that my husband may be greatly inflamed with desire for me —

CALONICE: — so that my husband may be greatly inflamed with desire for me —

LYSISTRATA: — and will never of my free will yield myself to my husband.

CALONICE: — and will never of my free will yield myself to my husband.

LYSISTRATA: And if he force me by force against my will —

CALONICE: And if he force me by force against my will —

LYSISTRATA: — I will submit grudgingly and will not thrust back.

CALONICE: — I will submit grudgingly and will not thrust back.

LYSISTRATA: I will not raise up my Persian slippers ceilingwards.

CALONICE: I will not raise up my Persian slippers ceilingwards.

LYSISTRATA: I will not stand in the lioness-on-a-cheesegrater position.

CALONICE: I will not stand in the lioness-on-a-cheesegrater position.

LYSISTRATA: If I fulfil all this, may I drink from this cup.

CALONICE: If I fulfil all this, may I drink from this cup.

LYSISTRATA· But if I transgress it, may the cup be filled with water.

CALONICE: But if I transgress it, may the cup be filled with water.

LYSISTRATA [*to the others*]: Do all of you join in swearing this oath?

ALL: We do.

DISCUSSION QUESTIONS

1. According to Aristophanes, how do women in Greece's Golden Age feel about sex? What, if anything, is surprising about Lysistrata's proposal to the group?

2. How does the play portray the role of women in Greek society? Are women cast in a positive and/or a negative light? Does the satirical and comedic intent of the playwright affect your interpretation?

3. How does Aristophanes use defined gender roles to make a political statement?

COMPARATIVE QUESTIONS

1. In what ways does the statue of the discus thrower embody the characteristics of Athenian society celebrated in Pericles' speech? In what ways does the statue of Atalanta complicate and challenge them?

2. According to Pericles, what are the virtues of Athenian democracy? Based on the inscription recording a slave auction in the city, how did slavery function within this democracy?

3. How did both Socrates and Hippocrates challenge traditional forms of wisdom in Greek society? What was the basis of their reasoning?

4. Both Euphiletus's defense and Aristophanes' comedy suggest that attempts to regulate women's contact with men from outside the family did not always work. Compare the women mentioned in the defense with the fictional heroines of the play. What do they have in common? What does Aristophanes exaggerate or make up to raise laughs from his audience and to advance his antiwar position?

CHAPTER 4

From the Classical to the Hellenistic World
400–30 B.C.E.

Following the end of the Peloponnesian War in 404 B.C.E., the Greek city-states fell victim to internal squabbling and disunity as each vied to dominate Greece. The first document elucidates how Macedonian kings seized this opportunity to become masters of the eastern Mediterranean and beyond. Their successors capitalized on this legacy, carving out individual kingdoms from the Macedonian Empire. The result was a mix of Greek and Near Eastern peoples and traditions that became a hallmark of the Hellenistic world. In the second document, we see this world through the eyes of an official working in one of its hubs, Egypt, to keep royal rule running smoothly at the local level. The third and fourth documents help us to understand women's roles in this new landscape. Against this backdrop of cultural expansion and internal disunity, Greek thinkers, including Epicurus (Document 5), reexamined the role of fate and chance in life while, as the final document attests, Hellenistic scientists likewise expanded the boundaries of knowledge with innovative methods and discoveries.

1. The Conquest of New Lands
Arrian, *The Campaigns of Alexander the Great*
(Fourth Century B.C.E.)

During his reign from 336 to 323 B.C.E., the Macedonian king Alexander the Great forever changed the eastern Mediterranean world. Following his father's lead, Alexander not only secured Macedonia's position as the leading power in Greece but also conquered the mighty Persian Empire. This excerpt from The Campaigns of Alexander *by Arrian of Nicomedia, written in the second century C.E., paints a vivid picture of Alexander as a warrior and king.*

From Arrian, *The Campaigns of Alexander*, trans. Aubrey de Sélincourt (London: Penguin Books, 1971), 360–66.

Despite errors and exaggerations, Arrian's account is the starting point for all modern research on Alexander. In this passage, Alexander has just returned to Persia in 324 b.c.e. from his expedition to India, where his exhausted soldiers had forced him to turn back because they wanted to return home. His decision to discharge disabled veterans had sparked anger among his Macedonian troops, who feared they were to be replaced by foreigners. According to Arrian, Alexander delivered the following speech to chastise them while glorifying his father's and his own accomplishments.

"My countrymen, you are sick for home — so be it! I shall make no attempt to check your longing to return. Go whither you will; I shall not hinder you. But, if go you must, there is one thing I would have you understand — what I have done for you, and in what coin you will have repaid me.

"First I will speak of my father Philip, as it is my duty to do. Philip found you a tribe of impoverished vagabonds, most of you dressed in skins, feeding a few sheep on the hills and fighting, feebly enough, to keep them from your neighbors — Thracians and Triballians and Illyrians. He gave you cloaks to wear instead of skins; he brought you down from the hills into the plains; he taught you to fight on equal terms with the enemy on your borders, till you knew that your safety lay not, as once, in your mountain strongholds, but in your own valor. He made you city-dwellers; he brought you law; he civilized you. He rescued you from subjection and slavery, and made you masters of the wild tribes who harried and plundered you; he annexed the greater part of Thrace, and by seizing the best places on the coast opened your country to trade, and enabled you to work your mines without fear of attack.[1] Thessaly, so long your bugbear and your dread, he subjected to your rule, and by humbling the Phocians he made the narrow and difficult path into Greece a broad and easy road.[2] The men of Athens and Thebes, who for years had kept watching for their moment to strike us down, he brought so low — and by this time I myself was working at my father's side[3] that they who once exacted from us either our money or our obedience, now, in their turn, looked to us as the means of their salvation. Passing into the Peloponnese, he settled everything there to his satisfaction, and when he was made supreme commander of all the rest of Greece for the war against Persia, he claimed the glory of it not for himself alone, but for the Macedonian people.

"These services which my father rendered you are, indeed, intrinsically great; yet they are small compared with my own. I inherited from him a handful of gold and silver cups, coin in the treasury worth less than sixty talents and over eight times that amount of debts incurred by him; yet to add to this burden I borrowed a further sum of eight hundred talents, and, marching out from a country too poor to maintain you decently, laid open for you at a blow, and in spite of Persia's naval supremacy, the gates of the Hellespont. My cavalry crushed the *satraps* [governors] of Darius, and I added all Ionia and Aeolia, the two Phrygias and Lydia to your empire. Miletus I reduced by siege; the other

---

[1]The gold and silver mines at Mount Pangaeum near Philippi are said to have brought Philip more than 1,000 talents a year.
[2]In 346 b.c.e.
[3]He refers principally, no doubt, to his part in the battle of Chaeronea in 338 b.c.e.

towns all yielded of their own free will — I took them and gave them you for your profit and enjoyment. The wealth of Egypt and Cyrene, which I shed no blood to win, now flows into your hands; Palestine and the plains of Syria and the Land between the Rivers are now your property; Babylon and Bactria and Susa are yours; you are masters of the gold of Lydia, the treasures of Persia, the wealth of India — yes, and of the sea beyond India, too. You are my captains, my generals, my governors of provinces.

"From all this which I have labored to win for you, what is left for myself except the purple and this crown? I keep nothing for my own; no one can point to treasure of mine apart from all this which you yourselves either possess, or have in safe keeping for your future use. Indeed, what reason have I to keep anything, as I eat the same food and take the same sleep as you do? Ah, but there are epicures among you who, I fancy, eat more luxuriously than I; and this I know, that I wake earlier than you — and watch, that you may sleep.

"Perhaps you will say that, in my position as your commander, I had none of the labors and distress which you had to endure to win for me what I have won. But does any man among you honestly feel that he has suffered more for me than I have suffered for him? Come now — if you are wounded, strip and show your wounds, and I will show mine. There is no part of my body but my back which has not a scar; not a weapon a man may grasp or fling the mark of which I do not carry upon me. I have sword cuts from close fight; arrows have pierced me, missiles from catapults bruised my flesh; again and again I have been struck by stones or clubs — and all for your sakes. for your glory and your gain. Over every land and sea, across river, mountain, and plain I led you to the world's end, a victorious army. I married as you married, and many of you will have children related by blood to my own. Some of you have owed money — I have paid your debts, never troubling to inquire how they were incurred, and in spite of the fact that you earn good pay and grow rich from the sack of cities. To most of you I have given a circlet of gold as a memorial for ever and ever of your courage and of my regard.[4] And what of those who have died in battle? Their death was noble, their burial illustrious; almost all are commemorated at home by statues of bronze; their parents are held in honor, with all dues of money or service remitted, for under my leadership not a man among you has ever fallen with his back to the enemy.

"And now it was in my mind to dismiss any man no longer fit for active service — all such should return home to be envied and admired. But you all wish to leave me. Go then! And when you reach home, tell them that Alexander your King, who vanquished Persians and Medes and Bactrians and Sacae; who crushed the Uxii, the Arachotians, and the Drangae, and added to his empire Parthia, the Chorasmian waste, and Hyrcania to the Caspian Sea; who crossed the Caucasus beyond the Caspian Gates, and Oxus and Tanais and the Indus, which none but Dionysus had crossed before him, and Hydaspes and Acesines and Hydraotes — yes, and Hyphasis too, had you not feared to follow; who by both mouths of the Indus burst into the Great Sea beyond, and traversed the desert of Gedrosia, untrodden before by any army; who made Carmania his own, as his troops swept by, and the country of the Oreitans; who was brought back by you to Susa, when his

---

[4]Surely an exaggeration.

ships had sailed the ocean from India to Persia — tell them, I say, that you deserted him and left him to the mercy of barbarian men, whom you yourselves had conquered. Such news will indeed assure you praise upon earth and reward in heaven. Out of my sight!"

As he ended, Alexander sprang from the rostrum and hurried into the palace. All that day he neither ate nor washed nor permitted any of his friends to see him. On the following day too he remained closely confined. On the third day he sent for the Persian officers who were in the highest favor and divided among them the command of the various units of the army. Only those whom he designated his kinsmen were now permitted to give him the customary kiss.[5]

On the Macedonians the immediate effect of Alexander's speech was profound. They stood in silence in front of the rostrum. Nobody made a move to follow the King except his closest attendants and the members of his personal guard; the rest, helpless to speak or act, yet unwilling to go away, remained rooted to the spot. But when they were told about the Persians and Mede — how command was being given to Persian officers, foreign troops drafted into Macedonian units, a Persian Corps of Guards called by a Macedonian name, Persian infantry units given the coveted title of Companions, Persian Silver Shields,[6] and Persian mounted Companions, including even a new Royal Squadron, in process of formation — they could contain themselves no longer. Every man of them hurried to the palace; in sign of supplication they flung their arms on the ground before the doors and stood there calling and begging for admission. They offered to give up the ringleaders of the mutiny and those who had led the cry against the King, and swore they would not stir from the spot day or night unless Alexander took pity on them.

Alexander, the moment he heard of this change of heart, hastened out to meet them, and he was so touched by their groveling repentance and their bitter lamentations that the tears came into his eyes. While they continued to beg for his pity, he stepped forward as if to speak, but was anticipated by one Callines, an officer of the Companions, distinguished both by age and rank. "My lord," he cried, "what hurts us is that you have made Persians your kinsmen — Persians are called Alexander's kinsmen — Persians kiss you. But no Macedonian has yet had a taste of this honor."

"Every man of you," Alexander replied, "I regard as my kinsman, and from now on that is what I shall call you."

Thereupon Callines came up to him and kissed him, and all the others who wished to do so kissed him too. Then they picked up their weapons and returned to their quarters singing the song of victory at the top of their voices.

To mark the restoration of harmony, Alexander offered sacrifice to the gods he was accustomed to honor, and gave a public banquet which he himself attended, sitting among the Macedonians, all of whom were present.[7] Next to them the Persians had their places, and next to the Persians distinguished foreigners of other nations; Alexander and his friends dipped their wine from the same bowl and poured the same libations, following the lead of the Greek seers and the Magi (Persian priests). The chief object of

---

[5]*Kinsman* was an honorific title bestowed by the Persian king on leading Persians.
[6]This is a later name for the Guards (*Hypaspists*).
[7]An evident exaggeration, unless only officers are meant.

his prayers was that Persians and Macedonians might rule together in harmony as an imperial power. It is said that 9,000 people attended the banquet; they unanimously drank the same toast, and followed it by the paean of victory.[8]

DISCUSSION QUESTIONS

1. According to Alexander, how did Philip II transform Macedonia from a minor kingdom into a great power?
2. What does Alexander reveal about the impact Macedonia's rise to power had on the Greek city-states?
3. Why does Alexander consider his achievements to be even greater than those of his father?
4. Based on Alexander's speech, how would you characterize his method of rule?

2. Imperial Bureaucracy

Zeno, Egyptian Official, *Records* (259–250 B.C.E.)

Although Alexander the Great's imperial glory was short-lived, it opened the door to a new, more international eastern Mediterranean world. Upon his death in 323 B.C.E., Alexander's army commanders divided his empire into separate kingdoms over which they assumed control. To rule effectively, these new kings and their successors relied on a hierarchical bureaucracy staffed by Greeks and local administrators to oversee local affairs. This document illuminates the busy life of a Greek named Zeno, who was an agent for Apollonius, the financial minister for Ptolemy Philadelphus of Egypt (r. 285–246 B.C.E.). At the time, Egypt was home to both Greeks and indigenous peoples who contributed to a vibrant urban culture and economy. These extracts include instructions from Apollonius, requests for help, a desk diary, and other records of Zeno's daily affairs.

Letter from Hierocles (257 B.C.E.)

Hierocles to Zeno greeting. If you are well, it would be excellent. I too am in good health. You wrote to me about Pyrrhus, telling me to train[1] him if I am quite certain of his success, but if not, to avoid incurring useless expense and distracting him from his studies. Now as for my being certain, the gods should know best, but it seems to Ptolemaeus, as far as a man can tell, that Pyrrhus is much better than those now being trained, though they started long before him, and that in a very short time he will be far ahead of them;

From *Select Papyri*, vol. 1, trans. A. S. Hunt and C. C. Edgar (London: William Heinemann, 1932), 269–77, 397–99, 409–15.

[8]This banquet was held to celebrate the reconciliation between Alexander and his Macedonians and (it was hoped) between them and the Persians.

[1]For competition in the public games.

moreover he is pursuing his other studies as well; and to speak with the gods' leave, I hope to see you crowned. Make haste to send him a bathing-apron, and if possible let it be of goatskin or, if not, of thin sheepskin, and a tunic and cloak, and the mattress, coverlet and pillows, and the honey. You wrote to me that you were surprised at my not understanding that all these things are subject to toll. I know it, but you are well able to arrange for them to be sent in perfect security.[2] (Addressed) To Zeno. (Docketed) Hierocles about Pyrrhus. Year 29, Xandicus 3, at Memphis.

Letter from Promethion (256 B.C.E.)

Promethion[3] to Zeno greeting. I suffered anxiety when I heard of your long protracted illness, but now I am delighted to hear that you are convalescent and already on the point of recovery. I myself am well. I previously gave your agent Heraclides 150 drachmae in silver from your account, as you wrote to me to do, and he is bringing you now 10 *hins* of perfume in 21 vases which have been sealed with my finger-ring. For though Apollonius wrote to me to buy and give him also 300 wild pomegranate wreaths, I did not manage to give him these at the same time, as they were not ready, but Pa . . . will bring them to him at Naucratis; for they will be finished before the 30th. I have paid the price both of these and of the perfume from your account, as Apollonius wrote. I have also paid a charge of 10 drachmae in copper for the boat in which he is sailing up. And 400 drachmae in silver have been paid to Iatrocles for the papyrus rolls which are being manufactured in Tanis for Apollonius. Take note then that these affairs have been settled thus. And please write yourself if ever you need anything here. Goodbye. Year 29, Choiach 28. (Addressed) To Zeno. (Docketed) Year 29, Peritius 3. Promethion about what he has paid.

Letter from Apollonius the Dioecetes (256 B.C.E.)

Apollonius to Zeno greeting. From the dry wood put on board a boat as many of the thickest logs as possible and send them immediately to Alexandria that we may be able to use them for the festival of Isis. Goodbye. Year 30, Dius 3, Phaophi 23. (Addressed) To Zeno. At once.[4] (Docketed by Zeno) Year 30, Dius 18, Hathur 18. Apollonius about wood for the Isis festival. (Docketed by sender) Wood for the Isis festival.

Letter from Plato (255 B.C.E.)

Plato to Zeno greeting. The father of Demetrius the bearer of this letter happens, it seems, to be residing in the Arsinoite nome,[5] and the lad therefore wishes to find employment there himself. On hearing of your kindly disposition some of his friends asked me to write to you about him, begging you to give him a post in your service. Please then do me a favor and provide some employment for him, whatever you may think suitable, and otherwise look after him, if you find him useful. As a token (of goodwill) I have sent you,

---

[2]That is, by using his influence as an agent of the financial minister.
[3]A banker in Mendes.
[4]An admonition to the persons concerned to send the letter immediately.
[5]**nome**: Region. [Ed.]

from Sosus, 2 artabae[6] of chick-peas bought at 5 drachmae each, and if there are any at Naucratis, I will try to buy you about 20 artabae more and bring them up to you myself. Goodbye. Year 31, Dius 12. (Addressed) To Zeno.

Letter from Artemidorus (252 B.C.E.)

Artemidorus[7] to Zeno greeting. If you are well, it would be excellent. I too am well and Apollonius is in good health and other things are satisfactory. As I write this, we have just arrived in Sidon after escorting the princess[8] to the frontier, and I expect that we shall soon be with you. Now you will do me a favor by taking care of your own health and writing to me if you want anything done that I can do for you. And kindly buy me, so that I may get them when I arrive, 3 metretae[9] of the best honey and 600 artabae of barley for the animals, and pay the cost of them out of the produce of the sesame and croton,[10] and also see to the house in Philadelphia in order that I may find it roofed when I arrive. Try also as best you can to keep watch on the oxen and the pigs and the geese and the rest of the stock there; I shall have a better supply of provisions if you do. Also see to it that the crops are harvested somehow, and if any outlay is required, do not hesitate to pay what is necessary. Goodbye. Year 33, intercalary Peritius 6. (Addressed) To Zeno. To Philadelphia. (Docketed) Year 33, Phamenoth 6. Artemidorus.

Letter from an Invalid (259–257 B.C.E.)

Memorandum to Zeno from Cydippus. If in accordance with the doctors' orders I could have purchased any of the following things in the market, I should not have troubled you; but as it is I have written you a note of what I require, as Apollonius thought I ought to do. So if you have them in store, send me a jar of wine, either Lesbian or Chian,[11] of the very sweetest, and if possible a chous[12] of honey or, if not, as much as you can, and order them to fill me the vessel with salt fish. For both these things they consider to be most needful. And if my health improves and I go abroad to Byzantium, I will bring you back some excellent salt fish. (On the back) Memorandum from Cydippus.

Letter from a House-Painter (c. 255 B.C.E.)

Memorandum to Zeno from Theophilus the . . . About the work in the house of Diotimus: for the portico, [I undertake] to have the cornice painted with a purple border, the upper part of the wall variegated, the lower course like vetch-seed,[13] and the pediment with

---

[6]**artabae**: Baskets. [Ed.]

[7]A physician in the service of the dioecetes.

[8]The princess Berenice, who was escorted to Syria by Apollonius on the occasion of her marriage to Antiochus II.

[9]**metretae**: Jars. [Ed.]

[10]The two oils chiefly used in Egypt at this period were made from sesame and croton (the castor-oil plant), the former for food and the latter for lamps.

[11]**Lesbian or Chian**: From the Greek islands of Lesbos and Chia. [Ed.]

[12]**chous**: Container. [Ed.]

[13]**vetch-seed**: Pea-colored. [Ed.]

circular veining, providing myself with all materials, for 30 drachmae. For the dining-room with seven couches, I will do the vault according to the pattern which you saw, and give the lower course an agreeable tint and paint the Lesbian cornice, providing myself with all materials, for 20 drachmae. And for the dining-rooms with five couches, I will paint the cornices, providing myself with all materials, for 3 drachmae. The sum total is 53 drachmae. But if you provide everything, it will come to 30 drachmae. Goodbye.

Zeno's Agenda (c. 250 B.C.E.)

To ask Herodotus about the goat hair. To ask Aminias at how much mina he sold it. The letter to Dioscurides about the boat. To make an agreement with Timaeus about the pigs. To draft the contract with Apollodorus and write to him to hand over. To load the boat with wool. To write to Jason to let Dionysius put the wool on board and take it down the river when cleaned; the fourth part of the Arabian wool; to let him take down the sour wine. To write to Meliton to plant shoots of the *bumastus* vine belonging to Neoptolemus, and to Alcimus to do likewise if he approves. To Theogenes about twelve yokes of bulls. To give Apollodorus and Callippus . . . [f]rom Metrodorus to Athenagoras about the same year's produce. To Theophilus granting a favor and about the state of the work. To write about corn to Iatrokles and Theodorus before the water from the canal. . . .

Zeno's Agenda (c. 250 B.C.E.)

To get the olive kernels. The oil from Heragoras. To buy for the horses 4 strigils, 4 rubbing cloths, 4 scrapers, and for Phatres 1 strigil. To get shoots of the walnut trees. To ascertain the registration of the wine carried down, for which nome it has been registered. To receive Hermon's boy.

List of Foreign Goods (257 B.C.E.)

Year 29, Xandicus 11, at Hermopolis.[14] We have left behind these articles which Charmus has handed over to Apollodotus: in a basket 5 small bags of nard sealed and 1 small wallet sealed, 1 small wallet, sealed, containing dice of gazelle bone; purple dye in one pillow-case; 1 strip of variegated cloth; 3 half-strips of variegated cloth; 2 strips of white cloth; 4 strips of purple cloth; 3 bags and 1 small bag of frankincense sealed; 3 small bags of myrrh sealed; 1 wallet containing dice of gazelle bone; 1 small wallet of purple dye sealed; 1 small wallet of saffron sealed.

List of Zeno's Clothes (c. 257 B.C.E.)

Zeno's trunk in which are contained: 1 linen wrap, washed; 1 clay-colored cloak, for winter, washed, and 1 worn, 1 for summer, half-worn, 1 natural-colored, for winter, washed, and 1 worn, 1 vetch-colored, for summer, new; 1 white tunic for winter, with sleeves, washed, 1 natural-colored, for winter, with sleeves, worn, 1 natural-colored, for winter, worn, 2 white, for winter, washed, and 1 half-worn, 3 for summer, white, new, 1 unbleached, 1 half-worn;

---

[14]Hermopolis Parva in the Delta.

1 outer garment, white, for winter, washed; 1 coarse mantle; 1 summer garment, white, washed, and 1 half-worn; 1 pair of Sardian pillow-cases; 2 pairs of socks, clay-colored, new, 2 pairs of white, new; 2 girdles, white, new. (Endorsed) From Pisicles, a list of Zeno's clothes.

DISCUSSION QUESTIONS

1. If you had to write a job description for Zeno based on these records, what responsibilities would it include?
2. What do Zeno's records reveal about the local economy?
3. What evidence do you find in Zeno's records of cross-cultural influences within the Hellenistic world?

3. Remembering the Dead

Funerary Inscriptions and Epitaphs (Fifth–First Centuries B.C.E.)

These inscriptions and epitaphs provide a glimpse of women's place in the classical and Hellenistic worlds as described by family members and admirers after their deaths. Originally written in Greek and Latin on tombs and funerary monuments dispersed throughout the Hellenistic world, the words preserved in this form do not simply mark each woman's passing from this world to the next, but they hold her up as an exemplar of female behavior. As in the past, a woman's identity revolved principally around her roles as daughter, wife, and mother. Yet not all women's lives were confined to domestic duties. Some were royal attendants, priestesses, and even physicians, whose daily activities extended into the public sphere.

Archedice, Athens, Fifth Century B.C.E.

This dust hides Archedice, daughter of Hippias, the most important man in Greece in his day. But though her father, husband, brothers, and children were tyrants, her mind was never carried away into arrogance.

Aspasia, Chios, c. 400 B.C.E.

Of a worthy wife this is the tomb — here, by the road that throngs with people — of Aspasia, who is dead; in response to her noble disposition Euopides set up this monument for her; she was his consort.

Dionysia, Athens, Fourth Century B.C.E.

It was not clothes, it was not gold that this woman admired during her lifetime; it was her husband and the good sense that she showed in her behavior. But in return for the youth you shared with him, Dionysia, your tomb is adorned by your husband Antiphilus.

From Mary R. Lefkowitz and Maureen B. Fant, eds., *Women's Life in Greece and Rome*, 2nd ed. (Baltimore: Johns Hopkins University Press, 1992), 16–17, 190, 206, 219, 221–22, 263, 266–67, 274.

Claudia, Rome, Second Century B.C.E.

Friend, I have not much to say; stop and read it. This tomb, which is not fair, is for a fair woman. Her parents gave her the name Claudia. She loved her husband in her heart. She bore two sons, one of whom she left on earth, the other beneath it. She was pleasant to talk with, and she walked with grace. She kept the house and worked in wool. That is all. You may go.

An Accomplished Woman, Sardis, First Century B.C.E.

[An inscription set up by the municipality of Sardis in honor of Menophila, daughter of Hermagenes.] This stone marks a woman of accomplishment and beauty. Who she is the Muses' inscriptions reveal: Menophila. Why she is honored is shown by a carved lily and an alpha, a book and a basket, and with these a wreath. The book shows that you were wise, the wreath that you wore on your head shows that you were a leader; the letter alpha that you were an only child; the basket is a sign of your orderly excellence; the flower shows the prime of your life, which Fate stole away. May the dust lie light on you in death. Alas; your parents are childless; to them you have left tears.

Posilla Senenia, Monteleone Sabino, First Century B.C.E.

Posilla Senenia, daughter of Quartus and Quarta Senenia, freedwoman of Gaius.

Stranger, stop and, while you are here, read what is written: that a mother was not permitted to enjoy her only daughter, whose life, I believe, was envied by some god.

Since her mother was not allowed to adorn her while she was alive, she does so just the same after death; at the end of her time, [her mother] with this monument honors her whom she loved.

Xenoclea, Piraeus, 360? B.C.E.

Leaving two young girls, Xenoclea, daughter of Nicarchus, lies here dead; she mourned the sad end of her son, Phoenix, who died out at sea when he was eight years old.

There is no one so ignorant of grief, Xenoclea, that he doesn't pity your fate. You left behind two young girls and died of grief for your son, who has a pitiless tomb where he lies in the dark sea.

Handiwork, Athens, after 350 B.C.E.

I worked with my hands; I was a thrifty woman, I, Nicarete who lie here.

A Storeroom Attendant, Cape Zoster, near Athens, 56–55 B.C.E.

[An epitaph by a mother for a daughter who worked for Cleopatra at the royal court of Alexandria.] Her mother, an Athenian woman, raised her to be an attendant of foreign storerooms. She too rushed for her child's sake to come to the palace of the king who had set her over his rich possessions. Yet still she could not bring her daughter back alive. But the daughter has a tomb in Athens instead of on Libyan sand.

Epitaph for a Woman Who Died While Pregnant, Egypt, Second–First Centuries B.C.E.

Dosithea, daughter of_____ Look at these letters on the polished rock. Thallo's son Chaeremon married me in his great house. I die in pain, escaping the pangs of childbirth, leaving the breath of life when I was twenty-five years old; from a disease which he died of before, I succumbed after. I lie here in Schedia. Wayfarers, as you go by, all of you, say: "Beloved Dosithea, stay well, also among the dead."

A Midwife and Physician, Athens, Fourth Century B.C.E.

[The memorial tablet represents two women, one seated, one standing, surrounded by infants of both sexes.] Phanostrate, a midwife and physician, lies here. She caused pain to none, and all lamented her death.

A Nurse, Athens, after 350 B.C.E.

[Epitaph for] Apollodorus the immigrant's daughter, Melitta, a nurse. Here the earth covers Hippostrate's good nurse; and Hippostrate still misses you. "I loved you while you were alive, nurse, I love you still now even beneath the earth and now I shall honor you as long as I live. I know that for you beneath the earth also, if there is reward for the good, honors will come first to you, in the realm of Persephone and of Pluto."

Epitaph for a Priestess, Miletus, Third Century B.C.E.

Bacchae[1] of the City, say, "Farewell you holy priestess." This is what a good woman deserves. She led you to the mountain and carried all the sacred objects and implements, marching in procession before the whole city. Should some stranger ask for her name: Alcmeonis, daughter of Rhodius, who knew her share of the blessings.

DISCUSSION QUESTIONS

1. Judging from these inscriptions and epitaphs, what particular qualities did people admire in women, and why?

2. Scholars have described Greek society at the time as patriarchal. Do the epitaphs and inscriptions support this view? Why or why not?

3. What do the epitaphs and inscriptions reveal about the social and economic standing of the women they describe?

---

[1]**Bacchae:** Women worshippers of Dionysus. [Ed.]

4. Modeling Femininity

SOURCES IN CONVERSATION | *Terracotta Figurines*
(Second to Third Century B.C.E.)

Material culture offers additional insights into the lives of Hellenistic women beyond the boundaries of the home. For centuries, small terracotta figurines had been produced in Athens for religious purposes and as theater souvenirs. Over the course of the fourth century B.C.E., this artistic form underwent a notable transformation. For reasons scholars are still uncertain about, depictions of well-to-do, fashionably attired women and girls in a variety of poses now dominated the genre. Often measuring from just under five inches to a foot in height, they typically were brightly painted and departed from earlier models by portraying

Gift of Mrs. Saidie Adler May, 1930 / The Metropolitan Museum of Art, New York, NY / agefotostock Art Collection / AGE Fotostock

their subjects with emotive facial expressions and naturalistic body language. As the two examples here suggest, these were women dressed to be noticed. In real life, the most likely occasion for women to wear such finery would have been at public religious festivals, and clothing regulations from the period suggest that they did. In this way, the figurines allow us

Saint Louis Art Museum, Missouri, USA / Museum purchase / Bridgeman Images

to imagine women beyond the scope of their private duties as mothers, wives, and household managers. Manufactured throughout the Hellenistic world, figurines of this type were in high demand among the buying public as commemorative and decorative objects and have been found by archaeologists in houses, shrines, and burial sites in great numbers.

DISCUSSION QUESTIONS

1. Look closely at the figurines. What details in their style of dress, body configurations, and gestures stand out?

2. In what ways do folds and texture of the drapery accentuate the bodies of the figurines? Why do you think the artists made these stylistic choices?

3. What insights, if any, can we draw from these figures about everyday life of the civic elite in the Hellenistic period?

5. In Pursuit of Happiness

Epicurus, *Letter to a Friend* (Late Third Century B.C.E.)

Born on the island of Samos, Epicurus (c. 341–270 B.C.E.) earned a reputation as an accomplished teacher in Asia Minor that eventually led him to Athens in 306. In the tradition of the schools of philosophy of Plato and Aristotle, the "Garden" of Epicurus attracted a strong following. Although the adjective epicurean *has often been taken to mean the enjoyment of life's pleasures, Epicurus's actual philosophy was based on the pursuit of true, spiritual happiness. In his* Letter to a Friend, *Epicurus explores the meaning of happiness and concludes that it is based on simple needs and a serene spirit.*

We must consider that of desires some are natural, others empty; that of the natural some are necessary, others not; and that of the necessary some are necessary for happiness, others for bodily comfort, and others for life itself. A right understanding of these facts enables us to direct all choice and avoidance toward securing the health of the body and tranquility of the soul; this being the final aim of a blessed life. For the aim of all actions is to avoid pain and fear; and when this is once secured for us the tempest of the soul is entirely quelled, since the living animal no longer needs to wander as though in search of something he lacks, hunting for that by which he can fulfill some need of soul or body. We feel a need of pleasure only when we grieve over its absence; when we stop grieving we are in need of pleasure no longer. Pleasure, then, is the beginning and end of the blessed life. For we recognize it as a good which is both primary and kindred to us. From pleasure we begin every act of choice and avoidance; and to pleasure we return again, using the feeling as the standard by which to judge every good.

Now since pleasure is the good that is primary and most natural to us, for that very reason we do not seize all pleasures indiscriminately; on the contrary we often pass over

From "Letter to Menoecius," in *The Way of Philosophy*, trans. Philip Wheelwright (Upper Saddle River, NJ: Pearson Education, 1960), 423–25.

many pleasures, when greater discomfort accrues to us as a result of them. Similarly we not infrequently judge pains better than pleasures, when the long endurance of a pain yields us a greater pleasure in the end. Thus every pleasure because of its natural kinship to us is good, yet not every pleasure is to be chosen; just as every pain also is an evil, yet that does not mean that all pains are necessarily to be shunned. It is by a scale of comparison and by the consideration of advantages and disadvantages that we must form our judgment on these matters. On particular occasions we may have reason to treat the good as bad, and the bad as good.

Independence of circumstance we regard as a great good: not because we wish to dispense altogether with external advantages, but in order that, if our possessions are few, we may be content with what we have, sincerely believing that those enjoy luxury most who depend on it least, and that natural wants are easily satisfied if we are willing to forego superfluities. Plain fare yields as much pleasure as a luxurious table, provided the pain of real want is removed; bread and water can give exquisite delight to hungry and thirsty lips. To form the habit of a simple and modest diet, therefore, is the way to health: it enables us to perform the needful employments of life without shrinking, it puts us in better condition to enjoy luxuries when they are offered, and it renders us fearless of fortune.

Accordingly, when we argue that pleasure is the end and aim of life, we do not mean the pleasure of prodigals and sensualists, as some of our ignorant or prejudiced critics persist in mistaking us. We mean the pleasure of being free from pain of body and anxiety of mind. It is not a continual round of drunken debauches and lecherous delights, nor the enjoyment of fish and other delicacies of a wealthy table, which produce a pleasant life; but sober reasoning, searching out the motives of choice and avoidance, and escaping the bondage of opinion, to which the greatest disturbances of spirit are due.

The first step and the greatest good is prudence — a more precious thing than philosophy even, for all the other virtues are sprung from it. By prudence we learn that we can live pleasurably only if we live prudently, honorably, and justly, while contrariwise to live prudently, honorably, and justly guarantees a life that is pleasurable as well. The virtues are by nature bound up with a pleasant life, and a pleasant life is inseparable from them in turn.

Is there any better and wiser man than he who holds reverent beliefs about the gods, is altogether free from the fear of death, and has serenely contemplated the basic tendencies (*telê*) of natural law? Such a man understands that the limit of good things is easy to attain, and that evils are slight either in duration or in intensity. He laughs at Destiny, which so many accept as all-powerful. Some things, he observes, occur of necessity, others by chance, and still others through our own agency. Necessity is irresponsible, chance is inconstant, but our own actions are free, and it is to them that praise and blame are properly attached. It would be better even to believe the myths about the gods than to submit to the Destiny which the natural philosophers teach. For the old superstitions at least offer some faint hope of placating the gods by worship, but the Necessity of the scientific philosophers is absolutely unyielding. As to chance, the wise man does not deify it as most men do; for if it were divine it would not be without order. Nor will he accept the view that it is a universal cause even though of a wavering kind; for he believes that what chance bestows is not the good and evil that determine a man's blessedness in life, but the starting-points from which each person can arrive at great good or great evil. He esteems the misfortune of the wise above the prosperity of a fool; holding it better that well chosen courses of action should fail than that ill chosen ones should succeed by mere chance.

Meditate on these and like precepts day and night, both privately and with some companion who is of kindred disposition. Thereby shall you never suffer disturbance, waking or asleep, but shall live like a god among men. For a man who lives constantly among immortal blessings is surely more than mortal.

DISCUSSION QUESTIONS

1. According to Epicurus, what is the relationship between pleasure and pain? What is pleasure? Why might someone choose pain over pleasure?
2. What guidelines should a human being follow in making life choices?
3. How could someone best reconcile the fact that destiny, or chance, is beyond his or her control?

6. Exacting Science

Archimedes, *Letter to Eratosthenes* (Third Century B.C.E.)
and
Marcus Vitruvius Pollio, *Archimedes' "Eureka!" Moment*
(c. 30–20 B.C.E.)

Scientific innovation blossomed during the Hellenistic period. Alexander the Great had ordered the city of Alexandria built, and it became the capital of the Hellenistic kingdom of the Ptolemies. Scientists flocked to the city's royally funded library and research institute, including the mathematician Archimedes of Syracuse (287–212 B.C.E.). It is there that he most likely met the library's director, Eratosthenes of Cyrene (c. 285–194 B.C.E.), a pioneer in mathematical geography. Upon returning home, Archimedes remained in contact with Eratosthenes, thereby promoting the exchange of ideas typical of the intellectual scene at the time. Archimedes included the letter excerpted below in the preface to his treatise Method. *Discovered in 1906, it is unusual in its focus when compared to works by other classical Greek geometers. As Archimedes writes to Eratosthenes, he did not simply want to present his discoveries as finished products, in this case certain geometric theorems; he wanted to pull back the veil on the steps of analysis he took to arrive at them. The second document recounts a story about Archimedes' thinking in action included in a first-century B.C.E. text. For its author, the Roman architect Vitruvius, the tale embodied the wisdom that past thinkers had to offer contemporary civilization. Together, the two documents illuminate the thrill of discovery through measurement, observation, and experimentation that helped to lay the foundation of later Western scientific thought.*

From *The Works of Archimedes*, ed. T. L. Heath (Mineola, NY: Dover Publications, 2002), 12–13, and *Vitruvius: Ten Books on Architecture*, trans. Ingrid D. Rowland (New York: Cambridge University Press, 1999), 108.

Archimedes

Archimedes to Eratosthenes greeting.

I sent you on a former occasion some of the theorems discovered by me, merely writing out the enunciations and inviting you to discover the proofs, which at the moment I did not give. . . .

. . . The proofs then of these theorems I have written in this book and now send to you. Seeing moreover in you, as I say, an earnest student, a man of considerable eminence in philosophy, and an admirer [of mathematical inquiry], I thought fit to write out for you and explain in detail in the same book the peculiarity of a certain method, by which it will be possible for you to get a start to enable you to investigate some of the problems in mathematics by means of mechanics. This procedure is, I am persuaded, no less useful even for the proof of the theorems themselves; for certain things first became clear to me by a mechanical method, although they had to be demonstrated by geometry afterwards because their investigation by the said method did not furnish an actual demonstration. But it is of course easier, when we have previously acquired, by the method, some knowledge of the questions, to supply the proof than it is to find it without any previous knowledge. . . .

Vitruvius

As for Archimedes, although in his limitless wisdom he discovered many wonderful things, nonetheless, of all of them, one in particular, which I shall now describe, seems to convey his boundless ingenuity. It is no surprise that Hieron,[1] after he had obtained immense kingly power in Syracuse, decided, because of the favorable turn of events, to dedicate a votive crown of gold to the immortal gods in a certain shrine. He contracted for the craftsman's wages, and he [himself] weighed out the gold precisely for the contractor. This contractor completed the work with great skill and on schedule; it was approved by the king, and the contractor seemed to have used up the furnished supply of gold. Later, charges were leveled that in the making of the crown a certain amount of gold had been removed and replaced by an equal amount of silver. Hieron, outraged that he should have been shown so little respect, and not knowing by what method he might expose the theft, requested that Archimedes take the matter under consideration on his behalf.

Now Archimedes, once he had charge of this matter, chanced to go to the baths, and there, as he stepped into the tub, he noticed that however much he immersed his body in it, that much water spilled over the sides of the tub. When the reason for this occurrence came clear to him, he did not hesitate, but in a transport of joy he leapt out of the tub, and as he rushed home naked, he let one and all know that he had truly found what he had been looking for — because as he ran he shouted over and over in Greek: "I found it! I found it!" (*Eurêka! Eurêka!*)

On the basis of this discovery he is said to have made two masses whose weight was equal to that of the crown: one of gold and one of silver. When he had done this, he filled

---

[1] **Hieron:** Hieron II was tyrant of Syracuse (270–215 B.C.E.). [Ed.]

a large vessel to the brim with water, into which he sank the mass of silver. Whatever amount of silver was submerged, that much water spilled out. Then, once the mass had been taken out, he poured back the missing amount of water so that it would be level with the brim in the same way as before, using a one-sextarius pitcher [= ½ liter] as a measure. From this procedure he discovered that a certain weight of silver corresponded to a certain measure of water. Once he had tried this, then in the same fashion he sank the gold mass into the full vessel, and when he had removed it, replacing the water by the same method, he discovered that not so much of the water had been lost, and less was required to replace it, as much less as a mass of gold will be smaller in body than a mass of silver which has the same weight. After this, once he had filled the vessel yet again, the crown itself was sunk into the water, and he discovered that more water was required to replace the crown than to replace the mass of gold of equal weight, and because there was more water in the crown's place than in the place of the mass of gold, he detected, by deduction, the mixture of silver in the crown and the contractor's flagrant theft.

DISCUSSION QUESTIONS

1. Why does Archimedes think it is valuable to describe his methods of discovery to Eratosthenes rather than just the discoveries themselves? What does he hope Eratosthenes will gain from the description?

2. What do Archimedes' methods suggest about his thinking process? Do you see evidence of this process at work in Vitruvius's account?

3. It was typical of Archimedes to include letters of this type in the introductions to his works. What does this say about the nature of the scientific community in the Hellenistic world?

4. What do these two sources suggest about the role of observation and mechanical methods in Hellenistic science?

COMPARATIVE QUESTIONS

1. How does Alexander the Great define "civilization" in his assessment of his father's and his own accomplishments? In what ways did Hellenistic kingdoms reflect and build on this definition as revealed in Zeno's Egyptian records?

2. What are the similarities and differences between Epicurus's views of the human condition and those expressed in the funerary inscriptions and epitaphs?

3. What sorts of representations of women are offered by the terracotta figures and the funerary inscriptions and epitaphs? What do these representations have in common, and where do they diverge?

4. What evidence can you find in these documents of increased interactions between Greek and Near Eastern peoples in the Hellenistic world?

The Rise of Rome and Its Republic
753–44 B.C.E.

W hen the Roman republic was founded in 509 B.C.E., few could have foreseen its future as a mighty imperialist state. At the time, Greece was on the threshold of its Golden Age, which was soon followed by Macedonia's meteoric rise to power. Yet throughout this period, the Romans gradually expanded their territories and wealth so that by the end of the second century B.C.E., they controlled most of southern Europe, North Africa, and beyond. Victory came at a price, however, as Roman politicians and military leaders came to value their individual successes more than that of the republic. The documents in this chapter help us chart the republic's development from several different angles. Together, they reveal the pillars of the republic — law, tradition, and communal values — while providing a glimpse of their ultimate demise.

1. Formalizing Roman Law
The Twelve Tables (451–449 B.C.E.)

Although Rome's elite successfully overthrew the Roman monarchy and established the republic in 509 B.C.E., more challenges lay ahead. For the next two centuries, the city's patricians and the rest of its citizens battled over the course the new government should take and their respective roles in it. Promulgated between 451 and 449 B.C.E., the Twelve Tables were a turning point in this struggle, marking the republic's first step toward establishing a fair system of justice. Surviving in fragments only, this code, the earliest in Roman law, was based largely on existing customs. The following excerpts illuminate not only the social and economic landscape of early Rome but also the foundation of Roman jurisprudence.

From *Ancient Roman Statutes*, trans. Allan Chester Johnson et al. (Austin: University of Texas Press, 1961), 9–17.

Table I. Proceedings Preliminary to Trial

If the plaintiff summons the defendant to court the defendant shall go. If the defendant does not go the plaintiff shall call a witness thereto. Only then the plaintiff shall seize the defendant.

If the defendant attempts evasion or takes flight the plaintiff shall lay hand on him.

If sickness or age is an impediment he who summons the defendant to court shall grant him a vehicle. If he does not wish he shall not spread a carriage with cushions.

For a freeholder[1] a freeholder shall be surety;[2] for a proletary[3] anyone who wishes shall be surety.

There shall be the same right of bond and of conveyance with the Roman people for a steadfast person and for a person restored to allegiance.[4]

When the parties agree on the matter the magistrate shall announce it.

If they agree not on terms the parties shall state their case before the assembly in the meeting place or before the magistrate in the market place before noon. Both parties being present shall plead the case throughout together.

If one of the parties does not appear the magistrate shall adjudge the case, after noon, in favor of the one present.

If both parties are present sunset shall be the time limit of the proceedings. . . .

Table II. Trial

The penal sum[5] in an action by solemn deposit shall be either 500 asses or 50 asses.[6] . . . It shall be argued by solemn deposit with 500 asses, when the property is valued at 1,000 asses or more, but with 50 asses, when the property is valued at less than 1,000 asses. But if the controversy is about the freedom of a person, although the person may be very valuable, yet the case shall be argued by a solemn deposit of 50 asses. . . .

Table III. Execution of Judgment

Thirty days shall be allowed by law for payment of confessed debt and for settlement of matters adjudged in court.

---

[1]A taxpayer whose fortune is valued at not less than 1,500 asses.

[2]That is, for his appearance at trial.

[3]A "proletary" is a nontaxpayer whose fortune is rated at less than a freeholder's.

[4]This apparently allows the Latin allies who had revolted and later returned into allegiance to enjoy the same rights and to use the same legal formulas in contractual matters and in transferring property as those who had remained loyal.

[5]Each litigant deposited a sum with the court as a kind of "wager on oath" that his cause was right. The defeated party forfeited his deposit to the state. On account of the desire to show special favor to persons illegally held as slaves and claiming their freedom, the law made the deposit for them very low, typically only fifty asses in such cases.

[6]**asses:** An as was a bronze coin. At the time the Twelve Tables were composed, an as was a one-foot-long bar of copper. It took the form of a coin later, around 269 b.c.e. [Ed.]

After this time the creditor shall have the right of laying hand on the debtor. The creditor shall hale the debtor into court.

Unless the debtor discharges the debt adjudged or unless someone offers surety for him in court the creditor shall take the debtor with him. He shall bind him either with a thong or with fetters of not less than fifteen pounds in weight, or if he wishes he shall bind him with fetters of more than this weight.

If the debtor wishes he shall live on his own means. If he does not live on his own means the creditor who holds him in bonds shall give him a pound of grits daily. If he wishes he shall give him more.

. . . Meanwhile they shall have the right to compromise, and unless they make a compromise the debtors shall be held in bonds for sixty days. During these days they shall be brought to the praetor[7] into the meeting place on three successive market days, and the amount for which they have been judged liable shall be declared publicly. Moreover, on the third market day they shall suffer capital punishment or shall be delivered for sale abroad across the Tiber River.

On the third market day the creditors shall cut shares. If they have cut more or less than their shares it shall be without prejudice.

Table IV. Paternal Power

A notably deformed child shall be killed immediately.

To a father . . . shall be given over a son the power of life and death.

If a father thrice surrenders a son for sale the son shall be free from the father.[8]

To repudiate his wife her husband shall order her . . . to have her own property for herself, shall take the keys, shall expel her.[9]

A child born within ten months of the father's death shall enter into the inheritance. . . .

Table V. Inheritance and Guardianship

. . . Women, even though they are of full age,[10] because of their levity of mind shall be under guardianship . . . except vestal virgins, who . . . shall be free from guardianship. . . .

---

[7]**praetor**: A high elected official. [Ed.]

[8]In the early days of Rome, a Roman father could sell his son into slavery. If the buyer freed the son, the son reentered his father's control (*patria potestas*).

[9]The formula for a valid repudiation of the other by either the husband or the wife is said to have contained the words "have (*or* manage) your own property for yourself." Dissolution of marriage by mutual consent is divorce (*divortium*). In either event, an essential feature is the husband's return of the wife's dowry, if any, whose investment he had controlled during marriage.

[10]For females "full age" was twenty-five years. According to the law of this period, a woman never has legal independence: if she is not in her father's power (*potestas*), she is dependent on her husband's control (*manus*) or, if unmarried and fatherless, she is subject to her guardian's governance (*tutela*).

The conveyable possessions of a woman who is under guardianship of male agnates[11] shall not be acquired by prescriptive right unless they are transferred by the woman herself with the authorization of her guardian. . . .

According as a person has made bequest regarding his personal property or the guardianship of his estate so shall be the law.

If anyone who has no direct heir dies intestate the nearest male agnate shall have the estate.

If there is not a male agnate the male clansmen shall have the estate.

Persons for whom by will . . . a guardian is not given, for them . . . their male agnates shall be guardians.

If a person is insane authority over him and his personal property shall belong to his male agnates and in default of these to his male clansmen. . . .

If a Roman citizen freedman dies intestate without a direct heir, to his patron shall fall the inheritance . . . from said household . . . into said household. . . .

Table VI. Ownership and Possession

. . . If any woman is unwilling to be subjected in this manner[12] to her husband's marital control she shall absent herself for three successive nights in every year and by this means shall interrupt his prescriptive right of each year.[13] . . .

One shall not take from framework timber fixed in buildings or in vineyards. . . . One shall be permitted neither to remove nor to claim stolen timber fixed in buildings or in vineyards, . . . but against the person who is convicted of having fixed such timber there an action for double damages shall be given. . . .

Table VII. Real Property

If a watercourse conducted through a public place does damage to a private person the said person shall have the right to bring an action . . . that security against damage may be given to the owner.

. . . Branches of a tree shall be pruned all around to a height of fifteen feet.

If a tree from a neighbor's farm has been felled by the wind over one's farm, . . . one rightfully can take legal action for that tree to be removed.

. . . It shall be lawful to gather fruit falling upon another's farm. . . .

A slave is ordered in a will to be a free man under this condition: "if he has given 10,000 asses to the heir"; although the slave has been alienated by the heir, yet the slave by giving the said money to the buyer shall enter into his freedom. . . .

---

[11]**agnates:** Relatives from the father's family. [Ed.]

[12]That is, by prescriptive right (*usus*).

[13]This method, the so-called *ius trinoctii* (right of three nights; that is, the right acquired by an absence of three successive nights), enabled a wife to remain married to her husband and yet neither to come into nor to remain in his marital control. If the prescriptive right has been interrupted for three consecutive nights annually, the time of *usus* must commence afresh because the husband's previous possession is considered to be canceled.

Table VIII. Torts or Delicts

. . . If anyone sings or composes an incantation that can cause dishonor or disgrace to another . . . he shall suffer a capital penalty.[14]

If anyone has broken another's limb there shall be retaliation in kind unless he compounds for compensation with him.

. . . If a person breaks a bone of a freeman with hand or by club, he shall undergo a penalty of 300 asses; or of 150 asses, if of a slave.

If one commits an outrage against another the penalty shall be twenty-five asses.

. . . One has broken. . . . One shall make amends.

If a quadruped is said to have caused damage an action shall lie therefore . . . either for surrendering that which did the damage to the aggrieved person . . . or for offering an assessment of the damage.

If fruit from your tree falls onto my farm and if I feed my flock off it by letting the flock onto it . . . no action can lie against me either on the statute concerning pasturage of a flock, because it is not being pastured on your land, or on the statute concerning damage caused by an animal. . . .

If anyone pastures on or cuts by night another's crops obtained by cultivation the penalty for an adult shall be capital punishment and after having been hung up, death as a sacrifice to Ceres. . . . A person below the age of puberty at the praetor's decision shall be scourged and shall be judged as a person either to be surrendered to the plaintiff for damage done or to pay double damages.

Whoever destroys by burning a building or a stack of grain placed beside a house . . . shall be bound, scourged, burned to death, provided that knowingly and consciously he has committed this crime; but if this deed is by accident, that is, by negligence, either he shall repair the damage or if he is unable he shall be corporally punished more lightly.

Whoever fells unjustly another's trees shall pay twenty-five asses for each tree.

If a thief commits a theft by night, if the owner kills the thief, the thief shall be killed lawfully.

By daylight . . . if a thief defends himself with a weapon . . . and the owner shall shout.

In the case of all other . . . thieves caught in the act freemen shall be scourged and shall be adjudged as bondsmen to the person against whom the theft has been committed provided that they have done this by daylight and have not defended themselves with a weapon; slaves caught in the act of theft . . . shall be whipped with scourges and shall be thrown from the rock;[15] but children below the age of puberty shall be scourged at the praetor's decision and the damage done by them shall be repaired. . . .

If a patron defrauds a client he shall be accursed.[16]

---

[14]According to one ancient account the infliction of this penalty perhaps may have included clubbing to death.

[15]A southern spur of the Capitoline Hill, which overlooks the Forum.

[16]That is, declared forfeited to the lower gods and liable to be slain by anyone with impunity.

Unless he speaks his testimony whoever allows himself to be called as a witness or is a scales-bearer shall be dishonored and incompetent to give or obtain testimony. . . .

If anyone pastures on or cuts stealthily by night . . . another's crops . . . the penalty shall be capital punishment, and, after having been hung up, death as a sacrifice to Ceres, a punishment more severe than in homicide. . . .

Table IX. Public Law

Laws of personal exception shall not be proposed. Laws concerning capital punishment of a citizen shall not be passed . . . except by the Greatest Assembly. . . .

. . . Whoever incites a public enemy or whoever betrays a citizen to a public enemy shall be punished capitally.

For anyone whomsoever to be put to death without a trial and unconvicted . . . is forbidden.

Table X. Sacred Law

A dead person shall not be buried or burned in the city.[17] . . .

. . . Expenses of a funeral shall be limited to three mourners wearing veils and one mourner wearing an inexpensive purple tunic and ten flutists. . . .

Women shall not tear their cheeks or shall not make a sorrowful outcry on account of a funeral.

A dead person's bones shall not be collected that one may make a second funeral.

An exception is for death in battle and on foreign soil. . . .

Table XI. Supplementary Laws

. . . There shall not be intermarriage between plebeians and patricians.

Table XII. Supplementary Laws

It is forbidden to dedicate for consecrated use a thing concerning whose ownership there is a controversy; otherwise a penalty of double the value involved shall be suffered. . . .

DISCUSSION QUESTIONS

1. What are the principal concerns expressed in this code?

2. What do these concerns suggest about Roman society at the time?

3. In what ways did these laws represent a triumph for the plebeian class?

---

[17]Inhumation on a large scale and in a crowded community not only was insanitary but also took too much space. Cremation could involve hazards from fire.

2. Artistic Influences

SOURCES IN CONVERSATION | *Etruscan Statuette of a Rider* (c. 434–400 B.C.E.) **and** *Roman Bust of Lucius Junius Brutus* (c. 300 B.C.E.)

Within two decades of its foundation, the Roman republic relied on an aggressive policy of territorial expansion in Italy and abroad to enhance its wealth and power. Unlike the practice of Greek city-states, the Romans absorbed conquered peoples into their population as citizens or allies. In the process, they were also exposed to new forms of art, literature, and language that helped to shape Rome's own cultural development. The Etruscans were an especially important cross-cultural influence, as the two images that follow suggest. The first displays a bronze statuette of a male rider, dating from c. 434–400 B.C.E. A wealthy and urbanized people, the Etruscans were fine craftsmen as well as avid importers of luxury goods from throughout the Mediterranean, including Greece. The second, a bust thought to be of Lucius Junius Brutus, one of the founders of the republic, dates from c. 300 B.C.E., after the Roman conquest of Etruscan territory.

Detroit Institute of Arts, Michigan, USA / Bridgeman Images

Musei Capitolini, Rome, Italy / Scala / Art Resource, NY

DISCUSSION QUESTIONS

1. How would you describe the facial features of the Etruscan rider? How do they compare to those of the bust of Brutus?

2. In choosing to portray human faces in this way, what emotions do you think the sculptors sought to provoke within the viewer?

3. Unlike the Etruscan statuette, the Roman bust probably depicts a known individual. How do you think this fact may have influenced the sculptor's design, and why?

3. Status and Discrimination

Livy, *Roman Women Demonstrate against the Oppian Law* (195 B.C.E.)

Women in ancient Rome were most valued as wives and mothers, yet sometimes they stepped outside the boundaries of family life to make their voices heard. In his History of Rome, *the Roman historian Livy (59 B.C.E.–17 C.E.) reconstructs a heated debate that erupted on one such occasion. In 195 B.C.E., upper-class women from the city and its environs joined together to demonstrate publicly against the Oppian law, which had been passed during wartime and restricted the amount of finery women could wear and their use of carriages in an effort to reduce friction between rich and poor. Their demand for the law's repeal so that they could once again display their elite status sparked both disdain and sympathy among various leaders, to whom they appealed for support. Each camp, represented here by the consul Cato and the tribune Valerius, claimed to have tradition on its side.*

Amid the anxieties of great wars, either scarce finished or soon to come, an incident occurred, trivial to relate, but which, by reason of the passions it aroused, developed into a violent contention. Marcus Fundanius and Lucius Valerius, tribunes of the people, proposed to the assembly the abrogation of the Oppian law. The tribune Gaius Oppius had carried this law in the heat of the Punic War, in the consulship of Quintus Fabius and Tiberius Sempronius, that no woman should possess more than half an ounce of gold or wear a parti-coloured garment or ride in a carriage in the City or in a town within a mile thereof, except on the occasion of a religious festival. The tribunes Marcus and Publius Iunius Brutus were supporting the Oppian law, and averred that they would not permit its repeal; many distinguished men came forward to speak for and against it; the Capitoline was filled with crowds of supporters and opponents of the bill. The matrons could not be kept at home by advice or modesty or their husbands' orders, but blocked all the streets and approaches to the Forum, begging the men as they came down to the Forum that, in the prosperous condition of the state, when the private fortunes of all men were daily increasing, they should allow the women too to have their former distinctions restored. The crowd of women grew larger day by day; for they were now coming in from the towns and rural districts. Soon they dared even to approach and appeal to the consuls, the praetors, and the other officials, but one consul, at least, they found adamant, Marcus Porcius Cato, who spoke thus in favor of the law whose repeal was being urged.

"If each of us, citizens, had determined to assert his rights and dignity as a husband with respect to his own spouse, we should have less trouble with the sex as a whole; as it is, our liberty, destroyed at home by female violence, even here in the Forum is crushed and trodden underfoot, and because we have not kept them individually under control, we dread them collectively. . . .

"For myself, I could not conceal my blushes a while ago, when I had to make my way to the Forum through a crowd of women. Had not respect for the dignity and modesty of some individuals among them rather than of the sex as a whole kept me silent, lest they should seem to have been rebuked by a consul, I should have said, 'What sort of practice is this, of running out into the streets and blocking the roads and speaking to other women's husbands? Could you not have made the same requests, each of your own husband, at home? Or are you more attractive outside and to other women's husbands than to your own? And yet, not even at home, if modesty would keep matrons within the limits of their proper rights, did it become you to concern yourselves with the question of what laws should be adopted in this place or repealed.' Our ancestors permitted no woman to conduct even personal business without a guardian to intervene in her behalf;[1] they wished them to be under the control of fathers, brothers, husbands; we (Heaven help us!) allow them now even to interfere in public affairs, yes, and to visit the Forum and our informal and formal sessions. What else are they doing now on the streets and at the corners except urging the bill of the tribunes and voting for the repeal of the law? Give loose rein to their uncontrollable nature and to this untamed creature and expect that they will themselves set bounds to their license; unless you act, this is the least of the things enjoined upon women by custom or law and to which they submit with a feeling of injustice. It is complete liberty or, rather, if we wish to speak the truth, complete license that they desire.

"If they win in this, what will they not attempt? Review all the laws with which your forefathers restrained their license and made them subject to their husbands; even with all these bonds you can scarcely control them. What of this? If you suffer them to seize these bonds one by one and wrench themselves free and finally to be placed on a parity with their husbands, do you think that you will be able to endure them? The moment they begin to be your equals, they will be your superiors. . . . No law is entirely convenient for everyone; this alone is asked, whether it is good for the majority and on the whole. If every law which harms anyone in his private affairs is to be repealed and discarded, what good will it do for all the citizens to pass laws which those at whom they are aimed will at once annul? . . . What pretext, respectable even to mention, is now given for this insurrection of the women? 'That we may glitter with gold and purple,' says one, 'that we may ride in carriages on holidays and ordinary days, that we may be borne through the city as if in triumph over the conquered and vanquished law and over the votes which we have captured and wrested from you; that there may be no limits to our spending and our luxury.' . . .

"She who can buy from her own purse will buy; she who cannot will beg her husband. Poor wretch that husband, both he who yields and he who yields not, since what he will not himself give he will see given by another man. Now they publicly address other women's husbands, and, what is more serious, they beg for a law and votes, and from sundry men they get what they ask. In matters affecting yourself, your property, your children, you, Sir, can be importuned; once the law has ceased to set a limit to your wife's expenditures you will never set it yourself. Do not think, citizens, that the situation which existed before the law was passed will ever return. It is safer for a criminal to go unaccused than to be acquitted; and luxury, left undisturbed, would have been more endurable then than it will be now, when it has been, like a wild beast, first rendered angry by its very fetters

---

[1]A woman was never independent and was not a person in the legal sense. If she was not under the power of a father or of a husband, a *tutor* was appointed to act for her in legal matters.

and then let loose. My opinion is that the Oppian law should on no account be repealed; whatever is your decision, I pray that all the gods may prosper it."

After this the tribunes of the people who had declared that they would veto the bill spoke briefly to the same effect, and then Lucius Valerius argued thus for the measure which he had proposed: . . . "Now, since that most influential man, the consul Marcus Porcius, has attacked our proposal not only with his authority, which unexpressed would have had enough of weight, but also in a long and carefully-prepared speech, it is necessary to make a brief reply. And yet he used up more words in reproving the matrons than he did in opposing our bill, and, in fact, left it in doubt whether the conduct for which he rebuked the matrons was spontaneous or inspired by us. I propose to defend the measure rather than ourselves, at whom the consul directed his insinuations, more to have something to say than to make a serious charge. This gathering of women he called a sedition and sometimes 'a female secession,' because the matrons, in the streets, had requested you to repeal, in a time of peace and in a rich and prosperous commonwealth, a law that was passed against them in the trying days of a war. . . .

"What new thing, pray, have the matrons done in coming out into the streets in crowds in a case that concerned them? Have they never before this moment appeared in public? Let me unroll your own *Origines* against you.[2] Hear how often they have done it and always, indeed, for the general good. . . . These cases, you say, are different. It is not my purpose to prove them similar; it suffices if I prove that this is nothing new. But what no one wonders that all, men and women alike, have done in matters that concern them, do we wonder what the women have done in a case peculiarly their own? What now have they done? We have proud ears, upon my word, if, although masters do not scorn to hear the petitions of slaves, we complain that we are appealed to by respectable women. . . .

"Laws passed in time of peace, war frequently annuls, and peace those passed in times of war, just as in handling a ship some means are useful in fair weather and others in a storm. Since they are so distinguished by nature, to which class, I ask, does the law which we are trying to repeal seem to belong? Well? Is it an ancient regal law, born with the City itself, or, what is next to that, one inscribed on the twelve tables by the decemvirs appointed to codify the law? Is it a law without which our ancestors held that a matron's virtue could not be preserved, and which we too must fear to repeal lest along with it we repeal the modesty and purity of our women? Who is there, then, who does not know that this is a new law, passed twenty years ago, in the consulship of Quintus Fabius and Tiberius Sempronius? Since for so many years our matrons lived virtuous lives without it, what danger is there that when it is repealed they will rush into riotous luxury? . . .

"Who fails to see that the poverty and distress of the state wrote that law, since all private property had to be diverted to public use, and that the law was to remain in force so long as the cause of its enactment lasted?[3]

---

[2] Although Valerius pretends to quote from Cato's own historical work *Origines*, which discussed early Roman history, the work had not actually been written at the time of the feminist agitation. The scroll form of the ancient book explains the choice of the verb *revolvam*.

[3] Valerius argues that the Oppian law was merely one of a series of emergency measures by which all elements in the state were affected. To leave this one law in force would mean continued discrimination against only women, after the other methods had been abandoned.

"All other orders, all men, will feel the change for the better in the state; shall our wives alone get no enjoyment from national peace and tranquillity? . . . By Hercules, there is mourning and anger among all when they see the wives of allies of the Latin confederacy permitted the ornaments which are refused to them, when they see them decked out in gold and purple, when they see them riding through the city, and themselves following on foot, as if dominion resided in the Latin towns and not in Rome. A thing like this would hurt the feelings even of men: what do you think is its effect upon weak women, whom even little things disturb? No offices, no priesthoods, no triumphs, no decorations, no gifts, no spoils of war can come to them; elegance of appearance, adornment, apparel — these are the woman's badges of honor; in these they rejoice and take delight; these our ancestors called the woman's world. What else do they lay aside in times of mourning than purple and jewelery? What do they put on when they have finished their time of mourning? What do they add save more splendid jewels in times of congratulations and thanksgiving? Of course, if you repeal the Oppian law, you will have no authority if you wish to forbid any of these things which now the law forbids; daughters, wives, even sisters of some will be less under control — never while their males survive is feminine slavery shaken off; and even they abhor the freedom which loss of husbands and fathers gives.[4] They prefer to have their finery under your control and not the law's; you too should keep them in control and guardianship and not in slavery, and should prefer the name of father or husband to that of master." . . .

When these speeches against and for the bill had been delivered, the next day an even greater crowd of women appeared in public, and all of them in a body beset the doors of the Bruti, who were vetoing their colleagues' proposal, and they did not desist until the threat of veto was withdrawn by the tribunes. After that there was no question that all the tribes would vote to repeal the law. The law was repealed twenty years after it was passed.

DISCUSSION QUESTIONS

1. Why did Cato object to repealing the Oppian law? What was the basis of his objections?

2. How did Valerius counter Cato's assertions? What evidence did he use?

3. What do both men reveal about contemporary attitudes toward women and their place in the republic?

4. What can we learn about the nature of government in the Roman republic from this debate?

---

[4]Under the stricter Roman law, a woman was throughout life under the *potestas* of her father or his representative or the *manus* of her husband. Valerius makes the point that this domestic authority will be resumed in full with the repeal of the law and that the same restrictions that the law provided can be enforced if desired.

4. Cultivating Humanity

Cicero, *In Defense of Archias* (62 B.C.E.)

During his illustrious public career in Rome, Marcus Tullius Cicero (106–43 B.C.E.) was a lawyer, statesman, author, and orator known for his keen intelligence, fierce patriotism, and high moral standards. In this speech in defense of the Greek-born poet Archias, who had been living in Rome for years, he highlights the role of education in shaping the core values and sense of destiny that he considered to be at the heart of the republic's greatness. Archias was on trial for allegedly using privileges of Roman citizenship without legal qualification. Rome's remarkable expansion was based on its willingness to incorporate outsiders into its citizenship body. Cicero argues that Archias should be no exception to this incorporation of outsiders. He bases his argument both on the law and, more importantly, on Archias's literary achievements and their ability to nurture the individual mind, the public good, and the republic's glory.

Gentlemen of the jury. It is only fair that my client here, Aulus Licinius,[1] should claim the use of my services above practically all others. He has a legitimate right to them. If I have any talent, and I am aware how small it is, he has a right to it. If I have any experience in the art of speaking, on which I admit I have spent considerable time, he has a right to it.

Permit me to use a somewhat new and unusual style of speaking, in a case concerning a figure of this type, who pursues his leisured studies out of the public eye, and for that reason has seldom been dealt with in the dangers of the court room.

[4] Do I sense that you have granted my wish and allowed me this license? Then I will convince you without delay that this man, Aulus Licinius, should not be severed from the citizen body, since he is indeed a citizen. In fact, when I am done you will think that if he were not a citizen, he ought to have been added to the rolls.

From the moment he left boyhood and completed the elementary studies that prepare the young for civilized culture, Archias applied himself to the writer's craft. He began at Antioch. That is where he was born, to a family of the high nobility. Even at Antioch, once a populous and wealthy city packed full with superb scholars of extremely refined literary tastes, he swiftly began to surpass them all in the fame acquired by his talent. Later he traveled throughout Asia Minor and all of mainland Greece in celebrated tours. His reputation there based on his writings was great. But that reputation was exceeded by the eager anticipation of a personal appearance. And that anticipation, immense as it was, was surpassed by the rapturous reception he received in person.

[12] You ask, Grattius,[2] why I take such delight in this man. Why? Because he furnishes me with the means to refresh my mind after the noise of the Forum. Thanks to him, my ears, worn out with verbal abuse, can at last have rest. How do you suppose I can

---

From Cicero, *In Defense of Archias,* from *Ancient Rome: An Anthology of Sources,* ed. and trans. by Christopher Francese and R. Scott Smith (Hackett, New York, 2014), 35-36, 38, 41-43.

[1]Cicero refers to Archias by the Roman names he adopted on becoming a citizen, rather than by his original Greek name, which he also kept as a cognomen. His full name was Aulus Licinius Archias. Frequently Cicero simply calls him "this man." The name Archias has been inserted as necessary for clarity.
[2]**Grattius:** The prosecutor of Archias. [Ed.]

find the words to speak every day on such a bewildering variety of affairs unless I develop my mind through study? How do you suppose I can find the energy to endure such strain if I cannot relax through that same study? I admit it. I am devoted to literature. Shame on those who have so buried themselves in literature that they can contribute nothing from it to the common good, nothing that they can bring out into public view. But why should I feel shame? I live, and have lived for so many years, gentlemen of the jury, in such a way that neither my own leisure, nor my own pleasure, nor even my sleep, has kept me from helping anyone in his time of need.

[23] Now, one might think that there is less to be gained from Greek poetry than from Latin. But he would be sorely mistaken. Greek literature is read in virtually every country, while Latin literature is confined to its own native territory, which is small indeed. So if Roman achievements are limited only by the extent of the earth, we ought to desire that our fame and glory penetrate everywhere our weapons have reached. On the one hand, such works do honor to the very peoples whose affairs are being written about. On the other hand, they provide a great incentive to those who are risking their lives for the sake of glory and undergoing dangerous and grueling work.

The fact is that merit requires no other reward for its labors and risks than that of glory and fame. But if this incentive is removed, gentlemen of the jury, what reason is there to wear ourselves out in so many labors during the ever so brief span of our lives? [29] Clearly if the human mind thought nothing of the future and limited all of its thoughts and aspirations to the circumscribed space of this life, it would never exhaust itself in so many labors; it would never allow itself to be afflicted by so many anxieties or sacrifice so much sleep; nor would it fight for its very life again and again.

In fact, a kind of inner voice of excellence lies within all the best men and spurs their minds with the incentive of fame. It tells them that the end of life must not be the end of one's name — rather that it should last as long as there are people to remember it. [30] Are we so small minded, those of us who take part in service to the state, with all its attendant trials and risk to life and limb? Are we so small-minded as to believe that, when we have drawn not a single tranquil and leisurely breath throughout our entire careers, it will all die with us? Many great men have been keen to leave behind statues and portraits, images not of their minds but of their bodies. Should we not far prefer to leave behind representations of our ideas and our virtues, elegantly expressed by great writers? As for me, I thought that everything I was doing, at the very moment when I was doing it, was spreading my reputation abroad and disseminating it into the eternal memory of the world. It may be that after I die I will perceive nothing, and this fame will mean nothing to me then. Or perhaps, as the wisest men have supposed, it will reach some part of my consciousness. Be that as it may, here and now I certainly delight in the contemplation and hope of it.

[31] And so, judges, save this defendant, whose sterling character is vouched for, as you can see, by the status of his friends and the length of his friendships with them. Save this defendant, whose literary gifts (to the extent that it's proper to take that into account) are sought after by the judgment of all the best people. Save a defendant whose case is of a type that is buttressed by the law, by the authority of his home city, by the testimony of Lucullus, and by the records of Metellus. You see how the matter stands, gentlemen of the jury. If Archias' genius serves as any recommendation in the eyes not just of men but of the gods themselves, I ask you to take under your protection a man who has always

showered fame on you, your generals, and on the achievements of the Roman people, and who promises that he will give eternal testimony to the glory won in these recent domestic dangers that you and I shared. He belongs to that class of men whom everyone has always considered and deemed holy. Take him under your protection. Let him be seen to be helped by your kindness, rather than injured by the cruelty of his enemies.

DISCUSSION QUESTIONS

1. What details about Archias's life and career does Cicero provide? Why are these details important to his argument?

2. How does Cicero describe his personal connection to Archias? How does he build on this connection to make his case?

3. What image of the republic does Cicero paint in this speech?

4. Cicero espoused a doctrine of *humanitas*, which scholars define as "humanness" or "the quality of being human." From this speech, what qualities defined Cicero's doctrine of *humanitas*?

5. Failure and Factionalism

Plutarch, *The Gracchan Reforms* (133 B.C.E.)

By the second century B.C.E., decades of war had exacted an economic toll on the Roman republic. Despite the vast territories and riches of the elite, many Roman citizens struggled to survive, especially veterans who had been displaced from their farms. In 133 B.C.E., the official newly elected by the plebs to protect their rights, Tiberius Gracchus (d. 133 B.C.E.), initiated a reform program to relieve the people's plight, described here by his biographer, Plutarch (c. 50–120 C.E.). As Plutarch vividly recounts, Tiberius's senatorial colleagues vehemently opposed him and viewed his efforts as a threat to their elite status and wealth. Tiberius paid for his reform initiative with his life and thereby opened a new and violent chapter in Roman politics. Henceforth, Roman citizens became increasingly more polarized, which set the stage for civil war.

But his brother Gaius has left it to us in writing, that when Tiberius went through Tuscany to Numantia, and found the country almost depopulated, there being hardly any free peasants or shepherds, but for the most part only barbarian, imported slaves, he then first conceived the course of policy which in the sequel proved so fatal to his family. Though it is also most certain that the people themselves chiefly excited his zeal and determination in the prosecution of it, by setting up writings upon the porches, walls, and monuments, calling upon him to reinstate the poor citizens in their former possessions.

However, he did not draw up his law without the advice and assistance of those citizens that were then most eminent for their virtue and authority; amongst whom were

From *Plutarch's Lives*, vol. 4, rev. trans. A. H. Clough (Boston: Little, Brown, 1909), 514–21.

Crassus, the high-priest, Mucius Scaevola, the lawyer, who at that time was consul, and Claudius Appius, his father-in-law. Never did any law appear more moderate and gentle, especially being enacted against such great oppression and avarice. For they who ought to have been severely punished for transgressing the former laws, and should at least have lost all their titles to such lands which they had unjustly usurped, were notwithstanding to receive a price for quitting their unlawful claims, and giving up their lands to those fit owners who stood in need of help. But though this reformation was managed with so much tenderness, that, all the former transactions being passed over, the people were only thankful to prevent abuses of the like nature for the future, yet, on the other hand, the moneyed men, and those of great estates, were exasperated, through their covetous feelings against the law itself, and against the law giver, through anger and party spirit. They therefore endeavored to seduce the people, declaring that Tiberius was designing a general redivision of lands, to overthrow the government, and put all things into confusion.

But they had no success. For Tiberius, maintaining an honorable and just cause, and possessed of eloquence sufficient to have made a less creditable action appear plausible, was no safe or easy antagonist, when, with the people crowding around the hustings, he took his place, and spoke in behalf of the poor. "The savage beasts," said he, "in Italy, have their particular dens, they have their places of repose and refuge; but the men who bear arms, and expose their lives for the safety of their country, enjoy in the mean time nothing more in it but the air and light; and having no houses or settlements of their own, are constrained to wander from place to place with their wives and children." He told them that the commanders were guilty of a ridiculous error, when, at the head of their armies, they exhorted the common soldiers to fight for their sepulchres and altars; when not any amongst so many Romans is possessed of either altar or monument, neither have they any houses of their own, or hearths of their ancestors to defend. They fought indeed, and were slain, but it was to maintain the luxury and the wealth of other men. They were styled the masters of the world, but in the mean time had not one foot of ground which they could call their own. An harangue of this nature, spoken to an enthusiastic and sympathizing audience, by a person of commanding spirit and genuine feeling, no adversaries at that time were competent to oppose. Forbearing, therefore, all discussion and debate, they addressed themselves to Marcus Octavius, his fellow-tribune, who, being a young man of a steady, orderly character, and an intimate friend of Tiberius, upon this account declined at first the task of opposing him; but at length, over persuaded with the repeated importunities of numerous considerable persons, he was prevailed upon to do so, and hindered the passing of the law; it being the rule that any tribune has a power to hinder an act, and that all the rest can effect nothing, if only one of them dissents. . . .

When the day appointed was come, and the people summoned to give their votes, the rich men seized upon the voting urns, and carried them away by force; thus all things were in confusion. . . .

But when the senate assembled, and could not bring the business to any result, through the prevalence of the rich faction, he [Tiberius] then was driven to a course neither legal nor fair, and proposed to deprive Octavius of his tribuneship, it being impossible for him in any other way to get the law brought to the vote. . . .

He referred the whole matter to the people, calling on them to vote at once, whether Octavius should be deposed or not; and when seventeen of the thirty-five tribes had already voted against him, and there wanted only the votes of one tribe more for his final deprivation, Tiberius put a short stop to the proceedings, and once more renewed his importunities; he embraced and kissed him before all the assembly, begging, with all the earnestness imaginable, that he would neither suffer himself to incur the dishonor, nor him to be reputed the author and promoter of so odious a measure. Octavius, we are told, did seem a little softened and moved with these entreaties; his eyes filled with tears, and he continued silent for a considerable time. But presently looking towards the rich men and proprietors of estates, who stood gathered in a body together, partly for shame, and partly for fear of disgracing himself with them, he boldly bade Tiberius use any severity he pleased. The law for his deprivation being thus voted, Tiberius ordered one of his servants, whom he had made a freeman, to remove Octavius from the rostra, employing his own domestic freed servants in the stead of the public officers. And it made the action seem all the sadder, that Octavius was dragged out in such an ignominious manner. The people immediately assaulted him, whilst the rich men ran in to his assistance. Octavius, with some difficulty, was snatched away, and safely conveyed out of the crowd; though a trusty servant of his, who had placed himself in front of his master that he might assist his escape, in keeping off the multitude, had his eyes struck out, much to the displeasure of Tiberius, who ran with all haste, when he perceived the disturbance, to appease the rioters.

This being done, the law concerning the lands was ratified and confirmed, and three commissioners were appointed, to make a survey of the grounds and see the same equally divided. These were Tiberius himself, Claudius Appius, his father-in-law, and his brother, Caius Gracchus, who at this time was not at Rome, but in the army under the command of Scipio Africanus before Numantia. These things were transacted by Tiberius without any disturbance, none daring to offer any resistance to him. . . .

About this time, king Attalus, surnamed Philometor, died, and Eudemus, a Pergamenian, brought his last will to Rome, by which he had made the Roman people his heirs. Tiberius, to please the people, immediately proposed making a law, that all the money which Attalus left, should be distributed amongst such poor citizens as were to be sharers of the public lands, for the better enabling them to proceed in stocking and cultivating their ground; and as for the cities that were in the territories of Attalus, he declared that the disposal of them did not at all belong to the senate, but to the people, and that he himself would ask their pleasure herein. By this he offended the senate more than ever he had done before.

DISCUSSION QUESTIONS

1. According to Plutarch, what specific factors prompted Tiberius to take action in the people's favor?

2. In his address to the crowd, how does Tiberius characterize his opponents, and why?

3. As portrayed by Plutarch, what fundamental Roman values did Tiberius embody?

6. Toward Empire

Julius Caesar, *The Gallic War* (52 b.c.e.)

The violent failure of the Gracchan reforms marked the end of political cooperation among the Roman elite and, in the process, opened the door for a new kind of leader in the republic — the general-politician — who used his own troops to gain wealth and power. After securing a special command in Gaul, Julius Caesar (100–44 b.c.e.) exhibited just such a strategy through a combination of military genius and political savvy. Between 58 and 50 b.c.e., he and his army pushed past Rome's northwest frontier, conquering much of modern-day France along the way. His success sparked a general rebellion among the peoples of central Gaul in 52 b.c.e., led by the tribal chief Vercingetorix (d. 46 b.c.e.). Caesar described the revolt and its climax at the fortress of Alesia in The Gallic War, *excerpted below. In his account, he provides a glimpse of the realities of warfare and, at the same time, of how he won loyalty both at home and abroad. He used this loyalty as leverage in the civil war brewing in Rome, which ultimately destroyed the republic.*

. . . When all the horsemen had been put to flight Vercingetorix drew his forces back from their position in front of the camps and at once began the march to Alexia, a town of the Mandubii, ordering the baggage to be brought speedily out of camp and to follow close after him. Caesar withdrew his baggage to the nearest hill and, leaving two legions to guard it, pursued as long as daylight allowed. Some three thousand of the enemy's rearguard were slain, and on the next day he pitched camp near Alesia. He reconnoitered the situation of the city, and as the enemy were terror-struck by the rout of their horsemen, the branch of their army on which they most relied, he urged his soldiers to the task and began the investment.[1]

The actual stronghold of Alesia was set atop of a hill, in a very lofty situation, apparently impregnable save by blockade. The bases of the hill were washed on two separate sides by rivers. Before the town a plain extended for a length of about three miles; on all the other sides there were hills surrounding the town at a short distance, and equal to it in height. Under the wall, on the side which looked eastward, the forces of the Gauls had entirely occupied all this intervening space, and had made in front a ditch and a rough wall six feet high. The perimeter of the siege-works which the Romans were beginning had a length of eleven miles. Camps had been pitched at convenient spots, and twenty-three forts had been constructed on the line. In these piquets[2] would be posted by day to prevent any sudden sortie; by night the same stations were held by sentries and strong garrisons.

. . . Vercingetorix now made up his mind to send away all his horsemen by night, before the Romans could complete their entrenchments. His parting instructions were

---

Adapted from Julius Caesar, *The Gallic War*, trans. H. J. Edwards (Cambridge, MA: Harvard University Press, 1917), 68, 69, 71, 72, 79, 84–90.

[1]This refers to Caesar's construction of fortifications on which weapons could be mounted to besiege the city. [Ed.]

[2]**piquet**: A small group of soldiers. [Ed.]

that each of them should proceed to his own state and impress for the campaign all men whose age allowed them to bear arms. He set forth his own claims upon them, and urged them to have regard for his personal safety, and not to surrender him to the torture of the enemy after his sterling service for the liberty of all. . . .

Caesar had report of this from deserters and prisoners, and determined on the following types of entrenchments. He dug a trench twenty feet wide with perpendicular sides, in such fashion that its bottom was just as broad as the distance from edge to edge at the surface. He set back the rest of the siege-works four hundred paces from the trench; for as he had of necessity included so large an area, and the whole of the works could not easily be manned by a ring-fence of troops, his intention was to provide against any sudden rush of the enemy's host by night upon the entrenchments, or any chance of directing their missiles by day upon our troops engaged on the works. Behind this interval he dug all round two trenches, fifteen feet broad and of equal depth; and the inner one, where the ground was level with the plain or sank below it, he filled with water diverted from the river. Behind the trenches he constructed a ramp and palisade twelve feet high; to this he added a protective wall and battlements, with large pointed stakes . . . to check the upward advance of the enemy; and all round the works he set turrets at intervals of eighty feet. . . .

Meanwhile Commius[3] and the other leaders entrusted with the supreme command reached the neighborhood of Alesia with all their force, and, seizing a hill outside, halted not more than a mile from our entrenchments. The day after they brought their horsemen out of camp and filled the whole of that plain . . . extending for a length of three miles; their force of footmen they posted a little way back from the spot, on the higher ground. There was a bird's-eye view from the town of Alesia over the plain. . . .

When from the citadel of Alesia Vercingetorix observed his countrymen, he moved out of the town, taking with him the hurdles, poles, mantlets, grappling-hooks, and all the other supplies prepared for the charge. The fight went on simultaneously in all places, and all expedients were attempted, with a rapid concentration on that section which was seen to be least strong. With lines so extensive the Roman army was strung out, and at several points defense proved difficult. The shouting which arose in the rear of the fighting line did much to scare our troops, as they saw that the risk to themselves depended on the success of others; for, as a rule, what is out of sight disturbs men's minds more seriously than what they see.

Caesar found a suitable spot from which he could see what was proceeding in each quarter. To parties distressed he sent up supports. Both sides felt that this was the hour of all others in which it was proper to make their greatest effort. The Gauls utterly despaired of safety unless they could break through the lines; the Romans anticipated an end of all toils if they could hold their own. . . . The unfavorable downward slope of the ground had great effect. Some of the enemy discharged missiles, others moved up in close formation under their shields; fresh men quickly replaced the exhausted. Earth cast by the whole body together over the entrenchments gave the Gauls a means of ascent and at the same time covered over the supplies which the Romans had concealed in the ground; and our troops had now neither arms nor strength enough.

---

[3]Before the uprising in Gaul, Commius had been an ally of Caesar's in Britain; in return, Caesar had made him king of the Atrebates. [Ed.]

When Caesar learned this, he sent Labienus with six cohorts to support them in their distress. He commanded him, if he could not hold his ground, to draw in the cohorts and fight his way out, but not to do so unless of necessity. He himself went up to the rest of the troops, and urged them not to give in to the strain, telling them that the fruit of all previous engagements depended upon that day and hour. The enemy on the inner side, despairing of success on the level ground, because of the size of the entrenchments, made an attempt to scale the precipitous parts. . . . They dislodged the defenders of the turrets by a swarm of missiles, filled in the trenches with earth and hurdles, tore down rampart and breastwork with grappling-hooks.

Caesar first sent young Brutus[4] with some cohorts, and then Gaius Fabius, lieutenant-general, with others; last of all, as the fight raged more fiercely, he himself brought up fresh troops to reinforce. The battle restored, and the enemy repulsed, he hastened to the quarter where he had sent Labienus. He withdrew four cohorts from the nearest fort, and ordered part of the cavalry to follow him, part to go round the outer entrenchments and attack the enemy in rear. Labienus, finding that neither ramps nor trenches could resist the rush of the enemy, collected together forty cohorts, which had been withdrawn from the nearest posts and by chance presented themselves, and sent messengers to inform Caesar what he thought it proper to do. Caesar hurried on to take part in the action.

His coming was known by the color of his cloak,[5] which it was his habit to wear in action as a distinguishing mark; and the troops of cavalry and the cohorts which he had ordered to follow him were noticed, because from the upper levels these down-ward slopes and depressions were visible. Thereupon the enemy joined battle: a shout was raised on both sides, and taken up by an answering shout from the rampart and the whole of the entrenchments. Our troops discarded their pikes and got to work with their swords. Suddenly the cavalry was noticed in the rear; other cohorts drew near. The enemy turned to flee; the cavalry met them in flight, and a great slaughter ensued. . . . The oth-ers beheld from the town the slaughter and rout of their countrymen and, in despair of safety, recalled their force from the entrenchments. After they heard what had happened, the Gauls fled from their camp. And if the troops had not been worn out by frequent reinforcing and the whole day's effort, the entire force of the enemy could have been destroyed. The cavalry were sent off just after midnight and caught up to the rearguard: a great number were taken and slain, the rest fled away into the different states.

The next day Vercingetorix summoned a council, at which he stated that he had undertaken that campaign, not for his own concerns, but for the general liberty; and as they must yield to fortune he offered himself to them for whichever course they pleased — to give satisfaction to the Romans by his death, or to deliver him alive. Deputies were dispatched to Caesar to talk about this matter. He ordered the arms to be delivered up, the chiefs to be brought out. He himself took his seat in the entrenchments in front of the camp: the leaders were brought out to him there. Vercingetorix was surrendered,

---

[4]Decimus Junius Brutus Albinus, a Roman politician and general and later one of the instigator's of Caesar's assassination. Not to be confused with Marcus Brutus, the most famous of Caesar's assassins. [Ed.]

[5]A reference to Caesar's scarlet cloak, worn only by the *imperator*. [Ed.]

arms were thrown down. Keeping back the Aedui and the Arverni, to see if through them Caesar could recover their states, he distributed the rest of the prisoners, one apiece to each man throughout the army, by way of plunder.

When these affairs were settled he started for the country of the Aedui and recovered the state. The Arverni sent deputies to him there who promised to carry out his commands.

DISCUSSION QUESTIONS

1. What does Caesar's description of the siege of Alesia reveal about the technology of war at the time? How did Caesar use this technology to his advantage?

2. What does Caesar's portrait of Vercingetorix suggest about Roman attitudes toward non-Romans?

3. Although Caesar wrote *The Gallic War* to describe his own deeds, he uses "he" (the third person) instead of "I" (the first person) in telling his story. Why do you think he made this choice? Does his use of the third person give you more confidence or less confidence in the truth of his account?

4. In writing this account, how do you think Caesar intended to shape his public image, and why?

COMPARATIVE QUESTIONS

1. Scholars have argued that although the Roman republic was not a democracy, its non-elite citizens were an important political force. What evidence can you find in *Roman Women Demonstrate against the Oppian Law* and *The Gracchan Reforms* to support this claim?

2. How do the documents in this chapter lend support to the argument that the importance of law was a basic Roman value? In what ways does Cicero both respect and challenge this value?

3. What do both Plutarch and Caesar reveal about the ways in which war shaped Roman society and politics?

4. Imagine that the sculptor of the Roman bust was designing a statue of Caesar. Based on Caesar's self-portrait in *The Gallic War* of his actions during the climax of the siege of Alesia, what features do you think the sculptor would include, and why?

CHAPTER 6

The Creation of the Roman Empire
44 B.C.E.–284 C.E.

T he civil wars sparked by the assassination of Julius Caesar in 44 B.C.E. may have marked the death of the Roman republic, but they also signaled the birth of the Roman Empire. Through masterful political and military maneuvering, Caesar's heir Octavian (63 B.C.E.–14 C.E.) emerged from the wars as Rome's undisputed leader. In recognition of this fact, in 27 C.E., the Senate granted him special powers and a new title, Augustus ("divinely favored"). He thereupon forged a new system of government that laid the foundations for two hundred years of peace and prosperity. The documents in this chapter bring the empire to life from a variety of perspectives — from Virgil's epic poem praising the glory of Rome to the graffiti of everyday people living under Roman rule. The final three documents cast light on the Roman religious landscape; it, too, would be swept up in currents of change as a new religion, Christianity, emerged to compete with traditional beliefs and practices.

1. An Empire Foretold
Virgil, *The Aeneid* (First Century B.C.E.)

When Augustus assumed power in 27 B.C.E., he did not cast himself as an innovator. Well aware of the Romans' reverence for tradition, he used republican customs to cloak his creation of a new political system anchored in the power of its "first man," the emperor. Despite the misgivings some Romans had with this transformation, they enjoyed a period of unrivaled prosperity and stability. During Augustus's reign, artists and writers celebrated Rome's glory and superiority. One of the emperor's favorites was the poet Virgil (70–19 B.C.E.), who regularly shared his work with Augustus. Inspired by Homer, Virgil composed an epic poem about the origins of Rome, The Aeneid. *He died before finishing it to his satisfaction and, in his*

From Virgil, *The Aeneid*, trans. Robert Fagles (New York: Penguin Group, 2006), 205–10.

will, requested that it be destroyed. Augustus intervened, however, thereby preserving The Aeneid *for posterity. The poem recounts the story of the legendary founder of Rome, the Trojan Aeneas. The first six books focus on his travels to Italy from Troy; as in* The Odyssey, *the hero's voyage takes longer than expected due to a variety of mishaps and diversions along the way. These include a visit to the Underworld, as described in the excerpt below. Guided by the Sibyl, here Aeneas meets his dead father, Anchises, who shows him a pageant of the spirits of the great Romans to come, who will establish the empire and peace throughout the world.*

Now father Anchises, deep in a valley's green recess,
was passing among the souls secluded there, reviewing them,
eagerly, on their way to the world of light above. By chance
he was counting over his own people, all his cherished heirs,
their fame and their fates, their values, acts of valor.
When he saw Aeneas striding toward him over the fields,
he reached out both his hands as his spirit lifted,
tears ran down his checks, a cry broke from his lips:
"You've come at last? Has the love your father hoped for
mastered the hardship of the journey? Let me look at your face,
my son, exchange some words, and hear your familiar voice.
So I dreamed, I knew you'd come, I counted the moments —
my longing has not betrayed me...."

   And now Aeneas sees in the valley's depths
a sheltered grove and rustling wooded brakes
and the Lethe[1] flowing past the homes of peace.
Around it hovered numberless races, nations of souls
like bees in meadowlands on a cloudless summer day
that settle on flowers, riots of color, swarming round
the lilies' lustrous sheen, and the whole field comes alive
with a humming murmur. Struck by the sudden sight,
Aeneas, all unknowing, wonders aloud, and asks:
"What is the river over there? And who are they
who crowd the banks in such a growing throng?"

   His father Anchises answers: "They are the spirits
owed a second body by the Fates. They drink deep
of the river Lethe's currents there, long drafts
that will set them free of cares, oblivious forever.
How long I have yearned to tell you, show them to you,
face-to-face, yes, as I count the tally out
of all my children's children. So all the more
you can rejoice with me in Italy, found at last." ...

---

[1]**Lethe**: One of the major rivers in the Underworld. [Ed.]

"Here,
a son of Mars, his grandsire Numitor's comrade — Romulus,
bred from Assaracus' blood by his mother, Ilia.
See how the twin plumes stand joined on his helmet?
And the Father of Gods himself already marks him out
with his own bolts of honor. Under his auspices, watch,
my son, our brilliant Rome will extend her empire far
and wide as the earth, her spirit high as Olympus.
Within her single wall she will gird her seven hills,
blest in her breed of men: like the Berecynthian Mother
crowned with her turrets, riding her victor's chariot
through the Phrygian cities, glad in her brood of gods,
embracing a hundred grandsons. All dwell in the heavens,
all command the heights.

"Now turn your eyes this way
and behold these people, your own Roman people.
Here is Caesar and all the line of Iulus
soon to venture under the sky's great arch.
Here is the man, he's here! Time and again
you've heard his coming promised — Caesar Augustus!
Son of a god, he will bring back the Age of Gold
to the Latian fields where Saturn once held sway,
expand his empire past the Garamants and the Indians
to a land beyond the stars, beyond the wheel of the year,
the course of the sun itself, where Atlas bears the skies
and turns on his shoulder the heavens studded with flaming stars.
Even now the Caspian and Maeotic kingdoms quake at his coming,
oracles sound the alarm and the seven mouths of the Nile
churn with fear. Not even Hercules[2] himself could cross
such a vast expanse of earth, though it's true he shot
the stag with its brazen hoofs, and brought peace
to the ravaged woods of Erymanthus, terrorized
the Hydra of Lerna with his bow. Not even Bacchus[3]
in all his glory, driving his team with vines for reins
and lashing his tigers down from Nysa's soaring ridge.
Do we still flinch from turning our valor into deeds?
Or fear to make our home on Western soil? . . .

"Others, I have no doubt,
will forge the bronze to breathe with suppler lines,

---

[2]**Hercules**: The son of Zeus. [Ed.]
[3]**Bacchus**: The god of wine, the vine, and ecstasy. [Ed.]

draw from the block of marble features quick with life,
plead their cases better, chart with their rods the stars
that climb the sky and foretell the times they rise.
But you, Roman, remember, rule with all your power
the peoples of the earth — these will be your arts:
to put your stamp on the works and ways of peace,
to spare the defeated, break the proud in war."

DISCUSSION QUESTIONS

1. What does the pageant of souls suggest about the values Romans believed fueled the empire's success?

2. How does Virgil describe Augustus? What does this description reveal about his understanding of the emperor's particular place in Roman history?

3. In the final verses of this passage, Anchises distinguishes between Roman "arts" and those of "Others" — an implicit reference to the Greeks. How does he distinguish between them? In what ways may he be conveying a broader message about Roman imperialism?

2. An Urban Empire

Notices and Graffiti Describe Life in Pompeii (First Century C.E.)

Among the remarkable features of the Roman Empire was its immense expanse and the many cities, both new and old, that dotted its landscape. The following messages, graffiti, and election notices from the Roman municipality of Pompeii illuminate the hustle and bustle of urban life in the first century of the empire. Located at the foot of Mount Vesuvius in southern Italy, Pompeii at the time was a thriving commercial city, with a fashionable resort nearby. In 79 C.E., Mount Vesuvius erupted, burying the city in cinders and ash. Although the local population was destroyed or fled, remarkably, the city's buildings were preserved, as were hundreds of announcements painted in red on whitewashed walls, along with the scribbles of passersby. Here we see many facets of people's daily lives within the empire, from political appeals to lovesick lamentations.

In the Arrius Pollio block owned by Gnaeus Alleius Nigidius Maius, to let from the fifteenth of next July, shops with their stalls, high-class second-story apartments, and a house. Prospective lessees may apply to Primus, slave of Gnaeus Alleius Nigidius Maius.

On the property owned by Julia Felix, daughter of Spurius, to let from the thirteenth of next August to the thirteenth of the sixth August hence, or five consecutive years, the elite Venus Baths, shops, stalls, and second-story apartments. Interested parties may apply to the lessor in the matter.

From Naphtali Lewis and Meyer Reinhold, eds., *Roman Civilization: Selected Readings*, 3rd ed., vol. 2 (New York: Columbia University Press, 1990), 126–27, 237–38, 276–78.

The fruit dealers together with Helvius Vestalis unanimously urge the election of Marcus Holconius Priscus as duovir[1] with judicial power.

The goldsmiths unanimously urge the election of Gaius Cuspius Pansa as aedile.[2]

I ask you to elect Gaius Julius Polybius aedile. He gets good bread [for us].

The muleteers urge the election of Gaius Julius Polybius as duovir.

The worshippers of Isis unanimously urge the election of Gnaeus Helvius Sabinus as aedile.

Proculus, make Sabinus aedile and he will do as much for you.

His neighbors urge you to elect Lucius Statius Receptus duovir with judicial power; he is worthy. Aemilius Celer, a neighbor, wrote this. May you take sick if you maliciously erase this!

Satia and Petronia support and ask you to elect Marcus Casellius and Lucius Albucius aediles. May we always have such citizens in our colony!

I ask you to elect Epidius Sabinus duovir with judicial power. He is worthy, a defender of the colony, and in the opinion of the respected judge Suedius Clemens and by agreement of the council, because of his services and uprightness, worthy of the municipality. Elect him!

If upright living is considered any recommendation, Lucretius Fronto is well worthy of the office.

Genialis urges the election of Bruttius Balbus as duovir. He will protect the treasury.

I ask you to elect Marcus Cerrinius Vatia to the aedileship. All the late drinkers support him. Florus and Fructus wrote this.

The petty thieves support Vatia for the aedileship.

I ask you to elect Aulus Vettius Firmus aedile. He is worthy of the municipality. I ask you to elect him, ballplayers. Elect him!

I wonder, O wall, that you have not fallen in ruins from supporting the stupidities of so many scribblers.[3]

---

[1]**duovir**: One of two chief magistrates of Roman municipalities. [Ed.]
[2]**aedile**: A municipal administrator. [Ed.]
[3]Unlike the others, this inscription is a *graffito*, scratched on the wall.

Twenty pairs of gladiators of Decimus Lucretius Satrius Valens, life-time flamen[4] of Nero son of Caesar Augustus, and ten pairs of gladiators of Decimus Lucretius Valens, his son, will fight at Pompeii on April 8, 9, 10, 11, 12. There will be a full card of wild beast combats, and awnings [for the spectators]. Aemilius Celer [painted this sign], all alone in the moonlight.

Market days: Saturday in Pompeii, Sunday in Nuceria, Monday in Atella, Tuesday in Nola, Wednesday in Cumae, Thursday in Puteoli, Friday in Rome.

> 6th: cheese 1, bread 8, oil 3, wine 3[5]
> 7th: bread 8, oil 5, onions 5, bowl 1, bread for the slave[?] 2, wine 2
> 8th: bread 8, bread for the slave[?] 4, grits 3
> 9th: wine for the winner 1 *denarius*, bread 8, wine 2, cheese 2
> 10th: . . . 1 *denarius*, bread 2, for women 8, wheat 1 *denarius*, cucumber 1, dates 1,
>   incense 1, cheese 2, sausage 1, soft cheese 4, oil 7

Pleasure says: "You can get a drink here for an *as*, a better drink for two, Falernian[6] for four."

A copper pot is missing from this shop. 65 sesterces reward if anybody brings it back, 20 sesterces if he reveals the thief so we can get our property back.

The weaver Successus loves the innkeeper's slave girl, Iris by name. She doesn't care for him, but he begs her to take pity on him. Written by his rival. So long.
    [Answer by the rival:] Just because you're bursting with envy, don't pick on a handsomer man, a lady-killer and a gallant.
    [Answer by the first writer:] There's nothing more to say or write. You love Iris, who doesn't care for you.

Take your lewd looks and flirting eyes off another man's wife, and show some decency on your face!

Anybody in love, come here. I want to break Venus's ribs with a club and cripple the goddess' loins. If she can pierce my tender breast, why can't I break her head with a club?
    I write at Love's dictation and Cupid's instruction;
    But damn it! I don't want to be a god without you.

[A prostitute's sign:] I am yours for two *asses* cash.

---

[4]**flamen**: A priest. [Ed.]

[5]The initial number is the day of the month, and the numbers following the items of food indicate expenditures in asses, except where *denarii* are specified. A *denarius* was a Roman silver coin originally valued at ten and, later, sixteen asses. It was the equivalent of the Greek drachma. [Ed.]

[6]One of the prized wines of the Italian countryside (named after a district in Campania), best known from the poems of Horace that sing its praises.

DISCUSSION QUESTIONS

1. Based on these messages and notices, how would you describe life in Pompeii? What did the city look like?

2. What are some of the things people did for a living?

3. What do the election announcements reveal about the residents' political expectations and their role in local politics?

3. New Influences to the North

Tacitus, *Germania* (c. 98 c.e.)

The historian Tacitus (c. 56–120) was a shrewd observer and scathing critic of imperial rule, often contrasting the reportedly superior lives and morals of foreign peoples with those of Romans. Alongside his major historical writings, his works include a short treatise describing the Germanic peoples in the Rhineland. Drawing on earlier descriptions, he paints a compelling picture of the public and private life of the Germanic tribes, who at the time lived outside of Roman rule. Although Tacitus's account was perhaps idealized because of his dissatisfaction with contemporary Roman society — in his view, the Roman emperor was too high-handed and Roman citizens too decadent — his description offers information about the early Germans found in no other contemporary literary source.

Germany and Its Tribes

The Inhabitants. Origin of the Name "Germany"

The Germans themselves I should regard as aboriginal, and not mixed at all with other races through immigration or intercourse. For, in former times, it was not by land but on shipboard that those who sought to emigrate would arrive; and the boundless and, so to speak, hostile ocean beyond us, is seldom entered by a sail from our world. And, beside the perils of rough and unknown seas, who would leave Asia, or Africa, or Italy for Germany, with its wild country, its inclement skies, its sullen manners and aspect, unless indeed it were his home? . . .

Physical Characteristics

For my own part, I agree with those who think that the tribes of Germany are free from all taint of intermarriages with foreign nations, and that they appear as a distinct, unmixed race, like none but themselves. Hence, too, the same physical peculiarities throughout so vast a population. All have fierce blue eyes, red hair, huge frames, fit only for a sudden exertion. They are less able to bear laborious work. Heat and thirst they cannot in the least endure; to cold and hunger their climate and their soil inure them. . . .

From *The Agricola and Germany of Tacitus*, trans. Alfred John Church and William Jackson Brodribb (London: Macmillan, 1885), 87–90, 92–101.

Government. Influence of Women

They choose their kings by birth, their generals for merit. These kings have not unlimited or arbitrary power, and the generals do more by example than by authority. If they are energetic, if they are conspicuous, if they fight in the front, they lead because they are admired. But to reprimand, to imprison, even to flog, is permitted to the priests alone, and that not as a punishment, or at the general's bidding, but, as it were, by the mandate of the god whom they believe to inspire the warrior. They also carry with them into battle certain figures and images taken from their sacred groves. And what most stimulates their courage is, that their squadrons or battalions, instead of being formed by chance or by a fortuitous gathering, are composed of families and clans. Close by them, too, are those dearest to them, so that they hear the shrieks of women, the cries of infants. *They are to every man the most sacred witnesses of his bravery — they* are his most generous applauders. The soldier brings his wounds to mother and wife, who shrink not from counting or even demanding them and who administer both food and encouragement to the combatants. . . .

Councils

About minor matters the chiefs deliberate, about the more important the whole tribe. Yet even when the final decision rests with the people, the affair is always thoroughly discussed by the chiefs. They assemble, except in the case of a sudden emergency, on certain fixed days, either at new or at full moon; for this they consider the most auspicious season for the transaction of business. . . . When the multitude think proper, they sit down armed. Silence is proclaimed by the priests, who have on these occasions the right of keeping order. Then the king or the chief, according to age, birth, distinction in war, or eloquence, is heard, more because he has influence to persuade than because he has power to command. If his sentiments displease them, they reject them with murmurs; if they are satisfied, they brandish their spears. . . .

Training of the Youth

They transact no public or private business without being armed. It is not, however, usual for anyone to wear arms till the state has recognized his power to use them. Then in the presence of the council one of the chiefs, or the young man's father, or some kinsman, equips him with a shield and a spear. These arms are what the "toga" is with us, the first honor with which youth is invested. Up to this time he is regarded as a member of a household, afterwards as a member of the commonwealth. Very noble birth or great services rendered by the father secure for lads the rank of a chief; such lads attach themselves to men of mature strength and of long approved valor. It is no shame to be seen among a chief's followers. Even in his escort there are gradations of rank, dependent on the choice of the man to whom they are attached. These followers vie keenly with each other as to who shall rank first with his chief, the chiefs as to who shall have the most numerous and the bravest followers. It is an honor as well as a source of strength to be thus always surrounded by a large body of picked youths; it is an ornament in peace and a defense in war. And not only in his own tribe but also in the neighboring states it is the renown and glory of a chief to be distinguished for the number and valor of his followers, for such a man is courted by embassies, is honored with presents, and the very prestige of his name often settles a war. . . .

Habits in Time of Peace

Whenever they are not fighting, they pass much of their time in the chase, and still more in idleness, giving themselves up to sleep and to feasting, the bravest and the most warlike doing nothing, and surrendering the management of the household, of the home, and of the land, to the women, the old men, and all the weakest members of the family. They themselves lie buried in sloth, a strange combination in their nature that the same men should be so fond of idleness, so averse to peace. . . .

Arrangement of Their Towns. Subterranean Dwellings

It is well known that the nations of Germany have no cities, and that they do not even tolerate closely contiguous dwellings. They live scattered and apart, just as a spring, a meadow, or a wood has attracted them. Their villages they do not arrange in our fashion, with the buildings connected and joined together, but every person surrounds his dwelling with an open space, either as a precaution against the disasters of fire, or because they do not know how to build. No use is made by them of stone or tile; they employ timber for all purposes, rude masses without ornament or attractiveness. Some parts of their buildings they stain more carefully with a clay so clear and bright that it resembles painting, or a colored design. . . .

Dress

They all wrap themselves in a cloak which is fastened with a clasp, or, if this is not forthcoming, with a thorn, leaving the rest of their persons bare. They pass whole days on the hearth by the fire. The wealthiest are distinguished by a dress which is not flowing, like that of the Sarmatæ and Parthi, but is tight, and exhibits each limb. They also wear the skins of wild beasts; the tribes on the Rhine and Danube in a careless fashion, those of the interior with more elegance, as not obtaining other clothing by commerce. These select certain animals, the hides of which they strip off and vary them with the spotted skins of beasts, the produce of the outer ocean, and of seas unknown to us. The women have the same dress as the men, except that they generally wrap themselves in linen garments, which they embroider with purple, and do not lengthen out the upper part of their clothing into sleeves. The upper and lower arm is thus bare, and the nearest part of the bosom is also exposed.

Marriage Laws

Their marriage code, however, is strict, and indeed no part of their manners is more praiseworthy. Almost alone among barbarians they are content with one wife, except a very few among them, and these not from sensuality, but because their noble birth procures for them many offers of alliance. The wife does not bring a dower to the husband, but the husband to the wife. The parents and relatives are present, and pass judgment on the marriage-gifts, gifts not meant to suit a woman's taste, nor such as a bride would deck herself with, but oxen, a caparisoned steed, a shield, a lance, and a sword. With these presents the wife is espoused, and she herself in her turn brings her husband a gift of arms. This they count their strongest bond of union, these their sacred mysteries, these their gods of marriage. Lest the woman should think herself to stand apart from aspirations after noble deeds and from the perils of war, she is reminded by the ceremony which inaugurates marriage that she is her husband's partner in toil and danger, destined to suffer and to dare with him alike both in peace and in war. The yoked oxen, the harnessed steed, the gift of arms, proclaim this fact. She must live and die with the feeling that she is receiving what she must hand down to her children neither tarnished nor depreciated, what future daughters-in-law may receive, and may be so passed on to her grandchildren.

DISCUSSION QUESTIONS

1. How does Tacitus portray the German tribes' way of life? What aspects does he admire? What aspects does he criticize?

2. What message do you think Tacitus was trying to convey to his audience in his assessment of the strengths and weaknesses of Germanic society?

3. What roles did women play in Germanic society? What was their relationship with men? Why do you think that Tacitus singled out this topic in particular for elaboration?

4. The Making of a New Religion

SOURCES IN CONVERSATION | *The Gospel according to Matthew: The Sermon on the Mount* (28 C.E.) **and Paul of Tarsus,** *Letter to the Galatians* (c. 50–60 C.E.)

Despite their immense power, Roman emperors faced various threats across the broad expanse of the empire. Palestine was especially troubled due to increasingly harsh Roman rule there. Resentful of Roman authority in their homeland, many Jews agitated for change. Jesus was among them, calling his fellow Jews to prepare for God's kingdom. The verses below from the Sermon on the Mount *in the* Gospel according to Matthew *reveal that Jesus's teachings drew explicitly on Jewish religious and moral traditions. So should his supporters be identified as Jews or something new? Paul of Tarsus (c. 10–65 C.E.), a Jew and a Roman citizen, helped to answer this question, and thirteen letters attributed to him, along with the four gospels, came to make up the core of the New Testament. After a revelation called him to follow Jesus as the Messiah, Paul devoted his life to spreading Jesus's teachings to both non-Jews and Jews throughout Asia Minor. The excerpt here is from his letter to a fledgling community of converts in Galatia, who were embroiled in a crisis over whether non-Jewish converts to Christianity needed to keep the Jewish law. Paul reacted passionately to the situation by setting forth key principles that came to define Christianity as a distinct religion.*

From *The Jerusalem Bible*, ed. Alexander Jones (New York: Doubleday, 1966), 322, 324–28.

The Sermon on the Mount

The Beatitudes

5 Seeing the crowds, he went up the hill.[1] There he sat down and was joined by his disciples. •Then he began to speak. This is what he taught them:

'How happy are the poor in spirit;
theirs is the kingdom of heaven.
Happy *the gentle:*
they shall have the earth for their heritage.
Happy those who mourn:
they shall be comforted.
Happy those who hunger and thirst for what is right:
they shall be satisfied.
Happy the merciful:
they shall have mercy shown them.
Happy the pure in heart:
they shall see God.
Happy the peacemakers:
they shall be called sons of God.
Happy those who are persecuted in the cause of right:
theirs is the kingdom of heaven.

'Happy are you when people abuse you and persecute you and speak all kinds of calumny against you on my account. •Rejoice and be glad, for your reward will be great in heaven; this is how they persecuted the prophets before you.[2]

Salt of the Earth and Light of the World

'You are the salt of the earth. But if salt becomes tasteless, what can make it salty again? It is good for nothing, and can only be thrown out to be trampled underfoot by men.

'You are the light of the world. A city built on a hill-top cannot be hidden. No one lights a lamp to put it under a tub; they put it on the lamp-stand where it shines for everyone in the house. •In the same way your light must shine in the sight of men, so that, seeing your good works, they may give the praise to your Father in heaven.

The Fulfilment of the Law

'Do not imagine that I have come to abolish the Law or the Prophets. I have come not to abolish but to complete them.[3] •I tell you solemnly, till heaven and earth disappear, not one

---

[1]One of the hills near Capernaum.
[2]Christ's disciples are the successors of the prophets.
[3]I.e. 'to bring to perfection'. Jesus is speaking not of carrying into effect each single injunction of the old Law but of bestowing on that Law a new and definitive form by raising it to a higher place through the spirit of the gospel.

dot, not one little stroke, shall disappear from the Law until its purpose is achieved. •Therefore, the man who infringes even one of the least of these commandments and teaches others to do the same will be considered the least in the kingdom of heaven; but the man who keeps them and teaches them will be considered great in the kingdom of heaven.

The New Standard Higher Than the Old

'For I tell you, if your virtue goes no deeper than that of the scribes and Pharisees, you will never get into the kingdom of heaven.

'You have learnt[4] how it was said to our ancestors: *You must not kill;* and if anyone does kill he must answer for it before the court. •But I say this to you: anyone who is angry with his brother will answer for it before the court; if a man calls his brother "Fool"[5] he will answer for it before the Sanhedrin;[6] and if a man calls him "Renegade"[7] he will answer for it in hell fire. •So then, if you are bringing your offering to the altar and there remember that your brother has something against you, •leave your offering there before the altar, go and be reconciled with your brother first, and then come back and present your offering. •Come to terms with your opponent in good time while you are still on the way to the court with him, or he may hand you over to the judge and the judge to the officer, and you will be thrown into prison. •I tell you solemnly, you will not get out till you have paid the last penny.

'You have learnt how it was said: *You must not commit adultery.* •But I say this to you: if a man looks at a woman lustfully, he has already committed adultery with her in his heart. •If your right eye should cause you to sin, tear it out and throw it away; for it will do you less harm to lose one part of you than to have your whole body thrown into hell. •And if your right hand should cause you to sin, cut it off and throw it away; for it will do you less harm to lose one part of you than to have your whole body go to hell.

'It has also been said: *Anyone who divorces his wife must give her a writ of dismissal.* •But I say this to you: everyone who divorces his wife, except for the case of fornication, makes her an adulteress; and anyone who marries a divorced woman commits adultery.

'Again, you have learnt how it was said to our ancestors: *You must not break your oath, but must fulfil your oaths to the Lord.* •But I say this to you: do not swear at all, either by *heaven*, since that is God's throne; •or by *the earth,* since that is *his footstool*; or by Jerusalem, since that is *the city of the great king.* •Do not swear by your own head either, since you cannot turn a single hair white or black. All you need say is "Yes" if you mean yes, "No" if you mean no; anything more than this comes from the evil one.

'You have learnt how it was said: *Eye for eye and tooth for tooth.* •But I say this to you: offer the wicked man no resistance. On the contrary, if anyone hits you on the right

---

[4]Lit. 'you have heard' i.e. (normally) in the synagogues where the teachings of tradition were given orally.

[5]The Aramaic word *raqa*, transliterated in Mt, translated here, means: empty-head, nitwit.

[6]Here the Great Sanhedrin which met in Jerusalem, as opposed to the minor courts (vv. 21–22) of the country districts.

[7]To the first meaning ('fool') of the Greek word, Jewish usage added the much more insulting one of 'impious.'

cheek, offer him the other as well; •if a man takes you to law and would have your tunic, let him have your cloak as well. •And if anyone orders you to go one mile, go two miles with him. •Give to anyone who asks, and if anyone wants to borrow, do not turn away.

'You have learnt how it was said: *You must love your neighbour* and hate your enemy. •But I say this to you: love your enemies and pray for those who persecute you; •in this way you will be sons of your Father in heaven, for he causes his sun to rise on bad men as well as good, and his rain to fall on honest and dishonest men alike. •For if you love those who love you, what right have you to claim any credit? Even the tax collectors do as much, do they not? •And if you save your greetings for your brothers, are you doing anything exceptional? Even the pagans do as much, do they not? •You must therefore be perfect just as your heavenly Father is perfect.

Letter to the Galatians

Address

From Paul to the churches of Galatia, and from all the brothers who are here with me, an apostle who does not owe his authority to men or his appointment to any human being but who has been appointed by Jesus Christ and by God the Father who raised Jesus from the dead. We wish you the grace and peace of God our Father and of the Lord Jesus Christ, who in order to rescue us from this present wicked world sacrificed himself for our sins, in accordance with the will of God our Father, to whom be glory for ever and ever. Amen. . . .

The Good News as Proclaimed by Paul

"Though we were born Jews and not pagan sinners, we acknowledge that what makes a man righteous is not obedience to the Law, but faith in Jesus Christ. We had to become believers in Christ Jesus no less than you had, and now we hold that faith in Christ rather than fidelity to the Law is what justifies us, and that *no one can be justified*[8] by keeping the Law. Now if we were to admit that the result of looking to Christ to justify us is to make us sinners like the rest, it would follow that Christ had induced us to sin, which would be absurd. If I were to return to a position I had already abandoned, I should be admitting I had done something wrong. In other words, through the Law I am dead to the Law, so that now I can live for God. I have been crucified with Christ, and I live now not with my own life but with the life of Christ who lives in me. The life I now live in this body I live in faith: faith in the Son of God who loved me and who sacrificed himself for my sake. I cannot bring myself to give up God's gift: if the Law can justify us, there is no point in the death of Christ."

Justification by Faith

Are you people in Galatia mad? Has someone put a spell on you, in spite of the plain explanation you have had of the crucifixion of Jesus Christ? Let me ask you one question: was it because you practised the Law that you received the spirit, or because you believed what was preached to you? Are you foolish enough to end in outward observances what you began in the Spirit? Have all the favours you received been wasted? And if this were

---

[8]Psalms 143:2.

so, they would most certainly have been wasted. Does God give you the Spirit so freely and work miracles among you because you practise the Law or because you believed what was preached to you?...

The Purpose of the Law

What then was the purpose of adding the Law? This was done to specify crimes, until the posterity came to whom the promise was addressed. The Law was promulgated by angels,[9] assisted by an intermediary. Now there can only be an intermediary between two parties, yet God is one. Does this mean that there is opposition between the Law and the promises of God? Of course not. We could have been justified by the Law if the Law we were given had been capable of giving life, but it is not: scripture makes no exceptions when it says that sin is master everywhere. In this way the promise can only be given through faith in Jesus Christ and can only be given to those who have this faith.

The Coming of Faith

Before faith came, we were allowed no freedom by the Law; we were being looked after till faith was revealed. The Law was to be our guardian until the Christ came and we could be justified by faith. Now that that time has come we are no longer under that guardian, and you are, all of you, sons of God through faith in Christ Jesus. All baptised in Christ, you have all clothed yourselves in Christ, and there are no more distinctions between Jew and Greek, slave and free, male and female, but all of you are one in Christ Jesus. Merely by belonging to Christ you are the posterity of Abraham,[10] the heirs he was promised. . . .

Liberty and Charity

My brothers, you were called, as you know, to liberty; but be careful, or this liberty will provide an opening for self-indulgence. Serve one another, rather, in works of love, since the whole of the Law is summarised in a single command: *Love your neighbour as yourself.*[11] If you go snapping at each other and tearing each other to pieces, you had better watch or you will destroy the whole community.

DISCUSSION QUESTIONS

1. The Ten Commandments (2.2 Monotheism and Mosaic Law, pages 22–25) were a fundamental component of Jewish law. What connection does Jesus make between his teachings and the commandments in the Sermon on the Mount? Why is this important to his overall message?

2. Why was Jewish law a source of conflict in Galatia? How does Paul use his understanding of the role of faith in Christianity to address this conflict?

3. Compare Jesus's and Paul's approaches to the law. What differences and/or similarities do you see? What do they reveal about the early development of Christianity?

---

[9]In Jewish tradition, angels were present at Sinai; the "intermediary" is Moses.
[10]**Abraham**: The father of the Israelites in the Christian and Jewish traditions. [Ed.]
[11]Leviticus 19:18.

5. Deadly Beliefs

The Martyrdom of Saints Perpetua and Felicitas (203 C.E.)

Despite significant obstacles, Christianity gradually spread through the Roman Empire in the three centuries following Jesus's death. Although Christianity was not illegal in this period, Romans harbored deep suspicions toward Christians for their rejection of the old gods and the imperial cult. Open refusal to bow to tradition, which Romans regarded as the foundation of public order, could tip the scales into outright persecution. This was the case for Vibia Perpetua, a young, married mother living in the North African colony of Carthage. By order of the Roman governor, Hilarianus, she was arrested in 203 C.E. along with others (including a slave named Felicitas) on the charge of civil disobedience, convicted, and condemned to die in the arena. At the time she was a catechumen, a not-yet-baptized student in the Christian religion. What follows is her own account based on a diary she kept during her imprisonment, one of the earliest known Christian writings by a woman. After her death, the diary was incorporated into an official story of her and Felicitas's martyrdom as a "witness to the non-believer and a blessing to the faithful."

3. While we were still under arrest (she said) my father out of love for me was trying to persuade me and shake my resolution. 'Father,' said I, 'do you see this vase here, for example or water-pot or whatever?'

'Yes, I do', said he.

And I told him: 'Could it be called by any other name than what it is?'

And he said: 'No.'

'Well, so too I cannot be called anything other than what I am, a Christian.'

At this my father was so angered by the word 'Christian' that he moved towards me as though he would pluck my eyes out. But he left it at that and departed, vanquished along with his diabolical arguments.

For a few days afterwards I gave thanks to the Lord that I was separated from my father, and I was comforted by his absence. During these few days I was baptized, and I was inspired by the Spirit not to ask for any other favour after the water but simply the perseverance of the flesh. A few days later we were lodged in the prison; and I was terrified, as I had never before been in such a dark hole. What a difficult time it was! With the crowd the heat was stifling; then there was the extortion of the soldiers; and to crown all, I was tortured with worry for my baby there.

Then Tertius and Pomponius, those blessed deacons[1] who tried to take care of us, bribed the soldiers to allow us to go to a better part of the prison to refresh ourselves for a few hours. Everyone then left that dungeon and shifted for himself. I nursed my baby, who was faint from hunger. In my anxiety I spoke to my mother about the child, I tried to comfort my brother, and I gave the child in their charge. I was in pain because I saw them suffering out of pity for me. These were the trials I had to endure for many days. Then I got permission for my baby to stay with me in prison. At once I recovered my health,

---

[1]In early Christianity, deacons served a variety of ministerial roles in support of fledgling congregations. [Ed.]

relieved as I was of my worry and anxiety over the child. My prison had suddenly become a palace, so that I wanted to be there rather than anywhere else.

5. A few days later there was a rumour that we were going to be given a hearing. My father also arrived from the city, worn with worry, and he came to see me with the idea of persuading me.

'Daughter,' he said, 'have pity on my grey head—have pity on me your father, if I deserve to be called your father, if I have favoured you above all your brothers, if I have raised you to reach this prime of your life. Do not abandon me to be the reproach of men. Think of your brothers, think of your mother and your aunt, think of your child, who will not be able to live once you are gone. Give up your pride! You will destroy all of us! None of us will ever be able to speak freely again if anything happens to you.'

This was the way my father spoke out of love for me, kissing my hands and throwing himself down before me. With tears in his eyes he no longer addressed me as his daughter but as a woman. I was sorry for my father's sake, because he alone of all my kin would be unhappy to see me suffer.

I tried to comfort him saying: 'It will all happen in the prisoner's dock as God wills; for you may be sure that we are not left to ourselves but are all in his power.'

And he left me in great sorrow.

6. One day while we were eating breakfast we were suddenly hurried off for a hearing. We arrived at the forum, and straight away the story went about the neighbourhood near the forum and a huge crowd gathered. We walked up to the prisoner's dock. All the others when questioned admitted their guilt. Then, when it came my turn, my father appeared with my son, dragged me from the step, and said: 'Perform the sacrifice—have pity on your baby!'

Hilarianus the governor, who had received his judicial powers as the successor of the late proconsul Minucius Timinianus, said to me: 'Have pity on your father's grey head; have pity on your infant son. Offer the sacrifice for the welfare of the emperors.'

'I will not,' I retorted.

'Are you a Christian?' said Hilarianus.

And I said: 'Yes, I am.'

When my father persisted in trying to dissuade me, Hilarianus ordered him to be thrown to the ground and beaten with a rod. I felt sorry for father, just as if I myself had been beaten. I felt sorry for his pathetic old age.

Then Hilarianus passed sentence on all of us: we were condemned to the beasts, and we returned to prison in high spirits.

DISCUSSION QUESTIONS

1. According to her diary, why did Perpetua refuse to submit to her father and the Roman officials' request for her to renounce Christianity?

2. Perpetua was a mother, daughter, sister, and wife. In what ways did she reshape these traditional female roles through her Christian faith?

3. What does this document suggest about the basis of Christianity's appeal at this time?

6. Private Piety

Household Shrine, Pompeii (First Century c.e.)

Even as Christianity gained new adherents in the Roman Empire, the vast majority of people remained firmly attached to polytheism. They worshiped an array of gods in many kinds of sanctuaries, all with the aim of gaining divine goodwill. While public worship of the state cults' major gods was an important element of polytheistic religion, private worship at household shrines dedicated to the gods of the house, called lares, *likewise played a significant role. These shrines survive in a variety of different shapes and forms in many Roman houses, from simple wall paintings to large shrines. Throughout the year, household members would make daily prayers and offerings to the* lares *for protection and prosperity. The shrine pictured here is found in the elaborately decorated House of the Vettii built in Pompeii by two Roman freedmen in the first century* c.e. *The shrine's columns and pediment mimic the form of a public temple and frame a simple but highly symbolic painting. At its center is the genius who represents the spirit of the male head of household. He is dressed in a toga and making a sacrifice with* lares *dancing on either side. Beneath them all is a serpent, another guardian spirit. These household gods were believed to guard the family from outside threats just as the Roman emperor was the protector of the Roman people. Indeed, Augustus had introduced a cult of his own genius as part of the official state imperial cult, assuming the role as the head of all Roman households.*

Werner Forman Archive / REX / Shutterstock

DISCUSSION QUESTIONS

1. The columns on the shrine imitate the form of a public temple. What could be some reasons for this design choice, and what does this choice suggest about the relationship between public and private worship in polytheistic religion?

2. What does the image of the male head of the household in the shrine suggest about the nature of Roman paternalism in the domestic sphere?

3. What does the form and function of this shrine suggest about polytheists' belief in the ability of the gods to affect everyday life?

COMPARATIVE QUESTIONS

1. As portrayed by Virgil, what was the basis of Rome's success as an imperial power? How had these perceptions of Roman rule changed by the time Tacitus was writing?

2. What everyday features of Roman life do the graffiti and household shrine from Pompeii bring to light? How do these depictions of daily life compare to those of the Germanic peoples described by Tacitus?

3. Saint Perpetua openly embraced martyrdom as a testament of her Christian faith. How does her understanding of faith compare to that conveyed in the *Sermon on the Mount* and Paul's *Letter to the Galatians*?

4. What attitudes do you think Virgil, Paul, and the author of *The Martyrdom of Saints Perpetua and Felicitas* hoped to inspire in their audiences? What reward or "promise" does each offer believers? What does this tell us about competing religious beliefs and attitudes at the time?

The Transformation of the Roman Empire
284–600 C.E.

The Roman Empire had faced many challenges since its formation at the end of the first century B.C.E., but by the fourth century C.E., the forces of change proved too powerful to resist, as the documents in this chapter attest. Christianity was spreading far and wide, even gaining the allegiance of the emperor Constantine (r. 306–337 C.E.). In the process, Christians also attempted to define doctrine and combat heresy in the Nicene Creed; this did not, however, end controversies. Although reminders of Rome's pluralistic past persisted, notably in Jewish communities, over the course of the fourth century Christianity gained the upper hand by calling on its followers to surrender themselves to God in both body and will. The success of this message permanently transformed Roman culture and society. At the same time, waves of Germanic peoples penetrated the empire's borders and migrated westward, eventually establishing their own kingdoms that replaced imperial government. These new regimes became the heirs of Roman civilization in the West, setting the stage for the development of medieval Europe, whereas in the East the imperial legacy lived on in the Byzantine Empire.

1. The Establishment of Roman Christian Doctrine

SOURCES IN CONVERSATION | Arius, *Letter to Alexander, Bishop of Alexandria* (c. 320 C.E.) and *The Nicene Creed* (325 C.E.)

Although Emperor Constantine (288–337 C.E.) had made Christianity a legal religion in the Roman Empire in 313 C.E., major controversies about doctrine and belief continued to rage. Arius (c. 260–336 C.E.), a priest and theologian of Alexandria, posed the most serious

From J. Stevenson, *A New Eusebius: Documents Illustrating the History of the Church to AD 337*, rev. ed. (London: SPCK, 1987), 326–27; and Patrick V. Reid, *Readings in Western Religious Thought: The Ancient World* (New York: Paulist Press, 1987), 376.

challenge to the developing church. Setting forth the belief that the Father and Son could not both be uncreated, Arius insisted that Jesus Christ was not God in the same manner as God the Father. He defended his views in the letter that follows, written circa 320 to the bishop of Alexandria after Arius's condemnation by the Synod of Egypt. As the doctrine of Arianism swept through the empire, sparking anger among many Christians, Constantine called the Council of Nicaea (325 C.E.) to resolve the issue. Two hundred to three hundred bishops attended the council, at which Arius explained his position. It was rejected, and the council formulated a creed — one that is still used in slightly different forms in most Western Christian churches today. Despite the creed's widespread acceptance, Arianism continued to spread and divide the church.

Letter of Arius to Alexander, Bishop of Alexandria

To our blessed Pope[1] and Bishop Alexander, the Presbyters and Deacons send greeting in the Lord.

Our faith from our forefathers, which we have learned also from thee, Blessed Pope, is this: We acknowledge One God, alone unbegotten, alone everlasting, alone unbegun, alone true, *alone having immortality*, alone wise, alone good, alone sovereign; judge, governor, and administrator of all, unalterable and unchangeable, just and good, God of Law and Prophets and New Testament; who begat an Only-begotten Son before eternal times, through whom he has made both the ages and the universe; and begat him not in semblance, but in truth: and that he made him subsist at his own will, unalterable and unchangeable; perfect creature of God, . . . created before times and before ages, and gaining life and being and his glories from the Father, who gave real existence to those together with him. For the Father did not, in giving to him the inheritance of all things, deprive himself of what he has ingenerately in himself; for he is the Fountain of all things. Thus there are three Subsistences. And God, being the cause of all things, is unbegun and altogether sole but the Son being begotten apart from time by the Father, and being created and found before ages, was not before his generation; but, being begotten apart from time before all things, alone was made to subsist by the Father. For he is not eternal or co-eternal or co-unoriginate with the Father, nor has he his being together with the Father, as some speak of relations, introducing two ingenerate beginnings, but God is before all things as being Monad and Beginning of all.

The Nicene Creed

We believe in one God, the Father Almighty, Maker of all things visible and invisible; and in one Lord Jesus Christ, the Son of God, the only-begotten of his Father, of the substance of the Father, God of God, Light of Light, very God of very God, begotten, not made, being of one substance with the Father. By whom all things were made, both which be in heaven and in earth. Who for us men and for our salvation came down [from heaven]

---

[1]Pope, a title of respect for distinguished churchmen.

and was incarnate and was made man. He suffered and the third day he rose again, and ascended into heaven. And he shall come again to judge both the quick and the dead.

And [we believe] in the Holy Ghost.

And whosoever shall say that there was a time when the Son of God was not, or that before he was begotten he was not, or that he was made of things that were not, or that he is of a different substance or essence [from the Father] or that he is a creature, or subject to change or conversion — all that so say, the Catholic and Apostolic Church anathematizes them.

DISCUSSION QUESTIONS

1. What does Arius mean that Jesus is "not eternal or co-eternal or co-unoriginate with the Father"? How is this statement central to his and his followers' faith?

2. How does the Nicene Creed refute the Arian position while defining essential doctrinal beliefs about Christianity?

3. By defining "correct belief," how does the church put into place a mechanism for dealing with heresy?

4. How does the Nicene Creed illustrate the changes in the church as it grew from relatively small, illegal communities into a major hierarchical institution?

2. The Struggle of Conversion

Augustine of Hippo, *Confessions* (c. 397 C.E.)

The establishment of a church hierarchy and uniform doctrine was not the only force driving the Christianization of the Roman Empire. It also depended on individuals abandoning tradition to embrace Christ. Augustine of Hippo reveals in his autobiographical work Confessions *that this choice was not always easy no matter how strong Christianity's appeal in the wake of Constantine's conversion. Although Augustine eventually became both a bishop and a renowned theologian, his path there was arduous. Born to a Christian mother and a pagan father in North Africa, Augustine was smart and eager to move up in the world. While pursuing his studies and a teaching career, he scoffed at the Christian scriptures, convinced that true wisdom lay elsewhere. He was also swept up in his own desire for fame, wealth, and sensual pleasure. Yet he struggled to break free from his sinful habits, which he considered to be obstacles to living a Christian life. As he recounts in this excerpt from* Confessions, *his struggles came to a climax while he was living in Milan. The setting of the scene below is his house, where he lived with several companions, including Alypius. A visitor has just finished telling them a story about two Roman officials who abandoned their*

From Saint Augustine, *Confessions*, trans. R. S. Pine-Coffin (London: Penguin Books, 1961), 170–71, 173, 175–78.

careers to serve Christ. The story gnaws at Augustine's conscience, and he retreats into the adjacent garden in a state of emotional turmoil. It is here that he finally receives the grace needed to devote himself to the Christian faith.

There was a small garden attached to the house where we lodged. We were free to make use of it as well as the rest of the house because our host, the owner of the house, did not live there. I now found myself driven by the tumult in my breast to take refuge in this garden, where no one could interrupt that fierce struggle, in which I was my own contestant, until it came to its conclusion. What the conclusion was to be you knew, O Lord, but I did not. Meanwhile I was beside myself with madness that would bring me sanity. I was dying a death that would bring me life. I knew the evil that was in me, but the good that was soon to be born in me I did not know. So I went out into the garden and Alypius followed at my heels. His presence was no intrusion on my solitude, and how could he leave me in that state? We sat down as far as possible from the house. I was frantic, overcome by violent anger with myself for not accepting your will and entering into your covenant. Yet in my bones I knew that this was what I ought to do. In my heart of hearts I praised it to the skies. And to reach this goal I needed no chariot or ship. I need not even walk as far as I had come from the house to the place where we sat, for to make the journey, and to arrive safely, no more was required than an act of will. But it must be a resolute and whole-hearted act of the will, not some lame wish which I kept turning over and over in my mind, so that it had to wrestle with itself, part of it trying to rise, part falling to the ground. . . .

When I was trying to reach a decision about serving the Lord my God, as I had long intended to do, it was I who willed to take this course and again it was I who willed not to take it. It was I and I alone. But I neither willed to do it nor refused to do it with my full will. So I was at odds with myself. . . .

Yet I did not fall back into my old state. I stood on the brink of resolution, waiting to take fresh breath. I tried again and came a little nearer to my goal, and then a little nearer still, so that I could almost reach out and grasp it. But I did not reach it. I could not reach out to it or grasp it, because I held back from the step by which I should die to death and become alive to life. My lower instincts, which had taken firm hold of me, were stronger than the higher, which were untried. And the closer I came to the moment which was to mark the great change in me, the more I shrank from it in horror. But it did not drive me back or turn me from my purpose: it merely left me hanging in suspense.

I was held back by mere trifles, the most paltry inanities, all my old attachments. They plucked at my garment of flesh and whispered, "Are you going to dismiss us? From this moment we shall never be with you again, for ever and ever. From this moment you will never again be allowed to do this thing or that, for evermore." What was it, my God, that they meant when they whispered "this thing or that"? Things so sordid and so shameful that I beg you in your mercy to keep the soul of your servant free from them! . . .

I probed the hidden depths of my soul and wrung its pitiful secrets from it, and when I mustered them all before the eyes of my heart, a great storm broke within me, bringing with it a great deluge of tears. I stood up and left Alypius so that I might weep and cry to my heart's content, for it occurred to me that tears were best shed in solitude. I moved away far enough to avoid being embarrassed even by his presence. He must have realized what my feelings were, for I suppose I had said something and he had known from the sound of my voice that I was ready to burst into tears. So I stood up and left him where we had been sitting, utterly bewildered. Somehow I flung myself down beneath a fig tree and gave way to the tears which now streamed from my eyes, the sacrifice that is acceptable to you.[1] I had much to say to you, my God, not in these very words but in this strain: *Lord, will you never be content?[2] Must we always taste your vengeance? Forget the long record of our sins.*[3] For I felt that I was still the captive of my sins and in my misery I kept crying "How long shall I go on saying 'tomorrow, tomorrow'? Why not now? Why not make an end of my ugly sins at this moment?"

I was asking myself these questions, weeping all the while with the most bitter sorrow in my heart, when all at once I heard the sing-song voice of a child in a nearby house. Whether it was the voice of a boy or a girl I cannot say, but again and again it repeated the refrain "Take it and read, take it and read." At this I looked up, thinking hard whether there was any kind of game in which children used to chant words like these, but I could not remember ever hearing them before. I stemmed my flood of tears and stood up, telling myself that this could only be a divine command to open my book of Scripture and read the first passage on which my eyes should fall. . . .

So I hurried back to the place where Alypius was sitting, for when I stood up to move away I had put down the book containing Paul's Epistles. I seized it and opened it, and in silence I read the first passage on which my eyes fell: *Not in revelling and drunkenness, not in lust and wantonness, not in quarrels and rivalries. Rather, arm yourselves with the Lord Jesus Christ; spend no more thought on nature and nature's appetites.*[4] I had no wish to read more and no need to do so. For in an instant, as I came to the end of the sentence, it was as though the light of confidence flooded into my heart and all the darkness of doubt was dispelled.

DISCUSSION QUESTIONS

1. Why is it so difficult for Augustine to make a decision about embracing the Christian faith? Why is he so at odds with himself?

2. How does his choice of language convey the depth of his emotion as he struggles with this decision?

3. What triggers Augustine's conversion? Why do you think he includes this account in his *Confessions*, which he wrote more than a decade after the events he describes?

---

[1] See Ps. 50:19 (51:17).
[2] Ps. 6:4 (6:3).
[3] Ps. 78:5, 8 (79:5, 8).
[4] Rom. 13:13, 14. Saint Augustine does not quote the whole passage, which begins "*Let us pass our time honourably, as by the light of day, not in revelling and drunkenness,*" etc.

3. The Development of Monasticism

Benedict of Nursia, *The Rule of Saint Benedict* (c. 540 C.E.)

The rise of monasticism was another important vehicle for religious change in the Roman Empire. Individual monks first appeared in third-century Egypt, where they rejected the everyday world and its comforts in pursuit of holiness. By the next century, communities of monks formed in the region, and their example spread to other parts of the empire. Discipline and communal self-sufficiency were hallmarks of life within monasteries, often resulting in harsh living conditions for members. Benedict of Nursia (c. 480–553) sought to balance the ascetic ideal with his own understanding of monks' spiritual and physical needs. The result was a code of conduct, called the Benedictine rule, which became the basis of monasticism in the West. The Rule *prescribed a regime centered on prayer, scriptural readings, and manual labor. A head monk, known as the abbot, was to oversee the community according to the* Rule's *instructions. As the excerpts here reveal, at the heart of these instructions was the goal of instilling obedience and humility within every monk; only then could a monastic community achieve its ultimate spiritual mission: salvation and service to God.*

Prologue

Listen carefully, my son, to the master's instructions, and attend to them with the ear of your heart. This is advice from a father who loves you; welcome it, and faithfully put it into practice. The labor of obedience will bring you back to him from whom you had drifted through the sloth of disobedience. This message of mine is for you, then, if you are ready to give up your own will, once and for all, and armed with the strong and noble weapons of obedience to do battle for the true King, Christ the Lord.

First of all, every time you begin a good work, you must pray to him most earnestly to bring it to perfection. In his goodness, he has already counted us as his sons, and therefore we should never grieve him by our evil actions. With his good gifts which are in us, we must obey him at all times that he may never become the angry father who disinherits his sons, nor the dread lord, enraged by our sins, who punishes us forever as worthless servants for refusing to follow him to glory. . . .

Clothed then with faith and the performance of good works, let us set out on this way, with the Gospel for our guide, that we may deserve to see him *who has called us to his kingdom* (1 Thess 2:12).

If we wish to dwell in the tent of this kingdom, we will never arrive unless we run there by doing good deeds. But let us ask the Lord with the Prophet: *Who will dwell in your tent, O Lord, who will find rest upon your holy mountain?* (Ps 14[15]:1) After this question, brothers, let us listen well to what the Lord says in reply, for he shows us the way to his tent. *One who walks without blemish,* he says, *and is just in all his dealings;*

From *The Rule of St. Benedict*, ed. Timothy Fry (Collegeville, MN: The Liturgical Press, 1981), 157, 159, 161, 163, 165, 167, 181, 183, 185, 187, 189.

who speaks the truth from his heart and has not practiced deceit with his tongue; who has not wronged a fellowman in any way, nor listened to slanders against his neighbor (Ps 14[15]:2–3). . . .

Brothers, now that we have asked the Lord who will dwell in his tent, we have heard the instruction for dwelling in it, but only if we fulfill the obligations of those who live there. We must, then, prepare our hearts and bodies for the battle of holy obedience to his instructions. What is not possible to us by nature, let us ask the Lord to supply by the help of his grace. If we wish to reach eternal life, even as we avoid the torments of hell, then — while there is still time, while we are in this body and have time to accomplish all these things by the light of life — we must run and do now what will profit us forever.

Therefore we intend to establish a school for the Lord's service. In drawing up its regulations, we hope to set down nothing harsh, nothing burdensome. The good of all concerned, however, may prompt us to a little strictness in order to amend faults and to safeguard love. Do not be daunted immediately by fear and run away from the road that leads to salvation. It is bound to be narrow at the outset. But as we progress in this way of life and in faith, we shall run on the path of God's commandments, our hearts overflowing with the inexpressible delight of love. Never swerving from his instructions, then, but faithfully observing his teaching in the monastery until death, we shall through patience share in the sufferings of Christ that we may deserve also to share in his kingdom. Amen.

Chapter 4. The Tools for Good Works

Your way of acting should be different from the world's way; the love of Christ must come before all else. You are not to act in anger or nurse a grudge. Rid your heart of all deceit. Never give a hollow greeting of peace or turn away when someone needs your love. Bind yourself to no oath lest it prove false, but speak the truth with heart and tongue. . . .

Place your hope in God alone. If you notice something good in yourself, give credit to God, not to yourself, but be certain that the evil you commit is always your own and yours to acknowledge.

Live in fear of judgment day and have a great horror of hell. Yearn for everlasting life with holy desire. Day by day remind yourself that you are going to die. Hour by hour keep careful watch over all you do, aware that God's gaze is upon you, wherever you may be. As soon as wrongful thoughts come into your heart, dash them against Christ and disclose them to your spiritual father. Guard your lips from harmful or deceptive speech. Prefer moderation in speech and speak no foolish chatter, nothing just to provoke laughter; do not love immoderate or boisterous laughter.

Listen readily to holy reading, and devote yourself often to prayer. Every day with tears and sights confess your past sins to God in prayer and change from these evil ways in the future. . . .

Do not aspire to be called holy before you really are, but first be holy that you may more truly be called so. Live by God's commandments every day; treasure chastity, harbor neither hatred nor jealousy of anyone, and do nothing out of envy. Do not love quarreling; shun arrogance. Respect the elders and love the young. Pray for your enemies out of love for Christ. If you have a dispute with someone, make peace with him before the sun goes down.

And finally, never lose hope in God's mercy.

These, then, are the tools of the spiritual craft. . . .

The workshop where we are to toil faithfully at all these tasks is the enclosure of the monastery and stability in the community.

Chapter 5. Obedience

The first step of humility is unhesitating obedience, which comes naturally to those who cherish Christ above all. Because of the holy service they have professed, or because of dread of hell and for the glory of everlasting life, they carry out the superior's order as promptly as if the command came from God himself. . . . Such people as these immediately put aside their own concerns, abandon their own will, and lay down whatever they have in hand, leaving it unfinished. With the ready step of obedience, they follow the voice of authority in their actions. Almost at the same moment, then, as the master gives the instruction the disciple quickly puts it into practice in the fear of God; and both actions together are swiftly completed as one.

It is love that impels them to pursue everlasting life; therefore, they are eager to take the narrow road of which the Lord says: *Narrow is the road that leads to life* (Matt 7:14). They no longer live by their own judgment, giving in to their whims and appetites; rather they walk according to another's decisions and directions, choosing to live in monasteries and to have an abbot over them. . . .

This very obedience, however, will be acceptable to God and agreeable to men only if compliance with what is commanded is not cringing or sluggish or half-hearted, but free from any grumbling or any reaction of unwillingness. For the obedience shown to superiors is given to God, as he himself said: *Whoever listens to you, listens to me* (Luke 10:16). Furthermore, the disciples' obedience must be given gladly, for *God loves a cheerful giver* (2 Cor 9:7). If a disciple obeys grudgingly and grumbles, not only aloud but also in his heart, then, even though he carries out the order, his action will not be accepted with favor by God, who sees that he is grumbling in his heart. He will have no reward for service of this kind; on the contrary, he will incur punishment for grumbling, unless he changes for the better and makes amends.

DISCUSSION QUESTIONS

1. How would you describe Benedict's tone in the Prologue? What does this suggest about his overall goal in composing his *Rule*?

2. As explained here, what general religious principles and goals were supposed to guide the monks' lives, and why?

3. Why does Benedict place such a strong emphasis on humility? Why did he consider it to be so important to doing God's work?

4. Community Worship

The Torah Niche, Dura-Europos Synagogue (c. 244–245 c.e.)

Polytheists were not alone in feeling the pressures of Christianization; Jews likewise were caught in between the currents of change and tradition. On the one hand, they warranted special treatment because Jesus was a Jew; on the other hand, their refusal to convert gradually set them apart as second-class citizens in a now Christian empire. Dispersed throughout the empire following the destruction of the Jerusalem temple in 70 c.e., Jews embraced community based worship and the study of sacred texts to maintain their identity, as the Torah niche from the Dura-Europas synagogue reveals. Located in the imperial frontier town of Dura-Europos in modern-day Syria and completed in the mid-third century, the synagogue is one of the oldest in the world. The Torah niche is located in the synagogue's western wall, which is oriented toward Jerusalem and is elaborately decorated with biblical scenes. Architecturally, the niche was designed to house a copy of the Torah, the first five books of the Hebrew Bible. Depictions of the Jerusalem temple and ritual implements decorated the space above the niche, along with an image of Abraham preparing to sacrifice Isaac. Originally a private home, the synagogue's inconspicuous exterior concealed a far more elaborate interior. Because of this, worshippers could blend into the surroundings more easily, making them less susceptible to persecution.

DISCUSSION QUESTIONS

1. What do both the direction of the Torah niche and its decorative elements reveal about the importance of tradition to Jewish identity during this period? What do both the direction of the Torah niche and its form and decoration suggest about the role that remembrance and place played for the now scattered Jewish community?

2. Jews lived side by side with Christians and polytheists in Dura. How might this help us to understand their decision to decorate their synagogue with images that appear to violate the *Book of Exodus*'s second commandment against graven images? (2.2 Monotheism and Mosaic Law, pages 22–25)

3. What does the fact that this niche was constructed to hold a text suggest about the role of the written word in Jewish worship at this time? In what ways did this differ from polytheistic practices as revealed in the image of the household shrine in the last chapter? (6.6 Private Piety, page 116)

Zev Radovan / www.BibleLandPictures.com / Alamy

5. Germanic Law in the Roman Empire

The Burgundian Code (c. 475–525 C.E.)

The migration of Germanic tribes into the West changed imperial politics and society just as profoundly as Christianity did. Members of these tribes gradually formed independent kingdoms based on a mixture of their own and Roman traditions, which soon superseded Roman provincial government. Law codes established by Germanic leaders from the fifth century on were a crucial component of their state-building efforts. Rome provided a powerful precedent in this regard, with its emphasis on written law as both the basis of social order and a manifestation of state authority. These excerpts are drawn from one of the most comprehensive early Germanic law codes, The Burgundian Code, *compiled by the kings of the Burgundians, an East Germanic tribe, in the late fifth and early sixth centuries. At this time, they ruled over a large kingdom encompassing much of the former Roman province of Gaul. Early Frankish and Anglo-Saxon societies that were developing during this period were plagued by feuds that undermined political authority and perpetuated increasing cycles of violence. In an effort to curb personal vendettas and increase stability, many rulers established law codes based on wergeld ("man money") that set fines based on the type of crime and a person's value in that society.*

First Constitution

In the name of God in the second year of the reign of our lord the most glorious king Gundobad, this book concerning laws past and present, and to be preserved throughout all future time, has been issued on the fourth day before the Kalends of April (March 29) at Lyons. . . .

For the love of justice, through which God is pleased and the power of earthly kingdoms acquired, we have obtained the consent of our counts (*comites*) and leaders (*proceres*), and have desired to establish such laws that the integrity and equity of those judging may exclude all rewards and corruptions from themselves.

Therefore all administrators (*administrantes*) and judges must judge from the present time on between Burgundians and Romans according to our laws which have been set forth and corrected by a common method, to the end that no one may hope or presume to receive anything by way of reward or emolument from any party as the result of the suits or decisions; but let him whose case is deserving obtain justice and let the integrity of the judge alone suffice to accomplish this. . . .

Therefore let all nobles (*obtimates*), counsellors (*consiliarii*), bailiffs (*domestici*), mayors of our palace (*maiores domus nostrae*), chancellors (*cancellarii*), counts (*comites*) of the cities or villages, Burgundian as well as Roman, and all appointed judges and military judges (*judices militantes*) know that nothing can be accepted in connection

From *The Burgundian Code*, trans. Katherine Fischer Drew (Philadelphia: University of Pennsylvania Press, 1972), 17–24, 30–33, 40–47.

with those suits which have been acted upon or decided, and that nothing can be sought in the name of promise or reward from those litigating; nor can the parties (to the suit) be compelled by the judge to make a payment in order that they may receive anything (from their suit). . . .

Indeed if any judge, barbarian as well as Roman, shall not render decisions according to those provisions which the laws contain because he has been prevented by ignorance or negligence, and he has been diverted from justice for this reason, let him know that he must pay thirty solidi[1] and that the case must be judged again on behalf of the aggrieved parties. . . .

Of Murders

If anyone presumes with boldness or rashness bent on injury to kill a native freeman of our people of any nation or a servant of the king, in any case a man of barbarian tribe, let him make restitution for the committed crime not otherwise than by the shedding of his own blood.

We decree that this rule be added to the law by a reasonable provision, that if violence shall have been done by anyone to any person, so that he is injured by blows of lashes or by wounds, and if he pursues his persecutor and overcome by grief and indignation kills him, proof of the deed shall be afforded by the act itself or by suitable witnesses who can be believed. Then the guilty party shall be compelled to pay to the relatives of the person killed half his wergeld according to the status of the person: that is, if he shall have killed a noble of the highest class (*optimas nobilis*), we decree that the payment be set at one hundred fifty solidi, i.e., half his wergeld; if a person of Middle class (*mediocris*), one hundred solidi; if a person of the lowest class (*minor persona*), seventy-five solidi.

If a slave unknown to his master presumes to kill a native freeman, let the slave be handed over to death, and let the master not be made liable for damages.

If the master knows of the deed, let both be handed over to death.

If the slave himself flees (*defuerit*) after the deed, let his master be compelled to pay thirty solidi to the relatives of the man killed for the value (wergeld) of the slave.

Similarly in the case of royal slaves, in accordance with the status of such persons, let the same condition about murderers be observed.

In such cases let all know this must be observed carefully, that the relatives of the man killed must recognize that no one can be pursued except the killer; because just as we have ordered the criminals to be destroyed, so we will suffer the innocent to sustain no injury. . . .

Let Burgundians and Romans Be Held under the Same Condition in the Matter of Killing Slaves

If anyone kills a slave, barbarian by birth, a trained (select) house servant or messenger, let him compound sixty solidi; moreover, let the amount of the fine be twelve solidi.

---

[1]**solidi:** Plural of *solidus*, a gold coin. [Ed.]

If anyone kills another's slave, Roman or barbarian, either ploughman or swineherd, let him pay thirty solidi.

Whoever kills a skilled goldsmith, let him pay two hundred solidi.

Whoever kills a silversmith, let him pay one hundred solidi.

Whoever kills a blacksmith, let him pay fifty solidi.

Whoever kills a carpenter, let him pay forty solidi. . . .

Of the Stealing of Girls

If anyone shall steal a girl, let him be compelled to pay the price set for such a girl nine-fold, and let him pay a fine to the amount of twelve solidi.

If a girl who has been seized returns uncorrupted to her parents, let the abductor compound six times the wergeld of the girl; moreover, let the fine be set at twelve solidi.

But if the abductor does not have the means to make the above-mentioned payment, let him be given over to the parents of the girl that they may have the power of doing to him whatever they choose.

If indeed, the girl seeks the man of her own will and comes to his house, and he has intercourse with her, let him pay her marriage price threefold; if moreover, she returns uncorrupted to her home, let her return with all blame removed from him.

If indeed a Roman girl, without the consent or knowledge of her parents, unites in marriage with a Burgundian, let her know she will have none of the property of her parents. . . .

Of Succession

Among Burgundians we wish it to be observed that if anyone does not leave a son, let a daughter succeed to the inheritance of the father and mother in place of the son.

If by chance the dead leave neither son nor daughter, let the inheritance go to the sisters or nearest relatives.

It is pleasing that it be contained in the present law that if a woman having a husband dies without children, the husband of the dead wife may not demand back the marriage price (*pretium*) which had been given for her.

Likewise, let neither the woman nor the relatives of the woman seek back that which a woman pays when she comes to her husband if the husband dies without children.

Concerning those women who are vowed to God and remain in chastity, we order that if they have two brothers they receive a third portion of the inheritance of the father, that is, of that land which the father, possessing by the right of *sors* (allotment), left at the time of his death. Likewise, if she has four or five brothers, let her receive the portion due to her.

If moreover she has but one brother, let not a half, but a third part go to her on the condition that, after the death of her who is a woman and a nun, whatever she possesses in usufruct from her father's property shall go to the nearest relatives, and she will have no power of transferring anything therefrom, unless perhaps from her mother's goods, that is, from her clothing or things of the cell (*rescellulae*), or what she has acquired by her own labor.

We decree that this should be observed only by those whose fathers have not given them portions; but if they shall have received from their father a place where they can live, let them have full freedom of disposing of it at their will. . . .

Of Burgundian Women Entering a Second or Third Marriage

If any Burgundian woman, as is the custom, enters a second or third marriage after the death of her husband, and she has children by each husband, let her possess the marriage gift (*donatio nuptialis*) in usufruct while she lives; after her death, let what his father gave her be given to each son, with the further provision that the mother has the power neither of giving, selling, or transferring any of the things which she received in the marriage gift.

If by chance the woman has no children, after her death let her relatives receive half of whatever has come to her by way of marriage gift, and let the relatives of the dead husband who was the donor receive half.

But if perchance children shall have been born and they shall have died after the death of their father, we command that the inheritance of the husband or children belong wholly to the mother. Moreover, after the death of the mother, we decree that what she holds in usufruct by inheritance from her children shall belong to the legal heirs of her children. Also we command that she protect the property of her children dying intestate.

If any son has given his mother something by will or by gift, let the mother have the power of doing whatever she wishes therewith; if she dies intestate, let the relatives of the woman claim the inheritance as their possession.

If any Burgundian has sons (children?) to whom he has given their portions, let him have the power of giving or selling that which he has reserved for himself to whomever he wishes. . . .

Of Knocking Out Teeth

If anyone by chance strikes out the teeth of a Burgundian of the highest class, or of a Roman noble, let him be compelled to pay fifteen solidi.

For middle-class freeborn people, either Burgundian or Roman, if a tooth is knocked out, let composition be made in the sum of ten solidi.

For persons of the lowest class, five solidi.

If a slave voluntarily strikes out the tooth of a native freeman, let him be condemned to have a hand cut off; if the loss which has been set forth above has been committed by accident, let him pay the price for the tooth according to the status of the person.

If any native freeman strikes out the tooth of a freedman, let him pay him three solidi. If he strikes out the tooth of another's slave, let him pay two solidi to him to whom the slave belongs. . . .

Of Injuries Which Are Suffered by Women

If any native freewoman has her hair cut off and is humiliated without cause (when innocent) by any native freeman in her home or on the road, and this can be proved with witnesses, let the doer of the deed pay her twelve solidi, and let the amount of the fine be twelve solidi.

If this was done to a freedwoman, let him pay her six solidi.

If this was done to a maidservant, let him pay her three solidi, and let the amount of the fine be three solidi.

If this injury (shame, disgrace) is inflicted by a slave on a native freewoman, let him receive two hundred blows; if a freedwoman, let him receive a hundred blows; if a maidservant, let him receive seventy-five blows.

If indeed the woman whose injury we have ordered to be punished in this manner commits fornication voluntarily (i.e., if she yields), let nothing be sought for the injury suffered.

Of Divorces

If any woman leaves (puts aside) her husband to whom she is legally married, let her be smothered in mire.

If anyone wishes to put away his wife without cause, let him give her another payment such as he gave for her marriage price, and let the amount of the fine be twelve solidi.

If by chance a man wishes to put away his wife, and is able to prove one of these three crimes against her, that is, adultery, witchcraft, or violation of graves, let him have full right to put her away: and let the judge pronounce the sentence of the law against her, just as should be done against criminals.

But if she admits none of these three crimes, let no man be permitted to put away his wife for any other crime. But if he chooses, he may go away from the home, leaving all household property behind, and his wife with their children may possess the property of her husband.

Of the Punishment of Slaves Who Commit a Criminal Assault on Freeborn Women

If any slave does violence to a native freewoman, and if she complains and is clearly able to prove this, let the slave be killed for the crime committed.

If indeed a native free girl unites voluntarily with a slave, we order both to be killed.

But if the relatives of the girl do not wish to punish their own relative, let the girl be deprived of her free status and delivered into servitude to the king.

DISCUSSION QUESTIONS

1. What do these laws reveal about the social and political structure of the Burgundian kingdom? For example, do the laws place the same value on all social groups?
2. What does the code reveal about the role of women and of the family in Burgundian life?
3. Historians regard the interaction between Germanic and Roman peoples as a key component of the process by which Germanic kingdoms replaced imperial government in Western Europe. What evidence of such interaction can you find in this document?

6. Emergence of Byzantium

Procopius, *Secret History* (550 C.E.)

The emperors of the eastern Roman provinces successfully resisted the tides of change that engulfed the West. In the process, they forged a new empire, Byzantium. Emperor Justinian (r. 527–565 C.E.) played a pivotal role in shaping Byzantium's emerging identity as a bastion of Roman imperial glory and civilization. Byzantine historian and courtier Procopius of Caesarea (c. 490/510–560s C.E.) provides unrivaled information about Justinian's rule, including two official histories presenting the emperor's legal, military, and architectural accomplishments as expressions of his strong leadership and divine favor. Procopius also wrote a Secret History, *excerpted below, which likewise described the achievements of Justinian and his wife, Theodora (c. 500–548 C.E.). The book casts them in a highly unfavorable light, however, so much so that it was not published until after Procopius's death out of fear of reprisal for its contents.*

Character and Appearance of Justinian

I think this is as good a time as any to describe the personal appearance of the man. Now in physique he was neither tall nor short, but of average height; not thin, but moderately plump; his face was round, and not bad looking, for he had good color, even when he fasted for two days. . . .

Now such was Justinian in appearance; but his character was something I could not fully describe. For he was at once villainous and amenable; as people say colloquially, a moron. He was never truthful with anyone, but always guileful in what he said and did, yet easily hoodwinked by any who wanted to deceive him. His nature was an unnatural mixture of folly and wickedness. What in olden times a peripatetic philosopher said was also true of him, that opposite qualities combine in a man as in the mixing of colors. I will try to portray him, however, insofar as I can fathom his complexity.

This Emperor, then, was deceitful, devious, false, hypocritical, two-faced, cruel, skilled in dissembling his thought, never moved to tears by either joy or pain, though he could summon them artfully at will when the occasion demanded, a liar always, not only offhand, but in writing, and when he swore sacred oaths to his subjects in their very hearing. Then he would immediately break his agreements and pledges, like the vilest of slaves, whom indeed only the fear of torture drives to confess their perjury. A faithless friend, he was a treacherous enemy, insane for murder and plunder, quarrelsome and revolutionary, easily led to anything evil, but never willing to listen to good counsel, quick to plan mischief and carry it out, but finding even the hearing of anything good distasteful to his ears.

How could anyone put Justinian's ways into words? These and many even worse vices were disclosed in him as in no other mortal: nature seemed to have taken the wickedness of all other men combined and planted it in this man's soul. And besides this, he was too

From Procopius, *Secret History*, trans. Richard Atwater (Ann Arbor: University of Michigan Press, 1961), 40–44, 55, 58, 60, 75–76.

prone to listen to accusations; and too quick to punish. For he decided such cases without full examination, naming the punishment when he had heard only the accuser's side of the matter. Without hesitation he wrote decrees for the plundering of countries, sacking of cities, and slavery of whole nations, for no cause whatever. So that if one wished to take all the calamities which had befallen the Romans before this time and weigh them against his crimes, I think it would be found that more men had been murdered by this single man than in all previous history.

He had no scruples about appropriating other people's property, and did not even think any excuse necessary, legal or illegal, for confiscating what did not belong to him. And when it was his, he was more than ready to squander it in insane display, or give it as an unnecessary bribe to the barbarians. In short, he neither held on to any money himself nor let anyone else keep any: as if his reason were not avarice, but jealousy of those who had riches. Driving all wealth from the country of the Romans in this manner, he became the cause of universal poverty.

Now this was the character of Justinian, so far as I can portray it. . . .

How the Defender of the Faith Ruined His Subjects

As soon as Justinian came into power he turned everything upside down. Whatever had before been forbidden by law he now introduced into the government, while he revoked all established customs: as if he had been given the robes of an Emperor on the condition he would turn everything topsy-turvy. Existing offices he abolished, and invented new ones for the management of public affairs. He did the same thing to the laws and to the regulations of the army; and his reason was not any improvement of justice or any advantage, but simply that everything might be new and named after himself. And whatever was beyond his power to abolish, he renamed after himself anyway.

Of the plundering of property or the murder of men, no weariness ever overtook him. As soon as he had looted all the houses of the wealthy, he looked around for others; meanwhile throwing away the spoils of his previous robberies in subsidies to barbarians or senseless building extravagances. And when he had ruined perhaps myriads in this mad looting, he immediately sat down to plan how he could do likewise to others in even greater number. . . .

Moreover, while he was encouraging civil strife and frontier warfare to confound the Romans, with only one thought in his mind, that the earth should run red with human blood and he might acquire more and more booty, he invented a new means of murdering his subjects. Now among the Christians in the entire Roman Empire, there are many with dissenting doctrines, which are called heresies by the established church: such as those of the Montanists and Sabbatians, and whatever others cause the minds of men to wander from the true path. All of these beliefs he ordered to be abolished, and their place taken by the orthodox dogma: threatening, among the punishments for disobedience, loss of the heretic's right to will property to his children or other relatives.

After this he passed a law prohibiting pederasty:[1] a law pointed not at offenses committed after this decree, but at those who could be convicted of having practiced the vice

---

[1]**pederasty**: Male homosexual relations. [Ed.]

in the past. The conduct of the prosecution was utterly illegal. Sentence was passed when there was no accuser: the word of one man or boy, and that perhaps a slave, compelled against his will to bear witness against his owner, was defined as sufficient evidence. Those who were convicted were castrated and then exhibited in a public parade. . . .

How All Roman Citizens Became Slaves

Theodora too unceasingly hardened her heart in the practice of inhumanity. What she did, was never to please or obey anyone else; what she willed, she performed of her own accord and with all her might: and no one dared to intercede for any who fell in her way. For neither length of time, fullness of punishment, artifice of prayer, nor threat of death, whose vengeance sent by Heaven is feared by all mankind, could persuade her to abate her wrath. Indeed, no one ever saw Theodora reconciled to any one who had offended her, either while he lived or after he had departed this earth. Instead, the son of the dead would inherit the enmity of the Empress, together with the rest of his father's estate: and he in turn bequeathed it to the third generation. For her spirit was over ready to be kindled to the destruction of men, while cure for her fever there was none.

To her body she gave greater care than was necessary, if less than she thought desirable. For early she entered the bath and late she left it; and having bathed, went to breakfast. After breakfast she rested. At dinner and supper she partook of every kind of food and drink; and many hours she devoted to sleep, by day till nightfall, by night till the rising sun. Though she wasted her hours thus intemperately, what time of the day remained she deemed ample for managing the Roman Empire.

And if the Emperor intrusted any business to anyone without consulting her, the result of the affair for that officer would be his early and violent removal from favor and a most shameful death.

It was easy for Justinian to look after everything, not only because of his calmness of temper, but because he hardly ever slept, as I have said, and because he was not chary with his audiences. For great opportunity was given to people, however, obscure and unknown, not only to be admitted to the tyrant's presence, but to converse with him, and in private.

But to the Queen's presence even the highest officials could not enter without great delay and trouble; like slaves they had to wait all day in a small and stuffy antechamber, for to absent himself was a risk no official dared to take. So they stood there on their tiptoes, each straining to keep his face above his neighbor's, so that eunuchs, as they came out from the audience room, would see them. Some would be called, perhaps, after several days; and when they did enter to her presence in great fear, they were quickly dismissed as soon as they had made obeisance and kissed her feet. For to speak or make any request, unless she commanded, was not permitted.

Not civility, but servility was the rule, and Theodora was the slave driver. So far had Roman society been corrupted, between the false geniality of the tyrant and the harsh implacability of his consort. For his smile was not to be trusted, and against her frown nothing could be done. There was this superficial difference between them in attitude and manner; but in avarice, bloodthirstiness, and dissimulation they utterly agreed. They were both liars of the first order.

DISCUSSION QUESTIONS

1. What might have been Procopius's goals in writing this book?

2. How does Procopius's animosity toward Justinian and Theodora shape his account of their reign? In what ways should you take this into account as you evaluate his book as a historical source?

3. Do you see any evidence embedded within Procopius's attacks that may explain the reasons for Justinian's short-term success at reuniting the empire and enhancing imperial rule and its long-term costs?

COMPARATIVE QUESTIONS

1. When viewed together, what do the documents in this chapter reveal about the spread and institutional development of Christianity in the Roman Empire between the fourth and sixth centuries? How do these documents illuminate the interplay between politics and religion?

2. Do you see any similarities between Augustine's and Benedict's understandings of what constituted a holy life? What appeal do you think their views may have had?

3. In what ways do the Nicene Creed, Augustine, and Benedict reflect early efforts to define the basis of Christian identity? In what ways did the orientation, form, and function of the Torah niche do the same for the Jewish community in Dura?

4. According to Procopius, Justinian's decisions defined law and were a bulwark of his authority. In what ways does the Burgundian Code reflect a similar attitude toward the function of law in government and society?

The Heirs of Rome: Islam, Byzantium, and Europe
600–750

The seventh and eighth centuries marked the beginning of a new era in Western civilization — the Middle Ages. By this time, the Roman Empire had fragmented into three different worlds: Muslim, Byzantine, and western European. Even so, these worlds were all rooted in Hellenistic and Roman traditions that each region adapted to its own interests and circumstances. The sources in this chapter reveal different dimensions of this process, beginning with Islam. The first document illuminates some of the fundamental beliefs uniting the Islamic community as recorded in the Muslim holy book, the Qur'an. Islamic armies rapidly expanded the boundaries of the Muslim world, bringing both change and continuity to everyday life in their newly conquered lands, as the second document reveals. The third document describes facets of religious and social life in the provinces of the Byzantine Empire on the eve of the Muslim invasion. Although the western kingdoms shared a common Roman heritage with Byzantium, their development followed a different course as various barbarian peoples built new societies and cultures. The final documents bring this development to life by illustrating the westward spread of Christian institutions and values, even as some communities clung tenaciously to their pagan roots.

1. The Foundations of Islam
Qur'an, Suras 1, 53, 98 (c. 610–632)

The remarkable rise of Islam during the seventh century had far-reaching consequences. Muhammad (c. 570–632), a merchant turned holy man from the Arabian city of Mecca, founded the new faith based on what he believed were direct revelations from God, which he first received around 610. The messages continued until his death and soon thereafter were

From *Approaching the Qur'an: The Early Revelations*, trans. Michael Sells (Ashland, OR: White Cloud Press, 1999), 35, 42, 44, 47, 104–6.

written down and compiled into what became the Qur'an, the holy book of Islam. Comprising 114 hymnic chapters (suras), the Qur'an begins with the Fatihah ("opening"), which emphasizes God's oneness and the believer's recourse to God alone. The "road straight" is the path of right worship. The first eighteen verses of the Star, among the earliest of Muhammad's revelations, explicitly reveal his position in the divine plan, casting him as God's companion and servant. The final selection, the Testament, represents the later period of Muhammad's prophecy when he and his followers confronted the challenges posed by people who resisted the new religion.

1 The Opening

In the name of God
    the Compassionate the Caring
Praise be to God
    lord sustainer of the worlds
the Compassionate the Caring
master of the day of reckoning[1]
To you we turn to worship
    and to you we turn in time of need
Guide us along the road straight
the road of those to whom you are giving
    not those with anger upon them
    not those who have lost the way

53:1–18 The Star

In the Name of God the Compassionate the Caring

By the star as it falls
Your companion[2] has not lost his way nor is he
    deluded
He does not speak out of desire
This is a revelation
taught him by one of great power
and strength that stretched out over
while on the highest horizon —

---

[1] The word translated here as *reckoning* (*dīn*) is related to a number of terms for borrowing and payment of debt, as well as to terms for religion and faith. The word for *day* (*yawm*) also can be a more general term for any length of time or a moment in time. The term has been translated as "day of judgment" and "day of accounting." But it also has an implication similar to the "moment of truth" — that is, a time of indeterminate duration in which each soul will encounter the fundamental reality that normal consciousness masks.

[2] "Your companion" is interpreted as Muhammad.

then drew near and came down
two bows' lengths or nearer
He revealed to his servant what he revealed
The heart did not lie in what it saw

Will you then dispute with him his vision?
He saw it[3] descending another time
at the lote[4] tree of the furthest limit
There was the garden of sanctuary
when something came down over the
      lote tree, enfolding
His gaze did not turn aside nor go too far
He had seen the signs of his lord, great signs

98 The Testament

In the Name of God the Compassionate the Caring

Those who denied the faith —
      from the peoples of the book[5]
      or the idolators —
      could not stop calling it a lie
      until they received the testament

A messenger of God
      reciting pages that are pure

Of scripture that are sure

Those who were given the book
      were not divided one against the other
      until they received the testament

And all they were commanded
      was to worship God sincerely
      affirm oneness, perform the prayer
      and give a share of what they have
      That is the religion of the sure

---

[3]When the Qur'an states "He saw it descending another time," the antecedent of the pronoun (*hu*, it/him) is unstated, and thus the referent of the "it" is not determinable from the passage. The identity of the referent became a matter of controversy, with the debate centering upon whether or not the deity can be seen in this world. Those for whom the vision of God can only occur in the afterlife tend to interpret the it/he as referring to the messenger angel Gabriel.

[4]**lote**: A thorny tree with edible fruit; it is also known as Christ-thorn. [Ed.]

[5]Those with written scriptures named in other passages of the Qur'an as the Jews, Christians, and Sabeans (the exact identity of whom has been a matter of controversy).

Those who deny the faith —
    from the peoples of the book
    or the idolators —
    are in Jahannam's[6] fire
    eternal there
    They are the worst of creation

Those who keep the faith
    and perform the prayer
    they are the best of creation

As recompense for them with their lord —
    gardens of Eden
    waters flowing underground
    eternal there forever
    God be pleased in them
    and they in God
    That is for those who hold their lord in awe

DISCUSSION QUESTIONS

1. Based on these excerpts, what beliefs and practices constitute the "right path" of Islam?

2. How does the Star portray Muhammad? What does this portrait reveal about his role in Islam?

3. The rejection of Islam by many Jews and Christians ("peoples of the book") in Arabia surprised and disappointed Muhammad since he brought his message in the name of the tradition of Abraham, Moses, and Jesus. How does the Testament give expression to these feelings and, at the same time, defend the truth of Muhammad's revelations?

4. What defining features of religion are articulated in the Opening and the Testament? What similarities and differences do you see?

2. Jihad and Jizya

Islamic Terms of Peace (633–639)

Despite facing some resistance, Muhammad's revelations soon gained widespread adherence across the Arabian Peninsula. Together, his converts formed a community united by the worship of God, expressed not only in individual prayer but also in the collective duty

---

Adapted from Muhammad ibn Jarir al-Tabari, *The History of al-Tabari*, trans. Khalid Yahya Blankinship (Albany State University of New York Press, 1993), 11:40; Muhammad ibn Jarir al-Tabari, *The History of al-Tabari*, trans. Yohanan Friedmann (Albany State University of New York Press, 1992) 12:191–92; Muhammad ibn Jarir al-Tabari, *The History of al-Tabari*, trans. Gauthier H. A. Juynboll (Albany State University of New York Press, 1993), 13:216–17.

[6]**Jahannam**: Hell. [Ed.]

to "strive" (jihad) against unbelievers, often in war. By the eighth century, the armies of the Umayyad Caliphate had conquered all of Persia and much of the Byzantine Empire. These letters dictate the terms of peace to conquered communities and illuminate the Muslims' method of conquest and rule in the decade following Muhammad's death. In exchange for the payment of a special tax (jizya), non-Muslim subjects were allowed to live much as they had before. Consequently, Islam became not the destroyer of Hellenistic and Roman traditions but rather their heir.

Bānqiyā and Basmā[1] (633)

In the name of God, the All-Compassionate, the Merciful. This is a letter from Khālid ibn al-Walīd to Salūba ibn Nastūnā and his people.

I give you a covenant on condition [of payment] of the *jizya* in return for protection. [This is a requirement] for whoever is able [to pay in] both Bānqiyā and Basmā, in the amount of ten thousand dīnārs, aside from the chosen spoils, the wealthy according to the amount of his wealth, and the poor according to the extent of his poverty, every year. You have been made your people's representative; they have accepted you. I and those with me have accepted. I am satisfied, and your people are also satisfied. Therefore, you have a guarantee of security and protection, so that, if we protect you, we are entitled to the *jizya*, but, if not, then not until we do protect you.

Witnessed by Hishām ibn al-Walīd, al-Qa 'qā 'ibn 'Amr, Jarīr ibn 'Abdallāh al Himyarī and Hanzala ibn al-Rabī' and written in the year 12 [633].

Jerusalem (636)

In the name of God, the Merciful, the Compassionate. This is the assurance of safety which the servant of God, 'Umar, the Commander of the Faithful, has granted to the city of Jerusalem. He has given them an assurance of safety for themselves, for their property, their churches, their crosses, the sick and the healthy of the city, and for all the rituals that belong to their religion. Their churches will not be inhabited [by Muslims] and will not be destroyed. Neither they, nor the land on which they stand, nor their crosses, nor their property will be damaged. They will not be forcibly converted. No Jew will live with them in Jerusalem.[2] The people of Jerusalem must pay *jizya* like the people of the [other] cities, and they must expel the Byzantines and the robbers. As for those who will leave the city, their lives and property will be safe until they reach . . . safety; and as for those who remain, they will be safe. They will have to pay *jizya* like the people of Jerusalem. Those of the people of Jerusalem who want to leave with the Byzantines, take their property, and abandon their churches and crosses, will be safe until they reach . . . safety. Those villagers who were in Jerusalem before the killing of so-and-so[3] may remain in the city if they

---

[1]Bānqiyā and Basmā: In modern-day Iraq. [Ed.]
[2]Following the Second Jewish Revolt (132–135 C.E.), Emperor Hadrian worked to cement imperial control by rebuilding Jerusalem along Roman lines. His efforts included building a sanctuary to Jupiter on the original site of the Jewish temple and banning all Jews from the city.
[3]The meaning of these words is not clear. . . . They are missing in the text of the letter.

wish, but they must pay *jizya* like the people of Jerusalem. Those who wish may go with the Byzantines, and those who wish may return to their families. Nothing will be taken from them before their harvest is reaped. If they pay *jizya* according to their obligations, then the contents of this letter are under the covenant of God, and are the responsibility of His Prophet, of the caliphs, and of the faithful.

Witnessed by Khālid ibn al-Walīd, 'Amr ibn al-'Aṣ, 'Abd al-Raḥmān ibn 'Awf, Mu'āwiya ibn Abī Sufyān, the last of whom wrote this document in the year 15 [636].

Basra and Kufa[4] (640)

In the name of God, the Merciful and the Compassionate.

This is the covenant that al-Nu'mān ibn Muqarrin has granted. . . . He has guaranteed them immunity for their person, their property and their lands; they need not give up any religious custom and they will not be prevented from implementing any of their own laws. They will also enjoy protection as long as every year they pay the *jizya* to the governor in charge. This is incumbent upon every adult in respect to himself and his possessions, each according to his ability. They will also enjoy protection as long as they show the way to travelers, keep the roads in good repair and extend hospitality for a day and a night to Muslim warriors who pass by and seek refuge with them, and as long as they fulfill their promises and give sound advice. But if they act dishonestly and change their conduct, our obligation to protect them will lapse.

Witnesses to this document were 'Abdallāh ibn Dhī al-Sahmayn, al-Qa'qā' ibn 'Amr and Jarīr ibn 'Abdallāh.

Written in the year 19 [640].

DISCUSSION QUESTIONS

1. Aside from the payment of a poll tax, what were some of the obligations Muslims imposed on their non-Muslim subjects?

2. What did the conquered people receive in exchange for the fulfillment of these obligations?

3. What does this system of exchange suggest about Muslim attitudes toward nonbelievers?

3. Byzantine Life

The Life of St. Theodore of Sykeon (Early Seventh Century)

Although Emperor Justinian (r. 527–565) had worked to revive the old Roman Empire, by 600 the eastern half began to change into something new, Byzantium. An emperor continued to rule from Constantinople, but his reach was smaller; the empire had shrunk in size, and its cities had decayed. Against this backdrop, rural life assumed greater importance

---

From Bernard Lewis, ed., *Islam from the Prophet Muhammad to the Capture of Constantinople,* vol. 1 (New York: Walker & Co., 1974), 234–36, 238–40.

[4]**Basra and Kufa:** In modern-day Iraq. [Ed.]

as the backbone of Byzantine society. Free and semifree peasant farmers grew food and herded cattle on small plots of land across the countryside. As the excerpt below from The Life of St. Theodore of Sykeon *reveals, among peasants' most frequent social contacts were monks in the local monasteries dotting the landscape. St. Theodore (c. 550–613) was a monk and bishop who lived in central Anatolia (modern Turkey). He gained a great following as a holy man and healer among the communities located on or near the Roman imperial road linking Constantinople to the eastern frontier of the empire. One of his disciples composed the* Life *in the early seventh century to honor Theodore's memory and to uphold him as a model of Christian virtue. In the process, the author also paints among the best pictures known to us of provincial life during this period, particularly villagers' deeply held belief in the omnipresent power of divine and demonic forces in the everyday world.*

After the Saint had returned to his monastery, it happened that he fell so ill of a desperate sickness that he saw the holy angels coming down upon him; and he began to weep and to be sorely troubled. Now above him there stood an icon of the wonder-working saints Cosmas and Damian. These saints were seen by him looking just as they did in that sacred icon and they came close to him, as doctors usually do; they felt his pulse and said to each other that he was in a desperate state as his strength had failed and the angels had come down from heaven to him. And they began to question him saying, "Why are you weeping and are sore troubled, brother?" He answered them, "Because I am unrepentant, sirs, and also because of this little flock which is only newly-instructed and is not yet established and requires much care." They asked him, "Would you wish us to go and plead for you that you may be allowed to live for a while?" He answered, "If you do this, you would do me a great service, by gaining for me time for repentance and you shall win the reward of my repentance and my work from henceforth." Then the saints turned to the angels and besought them to grant him yet a little time while they went to implore the King on his behalf. They agreed to wait. So the saints departed and entreated on his behalf the heavenly King, the Lord of life and death, Christ our God, Who granted unto Hezekiah the King an addition unto his life of fifteen years.[1] They obtained their request and came back to the Saint bringing with them a very tall young man, like in appearance to the angels that were there, though differing from them greatly in glory. He said to the holy angels, "Depart from him, for supplication has been made for him to the Lord of all and King of glory, and He has consented that he should remain for a while in the flesh." Straightway both they and the young man disappeared from his sight, going up to heaven. But the Saints, Cosmas and Damian, said to the Saint, "Rise up brother, and look to thyself and to thy flock; for our merciful Master who readily yields to supplication has received our petition on your behalf and grants you life to labor for 'the meat which perisheth not, but endureth to everlasting life'[2] and to care for many souls." With these words they, too, vanished.

---

[1]2 Kings xx. 6.
[2]John vi. 27.

Theodore immediately regained his health and strength; the sickness left him and glorifying God he resumed his life of abstinence and the regular recital of the psalms with still greater zeal and diligence.

Through the grace bestowed on him by God Theodore continued to work many miracles against every kind of illness and weakness, but especially did he make supplications to God for aid against unclean spirits; hence, if he merely rebuked them, or even sent them a threat through another, they would immediately come out of people. Some persons were so profoundly impressed by these miracles that they left their homes, journeyed to him, and entering upon a life of contemplation joined the monastery; others again who had obtained healing would not leave him but stayed with him, giving him such service as he needed. . . .

In the village of Buzaea, which belonged to the city of Kratianae, the inhabitants wanted to build a bridge over the torrent which ran through it, as the latter often became swollen by many streams and could not be crossed. They hired workmen and when the work had almost reached completion and only a few stone slabs were still needed to finish it the workmen at the Devil's instigation went to a certain hill not far off and dug out some slabs from it on the excuse, as some said, that they were needed for their work; but the majority said that they had stolen away a treasure that was hidden there. Then there issued from the place where they had dug for the stones a host of unclean spirits; some of them entered into sundry men and women of the village and afflicted them savagely, others again brought illnesses upon the remaining inhabitants, while yet others hung about the roads and the neighborhood and did injury to beasts and travelers; hence great misery arose in the village and despair at the misfortunes in their homes and in the countryside. Then they bethought themselves of Theodore, the servant of God, and by prayers in his name they tried to exorcize the unclean spirits when they showed signs of activity, and they found that the spirits showed no little fear when his name was uttered over them, and became docile and were reduced to subjection. With all speed, therefore, they made for the monastery and by dint of many supplications they persuaded him to come with them. When Theodore drew nigh to the village the spirits which were afflicting men felt his presence and met him howling out these words: "Oh violence! Why have you come here, you iron-eater, why have you quitted Galatia and come into Gordiane? There was no need for you to cross the frontier. We know why you have come, but we shall not obey you as did the demons of Galatia; for we are much tougher than they and not milder." When he rebuked them they at once held their peace. On the morrow all the inhabitants were gathered together, and those possessed by evil spirits surrounded the Saint who had ordered a procession of supplication to be formed which went right round the village and came to the hill from which they said the demons had come out. Then he tortured them by the divine grace of Christ and by the sign of the holy Cross and by beatings on his chest, and after offering up prayers for a long time he bade them come out of the people and return to their own abode. They uttered loud shouts and tore the garments which covered the sufferers and threw them down at his feet and then came out of them. But one very wicked spirit which was in a woman resisted and would not come out. Then the Saint caught hold of the woman's hair and shook her violently and rebuked the spirit by the sign of the Cross and by prayer to God and finally said, "I will not give way to you nor will I leave this spot until you come out of her!" Then the spirit began to shriek and say, "Oh violence, you are burning me, iron-eater! I am coming out, I will not resist you, only give us something that you are wearing." The Saint loosed a sandal from his foot and threw it into the hole in the hill whence they had entered into people and straightway the spirit hurled the woman down at the feet of the Saint and came out of her.

Then the Saint halted again and prayed to the Lord that He would drive together all the spirits, which were still remaining in the neighborhood and in the roads to the injury of travelers, and would shut them up once more in the place from which they came out. And through the grace of God they were all collected, and to some who saw them they looked like flying blue-bottles or hares or dormice, and they entered into the place where the stones had been dug out, which the Saint then sealed with prayer and the sign of the Cross, and bade the men fill up the hole and restore it as it was before. He then led the procession back to the village, and from that time on that place and the inhabitants of the village and all the neighborhood remained safe from harm to the glory of Christ our God, the prime author of healings.

And the Saint returned and came to his monastery.

DISCUSSION QUESTIONS

1. What role do icons play in Theodore's recovery? What does this reveal about the place of icons in Byzantine religious devotion?

2. Why did the villagers of Buzaea seek Theodore's help? What was the source of his power?

3. What does the *Life* reveal about Byzantine notions of sanctity? Why did Theodore command such prestige among local residents?

4. A Noblewoman's Life

The Life of Lady Balthild, Queen of the Franks
(Late Seventh Century)

With the collapse of imperial government in the West in the fifth and sixth centuries, the kings from the Frankish royal dynasty, the Merovingians, came to dominate Roman Gaul. Their queens also wielded power, as The Life of Lady Balthild *demonstrates. Lady Balthild (d. c. 680) was an Anglo-Saxon captive sold as a slave to the mayor of the palace in the Frankish kingdom of Neustria. He eventually offered her in marriage to King Clovis II (r. 638–657). On the king's death in 657, Lady Balthild acted as regent until her eldest son came of age in 663 or 664. She thereupon retired from court to a monastery. Although the author is unknown, his or her intent is clear: to hold Lady Balthild up as a model of Christian piety. Religious motives aside, the book illuminates women's place in court life as well as the growing influence of Christianity in Merovingian culture.*

From Paul Fouracre and Richard A. Gerberding, eds., *Late Merovingian France: History and Hagiography, 640–720* (Manchester: Manchester University Press, 1996), 119–27, 131–32.

*and long-distance trade networks. The creation of novel business agreements through part-
nerships and contracts fueled the economic boom. One in particular was essential to the
expansion of trade, the* commenda *contract, sometimes translated as "business venture."
The* commenda *had historical precedents, but beginning in the tenth century, it assumed
unique characteristics in the western Mediterranean, as illustrated in the examples below.
Although known by different names in different places,* commenda *contracts all served the
same purpose as legal tools for pooling capital and bringing together investors and managers for sea trade. Italy was a hub for these contracts as coastal cities like Genoa and Venice
sought to establish and expand their maritime markets. The types of goods being traded varied widely; they included cotton, silk, sugar, gold, and spices. Sometimes both the investors
and the traveling party provided capital for the venture (examples 1 and 3); other times, one
party was the sole lender (example 4). When the traveling party returned, the terms of the
contract were settled (example 2). In each instance, all parties involved shared the profits
and the risks associated with the undertaking.*

The Venetian Commenda or Collegantia

1

Venice, August, 1073

In the name of the Lord God and of our Savior, Jesus Christ. In the year of the Incarnation of the same Redeemer of 1073, in the month of August, eleventh indiction, at
Rialto,[1] I, Giovanni Lissado of Luprio together with my heirs, have received in *collegantia*[2]
from you, Sevasto Orefice, son of Ser Trudimondo, and from your heirs, this [amount]:
£200 [Venetian]. And I myself have invested £100 in it. And with this capital (*habere*) we
have [acquired] two shares (*sortes*) in the ship of which Gosmiro da Molino is captain.
And I am under obligation to bring all of this with me in *taxegio*[3] to Thebes in the ship
in which the aforesaid Gosmiro da Molino sails as captain. Indeed, by this agreement
and understanding of ours I promise to put to work this entire [capital] and to strive the
best way I can. Then, if the capital is saved, we are to divide whatever profit the Lord may
grant us from it by exact halves, without fraud and evil device. And whatever I can gain
with those goods from any source, I am under obligation to invest all [of it] in the *collegantia*. And if all these goods are lost because of the sea or of [hostile] people, and this is
proved — may this be averted — neither party ought to ask any of them from the other;
if, however, some of them remain, in proportion as we invested so shall we share. Let this
collegantia exist between us so long as our wills are fully agreed.

But if I do not observe everything just as is stated above, I, together with my heirs,
then promise to give and to return to you and your heirs everything in the double, both

---

[1]Rialto ("high creek") is the original name of some of the islands which are now called Venice.
Venice at first was the name of the entire region of which Rialto became the capital in the early
ninth century.
[2]*collegantia*: The contracts are called *collegantia* according to the Venetian use. [Ed.]
[3]*Taxegium* is a word of Byzantine origin and means "commercial voyage" or "commercial journey."

capital and profit (*caput et prode*), out of my land and my house or out of anything that I am known to have in this world.

Signature of the aforesaid Giovanni who requested this [instrument] to be made.

I, Pietro, witness, signed.

I, Lorenzo, witness, signed.

I, Gosmiro, witness, signed.

The full names of the witnesses are these: Pietro Gossoni; Lorenzo Scudaio; Gosmiro da Molino.

I, Domenico, cleric and notary, completed and certified [this instrument].

2

Venice, May, 1072[4]

In the name of the Lord God Almighty. In the year of the Incarnation of our Lord Jesus Christ 1072, in the month of May, tenth indiction, at Rialto. I, Domenico Zopulo, son of Vitale Zopulo junior, together with my heirs, do make to you, Giovanni Barozzi, son of Giovanni Barozzi, and to your heirs, full and irrevocable release[5] in regard to an instrument of record which you made to me, whereby I myself invested £50 in deniers[6] of good alloy and you by the same [instrument] invested £25, and [whereby] you went with all these goods in *taxegio* to Thebes in the ship of which Leone Orefice was captain. But now, since you have returned from said *taxegio*, you have rendered me a full, accurate, and true account of it, in regard to both the principal and the profit; under oath you have handed over everything to me and you have settled [accounts]. From now on you shall always remain released in regard to the principal and the profit or to the [penalty of the] double and to all that is stated in the said record, so that on no day and at no time [henceforth] are we to make any further demand or to exert [any more] pressure by any device, whether small or great. I, moreover, have returned to you the record itself. If a copy of it appears in my possession or in that of any man, it shall remain null and void, wholly without validity and force, because there is nothing left in it whereby we should make any further demand upon you. But if we at any time attempt to demand anything in regard to the clauses stated above, I, together with my heirs, promise to pay to you and to your heirs £5 in gold [as penalty], and this release shall [nevertheless] remain in force.

I, Domenico, signed by my hand.

I, Giovanni, witness, signed.

I, Domenico, witness, signed.

I, Leone, witness, signed.

The full names of the witnesses are these: Giovanni, son of Pietro Michiel and Domenico, his brother; Leone, son of Domenico Michiel.

I, Giovanni, subdeacon and notary, completed and certified [this instrument].

---

4. . . . The parties and the witnesses belonged to the highest merchant nobility in Venice.

5*Securitatem*, literally, "security."

6**denier**: Coin used as a money of account; one pound was valued at the equivalent of 240 deniers. [Ed.]

The Genoese Commenda and Societas

3

[Genoa,] September 29, 1163

Witnesses: Simone Bucuccio, Ogerio Peloso, Ribaldo di Sauro, and Genoardo Tasca. Stabile and Ansaldo Garraton have formed a *societas*[7] in which, as they mutually declared, Stabile contributed £88 [Genoese] and Ansaldo £44. Ansaldo carries this *societas*, in order to put it to work, to Tunis or to wherever goes the ship in which he shall go — namely, [the ship] of Baldizzone Grasso and Girardo. On his return [he will place the proceeds] in the power of Stabile or of his messenger for [the purpose of] division. After deducting the capital, they shall divide the profits in half. Done in the chapter house, September 29, 1163, eleventh indiction.

In addition, Stabile gave his permission to send that money to Genoa by whatever ship seems most convenient to him [to Ansaldo].

4

[Genoa,] October 7, 1163

Witnesses: Bernizone Serra, Raimondo, Crispino and Pietro Vinattiere. I, Ingo Bedello, declare publicly that I am carrying £41 s.6 [Genoese] of goods belonging to Guglielmotto Ciriolo [invested] in silk and paper to Tunis, and from there to Genoa [where I shall place the proceeds] in the power of Guglielmotto or of his messenger. And he is not under obligation to contribute toward expenses in regard to them except in furnishing the [original] money. [Ingo] on his return [will place the proceeds] in the power of Guglielmotto or of his messenger and, after deducting the capital, he is to have one fourth of the profit. And Guglielmotto himself reserved as his right that there will be no expense for him in it. Done in the chapter house, October 7, 1163, eleventh indiction.

DISCUSSION QUESTIONS

1. The rise of a profit-based economy is one of the most distinctive features of this time period. How did the business arrangements described in these documents seek to maximize the profit of all parties involved?

2. What do these documents suggest about the extent of trade networks at the time and the types of goods being traded?

3. What comparisons could you make between these documents and modern business practices? How are they similar? How are they different?

---

[7] *societas*: A bilateral commenda was called *societas* in Genoa, while *commenda* applied exclusively to the unilateral contract. [Ed.]

2. Sources of the Investiture Conflict

SOURCES IN CONVERSATION | Emperor Henry IV,
***Letter* and Pope Gregory VII,**
***Excommunication* (1076)**

The commercial revolution helped spark not only economic changes but also religious ones. Pope Gregory VII (r. 1073–1085) became the driving force behind a movement for church reform, which strove to liberate the church from secular influence and wealth. His zeal brought him head-to-head with Emperor Henry IV (r. 1056–1106), who, claiming to be crowned by God, asserted the traditional right to oversee the church in his realm. These two documents illuminate each side of the debate. The first is a letter that Henry sent to the pope in January 1076 after Gregory had denounced him for not obeying papal mandates prohibiting, among other things, laymen from "investing" (that is, appointing) church leaders. In response, the pope excommunicated and deposed Henry. The lines of the conflict were thus drawn, pitting imperial and papal claims of authority against each other. Although the battle ended in 1122 with a compromise, the papacy emerged as a more powerful force than ever.

Henry IV: Letter to Gregory VII

Henry, King not by usurpation, but by the pious ordination of God, to Hildebrand, now not Pope, but false monk:

You have deserved such a salutation as this because of the confusion you have wrought; for you left untouched no order of the Church which you could make a sharer of confusion instead of honor, of malediction instead of benediction.

For to discuss a few outstanding points among many: Not only have you dared to touch the rectors of the holy Church — the archbishops, the bishops, and the priests, anointed of the Lord as they are — but you have trodden them under foot like slaves who know not what their lord may do. In crushing them you have gained for yourself acclaim from the mouth of the rabble. You have judged that all these know nothing, while you alone know everything. In any case, you have sedulously used this knowledge not for edification, but for destruction, so greatly that we may believe Saint Gregory, whose name you have arrogated to yourself, rightly made this prophesy of you when he said: "From the abundance of his subjects, the mind of the prelate is often exalted, and he thinks that he has more knowledge than anyone else, since he sees that he has more power than anyone else."

And we, indeed, bore with all these abuses, since we were eager to preserve the honor of the Apostolic See. But you construed our humility as fear, and so you were emboldened to rise up even against the royal power itself, granted to us by God. You dared to threaten

From *The Correspondence of Pope Gregory VII*, trans. Ephraim Emerton (New York: Columbia University Press, 1932), 90–91, and *Imperial Lives and Letters of the Eleventh Century*, trans. Theodor E. Mommsen and Karl F. Morrison (New York: Columbia University Press, 1962), 150–51.

to take the kingship away from us — as though we had received the kingship from you, as though kingship and empire were in your hand and not in the hand of God.

Our Lord, Jesus Christ, has called us to kingship, but has not called you to the priesthood. For you have risen by these steps: namely, by cunning, which the monastic profession abhors, to money; by money to favor; by favor to the sword. By the sword you have come to the throne of peace, and from the throne of peace you have destroyed the peace. You have armed subjects against their prelates; you who have not been called by God have taught that our bishops who have been called by God are to be spurned; you have usurped for laymen the bishops' ministry over priests, with the result that these laymen depose and condemn the very men whom the laymen themselves received as teachers from the hand of God, through the imposition of the hands of bishops.

You have also touched me, one who, though unworthy, has been anointed to kingship among the anointed. This wrong you have done to me, although as the tradition of the holy Fathers has taught, I am to be judged by God alone and am not to be deposed for any crime unless — may it never happen — I should deviate from the Faith. For the prudence of the holy bishops entrusted the judgment and the deposition even of Julian the Apostate not to themselves, but to God alone. The true pope Saint Peter also exclaims, "Fear God, honor the king." You, however, since you do not fear God, dishonor me, ordained of Him.

Wherefore, when Saint Paul gave no quarter to an angel from heaven if the angel should preach heterodoxy, he did not except you who are now teaching heterodoxy throughout the earth. For he says, "If anyone, either I or an angel from heaven, preach any other gospel unto you than that which we have preached unto you, let him be accursed." Descend, therefore, condemned by this anathema and by the common judgment of all our bishops and of ourself. Relinquish the Apostolic See which you have arrogated. Let another mount the throne of Saint Peter, another who will not cloak violence with religion but who will teach the pure doctrine of Saint Peter.

I, Henry, King by the grace of God, together with all our bishops, say to you: Descend! Descend!

Gregory VII: Excommunication of Henry IV

O blessed Peter, prince of the Apostles, mercifully incline thine ear, we [sic] pray, and hear me, thy servant, whom thou hast cherished from infancy and hast delivered until now from the hand of the wicked who have hated and still hate me for my loyalty to thee. Thou art my witness, as are also my Lady, the Mother of God, and the blessed Paul, thy brother among all the saints, that thy Holy Roman Church forced me against my will to be its ruler. I had no thought of ascending thy throne as a robber, nay, rather would I have chosen to end my life as a pilgrim than to seize upon thy place for earthly glory and by devices of this world. Therefore, by thy favor, not by any works of mine, I believe that it is and has been thy will, that the Christian people especially committed to thee should render obedience to me, thy especially constituted representative. To me is given by thy grace the power of binding and loosing in Heaven and upon earth.

Wherefore, relying upon this commission, and for the honor and defense of thy Church, in the name of Almighty God, Father, Son and Holy Spirit, through thy power and authority, I deprive King Henry, son of the emperor Henry, who has rebelled against thy

Church with unheard of audacity, of the government over the whole kingdom of Germany and Italy, and I release all Christian men from the allegiance which they have sworn or may swear to him, and I forbid anyone to serve him as king. For it is fitting that he who seeks to diminish the glory of thy Church should lose the glory which he seems to have.

And, since he has refused to obey as a Christian should or to return to the God whom he has abandoned by taking part with excommunicated persons, has spurned my warnings which I gave him for his soul's welfare, as thou knowest, and has separated himself from thy Church and tried to rend it asunder, I bind him in the bonds of anathema in thy stead and I bind him thus as commissioned by thee, that the nations may know and be convinced that thou art Peter and that upon thy rock the son of the living God has built his Church and the gates of hell shall not prevail against it.

DISCUSSION QUESTIONS

1. What does Henry IV mean by denouncing the pope as a "false monk"?

2. What do Henry's denunciations reveal about his conception of the source and the scope of his power as emperor?

3. How did Henry's self-image conflict with Gregory's understanding of his own authority as reflected in his excommunication and deposition of the emperor?

3. Calling the First Crusade

Fulcher of Chartres, *Pope Urban II's Speech at Clermont* (1095)

The papacy emerged from the Gregorian reforms with enhanced power and prestige as the head of Western Christendom. Pope Urban II (r. 1088–1099) embraced his position of leadership and directed it toward a new cause: the liberation of Jerusalem and the Holy Land. At the time, these lands were under the control of the Seljuk Turks, who had gained control as part of their broader expansionist campaign in Asia Minor. In need of military reinforcements to counter the threat that the Seljuks posed to Byzantium, the Byzantine emperor called on the pope for help. Urban II's response is captured in the document that follows. It is a version of a speech he delivered to a large crowd in Clermont, France, in 1095 urging them to put down their weapons against one another and use them instead against the "infidel" in the Holy Land. Cleric Fulcher of Chartres (c. 1059–c. 1127) was present at the speech and was one of the tens of thousands who took up the pope's call to fight for God. He served as chaplain for one of the crusade leaders and recorded his experiences, including what he heard that day in Clermont, in a three-volume Chronicle. *His firsthand knowledge of events combined with the richness of his account make his* Chronicle *among the most reliable of all sources on the First Crusade.*

From Oliver J. Thatcher and Edgar Holmes McNeal, *A Source Book for Medieval History* (New York: Charles Scribner's Sons, 1905), 516–17.

Although, O sons of God, you have promised more firmly than ever to keep the peace among yourselves and to preserve the rights of the church, there remains still an important work for you to do. Freshly quickened by the divine correction, you must apply the strength of your righteousness to another matter which concerns you as well as God. For your brethren who live in the east are in urgent need of your help, and you must hasten to give them the aid which has often been promised them. For, as the most of you have heard, the Turks and Arabs have attacked them and have conquered the territory of Romania [the Greek empire] as far west as the shore of the Mediterranean and the Hellespont, which is called the Arm of St. George. They have occupied more and more of the lands of those Christians, and have overcome them in seven battles. They have killed and captured many, and have destroyed the churches and devastated the empire. If you permit them to continue thus for awhile with impunity, the faithful of God will be much more widely attacked by them. On this account I, or rather the Lord, beseech you as Christ's heralds to publish this everywhere and to persuade all people of whatever rank, foot-soldiers and knights, poor and rich, to carry aid promptly to those Christians and to destroy that vile race from the lands of our friends. I say this to those who are present, it is meant also for those who are absent. Moreover, Christ commands it.

All who die by the way, whether by land or by sea, or in battle against the pagans, shall have immediate remission of sins. This I grant them through the power of God with which I am invested. O what a disgrace if such a despised and base race, which worships demons, should conquer a people which has the faith of omnipotent God and is made glorious with the name of Christ! With what reproaches will the Lord overwhelm us if you do not aid those who, with us, profess the Christian religion! Let those who have been accustomed unjustly to wage private warfare against the faithful now go against the infidels and end with victory this war which should have been begun long ago. Let those who, for a long time, have been robbers, now become knights. Let those who have been fighting against their brothers and relatives now fight in a proper way against the barbarians. Let those who have been serving as mercenaries for small pay now obtain the eternal reward. Let those who have been wearing themselves out in both body and soul now work for a double honor. Behold! on this side will be the sorrowful and poor, on that, the rich; on this side, the enemies of the Lord, on that, his friends. Let those who go not put off the journey, but rent their lands and collect money for their expenses; and as soon as winter is over and spring comes, let them eagerly set out on the way with God as their guide.

DISCUSSION QUESTIONS

1. Why does Urban II urge his audience to fight against the Turks? What language does he use to describe the crusaders and their journey? What language does he use to describe the Turks?

2. Why do you think this language motivated people in the audience like Fulcher of Chartres to join the crusade? What did the crusade have to offer them?

3. How does Urban II cast himself in this speech? How may it have strengthened the papacy's position in the church hierarchy?

4. Arab Response to the First Crusade

Ibn al-Athīr, *A Complete History* (1097–1099)

In preaching the First Crusade, Pope Urban II called on the entire "race of Franks" to expel the enemies of God ("Turks" and "Arabs") from the Holy Land. As official accounts of the crusade make clear, Urban's words shaped the attitudes and actions of the crusaders as they made their way through Constantinople, south to the Seljuk capital of Nicaea, and then onward to Jerusalem, which they conquered in early June 1099. They saw themselves as God's army, which had the right and obligation to destroy "infidels." The document that follows reveals an entirely different perspective, that of Muslim leaders and soldiers fighting the crusaders along the way. It is drawn from a sweeping chronicle of Islamic history by Arab historian Ibn al-Athīr (1160–1233), who used a range of sources to describe the crusaders' activities and the Muslim response to them. For him, the crusaders were not men of God but rather ruthless invaders who wreaked havoc on local peoples and holy sites.

How the Franks Took the City of Antioch

The power of the Franks and their increased importance were first manifested by their invasion of the lands of Islam and their conquest of part of them in the year 478 [1085–6], for [that was when] they took the city of Toledo and other cities of Spain, as we have already mentioned.

Then in the year 484 [1091–2] they attacked and conquered the island of Sicily, as we have also mentioned. They descended on the coasts of Ifrīqiya¹ and seized some part, which was then taken back from them. Later they took other parts, as you shall see.

When it was the year 490 [1096–7] they invaded Syria. The reason for their invasion was that their ruler, Baldwin, a relative of Roger the Frank who had conquered Sicily, gathered a great host of Franks and sent to Roger saying, "I have gathered a great host and I am coming to you. I shall proceed to Ifrīqiya to take it and I shall be a neighbor of yours." Roger assembled his men and consulted them about this. They said, "By the truth of the Gospel, this is excellent for us and them. The lands will become Christian lands." Roger raised his leg and gave a loud fart. "By the truth of my religion," he said, "there is more use in that than in what you have to say!" "How so?" they asked. "If they come to me," he replied, "I shall require vast expenditure and ships to convey them to Ifrīqiya and troops of mine also. If they take the territory it will be theirs and resources from Sicily will go to them. I shall be deprived of the money that comes in every year from agricultural revenues. If they do not succeed, they will return to my lands and I shall suffer from them. Tamīm will say, 'You have betrayed me and broken the agreement I have [with you].' Our mutual contacts and visits will be interrupted. The land of Ifrīqiya will be waiting for us. Whenever we find the strength we will take it."

From Ibn al-Athīr, *The Chronicle of Ibn al-Athīr for the Crusading Period* from *al-Kamil fi'l-Ta'rikh*, part 1, trans. D. S. Richards (Burlington, VT: Ashgate, 2006), 13–17, 21–22.

¹The loose term for the eastern part of the Maghrib.

He summoned Baldwin's envoy and said to him, "If you are determined to wage holy war on the Muslims, then the best way is to conquer Jerusalem. You will free it from their hands and have glory. Between me and the people of Ifrīqiya, however, are oaths and treaties." They therefore made their preparations and marched forth to Syria.

It has been said that the Alid rulers of Egypt[2] became fearful when they saw the strength and power of the Saljuq state, that it had gained control of Syrian lands as far as Gaza, leaving no buffer state between the Saljuqs and Egypt to protect them, and that Aqsīs[3] had entered Egypt and blockaded it. They therefore sent to the Franks to invite them to invade Syria, to conquer it and separate them and the [other] Muslims, but God knows best.

After they had decided to march to Syria, they went to Constantinople to cross the straits into Muslim lands, to travel on by land, for that would be easier for them. When they arrived, the Byzantine emperor refused them passage through his territory. He said, "I will not allow you to cross into the lands of Islam until you swear to me that you will surrender Antioch to me." His aim was to urge them to move into Islamic lands, assuming that Turks would not spare a single one of them, because he had seen how fierce they were and their control of the lands. They agreed to that and crossed the Bosphorus at Constantinople in the year 490 [1096–7].

They reached the lands of Qilij Arslān ibn Sulaymán ibn Qutlumish[4] namely Konya and other cities. Having arrived there, they were met by Qilij Arslān with his hosts, who resisted them. They put him to flight in Rajab 490 [July 1097] after a battle[5] and then traversed his lands into those of the son of the Armenian[6] which they marched through before emerging at Antioch and putting it under siege.

When the ruler Yaghī Siyān[7] heard of their coming, he feared the Christians in the city. He sent out the Muslim inhabitants by themselves and ordered them to dig the moat. Then the next day he sent out the Christians also to dig the moat, unaccompanied by any Muslim. They labored on it until the evening but when they wished to enter the city he prevented them and said, "You can give me Antioch until I see how things will be with us and the Franks." They asked, "Who will look after our sons and our wives?" "I will look after them in your place," he replied. So they held back and took up residence in the Frankish camp. The Franks besieged the city for nine months. Yaghī Siyān displayed such courage, excellent counsel, resolution, and careful planning as had never been seen from anyone else. Most of the Franks perished. Had they remained in the numbers they set out with, they would have overwhelmed the lands of Islam. Yaghī Siyān protected the families of those Christians of Antioch, whom he had expelled, and restrained the hands that would do them harm.

After their siege of Antioch had lasted long, the Franks made contact with one of the men garrisoning the towers, who was an armorer, known as Rūzbah, and offered him money and grants of land. He was in charge of a tower next to the valley, which was built

---

[2]I.e., the Fatimid caliphs.
[3]Alternative name for Atsiz ibn Uvak, a Turkoman chief who attacked Egypt in 1077.
[4]Saljuq sultan of Asia Minor (Rūm), died 1107.
[5]This is the battle of Dorylaeum.
[6]Perhaps Constantine I, son of Rupen I (1095–1102) is intended.
[7]Turkish emir, given Aleppo as fief by Sultan Malikshāh.

with a window overlooking the valley. After they had made an arrangement with this cursed armorer, they came to the window, which they opened and through which they entered. A large number climbed up on ropes. When they numbered more than five hundred, they blew the trumpet. That was at dawn. The defenders were already tired from many sleepless nights on guard. Yaghī Siyān awoke and asked what was happening. He was told, "That trumpet is from the citadel. No doubt it has already been taken." However, it was not from the citadel but merely from that tower. He was seized with fear, opened the city gate and left in headlong flight with thirty retainers. His deputy as governor of the city came and asked after him. He was told that he had fled, so he himself fled by another gate. That was a boon for the Franks. Had he held firm for a while, they would have perished. The Franks entered the city through the gate and sacked it, killing the Muslims that were there. This was in Jumada I [April–May 1098].[8] . . .

How the Muslims Marched against the Franks and What Befell Them

When Qiwām al-Dawla Karbughā[9] heard of the Franks' doings and their conquest of Antioch, he gathered his forces and marched to Syria. He camped at Jarj Dābiq,[10] where the troops of Syria, both Turks and Arabs, rallied to him, apart from those who were in Aleppo. There assembled with him Duqāq ibn Tutush,[11] Tughtakīn the Atabeg,[12] Janāh al-Dawla the lord of Homs,[13] Arslān Tāsh the lord of Sinjār, Suqmān ibn Artuq and other emirs, the likes of whom are not to be found. Hearing of this, the Franks' misfortunes increased and they were fearful because of their weakness and their shortage of provisions. The Muslims came and besieged them in Antioch, but Karbughā behaved badly towards the Muslims with him. He angered the emirs and lorded it over them, imagining that they would stay with him despite that. However, infuriated by this, they secretly planned to betray him, if there should be a battle, and they determined to give him up when the armies clashed.

The Franks, after they had taken Antioch, were left there for twelve days with nothing to eat. The powerful fed on their horses, while the wretched poor ate carrion and leaves. In view of this, they sent to Karbughā, asking him for terms to leave the city, but he did not grant what they sought. He said, "My sword alone will eject you."

The following princes were with them: Baldwin,[14] [Raymond of] St. Gilles,[15] Count Godfrey, the Count lord of Edessa,[16] and Bohemond the lord of Antioch, their leader.

---

[8]The city fell in fact in early June 1098.

[9]Governor of Mosul and other Mesopotamian towns, supporter of Barkyāruq and patron of Zankī.

[10]The "plain" near Dābiq in North Syria.

[11]Saljuq prince of Damascus.

[12]Zāhir al-Dīn Abū Mansūr Tughtakīn, freedman of Tutush and atabeg (i.e., regent/guardian) of Duqāq. Founder of the short-lived Būrid dynasty in Damascus.

[13]Atabeg of Ridwān ibn Tutush, ruled independently in Homs from 490/1097.

[14]In Baldwin of Le Bourg, subsequently count of Edessa and then King Baldwin II.

[15]Count of Toulouse.

[16]Baldwin of Boulogne, count of Edessa and future Baldwin I, is meant, although he was not present at Antioch.

There was a monk there, of influence amongst them, who was a cunning man. He said to them, "The Messiah (blessings be upon Him) had a lance which was buried in the church at Antioch, which was a great building.[17] If you find it, you will prevail, but if you do not find it, then destruction is assured." He had previously buried a lance in a place there and removed the traces [of his digging]. He commanded them to fast and repent, which they did for three days. On the fourth day he took them all into the place, accompanied by the common people and workmen. They dug everywhere and found it as he had said. "Rejoice in your coming victory," he said to them.[18]

On the fifth day they went out of the gate in scattered groups of five or six or so. The Muslims said to Karbughā, "You ought to stand at the gate and kill all that come out, because now, when they are scattered, it is easy to deal with them." He replied, "No, do not do that. Leave them alone until they have all come out and then we can kill them." He did not allow his men to engage them. However, one group of Muslims did kill several that had come out but he came in person and ordered them to desist.

When the Franks had all come out and not one of them remained within, they drew up a great battle line. At that, the Muslims turned their backs in flight, firstly because of the contempt and the scorn with which Karbughā had treated them and secondly because he had prevented them from killing the Franks. Their flight was complete. Not one of them struck a blow with a sword, thrust with a spear or shot an arrow. The last to flee were Suqmān ibn Artuq and Janāḥ al-Dawla because they were stationed in ambush. Karbughā fled with them. When the Franks observed this, they thought that it was a trick, since there had been no battle such as to cause a flight and they feared to pursue them. A company of warriors for the faith stood firm and fought zealously, seeking martyrdom. The Franks slew thousands of them and seized as booty the provisions, money, furnishings, horses and weapons that were in the camp. Their situation was restored and their strength returned. . . .

How the Franks (God Curse Them) Took Jerusalem

Jerusalem had been held by Tāj al-Dawla Tutush who assigned it to Emir Suqmān ibn Artuq the Turkoman. When the Franks defeated the Turks at Antioch and made slaughter amongst them, the power of the Turks weakened and they lost cohesion. When the Egyptians saw their weakness, they marched to Jerusalem, led by al-Afdal ibn Badr al-Jamālī. There they besieged Suqmān and Īlghāzī, the sons of Artuq, and also their cousin Savanj and their nephew Yāqūtī. They set up forty and more trebuchets against the town and demolished parts of its wall. The inhabitants fought back and the fighting and the siege lasted somewhat over forty days, until the Egyptians took the city on terms in Sha'bān 489 [July 1096]. Al-Afdal treated Suqmān, Īlghāzī and their followers well, gave them generous gifts and sent them on their way to Damascus. Subsequently they crossed the Euphrates. Suqmān took up residence in Edessa but Īlghāzī moved to Iraq.

---

[17]This is the cathedral of St. Peter, called al-Qusyān.

[18]This lance, claimed to be the one used to pierce Jesus' side, was found in the Church of St. Peter by a Provencal, Peter Bartholomew.

The Egyptians appointed as deputy in Jerusalem a man called Iftikhār al-Dawla, who remained there until this present time, when the Franks attacked after they had besieged Acre but with no success. After their arrival they erected forty trebuchets or more and they constructed two towers, one on Mount Zion side but the Muslims burnt that one and killed all inside. After they had completely destroyed it by fire, their help was then called for, as the city defenses had been overwhelmed on the other side. The Franks did indeed take the city from the north in the forenoon of Friday, seven days remaining of Sha'bān [15 July 1099]. The inhabitants became prey for the sword. For a week the Franks continued to slaughter the Muslims. A group of Muslims took refuge in the Tower of David[19] and defended themselves there. They resisted for three days and then the Franks offered them safe-conduct, so they surrendered the place. The Franks kept faith with them and they departed at night for Ascalon, where they remained.

In the Aqsa Mosque the Franks killed more than 70,000, a large number of them being imams, ulema, righteous men, and ascetics, Muslims who had left their native lands and come to live a holy life in this august spot. The Franks took forty or more silver candlesticks from the Dome of the Rock, each of which weighed 3,600 dirhams, and also a silver candelabrum weighing forty Syrian rotls. They removed 150 small candlesticks of silver and twenty or so of gold. The booty they took was beyond counting.

DISCUSSION QUESTIONS

1. How does Ibn al-Athīr portray the crusaders and their leaders? What does he reveal about the organization and motives of the crusading armies in the process?

2. As described here, what factors contributed to the crusaders' military success against the Muslims?

3. According to Ibn al-Athīr, the Franks killed thousands of local residents when they took Jerusalem. How does Ibn al-Athīr describe the Franks' actions? How do you think his religious ideas may have shaped his account?

5. The Power of William I

The Anglo-Saxon Chronicle (1085–1086)
and
Domesday Book (1086–1087)

While the papacy was expanding its authority in the eleventh century, regional rulers were doing much the same. William I, duke of Normandy and king of England (r. 1066–1087), provides a case in point, and his efforts on this front helped to make his twelfth-century

---

From *The Anglo-Saxon Chronicle*, trans. Dorothy Whitelock (New Brunswick, NJ: Rutgers University Press, 1961), 161–65, and *Translations and Reprints from the Original Sources of European History*, vol. 3 (Philadelphia: Department of History, University of Pennsylvania, 1912), 6–7.

[19]I.e., the citadel, in Arabic called the Miḥrāb of David.

successors the mightiest kings in Europe. Upon conquering his rival to the throne in the battle of Hastings in 1066, William consolidated his rule by preserving existing institutions and establishing new ones. Below is a contemporary description of King William from the Anglo-Saxon Chronicle, a year-by-year account of English history from the birth of Christ to 1154. As it recounts, among William's many achievements was the commission of a comprehensive survey of England's land, livestock, taxes, and population, which was conducted in 1086–1087. Later condensed into two volumes, known as Domesday, the report paints a detailed picture of England's agricultural and urban landscape. An extract from the survey of the county of Norfolk follows. It bears witness not only to the minute level of record keeping the enterprise entailed but also to the king's immense resources and power.

Anglo-Saxon Chronicle

In this year people said and declared for a fact, that Cnut, king of Denmark, son of King Swein, was setting out in this direction and meant to conquer this country with the help of Robert, count of Flanders, because Cnut was married to Robert's daughter. When William, king of England, who was then in Normandy — for he was in possession of both England and Normandy — found out about this, he went to England with a larger force of mounted men and infantry from France and Brittany than had ever come to this country, so that people wondered how this country could maintain all that army. And the king had all the army dispersed all over the country among his vassals, and they provisioned the army each in proportion to his land. And people had much oppression that year, and the king had the land near the sea laid waste, so that if his enemies landed, they should have nothing to seize on so quickly. But when the king found out for a fact that his enemies had been hindered and could not carry out their expedition — then he let some of the army go to their own country, and some he kept in this country over winter.

Then at Christmas, the king was at Gloucester with his council, and held his court there for five days, and then the archbishop and clerics had a synod for three days. There Maurice was elected bishop of London, and William for Norfolk, and Robert for Cheshire — they were all clerics of the king.

After this, the king had much thought and very deep discussion with his council about this country — how it was occupied or with what sort of people. Then he sent his men over all England into every shire and had them find out how many hundred hides there were in the shire, or what land and cattle the king himself had in the country, or what dues he ought to have in twelve months from the shire.[1] Also he had a record made of how much land his archbishops had, and his bishops and his abbots and his earls — and though I relate it at too great length — what or how much everybody had who was occupying land in England, in land or cattle, and how much money it was worth. So very narrowly did he have it investigated, that there was no single hide nor virgate of land, nor indeed (it is a shame to relate but it seemed no shame to him to do) one ox nor one cow nor one pig which was there left out, and not put down in his record; and all these records were brought to him afterwards. . . .

---

[1]This initiative resulted in Domesday. A hide was a unit of land for taxation. [Ed.]

This King William of whom we speak was a very wise man,[2] and very powerful and more worshipful and stronger than any predecessor of his had been. He was gentle to the good men who loved God, and stern beyond all measure to those people who resisted his will. In the same place where God permitted him to conquer England, he set up a famous monastery and appointed monks for it,[3] and endowed it well. In his days the famous church at Canterbury was built,[4] and also many another over all England. Also, this country was very full of monks, and they lived their life under the rule of St. Benedict, and Christianity was such in his day that each man who wished followed out whatever concerned his order. Also, he was very dignified: three times every year he wore his crown, as often as he was in England. At Easter he wore it at Winchester, at Whitsuntide at Westminster, and at Christmas at Gloucester, and then there were with him all the powerful men over all England, archbishops and bishops, abbots and earls, thegns and knights. Also, he was a very stern and violent man, so that no one dared do anything contrary to his will. He had earls in his fetters, who acted against his will. He expelled bishops from their sees, and abbots from their abbacies, and put thegns in prison, and finally he did not spare his own brother, who was called Odo; he was a very powerful bishop in Normandy (his cathedral church was at Bayeux) and was the foremost man next the king, and had an earldom in England. And when the king was in Normandy, then he was master in this country; and he [the king] put *him* in prison. Amongst other things the good security he made in this country is not to be forgotten — so that any honest man could travel over his kingdom without injury with his bosom full of gold; and no one dared strike[5] another, however much wrong he had done him. And if any man had intercourse with a woman against her will, he was forthwith castrated.

He ruled over England, and by his cunning it was so investigated that there was not one hide of land in England that he did not know who owned it, and what it was worth, and then set it down in his record.[6] Wales was in his power, and he built castles there, and he entirely controlled that race. In the same way, he also subdued Scotland to himself, because of his great strength. The land of Normandy was his by natural inheritance, and he ruled over the county called Maine; and if he could have lived two years more, he would have conquered Ireland by his prudence and without any weapons. Certainly in his time people had much oppression and very many injuries:

He had castles built
And poor men hard oppressed.
The king was so very stark
And deprived his underlings of many a mark
Of gold and more hundreds of pounds of silver,
That he took by weight and with great injustice
From his people with little need for such a deed.

---

[2]The account that follows was clearly written by a man who had attended William's court.
[3]Battle Abbey.
[4]Lanfranc's rebuilding of Christ Church, Canterbury.
[5]Or "kill."
[6]Domesday.

Into avarice did he fall
And loved greediness above all.
He made great protection for the game
And imposed laws for the same,
That who so slew hart or hind
Should be made blind.

He preserved the harts and boars
And loved the stags as much
As if he were their father.
Moreover, for the hares did he decree that they should go free.
Powerful men complained of it and poor men lamented it,
But so fierce was he that he cared not for the rancour of them all,
But they had to follow out the king's will entirely
If they wished to live or hold their land,
Property or estate, or his favour great.
Alas! woe, that any man so proud should go,
And exalt himself and reckon himself above all men!
May Almighty God show mercy to his soul
And grant unto him forgiveness for his sins.

These things we have written about him, both good and bad, that good men may imitate their good points, and entirely avoid the bad, and travel on the road that leads us to the kingdom of heaven.

Extract from Domesday Survey of the County of Norfolk

The land of Robert Malet.

Fredrebruge Hundred and half. Glorestorp. Godwin, a freeman, held it. Two carucates[7] of land in the time of king Edward. Then and afterwards 8 villains[8]; now 3. Then and afterwards 3 bordars[9]; now 5. At all times 3 serfs, and 30 acres of meadow. At all times 2 carucates in demesne.[10] Then half a carucate of the men, and now. Woods for 8 swine, and 2 mills. Here are located 13 socmen,[11] of 40 acres of land. When it was received there were 2 horses, now 1. At all times 8 swine, then 20 sheep, and it is worth 60 shillings.

There is situated there, in addition, one berewick,[12] as the manor of Heuseda. In the time of king Edward, 1 carucate of land; then and afterwards 7 villains, now 5. At all

---

[7]**carucates**: Ploughland; in this part of England, a carucate was used as a unit of tax assessment in lieu of the hide. [Ed.]
[8]**villains**: Peasants living in a village. [Ed.]
[9]**bordars**: Peasants occupying a lower rung on the economic ladder than villains. [Ed.]
[10]**demesne**: Land in lordship, meaning it was in the lord's personal possession or exploited exclusively for his benefit. [Ed.]
[11]**socmen**: Freemen (often peasants) who owed service to a lord. [Ed.]
[12]**berewick**: An outlying estate or one with a special function. [Ed.]

times 12 bordars, and 3 serfs, and 40 acres of meadow; 1 mill. Woods for 16 swine and 1 salt pond and a half. Then 1 horse and now and 14 swine, 30 sheep, and 50 goats. In this berewick are located 3 socmen, of 10 acres of land, and it is worth 30 shillings. The two manors have 2 leagues in length and 4 firlongs in breadth. Whosoever is tenant there, returns 12 pence of the twenty shillings of geld.[13]

Scerpham Hundred Culverstestun Edric held it in the time of king Edward. Two carucates of land. At all times there were 4 villains, and 1 bordar, and 4 serfs; 5 acres of meadow and two carucates in the demesne. Then and afterwards 1 carucate, now one-half. At all times 1 mill and one fish-pond. Here is located 1 socmen of the king, of 40 acres of land; which his predecessors held only as commended and he claims his land from the gift of the king. Then and afterwards there was one carucate, now 2 oxen, and 2 acres of meadow. At all times two horses, and 4 geese; then 300 sheep, now 300 less 12; then 16 swine now 3. Then and afterwards it was worth 60 shillings, now 80; and there could be one plow. Walter of Caen holds it from Robert.

Heinstede Hundred. In Sasilingaham Edric, the predecessor of Robert Malet, held 2 sokes[14] and a half, of 66 acres of land, now Walter holds them. Then 9 bordars, now 13. At all times 3 carucates and a half among all, and 3 acres of meadow, and the eighth part of a mill; and under these 1 soke of 6 acres of land. At all times half a carucate. Then it was worth 30 shillings, now it returns 50 shillings.

In Scotessa Ulcetel was tenant, a free man commended to Edric, in the time of king Edward of 30 acres of land. At that time 1 bordar, afterward and now 2. Then half a carucate, none afterward nor now. It was at all times worth 5 shillings and 4 pence; the same.

DISCUSSION QUESTIONS

1. How does the *Anglo-Saxon Chronicle* describe William's method of rule in general? In what ways does the author present Domesday as a reflection of this rule?

2. Do you think that the Domesday extract supports the chronicle's account?

3. Do you think that the author of the chronicle was an objective observer? Why or why not? How does his account differ as a source from Domesday?

6. Living Close to the Land
Labors of the Month Zodiac Column, Souvigny Priory
(Mid-Twelfth Century)

As the Domesday survey suggests, even as new trade, wealth, and business institutions gained a foothold in cities, agricultural production was a key driver of the money economy in the late eleventh and twelfth centuries. It was also a way of life for the vast majority of people living at the time. Depictions of peasants engaged in agricultural work paired with

---

[13]**geld**: A land tax. [Ed.]
[14]**soke**: A lord's right of jurisdiction over specific places and people. [Ed.]

Gianni Dagli Orti / REX / Shutterstock

*signs of the Zodiac were commonly used by medieval artists to convey the changing seasons
and the passage of human time. The octagonal Zodiac column from the monastic church of
Souvigny in south-central France is one of many examples of this theme found in Roman-
esque ecclesiastical sculpture from the region. Measuring close to six feet in height, the column was originally topped by a sundial and housed in the church cloister. Two sides depict*

De Agostini Picture Library / Alfredo Dagli Orti / Bridgeman Images

fantastical beasts and creatures, a third portrays the labors of the months, and a fourth shows the corresponding signs of the Zodiac. The sculptures shown here are representations of the months of August (threshing oats) and December (Christmas dinner). Oats were one of the staple grains in the medieval agricultural economy, grown for food and, especially in this part of Europe, for animal feed. Two peasants are depicted here threshing oats with a flail, a physically demanding task. The December sculpture suggests that even at the darkest and coldest time of the year, peasant life was not without pleasure: a man warms himself between two braziers as he celebrates a Christmas feast, one arm outstretched as if to invite the viewer to join him.

DISCUSSION QUESTIONS

1. What details in these two sculptures stand out to you, and why?
2. Peasants were by far the largest segment of medieval society. Why might this be important to interpreting the broader meaning of these sculptures?
3. What do these two sculptures suggest about the basis of medieval notions of time?

COMPARATIVE QUESTIONS

1. What do the Domesday survey, *commenda* contracts, and Souvigny sculptures suggest about the basis of the medieval economy in the eleventh and twelfth centuries? What had changed from earlier periods? What remained the same?
2. How do you think Pope Gregory VII would have reacted to William I's relationship with the English church as described in the *Anglo-Saxon Chronicle*, and why?
3. In what ways do both the investiture conflict between Henry IV and Pope Gregory VII and the First Crusade reflect the new power of the medieval papacy?
4. Look closely at the language that Urban II and Ibn al-Athīr use to describe crusaders and Muslims. What similarities and differences do you see? What does this suggest about how the two sides viewed each other?

CHAPTER 11

The Flowering of the Middle Ages
1150–1215

Rowdy students, brave knights, pious women, enterprising tradesmen, and powerful kings were just a few of the people who infused medieval government, culture, and religion with new vitality and confidence in the twelfth and early thirteenth centuries. Some of the documents in this chapter illuminate how the vigor of the period found expression in new approaches to learning (Documents 1 and 2), literary and artistic styles (Documents 3 and 4), and religious movements (Document 5). Despite the diversity of these sources, they all share a heightened concern for regulating an individual's conduct as part of a larger group, another feature of this period. The drive to codify and control behavior and beliefs served a variety of purposes — from enhancing political authority and social prestige to gaining salvation. As the lines delineating who fit into certain groups became sharper, so, too, did those delineating who was to be excluded. Prejudice combined with religious zeal fueled violence and intolerance against an ever-widening array of enemies, including the Byzantine Greeks (Document 6).

1. New Learning

Peter Abelard, *The Story of My Misfortunes* (c. 1132)

As cities grew in size throughout twelfth-century Europe, so, too, did the number of people flocking to their gates, notably students hungry for knowledge. Schools associated with monasteries and cathedrals had been in place for centuries, but another model of learning gained prominence: the independent master with his own cohort of students. The career of Peter Abelard (1079–1142) embodied the intellectual vitality this second model had to offer. In his student days, he had wandered from school to school, increasingly dissatisfied with their

From *The Letters of Abelard and Heloise*, trans. Betty Radice, rev. ed. M. T. Clanchy (London: Penguin Group, 2003), 19–24, 254–55.

scholarship. Although Abelard was trained in a traditional liberal arts curriculum, he was especially interested in logic as an analytical tool. Ultimately, he gained a name for himself as a master in his own right because of his innovative style of thinking and teaching. As he describes in the excerpt below from his autobiography, The Story of My Misfortunes, *his methods attracted both friends and foes. The passage opens with a description of his success as a teacher and how it set the stage for a confrontation with church officials in 1121. By this point in his life, he had entered a monastery following the fallout of his love affair with his pupil and fellow scholar Heloise, but he remained deeply engaged in academic pursuits.*

When it became apparent that God had granted me the gift for interpreting the Scriptures as well as secular literature, the numbers in my school began to increase for both subjects, while elsewhere they diminished rapidly. This roused the envy and hatred of the other heads of schools against me; they set out to disparage me in whatever way they could, and two of them[1] especially were always attacking me behind my back for occupying myself with secular literature[2] in a manner totally unsuitable to my monastic calling, and for presuming to set up as a teacher of sacred learning when I had had no teacher myself. Their aim was for every form of teaching in a school to be forbidden me, and for this end they were always trying to win over bishops, archbishops, abbots, in fact anyone of account in the Church whom they could approach.

Now it happened that I first applied myself to lecturing on the basis of our faith by analogy with human reason, and composed a theological treatise on divine unity and trinity[3] for the use of my students who were asking for human and logical reasons on this subject, and demanded something intelligible rather than mere words. In fact they said that words were useless if the intelligence could not follow them, that nothing could be believed unless it was first understood, and that it was absurd for anyone to preach to others what neither he nor those he taught could grasp with the understanding: the Lord himself had criticized such "blind guides of blind men."[4] After the treatise had been seen and read by many people it began to please everyone, as it seemed to answer all questions alike on this subject. It was generally agreed that the questions were peculiarly difficult and the importance of the problem was matched by the subtlety of my solution.

My rivals were therefore much annoyed and convened a Council against me, prompted by my two old opponents, Alberic and Lotulf who, now that our former masters, William and Anselm, were dead, were trying to reign alone in their place and

---

[1]Presumably Alberic of Rheims and Lotulf of Lombardy. They ran a school together in Rheims and were two of Abelard's main opponents at the Council of Soissons, described below. [Ed.]

[2]**occupying myself with secular literature:** This refers to the controversy in Abelard's time about whether monks should be contemplative or active. Monks should withdraw from the world; it was the business of the secular clergy and canons to deal with the laity. Hugh of St. Victor argued that Abelard should be devoted to prayer and not to teaching, now that he had become a monk.

[3]**a theological treatise on divine unity and trinity:** The title that Abelard gave to this book was *Theologia* (*Theology*), meaning in Greek "discussion" (*logos*) about the nature of "God" (*theos*). He did not know Greek, but giving the book a Greek title made it look impressive. The book discusses the doctrine of the Trinity and whether non-Christians share this belief.

[4]**"blind guides of blind men":** Matthew 15:14.

succeed them as their heirs. Both of them were heads of the school in Rheims, and there, by repeated insinuations, they were able to influence their archbishop, Ralph, to take action against me and, along with Conan, bishop of Palestrina, who held the office of papal legate in France at the time, to convene an assembly, which they called a Council, in the city of Soissons, where I was to be invited to come bringing my treatise on the Trinity. This was done, but before I could make my appearance, my two rivals spread such evil rumours about me amongst the clerks and people that I and the few pupils who had accompanied me narrowly escaped being stoned by the people on the first day we arrived, for having preached and written (so they had been told) that there were three Gods.

I called on the legate as soon as I entered the town, handed him a copy of the treatise for him to read and form an opinion, and declared myself ready to receive correction and make amends if I had written anything contrary to the Catholic faith. But he told me at once to take the book to the archbishop and my opponents, so that my accusers could judge me themselves and the words "Our enemies are judges"[5] be fulfilled in me. However, though they read and reread the book again and again they could find nothing they dared charge me with at an open hearing, so they adjourned the condemnation they were panting for until the final meeting of the Council. For my part, every day before the Council sat, I spoke in public on the Catholic faith in accordance with what I had written, and all who heard me were full of praise both for my exposition and for my interpretation. When the people and clerks saw this they began to say "'Here he is, speaking openly,'[6] and no one utters a word against him. The Council which we were told was expressly convened against him is quickly coming to an end. Can the judges have found that the error is theirs, not his?" This went on every day and added fuel to my enemies' fury.

And so one day Alberic sought me out with some of his followers, intent on attacking me. After a few polite words he remarked that something he had noticed in the book had puzzled him very much; namely, that although God begat God, and there is only one God, I denied that God had begotten Himself. I said at once that if they wished I would offer an explanation on this point. "We take no account of rational explanation," he answered, "nor of your interpretation in such matters; we recognize only the words of authority." "Turn the page," I said, "and you will find the authority." There was a copy of the book at hand, which he had brought with him, so I looked up the passage which I knew but which he had failed to see — or else he looked only for what would damage me. By God's will I found what I wanted at once: a sentence headed "Augustine, *On the Trinity*, Book One." "Whoever supposes that God has the power to beget Himself is in error, and the more so because it is not only God who lacks this power, but also any spiritual or corporeal creature. There is nothing whatsoever which can beget itself."

When his followers standing by heard this they blushed in embarrassment, but he tried to cover up his mistake as best he could by saying that this should be understood in the right way. To that I replied that it was nothing new, but was irrelevant at the moment as he was looking only for words, not interpretation. But if he was willing to hear an interpretation and a reasoned argument I was ready to prove to him that by his own words he

[5]"Our enemies are judges": Deuteronomy 32:31.
[6]"Here he is, speaking openly": John 7:26.

had fallen into the heresy of supposing the Father to be His own Son. On hearing this he lost his temper and turned to threats, crying that neither my explanations nor my authorities would help me in this case. He then went off.

On the last day of the Council, before the session was resumed, the legate and the archbishop began to discuss at length with my opponents and other persons what decision to take about me and my book, as this was the chief reason for their being convened. They could find nothing to bring against me either in my words or in the treatise which was before them, and everyone stood silent for a while or began to retract his accusation, until Geoffrey, bishop of Chartres, who was outstanding among the other bishops for his reputation for holiness and the importance of his see, spoke as follows:

> All of you, Sirs, who are here today know that this man's teaching, whatever it is, and his intellectual ability have won him many followers and supporters wherever he has studied. He has greatly lessened the reputation both of his own teachers and of ours, and his vine has spread its branches from sea to sea. If you injure him through prejudice, though I do not think you will, you must know that even if your judgement is deserved you will offend many people, and large numbers will rally to his defence; especially as in this treatise before us we can see nothing which deserves any public condemnation. . . .

At once my rivals broke in with an outcry: "Fine advice that is, to bid us compete with the ready tongue of a man whose arguments and sophistries could triumph over the whole world!" (But it was surely far harder to compete with Christ, and yet Nicodemus[7] asked for him to be given a hearing, as sanctioned by the law.) However, when the bishop could not persuade them to agree to his proposal, he tried to curb their hostility by other means, saying that the few people present were insufficient for discussing a matter of such importance, and this case needed longer consideration. His further advice was that my abbot, who was present, should take me back to my monastery, the Abbey of St. Denis, and there a larger number of more learned men should be assembled to go into the case thoroughly and decide what was to be done. The legate agreed with this last suggestion, and so did everyone else. Soon after, the legate rose to celebrate Mass before he opened the Council. Through Bishop Geoffrey he sent me the permission agreed on: I was to return to my monastery and await a decision.

Then my rivals, thinking that they had achieved nothing if this matter were taken outside their diocese, where they would have no power to use force — it was plain that they had little confidence in the justice of their cause — convinced the archbishop that it would be an insult to his dignity if the case were transferred and heard elsewhere, and a serious danger if I were allowed to escape as a result. They hurried to the legate, made him reverse his decision and persuaded him against his better judgement to condemn the book without any inquiry, burn it immediately in the sight of all and condemn me to perpetual confinement in a different monastery. They said that the fact that I had dared to read the treatise in public and must have allowed many people to make copies without

---

[7]**Nicodemus:** The Pharisee who counselled that Jesus should be given a fair hearing (John 7:51). He was a secret supporter of Jesus (John 3:1–10) and assisted with his burial (John 19:39).

its being approved by the authority of the Pope the Church should be quite enough to condemn it, and that the Christian faith would greatly benefit if an example were made of me and similar presumption in many others were forestalled. As the legate was less of a scholar than he should have been, he relied largely on the advice of the archbishop, who in turn relied on theirs. When the bishop of Chartres saw what would happen he told me at once about their intrigues and strongly urged me not to take it too hard, as by now it was apparent to all that they were acting too harshly. He said I could be confident that such violence so clearly prompted by jealousy would discredit them and benefit me, and told me not to worry about being confined in a monastery as he knew that the papal legate was only acting under pressure, and would set me quite free within a few days of his leaving Soissons. So he gave me what comfort he could, both of us shedding tears.

I was then summoned and came at once before the Council. Without any questioning or discussion they compelled me to throw my book into the fire with my own hands, and so it was burnt.

DISCUSSION QUESTIONS

1. How would you describe Abelard's style of teaching? In his view, what should be the basis of all knowledge?

2. Why did some of Abelard's fellow scholars urge church officials to bring charges against him? What was the basis of their complaint? Why did they find him so threatening?

3. How did Abelard respond to the charges? What does his response reveal about the new ways of learning that were gaining ground during this period?

2. Scholarly Pursuits and Youthful Frolics

Royal Decrees of Special Privileges for Students and *Student Letters* (Twelfth–Early Thirteenth Centuries)

The development of permanent centers of learning in the twelfth and thirteenth centuries in cities across Europe attests to the vitality of the age. As the following documents suggest, royal patronage and the formation of a sense of common identity among students were key to the rise of medieval universities as self-governing institutions. The first two documents consist of special privileges granted in 1158 by King Frederick I (r. 1152–1190) of Germany to all students within his domains and in 1200 by King Philip II of France (r. 1180–1223) to students in Paris. In this way, students were enveloped within both rulers' growing bureaucracies as each strove to increase his power. The voices of students themselves are highlighted in the next set of documents, two letters included in an early thirteenth-century English handbook

From Dana Carleton Munro, ed., *Translations and Reprints from the Original Sources of European History*, vol. 2, no. 3 (Philadelphia: University of Pennsylvania Press, 1898), 2–7, and "A Student at Oxford Writes to His Father for Money," in *Lost Letters of Medieval Life: English Society, 1200–1250*, ed. Martha Carlin and David Crouch (Philadelphia: University of Pennsylvania Press, 2013), 249–50, 254.

of model texts. Handbooks of this type were a popular medieval genre. They served as guides to the art of letter writing for people from all walks of life and often preserved examples of actual correspondence considered to be useful to the given audience. Students in particular used them to convey a singular message — the need for money — while demonstrating their worthiness as diligent students.

From King Frederick I

After a careful consideration of this subject by the bishops, abbots, dukes, counts, judges, and other nobles of our sacred palace, we, from our piety, have granted this privilege to all scholars who travel for the sake of study, and especially, to the professors of divine and sacred laws, namely, that they may go in safety to the places in which the studies are carried on, both they themselves and their messengers, and may dwell there in security. For we think it fitting that, during good behavior, those should enjoy our praise and protection, by whose learning the world is enlightened to the obedience of God and of us, his ministers and the life of the subjects is moulded; and by a certain special love we defend them from all injuries.

For who does not pity those who exile themselves through love for learning, who wear themselves out in poverty in place of riches, who expose their lives to all perils and often suffer bodily injury from the vilest men—this must be endured with vexation. Therefore, we declare by this general and ever to be valid law, that in the future no one shall be so rash as to venture to inflict any injury on scholars, or to occasion any loss to them on account of a debt owed by an inhabitant of their province—a thing which we have learned is sometimes done by an evil custom. And let it be known to the violators of this constitution, and also to those who shall at the time be the rulers of the places, that a four-fold restitution of property shall be exacted from all and that, the mark of infamy being affixed to them by the law itself, they shall lose their office forever. . . .

We also order this law to be inserted among the imperial constitutions under the title, *ne filius pro patre, etc.*

Given at Roncaglia, in the year of our Lord 1158, in the month of November. . . .

From King Philip II

In the Name of the sacred and indivisible Trinity, amen. Philip, by the grace of God, King of the French.

Concerning the safety of the students at Paris in the future, by the advice of our subjects we have ordained as follows: we will cause all the citizens of Paris to swear that if any one sees an injury done to any student by any layman, he will testify truthfully to this, nor will any one withdraw in order not to see [the act]. And if it shall happen that any one strikes a student, except in self-defense, especially if he strikes the student with a weapon, a club or a stone, all laymen who see [the act] shall in good faith seize the malefactor or malefactors and deliver them to our judge; nor shall they withdraw in order not to see the act, or seize the malefactor, or testify to the truth. Also, whether the malefactor is seized in open crime or not, we will make a legal and full examination through clerks or laymen or certain lawful persons; and our count and our judges shall do the same. And if by a full examination we or our judges are able to learn that he who is accused, is guilty of the crime, then we or our judges shall immediately inflict a penalty, according to the quality and nature of the crime; notwithstanding the fact that the criminal may deny the deed and say that he is ready to defend himself in single combat, or to purge himself by the ordeal by water.

Also, neither our provost nor our judges shall lay hands on a student for any offense whatever; nor shall they place him in our prison, unless such a crime has been committed by the student, that he ought to be arrested. And in that case, our judge shall arrest him on the spot, without striking him at all, unless he resists, and shall hand him over to the ecclesiastical judge, who ought to guard him in order to satisfy us and the one suffering the injury. And if a serious crime has been committed, our judge shall go or shall send to see what is done with the student. . . .

In order, moreover, that these [decrees] may be kept more carefully and may be established forever by a fixed law, we have decided that our present provost and the people of Paris shall affirm by an oath, in the presence of the scholars, that they will carry out in good faith all the above-mentioned. And always in the future, whosoever receives from us the office of provost in Paris, among the other initiatory acts of his office, namely, on the first or second Sunday, in one of the churches of Paris,—after he has been summoned for the purpose,—shall affirm by an oath, publicly in the presence of the scholars, that he will keep in good faith all the above-mentioned. And that these decrees may be valid forever, we have ordered this document to be confirmed by the authority of our seal and by the characters of the royal name, signed below.

Students at Oxford Write to Their Parents for Money[1]

B. to his venerable master A., greeting. This is to inform you that I am studying at Oxford with the greatest diligence, but the matter of money stands greatly in the way of my promotion,[2] as it is now two months since I spent the last of what you sent me. The city is expensive and makes many demands; I have to rent lodgings, buy necessaries, and provide for many other things which I cannot now specify. Wherefore I respectfully beg Your Paternity that by the promptings of divine pity you may assist me, so that I may be able to complete what I have well begun. For you must know that without Ceres[3] and Bacchus[4] Apollo[5] grows cold. Therefore, I hope that you will act in such a way that, by your intercession, I may finish what I have well begun. Farewell.

To his father, his son sends greetings. Upon your scholar, O Pious Paternity, [may you cause] your affection to flow always — and abundantly. The course of nature is seriously distorted, and the laws of equity seem violated, in a father who does less than he might

---

[1]The student in this letter is studying at Oxford. He may be enrolled with a master at the university, then in its early years of development, or he may be taking a business course with a private instructor of *dictamen* (the art of letter writing) and other subjects related to estate management.
[2]**Promotion:** When a student has received his degree. [Ed.]
[3]**Ceres:** Roman goddess of grain. [Ed.]
[4]**Bacchus:** Roman god of wine. [Ed.]
[5]**Apollo:** Greek god of wisdom. [Ed.]

for his son. And, for God's sake! what sort of goodness is there in a man who is oblivious of his own offspring? Lions and tigers defend their young until they can thrive by their own natural fierceness, and are seen to teach their skills by demonstration while providing the necessities for life for them. More savage, therefore, than savage beasts is he who fails to come to the aid of his own son, especially one whose intention is to live honestly and, by living honestly, to be acceptable both to God and to his parents. I have received Your Paternity's letter by which you showed, so far as words go, that you hold us in tender paternal affection but, so that your affection is not expressed only in a literary form, some practical performance in the sending of necessities should generally follow it up, [lest] otherwise I regard ([or] *consider*) Your Paternity's assistance as valueless. Farewell.

DISCUSSION QUESTIONS

1. Why might both Frederick I and Philip II have been concerned for students' welfare? What benefits do you think they gained from guaranteeing students certain privileges? What evidence of these benefits can you find in the letters from the students?

2. What do the kings' privileges reveal about the process of state building at the time? What role did official records such as these play in the process?

3. What picture of student life do the letters paint? What similarities exist based on your own experiences as a student?

4. How do the two letters from students support the argument made by many historians that in the twelfth century, people became more aware of themselves as members of larger groups with similar concerns and objectives? In what ways do the kings' privileges define and perhaps limit identification with this group?

3. Courtly Love

Chrétien de Troyes, *Lancelot: The Knight of the Cart* (c. 1170s)

Students were not the only group to gain a sense of group solidarity in the twelfth century. Nobles forged a common class identity during this period in part through new forms of vernacular literature that flourished in aristocratic circles. Long poems examining the relationships between knights and their lady loves were especially popular. The following excerpt is from one such poem, Lancelot: The Knight of the Cart, *written in Old French by Chrétien de Troyes (c. 1150–1190) in the 1170s. Attached to the court of the count and countess of Champagne in the city of Troyes, located southeast of Paris, Chrétien used his poems to entertain his audiences while instructing them in the ways of courtliness and proper knightly*

From Chrétien de Troyes, *Lancelot: The Knight of the Cart*, trans. Burton Raffel (New Haven, CT: Yale University Press, 1997), 116–21.

behavior. Set against the backdrop of King Arthur's court, the poem recounts the adventures
of Arthur's best knight, Lancelot, in his quest to rescue Arthur's queen, Guinevere. She had
been kidnapped by the villain Méléagant and was being held hostage in his castle. Lancelot's
loyalty to his king was not the only emotion driving his quest; he was also passionately in
love with Guinevere. In the scene that follows, he has just arrived at Méléagant's castle,
where the two meet in combat as scores of people look on. Lancelot's strength is waning until
a servant girl calls his attention to Guinevere watching from on high from a castle window;
the tables then turn in the heroic knight's favor.

As soon as he heard his name,
Lancelot turned and looked
Behind him, and saw, seated
High at an open window,
What more than anything else
In the world he wanted to see.
And then, from the moment he saw her,
He neither moved his head
Nor looked in any other
Direction, fighting with his back
To his enemy, and Méléagant
Immediately began to press him
As hard as he could, delighted
To think that, now, the knight
Could no longer face him and defend
Himself. And his countrymen, too,
Were delighted, while the men of Logres
Were so sick at heart they could not
Stand, many falling
To their knees, but many fainting
Away, stretched on the ground.
Sorrow and excitement were everywhere.
But the girl, high at her window,
Shouted down once more:
"Ah, Lancelot! Can you really
Be as stupid as you look?
You seemed to be all
That a knight should be, till now:
You had me convinced that God
Had never made a knight
Who could challenge you for courage
And strength and virtue. And now
We see you fighting backwards,
Looking away from your enemy!
Do your fighting with your face

Turned to this tower, so you'll see her
Better! Let her shine on you!"
Outraged at the insult, and deeply
Shamed, Lancelot bitterly
Cursed himself for letting
The combat go against him,
Here in the sight of them all.
With a leap, he drove behind
Méléagant, forcing
His enemy to stand with his back
To the tower. Méléagant
Struggled to regain his ground,
But Lancelot charged him, striking
So many powerful strokes,
Swinging with all his strength,
That he forced a further retreat,
Two or three unwilling,
Unwelcome steps. Between
The strength Love had lent him,
Offered in willing assistance,
And the hate swelling in his heart
As the battle wore on, all
His powers and quickness had returned.
Love and his mortal hate—
Fiercer than any ever
Known—combined to make him
So fearsome that Méléagant
Was suddenly afraid,
For never in all his life
Had an enemy seemed so strong,
Or pressed and hurt him so badly
As this knight was doing. He tried
As hard as he could to keep him
At a distance, feinting, ducking,
Bobbing, badly hurt
Each time he was hit. Lancelot
Wasted no breath on threats,
Kept driving him toward the tower
And the queen, over and over
Coming as close as he could,
Forcing Méléagant back,
Each time, barely a foot
Away from stepping out
Of her sight. So Lancelot led him
Up and down, this way

And that, always making him
Stop in front of his lady,
The queen, who'd set his heart
On fire, just knowing she was
Watching—a fiercely roaring,
Burning-hot flame impelling him
Straight at Méléagant
And pushing his helpless enemy
Forward and back like a cripple,
Tugging him along like a blind man
Or a beggar at the end of a rope.
The king saw his son
Utterly overwhelmed
And was filled with pity and compassion:
He had to help, if he could.
But the queen, he knew, was the only
Possible source of assistance,
So he turned to her and spoke:
"Lady, for as long as you've been
In my land you've had my love
And honor; I've served you well,
And always gladly, in every
Way I could. Let me
Ask you, now, to repay me.
And the gift I ask you to give me
Could only be granted out
Of the purest love. I can see
Quite well—there's not the slightest
Doubt—that my son has lost
This battle. And I speak to you, now,
Not on this score, but because
It's clear that Lancelot
Could easily kill him, if he chose to.
I hope you want that no more
Than I do—not that my son
Has treated you well—he hasn't—
But simply because I beg you
For your mercy. Let him live.
Let the final blow be withheld.
And thus you can tell me, if you choose,
How you value the honor
I've shown you." "Dear sir, if that's
What you want, I want it, too.
I certainly hate and loathe
Your son, for the best of reasons,

But you indeed have served me
So well that it pleases me
To please you by stopping the battle."
They had not whispered private
Words; both Lancelot
And Méléagant heard them.
Lovers are obedient men,
Cheerfully willing to do
Whatever the beloved, who holds
Their entire heart, desires.
Lancelot had no choice,
For if ever anyone loved
More truly than Pyramus
It was him. Hearing her response,
As soon as the final word
Fell from her mouth, declaring,
"Dear sir, if you want the battle
Stopped, I want that, too,"
Nothing in the world could have made him
Fight, or even move,
No matter if it cost his life.

DISCUSSION QUESTIONS

1. Based on this scene, how would you describe Lancelot? What effect does Guinevere have on the outcome of his fight with Méléagant, and why is this important to understanding Lancelot's character?

2. In what ways do Lancelot's actions and attitudes embody the twelfth-century ideal of a chivalric hero?

3. Why do you think this ideal may have appealed to Chrétien's aristocratic audience? Do you think they saw themselves as living up to this ideal? Why or why not?

4. Early Bankers

Money Changers Window Panel, Chartres Cathedral
(Early Thirteenth Century)

Chivalric poetry reflected an ideal far removed from the economic and social realities transforming thirteenth-century Europe. With the rise of industry and commerce came new visibility for merchants and tradesmen, as the images below attest. They are from one of forty-two windows at Chartres Cathedral depicting tradesmen making, transporting, and selling their goods. The windows were created as part of a massive rebuilding campaign following a fire in 1194. Scholars long argued that tradesmen had donated the windows as a testament to their faith and solidarity with the community. In fact, at the time, many tradesmen were employed by the clergy, and more still were required to pay dues to help finance the project. Thus, it was the clergy's vision, not necessarily the tradesmen's, that shaped the windows' content. Just as pictorial depictions of the labors of the month in church sculpture acknowledged the place of agricultural workers in the divine plan, so now did the trade windows for new types of urban work. Money changers determined rates of exchange by measuring equal weights of the local currency with coins from a different district. In these signature panels from the lower window depicting the life of Joseph, money changers are shown behind the money changers' table (known as a banco, *the origins of the English word "bank"). In the first panel, the money changer on the left holds a scale, an essential tool of the trade, to weigh three cold coins in one basket with small gold weights in the other. He looks at the changer next to him, who gestures toward a pile of gold coins on the table. In the second panel, another money changer negotiates with a client, a merchant based on his attire. Behind him, a second money changer is seated as he checks a coin.*

Alfredo Dagli Orti / Art Resource, NY

Alfredo Dagli Orti / Art Resource, NY

DISCUSSION QUESTIONS

1. Describe the faces, bodies, and dress of the figures. What do these details tell you about these figures, and why?

2. Located fifty miles from Paris, Chartres was a growing economic hub in the thirteenth century. Based on this window panel, what role do you think money changers played in the local economy, and why?

3. In the second panel, both the money changer and the customer are depicted gesturing at one another. What do you think the artist was trying to convey with the gestures? What do they add to the scene as a whole?

5. Franciscan Piety

SOURCES IN CONVERSATION | St. Francis and St. Clare of Assisi, *Selected Writings*
(Thirteenth Century)

The church was very much entwined in the world of wealth, power, and splendor celebrated in the art and literature of the twelfth and early thirteenth centuries. A variety of new religious movements emerged in reaction against the church's perceived worldliness and neglect of its pastoral mission. St. Francis of Assisi (c. 1182–1226) founded what became the most popular and largest of these movements in Europe, the Franciscans. These excerpts from his Rule, *written in 1223, illuminate the fundamental principles guiding the order. Unlike their Benedictine counterparts, Franciscans actively engaged in the world, particularly through the ministry of preaching. The Franciscans' message of poverty, humility, and penance prompted people from all walks of life to follow their path, including St. Clare of Assisi (1194–1253). Upon hearing St. Francis preach in 1212, she established a community of pious women modeled after his ideals, which became the Order of the Sisters of St. Francis. Although the sisters were eventually cloistered, the following passages from St. Clare's Testament reveal not only how their ideals remained true to those of St. Francis but also how medieval women played an important role in cultivating new forms of piety.*

From Francis's *Rule*

This is the rule and way of living of the minorite brothers: namely to observe the holy Gospel of our Lord Jesus Christ, living in obedience, without personal possessions, and in chastity. Brother Francis promises obedience and reverence to our lord pope Honorius, and to his successors who canonically enter upon their office, and to the Roman Church. And the other brothers shall be bound to obey brother Francis and his successors.

If any persons shall wish to adopt this form of living, and shall come to our brothers, they shall send them to their provincial ministers; to whom alone, and to no others, permission is given to receive brothers. But the ministers shall diligently examine them in the matter of the catholic faith and the ecclesiastical sacraments. And if they believe all these, and are willing to faithfully confess them and observe them steadfastly to the end; and if they have no wives, or if they have them and the wives have already entered a monastery, or if they shall have given them permission to do so . . . the ministers shall say unto them the word of the holy Gospel, to the effect that they shall go and sell all that they have and strive to give it to the poor. But if they shall not be able to do this, their good will is enough. And the brothers and their ministers shall be on their guard and not concern themselves for their temporal goods; so that they may freely do with those goods exactly as God inspires them. . . . Afterwards there shall be granted to them the garments

From Ernest Henderson, ed., *Select Historical Documents of the Middle Ages* (London: G. Bell & Sons, 1921), 344–49, and *Francis and Clare: The Complete Works*, trans. Regis J. Armstrong and Ignatius C. Brady (New York: Paulist Press, 1982), 226–32.

of probation: namely two gowns without cowls and a belt, and hose and a cape down to the belt; unless to these same ministers something else may at some time seem to be preferable in the sight of God. But, when the year of probation is over, they shall be received into obedience; promising always to observe that manner of living, and this Rule. . . .

I firmly command all the brothers by no means to receive coin or money, of themselves or through an intervening person. But for the needs of the sick and for clothing the other brothers, the ministers alone and the guardians shall provide through spiritual friends, as it may seem to them that necessity demands, according to time, place and cold temperature. This one thing being always regarded, that, as has been said, they receive neither coin nor money.

Those brothers to whom God has given the ability to labor, shall labor faithfully and devoutly; in such way that idleness, the enemy of the soul, being excluded, they may not extinguish the spirit of holy prayer and devotion; to which other temporal things should be subservient. As a reward, moreover, for their labor, they may receive for themselves and their brothers the necessaries of life, but not coin or money; and this humbly, as becomes the servants of God and the followers of most holy poverty.

The brothers shall appropriate nothing to themselves, neither a house, nor a place, nor anything; but as pilgrims and strangers in this world, in poverty and humility serving God, they shall confidently go seeking for alms. Nor need they be ashamed, for the Lord made Himself poor for us in this world. This is that height of most lofty poverty, which has constituted you my most beloved brothers heirs and kings of the kingdom of Heaven, has made you poor in possessions, has exalted you in virtues. . . .

All the brothers shall be bound always to have one of the brothers of that order as general minister and servant of the whole fraternity, and shall be firmly bound to obey him. . . .

The brothers may not preach in the bishopric of any bishop if they have been forbidden to by him. And no one of the brothers shall dare to preach at all to the people, unless he have been examined and approved by the general minister of this fraternity, and the office of preacher have been conceded to him. I also exhort those same brothers that, in the preaching which they do, their expressions shall be chaste and chosen, to the utility and edification of the people; announcing to them vices and virtues, punishment and glory, with briefness of discourse; for the words were brief which the Lord spoke upon earth.

The brothers who are the ministers and servants of the other brothers shall visit and admonish their brothers and humbly and lovingly correct them; not teaching them anything which is against their soul and against our Rule. But the brothers who are subjected to them shall remember that, before God, they have discarded their own wills. Wherefore I firmly command them that they obey their ministers in all things which they have promised God to observe, and which are not contrary to their souls and to our Rule. . . .

I firmly command all the brothers not to have suspicious intercourse or to take counsel with women. And, with the exception of those to whom special permission has been given by the Apostolic Chair, let them not enter nunneries. Neither may they become fellow god-parents with men or women, lest from this cause a scandal may arise among the brothers or concerning brothers.

Whoever of the brothers by divine inspiration may wish to go among the Saracens and other infidels, shall seek permission to do so from their provincial ministers. But to none shall the ministers give permission to go, save to those whom they shall see to be fit for the mission.

Furthermore, through their obedience I enjoin on the ministers that they demand from the lord pope one of the cardinals of the holy Roman Church, who shall be the governor, corrector and protector of that fraternity, so that, always subjected and lying at the feet of that same holy Church, steadfast in the catholic faith, we may observe poverty and humility, and the holy Gospel of our Lord Jesus Christ; as we have firmly promised.

From Clare's *Testament*

In the name of the Lord!

Among all the other gifts which we have received and continue to receive daily from our benefactor, *the Father of mercies* (2 Cor. 1:3), and for which we must express the deepest thanks to our glorious God, our vocation is a great gift. Since it is the more perfect and greater, we should be so much more thankful to Him for it. For this reason the Apostle writes: "Acknowledge your calling" (1 Cor. 1:26).

The Son of God became for us *the Way* which our Blessed Father Francis, His true lover and imitator, has shown and taught us by word and example.

Therefore, beloved Sisters, we must consider the immense gifts which God has bestowed on us, especially those which He has seen fit to work in us through His beloved servant, our blessed Father Francis, not only after our conversion but also while we were still [living among] the vanities of the world.

For, almost immediately after his conversion, while he had neither brothers nor companions, when he was building the Church of San Damiano in which he was totally filled with divine consolation, he was led to abandon the world completely. This holy man, in the great joy and enlightenment of the Holy Spirit, made a prophecy about us which the Lord fulfilled later. Climbing the wall of that church he shouted in French to some poor people who were standing nearby: "Come and help me build the Monastery of San Damiano, because ladies will dwell here who will glorify our heavenly Father throughout His holy Church by their celebrated and holy manner of life."

In this, then, we can consider the abundant kindness of God toward us. Because of His mercy and love, He saw fit to speak these words about our vocation and selection through His saint. And our most blessed Father prophesied not only for us, but also for those who were to come to this [same] holy vocation to which the Lord has called us.

With what solicitude and fervor of mind and body, therefore, must we keep the commandments of our God and Father, so that, with the help of the Lord, we may return to Him an increase of His *talents*. For the Lord Himself not only has set us as an example and mirror for others, but also for our [own] sisters whom the Lord has called to our way of life, so that they in turn will be a mirror and example to those living in the world. . . .

After the most high heavenly Father saw fit in His mercy and grace to enlighten my heart to do penance according to the example and teaching of our most blessed Father Francis, shortly after his own conversion, I, together with the few sisters whom the Lord had given me soon after my conversion, voluntarily promised him obedience, since the Lord had given us the Light of His grace through his holy life and teaching.

But when the Blessed Francis saw that, although we were physically weak and frail, we did not shirk deprivation, poverty, hard work, distress, or the shame or contempt of the world—rather, as he and his brothers often saw for themselves, we considered [all such trials] as great delights after the example of the saints and their brothers—he rejoiced greatly in the Lord. And moved by compassion for us, he promised to have always, both through himself and through his Order, the same loving care and special solicitude for us as for his own brothers.

And thus, by the will of God and our most blessed Father Francis, we went to dwell at the Church of San Damiano. There, in a short time, the Lord increased our number by His mercy and grace so that what He had predicted through His saint might be fulfilled. We had stayed in another place [before this], but only for a little while.

Later on he wrote a form of life for us, [indicating] especially that we should persevere always in holy poverty. And while he was living, he was not content to encourage us by many words and examples to love and observe holy poverty; [in addition] he also gave us many writings so that, after his death, we should in no way turn away from it. [In a similar way] the Son of God never wished to abandon this holy poverty while He lived in the world, and our most blessed Father Francis, following His footprints, never departed, either in example or teaching, from this holy poverty which he had chosen for himself and for his brothers.

Therefore, I, Clare, the handmaid of Christ and of the Poor Sisters of the Monastery of San Damiano—although unworthy—and the little plant of the holy Father, consider together with my sisters our most high profession and the command of so great a father. [We also take note] in some [sisters] of the frailty which we feared in ourselves after the death of our holy Father Francis, [He] who was our pillar of strength and, after God, our one consolation and support. [Thus] time and again, we bound ourselves to our Lady, most holy Poverty, so that, after my death, the Sisters present and to come would never abandon her.

And, as I have always been most zealous and solicitous to observe and to have the other sisters observe the holy poverty which we have promised the Lord and our holy Father Francis, so, too, the others who will succeed me in office should be bound always to observe it and have it observed by the other sisters. . . .

In the Lord Jesus Christ, I admonish and exhort all my Sisters, both those present and those to come, to strive always to imitate the way of holy simplicity, humility, and poverty and [to preserve] the integrity of [our] holy manner of life, as we were taught by our blessed Father Francis from the beginning of our conversion to Christ. Thus may they always remain *in the fragrance* of a good name, both among those who are afar off and those who are near. [This will take place] not by our own merits but solely by the mercy and grace of our Benefactor, the *Father of mercies*. . . .

I also beg that sister who will have the office [of caring for] the Sisters to strive to exceed others more by her virtues and holy life than by her office so that, encouraged by her example, the Sisters may obey her not so much out of duty but rather out of love. Let her also be prudent and attentive to her Sisters just as a good mother is to her daughters; and especially, let her take care to provide for them according to the needs of each one from the things which the Lord shall give. Let her also be so kind and so available that all [of them] may reveal their needs with trust and have recourse to her at any hour with confidence as they see fit, both for her sake and that of her Sisters.

But the sisters who are subjects should keep in mind that for the Lord's sake they have given up their own wills. Therefore I ask that they obey their mother as they have promised the Lord of their own free will so that, seeing the charity, humility, and unity they have toward one another, their mother might bear all the burdens of her office more lightly. Thus what is painful and bitter might be turned into sweetness for her because of their holy way of life. . . .

So that it may be observed better, I leave this writing for you, my dearest and most beloved Sisters, those present and those to come, as a sign of the blessing of the Lord and of our most blessed Father Francis and of my blessing—I who am your mother and servant.

DISCUSSION QUESTIONS

1. Based on his *Rule*, how would you characterize St. Francis's spirituality and sense of mission? Why might he have appealed to so many people at the time?
2. How does St. Clare echo Francis's ideals in her *Testament*?
3. What goals did Francis and Clare share in composing the *Rule* and *Testament*, respectively?
4. What do both documents reveal about contemporary attitudes toward women? How do these attitudes compare, and what do you think may account for their similarities and differences?

6. The Sack of Constantinople
Annals of Niketas Choniatēs (1204)

As Europe became more confident and aggressive in the twelfth century, cracks began to appear in the edifice of the Byzantine state. The army and navy had lost much of their strength, and, to make matters worse, in 1201 rival claimants to the imperial throne were embroiled in a dispute. This crisis coincided with the Roman Catholic pope's call for a new crusade to the Holy Land and served as a pretext for a detour by the crusaders to the Byzantine capital of Constantinople (present-day Istanbul). Fueled by religious zeal and prejudice, in April 1204 the crusaders swiftly and savagely sacked the city. Greek historian and imperial official Niketas Choniatēs (c. 1155–1215) witnessed the rampage firsthand, which he describes in the excerpt from his Annals *that follows. Other sources confirm many of the details of Niketas Choniatēs' account, although he clearly viewed the crusaders through a distinctive lens. Steeped in classical Greek, Christian, and Byzantine traditions, he was highly critical not only of the crusaders' violent acts but also of what he perceived as the barbarity underlying them. His criticism had little effect. Although the empire regained control of Constantinople in 1261, it was never again a dominant political force in the West.*

From Niketas Choniatēs, *Alexii Ducae Imperium*, in *Recueil des historiens des Croisades*: *Historiens grecs*, vol. 1 (Paris, 1875), 397, quoted in Dana Carleton Munro, trans. and ed., "The Fourth Crusade," *Translations and Reprints from the Original Sources of European History* (Philadelphia: University of Pennsylvania Press, 1912), 3: 15–16.

. . . How shall I begin to tell of the deeds wrought by these nefarious men! Alas, the images, which ought to have been adored, were trodden under foot! Alas, the relics of the holy martyrs were thrown into unclean places! Then was seen what one shudders to hear, namely, the divine body and blood of Christ was spilled upon the ground or thrown about. They snatched the precious reliquaries, thrust into their bosoms the ornaments which these contained, and used the broken remnants for pans and drinking cups, — precursors of Anti-christ, authors and heralds of his nefarious deeds which we momentarily expect. Manifestly, indeed, by that race then, just as formerly, Christ was robbed and insulted and His garments were divided by lot; only one thing was lacking, that His side, pierced by a spear, should pour rivers of divine blood on the ground.

Nor can the violation of the Great Church[1] be listened to with equanimity. For the sacred altar, formed of all kinds of precious materials and admired by the whole world, was broken into bits and distributed among the soldiers, as was all the other sacred wealth of so great and infinite splendor.

When the sacred vases and utensils of unsurpassable art and grace and rare material, and the fine silver, wrought with gold, which encircled the screen of the tribunal and the ambo,[2] of admirable workmanship, and the door and many other ornaments, were to be borne away as booty, mules and saddled horses were led to the very sanctuary of the temple. Some of these which were unable to keep their footing on the splendid and slippery pavement, were stabbed when they fell, so that the sacred pavement was polluted with blood and filth.

Nay more, a certain harlot,[3] a sharer in their guilt, a minister of the furies, a servant of the demons; a worker of incantations and poisonings, insulting Christ, sat in the patriarch's seat, singing an obscene song and dancing frequently. Nor, indeed, were these crimes committed and others left undone, on the ground that these were of lesser guilt, the others of greater. But with one consent all the most heinous sins and crimes were committed by all with equal zeal. Could those, who showed so great madness against God Himself, have spared the honorable matrons and maidens or the virgins consecrated to God?

Nothing was more difficult and laborious than to soften by prayers, to render benevolent, these wrathful barbarians, vomiting forth bile at every unpleasing word, so that nothing failed to inflame their fury. Whoever attempted it was derided as insane and a man of intemperate language. Often they drew their daggers against anyone who opposed them at all or hindered their demands.

No one was without a share in the grief. In the alleys, in the streets, in the temples, complaints, weeping, lamentations, grief, the groaning of men, the shrieks of women, wounds, rape, captivity, the separation of those most closely united. Nobles wandered about ignominiously, those of venerable age in tears, the rich in poverty. Thus it was in the streets, on the corners, in the temple, in the dens, for no place remained unassailed or defended the suppliants. All places everywhere were filled full of all kinds of crime. Oh, immortal God, how great the afflictions of the men, how great the distress!

---

[1] Hagia Sophia.
[2] **Ambo**: elevated pulpit. [Ed.]
[3] See 1 Timothy 5:11.

DISCUSSION QUESTIONS

1. What language does Choniatēs use to describe the crusaders and their actions?

2. What does this language suggest about Greek attitudes toward western Europeans and their culture?

3. Why does Choniatēs focus in particular on the crusaders' destruction of religious property? Why would this have been especially disturbing to him and other Byzantine Greeks?

COMPARATIVE QUESTIONS

1. What do Abelard's story and the privileges granted to students by Frederick I and Philip II suggest about the culture of learning at the time? Why was it so appealing to students? Why do you think political authorities were willing to grant them special privileges?

2. In what ways does the money changers window reflect the increase in wealth and the circulation of cash in the medieval economy? How did these changes shape the ideals of Chrétien de Troyes and St. Francis?

3. How would you describe the roles of students as defined in Document 2 and of St. Francis and his followers in Document 5? What features do they share? How do they differ? Do you see any potential points of conflict?

4. Compare the behavior of the fictional hero Lancelot to that of the real-life crusaders described in the *Annals of Niketas Choniatēs*. What similarities and/or differences do you see? What do both sources suggest about Western aristocratic values and measures of self-worth at the time?

CHAPTER 12

The Medieval Synthesis — and Its Cracks

1215–1340

H armony, order, and unity were the ideals sought by people from all walks of life in the medieval West between 1215 and 1340. Guided by the papacy, the church drove these efforts as it worked to codify religious doctrine and reform the laity. The first document illuminates scholasticism, an important force underlying these efforts that strove to summarize and reconcile all knowledge. Responding in kind, many laypeople, especially women, sought greater involvement in their religion and a deeper relationship with Christ. The second document captures the voice of one of these women, Hadewijch of Brabant (?–1248). The third document reveals the dark side of this trend as anti-Jewish feelings grew across Europe. The search for meaning in a world looking for unity also found literary and political expression. As reflected in the fourth document, vernacular literature blossomed beneath the pen of Italian poet Dante Alighieri (1265–1321), who harmonized heaven and earth through the language of poetry. At the same time, the fifth document set demonstrates how some monarchs instituted their own politics of control to broaden both the scope and the basis of their power. Their success on this front brought them into conflict with other established authorities, notably the pope, who saw his influence severely weakened as a result. The final document suggests how the melding of the secular and profane found concrete expression in people's understanding of the world's geography.

1. Reconciling Faith and Reason

Thomas Aquinas, *Summa Theologiae* (1273)

Dominican theologian and university professor Thomas Aquinas (c. 1225–1274) embodied the general search for harmony and order characteristic of the period 1215–1340. Guided by

---

From *The Library of Original Sources: Ideas That Have Influenced Civilization, in the Original Documents, Translated*, vol. IV, ed. Oliver J. Thatcher (Metuchen, NJ: Mini-Print Corporation, 1971), 359–63.

the works of Aristotle, Aquinas embraced the power of human reason to examine important issues, both natural and divine. The title of his most famous work, Summa Theologiae, *reflects the confidence that he and other scholastics had in their ability to summarize knowledge for the benefit of teachers and students alike. Aquinas's systematic approach to this monumental task is embedded within the organization of the* Summa *itself. The material is divided into major topics, which in turn are divided into subtopics. He breaks down the content further still with "articles" where he poses a series of questions related to the corresponding subtopic. He then lays out the evidence for yes and no responses, ultimately guiding his reader to what he considers to be the correct conclusion. In doing so, Aquinas sought to convey not only theological fundamentals but also a way of thinking about complex issues in a logical and orderly way. The excerpt below is from the* Summa's *examination of the question of how we know that God exists, which for Aquinas was the essential starting point for understanding and explaining God's teachings.*

On the Existence of God

Article II. Whether the existence of God is demonstrable.

Let us proceed to the second point. It is objected (1) that the existence of God is not demonstrable: that God's existence is an article of faith, and that articles of faith are not demonstrable, because the office of demonstration is to prove, but faith pertains (only) to things that are not to be proven, as is evident from the Epistle to the Hebrews, XI. Hence that God's existence is not demonstrable.

Again, (2) that the subject matter of demonstration is that something exists, but in the case of God we cannot know what exists, but only what does not, as Damascenus[1] says (Of the Orthodox Faith, I.,4.). Hence that we cannot demonstrate God's existence.

Again, (3) that if God's existence is to be proved it must be from what He causes, and that what He effects is not sufficient for His supposed nature, since He is infinite, but the effects finite, and the finite is not proportional to the infinite. Since, therefore, a cause cannot be proved through an effect not proportional to itself, it is said that God's existence cannot be proved.

But against this argument the apostle says (Rom. I., 20), "The unseen things of God are visible through His manifest works." But this would not be so unless it were possible to demonstrate God's existence through His works. What ought to be understood concerning anything, is first of all, whether it exists.

Conclusion. It is possible to demonstrate God's existence, although not a priori (by pure reason), yet a posteriori from some work of His more surely known to us.[2]

In answer I must say that the proof is double. One is through the nature of a cause and is called *propter quid*:[3] this is through the nature of preceding events simply.

---

[1]John of Damascus (c. 676–749), a Christian theologian. [Ed.]

[2]Here Aquinas is distinguishing between knowledge obtained through logic and reason (a priori) as opposed to from facts and observation (a posteriori). [Ed.]

[3]***propter quid***: A type of Aristotelian logic that begins with a cause and concludes with an effect. Considered to be a very sound type of logical reasoning. [Ed.]

The other is through the nature of the effect, and is called *quia*,[4] and is through the nature of preceding things as respects us.

Since the effect is better known to us than the cause, we proceed from the effect to the knowledge of the cause. From any effect whatsoever it can be proved that a corresponding cause exists, if only the effects of it are sufficiently known to us, for since effects depend on causes, the effect being given, it is necessary that a preceding cause exists. Whence, that God exists, although this is not itself known to us, is provable through effects that are known to us.

To the first objection above, I reply, therefore, that God's existence, and those other things of this nature that can be known through natural reason concerning God, as is said in Rom. I., are not articles of faith, but preambles to these articles. So faith presupposes natural knowledge, so grace nature, and perfection a perfectible thing. Nothing prevents a thing that is in itself demonstratable and knowable, from being accepted as an article of faith by someone that does not accept the proof of it.

To the second objection, I reply that, since the cause is proven from the effect, one must use the effect in the place of a definition of the cause in demonstrating that the cause exists; and that this applies especially in the case of God, because for proving that anything exists, it is necessary to accept in this method what the name signifies, not however that anything exists, because the question *what it is* is secondary to the question *whether it exists at all*. The characteristics of God are drawn from His works as shall be shown hereafter. Whence by providing that God exists through His works as shall be shown hereafter. Whence by proving that God exists through His works, we are able by this very method to see what the name God signifies.

To the third objection, I reply that, although a perfect knowledge of the cause cannot be had from inadequate effects, yet that from any effect manifest to us it can be shown that a cause does exist, as has been said. And thus from the works of God His existence can be proved, although we cannot in this way know Him perfectly in accordance with His own essence.

Article III. Whether God exists.

Let us proceed to the third article. It is objected (1) that God does not exist, because if one of two contradictory things is infinite, the other will be totally destroyed; that it is implied in the name God that there is a certain infinite goodness: if then God existed, no evil would be found. But evil is found in the world; therefore it is objected that God does not exist.

Again, that what can be accomplished through a less number of principles will not be accomplished through more. It is objected that all things that appear on the earth can be accounted for through other principles, without supposing that God exists, since what is natural can be traced to a natural principle, and what proceeds from a proposition can be traced to the human reason or will. Therefore that there is no necessity to suppose that God exists.

But as against this note what is said of the person of God (Exod. III., 14) *I am that I am.*

---

[4]*quia*: Another type of Aristotelian logic that begins with a cause as its premise and concludes with an effect. Considered to be less logically sound than *propter quid* arguments. [Ed.]

Conclusion. There must be found in the nature of things one first immovable Being, a primary cause, necessarily existing, not created; existing the most widely, good, even the best possible; the first ruler through the intellect, and the ultimate end of all things, which is God.

I answer that it can be proved in five ways that God exists. The first and plainest is the method that proceeds from the point of view of motion. It is certain and in accord with experience, that things on earth undergo change. Now everything that is moved is moved by something; nothing, indeed, is changed, except it is changed to something which it is in potentiality. Moreover, anything moves in accordance with something actually existing; change itself, is nothing else than to bring forth something from potentiality into actuality. Now nothing can be brought from potentiality to actual existence except through something actually existing: thus heat in action, as fire, makes fire-wood, which is hot in potentiality, to be hot actually, and through this process, changes itself. The same thing cannot at the same time be actually and potentially the same thing, but only in regard to different things. What is actually hot cannot be at the same time potentially hot, but it is possible for it at the same time to be potentially cold. It is impossible, then, that anything should be both mover and the thing moved, in regard to the same thing and in the same way, or that it should move itself. Everything, therefore, is moved by something else. If, then, that by which it is moved, is also moved, this must be moved by something still different, and this, again, by something else. But this process cannot go on to infinity (1) because there would not be any first mover, nor, because of this fact, anything else in motion, as the succeeding things would not move except because of what is moved by the first mover, just as a stick is not moved except through what is moved from the hand. Therefore it is necessary to go back to some first mover, which is itself moved by nothing, and this all men know as God.

The second proof is from the nature of the efficient cause. We find in our experience that there is a chain of causes: nor is it found possible for anything to be the efficient cause of itself, since it would have to exist before itself, which is impossible. Nor in the case of efficient causes can the chain go back indefinitely, because in all chains of efficient causes, the first is the cause of the middle, and these of the last, whether they be one or many. If the cause is removed, the effect is removed. Hence if there is not a first cause, there will not be a last, nor a middle. But if the chain were to go back infinitely, there would be no first cause, and thus no ultimate effect, nor middle causes, which is admittedly false. Hence we must presuppose some first efficient cause, which all call God.

The third proof is taken from the natures of the merely possible and necessary. We find that certain things either may or may not exist, since they are found to come into being and be destroyed, and in consequence potentially, either existent or non-existent. But it is impossible for all things that are of this character to exist eternally, because what *may* not exist, at length *will* not. If, then, all things were merely possible (mere accidents), eventually nothing among things would exist. If this is true, even now there would be nothing, because what does not exist, does not take its beginning except through something that does exist. If then nothing existed, it would be impossible for anything to begin, and there would now be nothing existing, which is admittedly false. Hence not all things are mere accidents, but there must be one necessarily existing being. Now every necessary thing either has a cause of its necessary existence, or has not. In the case of necessary things that have a cause for their necessary existence, the chain of causes cannot go back infinitely, just as not in the case of efficient causes, as proved. Hence there must be presupposed something necessarily existing through its own nature, not having a cause elsewhere but being itself the cause of the necessary existence of other things, — which all call God.

The fourth proof arises from the degrees that are found in things. For there is found a greater and a less degree of goodness, truth, nobility, and the like. But more or less are terms spoken of various things as they approach in diverse ways toward something that is the greatest, just as in the case of hotter (more hot) which approaches nearer the greatest heat. There exists therefore something that is the truest, and best, and most noble, and in consequence, the greatest being. For what are the greatest truths are the greatest beings, as is said in the Metaphysics Bk. II. 2. What moreover is the greatest in its way, in another way is the cause of all things of its own kind (or genus); thus fire, which is the greatest heat, is the cause of all heat, as is said in the same book (cf. Plato and Aristotle). Therefore there exists something that is the cause of the existence of all things and of the goodness and of every perfection whatsoever — and this we call God.

The fifth proof arises from the ordering of things for we see that some things which lack reason such as natural bodies are operated in accordance with a plan. It appears from this that they are operated always or the more frequently in this same way the closer they follow what is the Highest; whence it is clear that they do not arrive at the result by chance but because of a purpose. The things, moreover, that do not have intelligence do not tend toward a result unless directed by some one knowing and intelligent; just as an arrow is sent by an archer. Therefore there is something intelligent by which all natural things are arranged in accordance with a plan, — and this we call God.

In response to the first objection, then, I reply what Augustine says; that since God is entirely good, He would permit evil to exist in His works only if He were so good and omnipotent that He might bring forth good even from the evil. It therefore pertains to the infinite goodness of God that he permits evil to exist and from this brings forth good.

My reply to the second objection is that since nature is ordered in accordance with some defined purpose by the direction of some superior agent, those things that spring from nature must be dependent upon God, just as upon a first cause. Likewise what springs from a proposition must be traceable to some higher cause which is not the human reason or will, because this is changeable and defective and everything changeable and liable to non-existence is dependent upon some unchangeable first principle that is necessarily self-existent as has been shown.

DISCUSSION QUESTIONS

1. What objections does Aquinas think some people may have to the idea of God's existence?

2. What does he offer as proof against such objections? Summarize one of them in your own words.

3. In its most basic form, scholasticism was a method of logical inquiry and exposition. In what ways do both the content of this excerpt and its organization, notably Aquinas's use of objections and proofs, reflect these characteristics?

2. A Female Mystic

Hadewijch of Brabant, *Letters and Poems* (1220–1240)

The body of religious work written or dictated by women during the thirteenth century is considerable and attests to heightened piety of laypeople across Europe. Often the line between the genres of writing was blurred as ordinary women explored different means of religious expression. Hadewijch of Brabant was one of many such women writers, and our knowledge of her comes primarily from her writings in her native Dutch, which include thirty-one letters, fourteen visions, forty-five stanzaic poems, and several other poems. Although criticized by members of her own, probably Beguine, community, Hadewijch nonetheless typifies many women writers of this period. She uses mystical and seemingly erotic language to describe a relationship with Christ. Love is a central concept throughout her work, which she consistently genders as female. For her, the word refers to her experience of the divine, far removed from the systematic doctrine of scholastic summas. Although some Beguines bordered on the edge of unorthodoxy and were at times accused of heresy, most works by female mystics fit harmoniously with the writings of such church leaders as St. Bernard of Clairvaux (1090–1153) and Richard (1123–1173) and Hugh of St. Victor (1096–1141).

Letter 11

Ah, dear child, may God give you what my heart desires for you, and may you love Him as He deserves. Still, I could never endure, dear child, that someone before me loved God as dearly as I. I believe that many loved Him as fondly and dearly, yet I could hardly bear that someone would know Him with such passion.

From the age of ten I have been overwhelmed with such passionate love that I would have died during the first two years of this experience if God had not granted me a power unknown to common people and made me recover with His own being. For He soon granted me reason, sometimes enlightened with many wonderful revelations, and I received many wonderful gifts from Him, when He let me feel His presence and showed Himself to me. I was aware of many signs that were between Him and me, as with friends who are used to concealing little and revealing much when their feelings for each other have grown most intimate, when they taste, eat, and drink and consume each other wholly. Through these many signs God, my lover, showed to me early in life, He made me gain much confidence in Him, and I often thought that no one loved Him as dearly as I. But meanwhile reason made me see that my love for Him was not the dearest, though the strong bonds of our loving had prevented me from sensing or even believing this. Such then is my present state. I do no longer believe that my love for Him is the dearest, nor do I believe that there is one alive who loves God as dearly as I. Sometimes I am so enlightened with love that I realize my failure to give my beloved what He deserves; sometimes when I am blinded with love's sweetness, when I am tasting and feeling her, I realize she is enough for me; and sometimes when I am feeling so fulfilled in her presence, I secretly admit to her that she is enough for me.

From "The Brabant Mystic: Hadewijch," in *Medieval Women Writers*, ed. Katherina M. Wilson (Athens: University of Georgia Press, 1984), 193–95, 198–201.

COMPARATIVE QUESTIONS

1. What common assumptions about Europeans' religious and political identities do these documents share? In what ways does the conflict between Pope Boniface and King Philip IV of France reflect a shift in these assumptions?

2. How do Dante's *Divine Comedy* and the Hereford map each conceive of the connection between the heavenly and earthly realms they describe? What do these depictions tell us about broader efforts at the time to harmonize the sacred and secular?

3. How would you compare Hadewijch's search for religious understanding to that of Aquinas and Dante? What similarities and differences do you see in their styles and use of language?

4. Hadewijch embodied the rise of intense lay piety in the twelfth and thirteenth centuries. How does this development relate to the intolerance for Jews revealed in *The Life and Martyrdom of St. William of Norwich*?

Crisis and Renaissance
1340–1492

Currents of both crisis and renewal swept through medieval society in the years 1340–1492. On the one hand, throughout the fourteenth century, Europeans faced myriad challenges, from pestilence to war to rebellions. On the other hand, the city-states of the northern Italian peninsula helped to spark a period of great creativity that historians often refer to as the Renaissance, which reached its peak in the 1400s. The documents in this chapter capture these twin themes, beginning with contemporary accounts of the catastrophic effects of the Black Death and the search for scapegoats, though many people viewed the plague as divine punishment (Document 1). The Hundred Years' War (1337–1453) added to people's troubles as the kings of France and England battled for land and prestige. Mercenaries on both sides ravaged the French countryside, leading to widespread rebellion emblematic of broader currents of discontent among the lower classes (Document 2). The very church that at its height had claimed to be the spiritual and temporal head of Christendom could not help because it was a house divided and threatened by abuses and calls for reform, as the selections by Geoffrey Chaucer (c. 1342–1400; Document 3) and letters of Jan Hus (1369–1415; Document 4) demonstrate. At the same time, however, men of the upper classes in Italy defined themselves self-consciously as living in new times. For such men (and a few women), this was a time of rebirth, distinct from what they viewed as a millennium of barbarism. Imitating the values and styles of antiquity, the Renaissance was defined by the *studia humanitatis* (roughly, the liberal arts), from which the term *humanism* was derived. The fifth document illustrates the application and possibilities of humanism, whereas the sixth document suggests that the realities of Italian life often did not match Renaissance ideals. The final document looks to the expansion of the Renaissance, where, north of the Alps, artists were also imagining the world around them in new ways.

1. Demographic Catastrophe

The Black Death (Fourteenth Century)

Few events in history have had such a shattering impact on every aspect of society as the plague, which reached Europe in 1347. The Black Death decimated a society already weakened by a demographic crisis, famines, and climatic disasters. It is estimated that one-third of

To a
Now
By C
On s
For,
Don
Here
Now

DISC

1. W
m.

2. Fr

3. Al
da

*Like
Grea
profe
appo
gap i
hear
Engli
inclu
the v
comn
his v
mate
Cons
upon
his se
death
Pragi*

Adapt
Herbe
230–3

because you are not of the world, therefore the world hates you. Remember my word that I said to you: The servant is not greater than his master. If they have persecuted me, they will also persecute you: if they have kept my word, they will keep yours also. But all these things they will do to you for my name's sake, because they know not him that sent me."[4] ...

These words the Lord spoke to His disciples that they might be able to escape such snares, cheering their minds that they might be wise and recognise by their works the ravening wolves that would swallow up the whole world in their greed.

Besides, He taught them how false prophets are recognised — namely, by the fact that they do not agree with the true prophets either in their writings or in their works. Thus, there are false Christs who assert that they are Christ's chief disciples, while in their works they are His chief foes and adversaries. Therefore in all possible ways they attempt to crush God's word, because it reproves their contumacy, pride, greed, luxury, simony, and other evil works.

They have accordingly attacked certain places of worship and chapels to prevent the word of God being preached in them;[5] but Christ has not suffered them to commit such a crime. I hear that they are now devising the destruction of the Bethlehem Chapel[6] and are preventing preaching in other places of worship, where God's word is wont to be taught; but I trust God that they will accomplish nothing. At first they laid their gins, their citations, and anathemas for the Goose[7], and now they are lying in wait for some of you; but since the Goose, a tame creature and a domestic fowl with no power to reach great heights in his flight, has yet broken through their nets, we may the more confidently expect that other birds, which by God's word and by their lives soar to high places, will break their traps in pieces. They spread out their nets and struck terror with their anathema as with a wooden toy-hawk and they shot their fiery bolt from Antichrist's quiver, provided only they might hinder God's word and worship. But the more they seek to conceal their true nature more often it betrays itself, and the more they strive to lay out their traditions like a net, the more they are broken through. In seeking to have the peace of the world, they lose both that and spiritual peace; in seeking to hurt others, they chiefly thwart themselves....

This letter, dear brothers and sisters beloved, I write that you may be steadfast in the truth you have learned and may have no fear of citations, and pay no less heed than before to the hearing of God's word by reason of the cruel threats they utter....

Finally, beloved, I beseech you to pray for them who proclaim God's truth with grace. Pray for me also that I too may write and preach in fuller measure against the malice of Antichrist, and that God may put me in the forefront of the battle, if needs be, to defend His truth.

[4]John 15:18-21.

[5]This references Pope Alexander V's 1409 decree prohibiting preaching in churches other than parochial, cathedral, and monastic ones. [Ed.]

[6]**Bethlehem Chapel:** A church in Prague where services were held in the Czech vernacular language. Jan Hus had preached before his exile. By the end of September 1412, the papal command to cease holding services had been received in Prague. [Ed.]

[7]**The Goose:** This refers to Hus, whose name means "goose." [Ed.]

For be assured I shrink not from yielding up this poor body to peril or death for the sake of God's truth, though I know that God's word has no need of us, nay, rather the truth of the gospel is spreading from day to day.

But I desire to live for the sake of those who suffer violence and need the preaching of God's word, that the malice of Antichrist may be exposed in such wise that the godly can escape it. That is why I am preaching elsewhere and ministering to all such, knowing that the will of God is fulfilled in me. ...

To All the People of Bohemia

Constance, Franciscan monastery
10 June 1415

Faithful and beloved of God, lords and ladies, rich and poor! I entreat you and exhort you to love God, to spread abroad His word, and to hear and observe it more willingly. I entreat you to hold fast the truth of God, which I have written and preached to you from the Holy Scriptures and the utterances of His saints. I entreat you also, if any have heard in my preaching or private conversation that which is opposed to God's truth, or if I have ever written anything of that kind — I trust God that it is not so — not to hold to it. I entreat you, if any have noticed frivolity in my words or actions, not to imitate it, but to pray God that it may please Him to pardon me. I entreat you to love and commend and cultivate priests of good life — especially those that are earnest students of Holy Writ. I entreat you to beware of deceitful men, and particularly of wicked priests. [...]

I entreat you to be kind to the poor and to rule them justly. I entreat all citizens to be righteous in their business dealings. I entreat all artisans faithfully to follow their craft and take delight in it. I entreat all servants to be faithful servants of their masters and mistresses. I entreat masters to live a good life and faithfully to instruct their scholars, especially that they may love God and learn to give themselves to knowledge, in order to promote His honour, the welfare of the state, and their own salvation, but not for the sake of avarice or the praise of man. I entreat students of letters and other scholars to obey their masters in things good, to imitate them, and diligently apply themselves to letters for the sake of God's honour and their own salvation and that of other men.

I entreat all the people to give thanks to Baron Wenzel of Duba, otherwise of Leštna, Baron John of Chlum, Lord Henry of Plumlow, Lord William Zajiic, Lord Myssa,[8] and the other nobles in Bohemia and Moravia, and the faithful nobles of the kingdom of Poland, and ever gratefully to remember their zeal in having often resisted, as God's brave defenders and helpers of His truth, the whole of the Council, telling them what they ought to do, and making replies with a view to my liberty, more especially Baron Wenzel of Duba and Baron John of Chlum. Give credence to them, whatever their account of the proceedings shall be; for they were present at the Council when I pleaded my cause, for several days. They know which of the Bohemians trumped up disgraceful charges against me, and how many those charges were, how the whole Council shouted against me, and how I replied to the questions which were put to me. [...]

---

[8]Henry of Plumlow was a principal noble from Moravia; Zajiic and Myssa were members of King Sigismund's inner circle.

I write this letter to you in prison, bound with chains and expecting on the morrow the sentence of death, yet fully trusting in God that I shall not swerve from His truth nor swear denial of the errors, whereof I have been charged by false witnesses. What grace God has shown me, and how He helps me in the midst of strange temptations, you will know when by His mercy we meet in joy in His presence.

Also I entreat you, especially people of Prague, to support the chapel at Bethlehem, so far as God shall permit His holy word to be preached there. It is on account of that chapel that the devil has blazed forth with anger, and it is against it that he has aroused parish priests and cathedral clergy; in truth he felt that his kingdom was being overthrown in that place. I trust that God will preserve that chapel as long as it is His pleasure, and cause greater good to be done there by others than by me, His unprofitable servant.

I entreat this too of you, that you love one another, defend good men from violent oppression, and give everyone an opportunity of hearing the truth.

DISCUSSION QUESTIONS

1. What aspects of the contemporary church did Hus criticize, and why? What do his criticisms reveal about his vision for the church and its pastors? In what ways did he himself seek to live out this vision?

2. What specific actions did Hus's detractors take against him and his supporters? Why do you think the archbishop of Prague and other church officials may have found his views threatening?

3. What advice did Hus give to his supporters in Prague while he was imprisoned in Constance? What does this letter suggest about the basis of his support? How might this help to explain why many people in Bohemia reacted angrily to his execution?

5. Extolling Humanism

Giovanni Rucellai and Leonardo Bruni,
Florence in the Quattrocento (1427 and 1457)

The Petrarchan ideal of humanism, which had refocused attention on the classics with special attention to language and letters, was given new expression in the 1400s. While Francesco Petrarch (1304–1374) had found answers to many of his life questions through introspection, civic humanists felt that a true life could be lived only within the hustle and bustle of Italian city politics. A civic humanist was one who applied humanism's academic principles to the active, political life. The first document is by Giovanni Rucellai (1403–1481), a merchant connected through marriage and patronage to two great families of Florence, the

---

From Stefano Ugo Baldassarri and Arielle Saiber, eds., *Images of Quattrocento Florence: Selected Writings in Literature, History, and Art* (New Haven, CT: Yale University Press, 2000), 73–75, and Benjamin G. Kohl and Alison Andrews Smith, eds., *Major Problems in the History of the Italian Renaissance* (Lexington, MA: D. C. Heath, 1995), 279–82.

Strozzis and Medicis, who made their fortunes in business and banking, respectively. The second document is a funeral oration for a leading citizen, given in the midst of the wars with Milan by Leonardo Bruni (1369–1444), a noted scholar of the Greek language who served as Florence's chancellor and official historian. Both men paint portraits of Florence and the ideal Renaissance man.

Rucellai's "A Merchant's Praise of Florence"

Most people believe that our age, from 1400 onward, is the most fortunate period in Florence's history. I shall now explain why this is so. It is commonly believed that since 1400 the Italians have been superior to all other nations in the art of war, whereas before 1400 the northern Europeans were thought to be peerless. Thanks to their intelligence, astuteness, cunning, and strategic ability, the Italians are now the best at seizing cities and winning battles. In this age, moreover, there are more outstanding scholars of Greek, Latin, and Hebrew in Florence than ever before. . . . Our men of letters have revived the elegance of the ancient style that has long been lost and forgotten. Those who have participated in the government of the city since 1400 have surpassed all their predecessors. Likewise, the dominion of Florence has considerably expanded. . . .

There have not been such accomplished masters in joinery and woodcarving since the days of antiquity: they are able to produce such skillfully designed works in perspective that a painter could not do any better. The same can be said of our masters in painting and drawing, whose ability, sense of proportion, and precision are so great that Giotto and Cimabue would not even be accepted as their pupils. Similarly, we cannot forget to mention our excellent tapestry makers and goldsmiths.

Never before have men and women dressed in such expensive and elegant clothing. Women wear brocade and embroidered gowns covered with jewels and saunter through the streets in their French-style hats that cost at least two hundred florins apiece. Neither the city nor the countryside has ever had such an abundance of household goods. . . .

This age has also had four notable citizens who deserve to be remembered. The first one is Palla di Nofri Strozzi, who possessed all seven of the things necessary for a man's happiness: a worthy homeland, noble and distinguished ancestors, a good knowledge of Greek and Latin, refinement, physical beauty, a good household, and honestly earned wealth. . . . Then we have Cosimo de' Medici, probably not only the richest Florentine, but the richest Italian of all time. . . . The third citizen I shall mention is Messer Leonardo di Francesco Bruni. Although he was born in Arezzo, he was an honorary citizen of Florence. He had a unique knowledge of and expertise in Greek, Hebrew, and Latin and was more famous than any rhetorician after Cicero. . . . Finally, Filippo, son of Ser Brunellesco, was a master architect and sculptor. He was an accomplished geometer and . . . is the one who rediscovered ancient Roman building techniques.

The earnings of the Florentine commune are now greater than ever. In this period, both in our city and in its countryside, people have witnessed tremendous wars and political upheaval, the like of which were never seen in the past. Churches and hospitals are richer than ever, better supplied with gold and silk paraments and precious silver. There are numerous friars and priests caring for these places, which the faithful visit constantly. Men and women attend Mass and other religious ceremonies with greater devotion than ever. . . .

The citizens have never had so much wealth, merchandise, and property, nor have the Monte's[1] interests ever been so conspicuous; consequently, the sums spent on weddings, tournaments, and various forms of entertainment are greater than ever before. Between 1418 and 1423 Florence's wealth was probably at its height. At the time, in the Mercato Nuovo and the streets nearby, there were seventy-two exchange banks.

Bruni's Funeral Oration for Nanni Strozzi, 1427

This is an exceptional funeral oration because it is appropriate neither to weep or lament. . . . His first claim to fame is conferred on him because of his country's merit. For the homeland is the first and chief basis of human happiness and more worthy of our veneration than even our own parents. If we begin therefore by praising the motherland, we will be starting in the right order.

He was born in the most spacious and greatest of cities, wide-ruling and endowed with the mightiest power, without question the foremost of all the Etruscan cities. Indeed, it is second to none of the cities of Italy either in origin, wealth, or size. . . . The Tuscans had been the chief people of Italy and supreme both in authority and wealth. Before the foundation of the Roman empire their power was so great that they had the seas on both sides of Italy under their control and governed the whole length of the country. . . . Finally, this one people diffused the worship of the immortal gods as well as learning and letters throughout Italy. . . .

What city, therefore, can be more excellent, more noble? What descended from more glorious antecedents? . . . [Our fathers] so established and governed it that they were in no way inferior to their own fathers in virtue. Sustained by the most sacred laws, the state was ruled by them with such wisdom that they served as an example of good moral behavior for other peoples and had no need to take others as their model. . . .

Worthy of praise as well are those who are its present-day citizens. They have augmented the power received from their predecessors even more by adding Pisa and a number of other great cities to their empire through their virtue and valor in arms. . . .

Our form of governing the state aims at achieving liberty and equality for each and every citizen. Because it is equal in all respects it is called a popular government. We tremble before no lord nor are we dominated by the power of a few. All enjoy the same liberty, governed only by law and free from fear of individuals. Everyone has the same hope of attaining honors and of improving his condition provided he is industrious, has talent and a good sober way of life. For our city requires virtue and honesty in its citizens. . . .

This is true liberty and equality in a city to fear the power of no one nor dread injury from them; to experience equality of law among the citizens and the same opportunity of ruling the state. These advantages cannot be had where one man rules or a few. . . .

This capacity for a free people to attain honors and this ability to pursue one's goals serve in a marvelous way to excite men's talents. For with the hope of honors extended, men raise themselves and surge upward; excluded they become lifeless. . . . Our citizens

---

[1]Monte della Doti (dowry fund) was a credit fund established by Florence in 1425 to help well-to-do families finance in advance their daughters' marriages. [Ed.]

excel so greatly in talents and intelligence that few equal them and none surpass them. They have vivacity and industry and alacrity and agility in acting with a greatness of spirit equal to all challenges.

We thrive not only in governing the republic, in domestic arts, and in engaging in business everywhere, but we are also distinguished for military glory. . . .

What now shall I say about literature and scholarship in which all concede that Florence is the chief and most splendid leader? . . . But I am speaking about those more civilized and lofty studies which are considered more excellent and worthy of everlasting immortal glory. For who is able to name a poet in our generation or in the last one who is not Florentine? Who but our citizens recalled this skill at eloquence, already lost, to light, to practical use, and to life? Who but they understood Latin literature, already abject, prostrate and almost dead, and raised it up, restored and reclaimed it from destruction? . . . For the same reason, should not our city be proclaimed the parent of the Latin language . . . ? Now the knowledge of Greek literature, which had decayed in Italy for more than seven hundred years, has been revived and restored by our city. . . . Finally, these humanities most excellent and of highest value, especially relevant for human beings, necessary both for private and public life, adorned with a knowledge of letters worthy of free men, have originated in our city and are now thriving throughout Italy. The city enjoys such resources and wealth that I fear to arouse jealousy by referring to its inexhaustible supply of money. This is demonstrated by the long Milanese war waged at an almost incredible cost. . . . Now at the end of the war men are more prompt in paying their taxes than they were at the beginning of the war.

DISCUSSION QUESTIONS

1. Bruni's funeral oration for Nanni Strozzi spends little time discussing Strozzi himself. What might be its true subject? What are its possible purposes?

2. What do both Bruni and Rucellai see as the desirable attributes of a citizen? Why do they portray the city of Florence as a model for other cities?

3. What role does wealth play in both Petrarchan and civic humanism?

4. In these documents, how do Greece and Rome serve as models for Florence?

6. Women's Place in Renaissance Italy

Alessandra, *Letters from a Widow* and *Matriarch of a Great Family* (1450–1465)

Although there were regional differences, women in medieval and Renaissance Europe were usually under legal guardianship — typically that of a father or husband. Although women of the lower classes may have had more freedom in terms of work and marriage early in

From Eric Cochrane and Julius Kirshner, eds., *University of Chicago Readings in Western Civilization, 5: The Renaissance* (Chicago: University of Chicago Press, 1986), 109, 113–17.

their lives, their upper-class counterparts gained their greatest prestige and power through widowhood. Alessandra (1407–1471) married Matteo Strozzi (c. 1397–1435), a wealthy merchant whose business had branches throughout Europe. But when Matteo died of the effects of the plague while exiled for being in opposition to Cosimo de' Medici (1389–1464), Alessandra's financial situation became more difficult because she had sons and daughters to marry and a great household to maintain. She engaged in lengthy correspondence with her sons about political, marital, and economic conditions that affected the family. The following excerpts from letters to her son Filippo show some of the realities of Italian life during the Renaissance: exile; political danger if one did not agree with the ruling faction; marriages that were contracted solely for reasons of politics, honor, and clientage; and slavery.

To Filippo, 1450

Really, as long as there are young girls in the house, you do nothing but work for them, so when she leaves I will have no one to attend to but you three. And when I get the house in a little better shape I would love it if you would think about coming home. You would have no cause to be ashamed with what there is now, and you could do honor to any friend who dropped in to see you at home. But two or three years from now it will all be much better. And I would love to get you a wife; you're of an age now to know how to manage the help and to give me some comfort and consolation. I have none. . . .

   You know that some time ago I bought Cateruccia, our slave, and for several years now, though I haven't laid a hand on her, she has behaved so badly toward me and the children that you wouldn't believe it if you hadn't seen it. Our Lorenzo could tell you all about it. . . . I've always suffered it because I can't chastise her, and besides I thought you would come once a month so that we could come to a decision together or she could be brought to better obedience. For several months now she has been saying and is still saying that she doesn't want to stay here, and she is so moody that no one can do a thing with her. If it weren't for love of Lesandra, I would have told you to sell her, but because of her malicious tongue, I want to see Lesandra safely out of the house first. But I don't know if I can hold out that long: mark my words, I'm going to get her out of my sight because I don't want this constant battle. She pays no more attention to me than if I were the slave and she were the mistress, and she threatens us all so that Lesandra and I are both afraid of her.

To Filippo, 1459

It grieves me, my son, that I'm not near you to take some of these troublesome things off your hands. You should have told me the first day Matteo fell sick so I could have jumped on a horse and been there in just a few days. But I know that you didn't do it for fear I would get sick or would be put to trouble. . . . I have been told that in the honors you arranged for the burial of my son you did honor to yourself as well as to him. You did all the better to pay him such honor there, since here they don't usually do anything for those who are in your condition [that is, in exile]. Thus I am pleased that you did so. Here these two girls, who are unconsolable over the death of their brother, and I have gone into mourning, and because I had not yet gotten the woolen cloth to make a mantle for myself, I have gotten it now and I will pay for it.

To Filippo, 1465

I told you in my other [letter] what happened about 60[1] [the daughter of Francesco Tanagli], and there's nothing new there. And you have been advised that there is no talk of 59 [a woman who belonged to the Adimari family] until we have placed the older girl. 13 [Marco Parenti] believes we should do nothing further until we can see our way clearly concerning these two and see what way they will go. Considering their age, this shouldn't take too long. It's true that my wish would be to see both of you with a companion, as I have told you many times before. That way when I die I would think you ready to take the step all mothers want — seeing their sons married — so your children could enjoy what you have acquired with enormous effort and stress over the long years. To that end, I have done my very best to keep up the little I have had, foregoing the things that I might have done for my soul's sake and for that of our ancestors. But for the hope I have that you will take a wife (in the aim of having children), I am happy to have done so. So what I would like would be what I told you. Since then I have heard what Lorenzo's wants are and how he was willing to take her to keep me happy, but that he would be just as glad to wait two years before binding himself to the lady. I have thought a good deal about the matter, and it seems to me that since nothing really advantageous to us is available, and since we have time to wait these two years, it would be a good idea to leave it at that unless something unexpected turns up. Otherwise, it doesn't seem to me something that requires immediate thought, particularly considering the stormy times we live in these days, when so many young men on this earth are happy to inhabit it without taking a wife. The world is in a sorry state, and never has so much expense been loaded on the backs of women as now. No dowry is so big that when the girl goes out she doesn't have the whole of it on her back, between silks and jewels. . . . If 60 works out well, we could sound out the possibility of the other girl for him. There's good forage there if they were to give her, and at any [other] time it would have been a commendable move. As things are going now, it seems to me better to wait and see a while for him. . . . This way something may come of it, and they will not offer a wife without money, as people are doing now, since it seems superfluous to those who are giving 50 to give her a dowry. 13 wrote you that 60's father touched on the matter with him in the way I wrote you about. He says that you should leave it to us to see to it and work it out. For my part, I've done my diligent best, and I can't think what more I could have done — for your consolation than my own. . . .

Niccolò has gone out of office, and although he did some good things, they weren't the ones I would have wanted. Little honor has been paid to him or to the other outgoing magistrates, either when they were in office, or now that they have stepped down. Our scrutineer was quite upset about it, as were we, but I feel that what was done will collapse, and it is thought they will start fresh. This Signoria has spent days in deliberation, and no one can find out anything about them. They have threatened to denounce whoever reveals anything as a rebel, so things are being done in total secrecy. I have heard that 58 [the Medici] is everything and 54 [the Pitti] doesn't stand a chance. For the moment, it

---

[1]Because much of her family was already in exile or in political danger, Alessandra used numbers to refer to possible marriage alliances, eliminating the danger of seeming to be associated with certain factions, even during the negotiation phase.

looks to me as if they will get back to 56 [the Pucci] in the runoffs, if things continue to go as now. May God, who can do all, set this city right, for it is in a bad way. Niccolò went in proudly and then lost heart — as 14's [Soderini] brother said, "He went in a lion and he will go out a lamb," and that's just what happened to him. When he saw the votes were going against him, he began to humble himself. Now, since he left office, he goes about accompanied by five or six armed men for fear. . . . It would have been better for him if [he had never been elected], for he would never have made so many enemies. . . .

[T]hink about having Niccolò Strozzi touch on the matter with Giovanfrancesco for 45 [Lorenzo], if you think it appropriate. Although I doubt that she would deign [to marry] so low, still, it sometimes happens that you look in places that in other times you wouldn't have dreamed of, by the force of events — deaths or other misfortunes. So think about it.

DISCUSSION QUESTIONS

1. What is Alessandra's role as matriarch of her family?

2. What is her view of the politics of the city in her day?

3. What is Alessandra's relation to the enslaved person she owned? How does the existence of slavery complicate Florence's vaunted ideal of "liberty for all"?

4. How were marriages formed among the middle and upper classes? What was required before one could marry?

7. Artistic Innovation

SOURCES IN CONVERSATION | Jan Van Eyck, *Arnolfini Double Portrait* (1434) and Bartolommeo Fazio, *On Famous Men* (1456)

While Italy was the hub of the Renaissance, northern Europe experienced its own form of "rebirth" in the fine arts, notably in the Netherlands between 1430 and 1580. Unlike their Italian counterparts, northern European artists were less interested in resuscitating the classical past than in observing and capturing the everyday in minute detail. Their medium of choice was oil, and they became masters at using it to paint what they observed in the world around them. Jan Van Eyck's painting, the Arnolfini Double Portrait, *completed in 1434, is an outstanding example of the rapid artistic developments that came to define the northern Renaissance. Van Eyck's foremost patron was the duke of Burgundy, but he also painted on commission for people connected to the court. Depicted are Giovanni di Nicolao Arnolfini, an Italian merchant living in Bruges, and his wife, Constanza. Originally inter- preted as a record of their wedding, scholars now believe it is a double portrait in memory of Constanza, who died before the painting was finished. Despite how it may appear to the*

From Bartolommeo Fazio, "On Famous Men" (1456), in Wolfgang Stechow, ed. *Northern Renaissance Art, 1400–1600: Sources and Documents* (Evanston IL: Northwestern University Press, 1966), 4–5.

modern eye, Constanza is not pregnant but is rather holding up a full-skirted dress fashionable at the time. The setting is an elegantly appointed bedroom, which Van Eyck infused with religious meaning that would not have been lost on contemporary viewers. Clogs and a dog, which symbolized faith and fidelity, and the mirror, which symbolized the eye of God, encapsulate a melding of sacred and ordinary typical of northern Renaissance paintings. Italian humanist Bartolommeo Fazio was among the first Italians to see Van Eyck's paintings while serving as the historian and secretary of King Alfonso of Naples. As the excerpt from his 1456 book On Famous Men *("De Viris Illustribus") reveals, he was an ardent admirer of Van Eyck's distinctive style and technique.*

Jan of Gaul has been judged the leading painter of our time. He was not unlettered, particularly in geometry[1] and such arts as contribute to the enrichment of painting, and he is thought for this reason to have discovered many things about the properties of colors recorded by the ancients and learned by him from reading Pliny and other authors. His is a remarkable picture in the private apartments of King Alfonso,[2] in which there is a Virgin Mary notable for its grace and modesty, with an Angel Gabriel, of exceptional beauty and with hair surpassing reality, announcing that the Son of God will be born of her; and a John the Baptist that declares the wonderful sanctity and austerity of his life, and Jerome like a living being in a library done with rare art: for if you move away from it a little it seems that it recedes inward and that it has complete books laid open in it, while if you go near it is evident that there is only a summary of these. On the outer side of the same picture is painted Battista Lomellini,[3] whose property it was — you would judge he lacked only a voice — and the woman whom he loved, of outstanding beauty; and she too is portrayed exactly as she was. Between them, as if through a chink in the wall, falls a ray of sun that you would take to be real sunlight. His is a circular representation of the world, which he painted for Philip, Prince of the Belgians, and it is thought that no work has been done more perfectly in our time; you may distinguish in it not only places and the lie of continents, but also, by measurement, the distances between places. There are also fine paintings of his in the possession of that distinguished man, Ottaviano della Carda:[4] women of uncommon beauty emerging from the bath, the more intimate parts of the body being with excellent modesty veiled in fine linen, and of one of them he has shown only the face and breast but has then represented the hind parts of her body in a mirror painted on the wall opposite, so that you may see her back as well as her breast. In the same picture, there is a lantern in the bath chamber, just like one lit, and an old woman seemingly sweating, a puppy lapping up water, and also horses, minute figures of men, mountains, groves, hamlets, and castles carried out with such skill you would believe one was fifty miles distant from another. But almost nothing is more wonderful in this work than the mirror painted in the picture, in which you see whatever is represented as in a real mirror. He is said to have done many other works, but of these I have been able to obtain no complete knowledge.

---

[1]Perspective. This must be understood in a strictly empirical sense.
[2]Alfonso V of Aragon, King of Naples. This triptych has not survived.
[3]Member of a Genoese family with business connections in Bruges, friend of Fazio.
[4]Ottaviano della Carda was a nephew and adviser of Federigo da Montefeltre (Baxandall). The picture is lost.

Universal History Archive / Universal Images Group / REX / Shutterstock

DISCUSSION QUESTIONS

1. Van Eyck's work is an early example of a portrait painted solely as a representation of its subjects. What details of his subjects' physical appearance does Van Eyck include to highlight their individuality?

2. Look closely at the details included in Van Eyck's painting. What does this portrait suggest about the lifestyle of the merchant class living in the Netherlands at the time?

3. What commonalities are there between the subject matter and technique of the Van Eyck paintings described by Fazio and that of the *Arnolfini Double Portrait*?

4. What does Fazio's praise for Van Eyck suggest about the broader impact of the northern Renaissance?

COMPARATIVE QUESTIONS

1. What connections can you draw between the plague and peasant rebellions, such as the *Jacquerie*, that swept over Europe during the decades after 1347?

2. What do Hus's and Chaucer's views of the church have in common? What does this suggest about the effects of the Great Schism and perceived abuses within the church on Europeans' spiritual life?

3. Compare the portraits of Florentine life and politics painted in Documents 5 and 6. What similarities and differences do you see? What does this suggest about the limitations of Italian Renaissance ideals?

4. One of historian Jacob Burckhardt's chapters in *The Civilization of the Renaissance* is titled "The Discovery of Man and the World." What was "new" about the northern and Italian Renaissance? What could be considered a continuation of medieval ideas?

CHAPTER 14

Global Encounters and the Shock of the Reformation
1492–1560

I n the late fifteenth century, Europe stood on the threshold of profound transformations both within its borders and beyond. Portuguese fleets had opened up new trade routes extending along the West African coast to Calicut, India, the hub of the spice trade. Their success whet Europeans' appetite for maritime exploration, with Spain ultimately taking the lead. The Spaniards' colonization of the Caribbean was in full gear by 1500, and from there they moved westward into Mexico. The first two documents illuminate aspects of the Spanish conquest of Mexico from both Spanish and indigenous perspectives. As they suggest, European colonization permanently changed the lives of indigenous peoples of the Americas, often with devastating results. The third document reveals that some Europeans openly criticized colonization while at the same time embracing the opportunities it provided to spread Catholic Christianity. Catholicism had long been a unifying force in the West. In the early sixteenth century, however, the religious landscape shifted dramatically. Problems within the Catholic Church combined with the spirit and methods of the Renaissance to usher in the Protestant Reformation, a time of questioning, reform, and revolt. Documents 4 and 5 allow us to see the Reformation through the eyes of two of its leaders, Martin Luther and John Calvin, as well as its impact on everyday life. Together, their ideas helped to shatter the religious unity of Europe. As the final document attests, despite the many challenges it faced, Catholicism underwent its own process of change and renewal.

1. Worlds Collide

Bernal Díaz del Castillo,
The True History of the Conquest of New Spain (c. 1567)

By the mid-sixteenth century, Spain had built an empire in the Americas that extended from Mexico to Chile. The Spanish crown especially prized Mexico, then called "New Spain," because of the precious metals (gold and silver) found there. Numerous Spanish accounts of the conquest of Mexico have survived, perhaps none more vivid than that of Bernal Díaz del Castillo (1495–1583). Díaz had been in the thick of colonization from an early age, having joined a Spanish expedition to Panama in 1514 and two more to Mexico before meeting up with Hernán Cortés (1485–1547) in Cuba. In 1519, Cortés led a group of conquistadors, including Díaz, to the Mexican heartland, which they ultimately brought under Spanish control. By the mid-1550s, Díaz had begun to record his version of events, which he called The True History of the Conquest of New Spain, *to counter what he considered to be "false" histories by people who had not participated in the conquest. Díaz was also sensitive to critics of the colonists' treatment of indigenous peoples. Completed around 1567, the book languished in obscurity until its publication in 1632. In the excerpt that follows, Díaz recounts a key moment in the conquest: the Spaniards' arrival in Tenochtitlán, the Aztec capital, on November 8, 1519. Here Cortés and his men were greeted by the Aztec leader, Moctezuma, with great hospitality. In its close attention to detail, Díaz's description reveals a blend of wonder and disdain underlying Spanish attitudes toward Aztec civilization.*

When Cortés was told that the Great Montezuma was approaching, and he saw him coming, he dismounted from his horse, and when he was near Montezuma, they simultaneously paid great reverence to one another. Montezuma bade him welcome and our Cortés replied through Doña Marina[1] wishing him very good health. And it seems to me that Cortés, through Doña Marina, offered him his right hand, and Montezuma did not wish to take it, but he did give his hand to Cortés and then Cortés brought out a necklace which he had ready at hand, made of glass stones, which I have already said are called Margaritas, which have within them many patterns of diverse colors, these were strung on a cord of gold and with musk so that it should have a sweet scent, and he placed it round the neck of the Great Montezuma and when he had so placed it he was going to embrace him, and those great Princes who accompanied Montezuma held back Cortés by the arm so that he should not embrace him, for they considered it an indignity.

Then Cortés through the mouth of Doña Marina told him that now his heart rejoiced at having seen such a great Prince, and that he took it as a great honor that he had come in person to meet him and had frequently shown him such favor.

Then Montezuma spoke other words of politeness to him, and told two of his nephews who supported his arms, the Lord of Texcoco and the Lord of Coyoacan, to go with us and show us to our quarters, and Montezuma with his other two relations, the Lord of Cuitlahuac and the Lord of Tacuba who accompanied him, returned to the

---

From Bernal Díaz del Castillo, *The True History of the Conquest of New Spain*, vol. 2, trans. Alfred Percival Maudslay (London: The Hakluyt Society, 1910), 41–44, 55–59.

[1]A Nahua slave of a Maya cacique, she was given to Cortés by the Maya after their defeat at Potonchan. Speaking both Nahuatl and Yucatec Maya, she (and the ex-Maya captive Gerónimo de Aguilar) became crucial interpreters for Cortés as he entered the world of the Mexica. She was also the mother of Cortés's illegitimate son, Martín. See Stuart B. Schwartz, ed., *Victors and Vanquished: Spanish and Nahua Views of the Conquest of Mexico* (Boston: Bedford/St. Martin's, 2000), 251. [Schwartz's note.]

city, and all those grand companies of Caciques[2] and chieftains who had come with him returned in his train. . . . Thus space was made for us to enter the streets of Mexico, without being so much crowded. But who could now count the multitude of men and women and boys who were in the streets and on the azoteas, and in canoes on the canals, who had come out to see us. It was indeed wonderful, and, now that I am writing about it, it all comes before my eyes as though it had happened but yesterday. Coming to think it over it seems to be a great mercy that our Lord Jesus Christ was pleased to give us grace and courage to dare to enter into such a city; and for the many times He has saved me from danger of death, as will be seen later on, I give Him sincere thanks, and in that He has preserved me to write about it, although I cannot do it as fully as is fitting or the subject needs. Let us make no words about it, for deeds are the best witnesses to what I say here and elsewhere.

Let us return to our entry to Mexico. They took us to lodge in some large houses, where there were apartments for all of us, for they had belonged to the father of the Great Montezuma, who was named Axayaca, and at that time Montezuma kept there the great oratories for his idols, and a secret chamber where he kept bars and jewels of gold, which was the treasure that he had inherited from his father Axayaca, and he never disturbed it. They took us to lodge in that house, because they called us Teules, and took us for such, so that we should be with the Idols or Teules which were kept there. However, for one reason or another, it was there they took us, where there were great halls and chambers canopied with the cloth of the country for our Captain, and for every one of us beds of matting with canopies above, and no better bed is given, however great the chief may be, for they are not used. And all these palaces were [coated] with shining cement and swept and garlanded.

As soon as we arrived and entered into the great court, the Great Montezuma took our Captain by the hand, for he was there awaiting him, and led him to the apartment and saloon where he was to lodge, which was very richly adorned according to their usage, and he had at hand a very rich necklace made of golden crabs, a marvelous piece of work, and Montezuma himself placed it round the neck of our Captain Cortés, and greatly astonished his [own] Captains by the great honor that he was bestowing on him. When the necklace had been fastened, Cortés thanked Montezuma through our interpreters, and Montezuma replied—"Malinche, you and your brethren are in your own house, rest awhile," and then he went to his palaces which were not far away, and we divided our lodgings by companies, and placed the artillery pointing in a convenient direction, and the order which we had to keep was clearly explained to us, and that we were to be much on the alert, both the cavalry and all of us soldiers. A sumptuous dinner was provided for us according to their use and custom, and we ate it at once. So this was our lucky and daring entry into the great city of Tenochtitlan, Mexico. . . .

Thanks to our Lord Jesus Christ for it all. . . .

---

[2]A Taino word meaning ruler, brought from the Indies to Mexico by the Spanish and used to refer to native rulers in Mexico and Latin America in general. See Schwartz, *Victors and Vanquished*, 254. [Schwartz's note.]

Let us leave this talk and go back to our story of what else happened to us, which I will go on to relate. . . .

The next day Cortés decided to go to Montezuma's palace, and he first sent to find out what he intended doing and to let him know that we were coming. . . .

When Montezuma knew of our coming he advanced to the middle of the hall to receive us, accompanied by many of his nephews, for no other chiefs were permitted to enter or hold communication with Montezuma where he then was, unless it were on important business. Cortés and he paid the greatest reverence to each other and then they took one another by the hand and Montezuma made him sit down on his couch on his right hand, and he also bade all of us to be seated on seats which he ordered to be brought.

Then Cortés began to make an explanation through our interpreters Doña Marina and Aguilar, and said that he and all of us were rested, and that in coming to see and converse with such a great Prince as he was, we had completed the journey and fulfilled the command which our great King and Prince had laid on us. But what he chiefly came to say on behalf of our Lord God had already been brought to his [Montezuma's] knowledge through his ambassadors, Tendile, Pitalpitoque and Quintalbor, at the time when he did us the favor to send the golden sun and moon to the sand dunes; for we told them then that we were Christians and worshipped one true and only God, named Jesus Christ, who suffered death and passion to save us, and we told them that a cross (when they asked us why we worshipped it) was a sign of the other Cross on which our Lord God was crucified for our salvation, and that the death and passion which He suffered was for the salvation of the whole human race, which was lost, and that this our God rose on the third day and is now in heaven, and it is He who made the heavens and the earth, the sea and the sands, and created all the things there are in the world, and He sends the rain and the dew, and nothing happens in the world without His holy will. That we believe in Him and worship Him, but that those whom they look upon as gods are not so, but are devils, which are evil things, and if their looks are bad their deeds are worse, and they could see that they were evil and of little worth, for where we had set up crosses such as those his ambassadors had seen, they dared not appear before them, through fear of them, and that as time went on they would notice this.

The favor he now begged of him was his attention to the words that he now wished to tell him; then he explained to him very clearly about the creation of the world, and how we are all brothers, sons of one father, and one mother who were called Adam and Eve, and how such a brother as our great Emperor, grieving for the perdition of so many souls, such as those which their idols were leading to Hell, where they burn in living flames, had sent us, so that after what he [Montezuma] had now heard he would put a stop to it and they would no longer adore these Idols or sacrifice Indian men and women to them, for we were all brethren, nor should they commit sodomy or thefts. He also told them that, in course of time, our Lord and King would send some men who among us lead very holy lives, much better than we do, who will explain to them all about it, for at present we merely came to give them due warning, and so he prayed him to do what he was asked and carry it into effect.

As Montezuma appeared to wish to reply, Cortés broke off his argument, and to all of us who were with him he said: "with this we have done our duty considering it is the first attempt."

Montezuma replied—"Señor Malinche, I have understood your words and arguments very well before now, from what you said to my servants at the sand dunes, this about three Gods and the Cross, and all those things that you have preached in the towns through which you have come. We have not made any answer to it because here throughout all time we have worshipped our own gods, and thought they were good, as no doubt yours are, so do not trouble to speak to us any more about them at present. Regarding the creation of the world, we have held the same belief for ages past, and for this reason we take it for certain that you are those whom our ancestors predicted would come from the direction of the sunrise." . . .

. . . Then Cortés and all of us answered that we thanked him sincerely for such signal good will, and Montezuma said, laughing, for he was very merry in his princely way of speaking: "Malinche, I know very well that these people of Tlaxcala with whom you are such good friends have told you that I am a sort of God or Teul, and that everything in my houses is made of gold and silver and precious stones, I know well enough that you are wise and did not believe it but took it as a joke. Behold now, Señor Malinche, my body is of flesh and bone like yours, my houses and palaces of stone and wood and lime; that I am a great king and inherit the riches of my ancestors is true, but not all the nonsense and lies that they have told you about me, although of course you treated it as a joke, as I did your thunder and lightning."

Cortés answered him, also laughing, and said that opponents and enemies always say evil things, without truth in them, of those whom they hate, and that he well knew that he could not hope to find another Prince more magnificent in these countries, and, that not without reason had he been so vaunted to our Emperor.

While this conversation was going on, Montezuma secretly sent a great Cacique, one of his nephews who was in his company, to order his stewards to bring certain pieces of gold, which it seems must have been put apart to give to Cortés, and ten loads of fine cloth, which he apportioned, the gold and mantles between Cortés and the four captains, and to each of us soldiers he gave two golden necklaces, each necklace being worth ten pesos, and two loads of mantles. The gold that he then gave us was worth in all more than a thousand pesos and he gave it all cheerfully and with the air of a great and valiant prince.

DISCUSSION QUESTIONS

1. How does Díaz describe Tenochtitlán and the Aztec leader Moctezuma? What impressed him in particular? What does he seem to criticize, and why?

2. How does Díaz portray Cortés and his interactions with Moctezuma? What was the role of Doña Marina in their exchanges?

3. In what ways is Díaz's account colored by his own preconceptions and beliefs as a European in a foreign land?

4. Based on this account, what motivated Díaz and other conquistadors? What did the New World have to offer them?

2. Illustrating an Indigenous Perspective

Lienzo de Tlaxcala (c. 1560)

Like Bernal Díaz del Castillo, the peoples of central Mexico had a stake in recording the momentous events unfolding around them, for they had long believed that remembering the past was essential to their cultural survival. Traditionally, local peoples used pictoriographic representations to record legends, myths, and historical events. After the Spaniards' arrival, indigenous artists borrowed from this tradition to produce their own accounts of the conquest, including the image below. It is one of a series contained in the Lienzo de Tlaxcala, *painted on cloth in the mid-sixteenth century. Apparently, the* Lienzo *was created for the Spanish viceroy to commemorate the alliance of the Tlaxcalans with the Spaniards. The Tlaxcalans were enemies of the Aztecs and, after initial resistance to the Spanish invasion, decided to join their forces. This particular image depicts two related events. The first is the meeting between the Aztec leader Moctezuma and Hernán Cortés in Tenochtitlán in August 1519. Cortés is accompanied by Doña Marina, his translator and cultural mediator; Moctezuma appears with warriors at his side. Rather than showing Moctezuma in his traditional garb, the artist dressed him in the manner of the Tlaxcalans. Both sit in European-style chairs, a nod to European artistic influence, and a Tlaxcalan headdress is suspended in the air between them. Game and fowl offered to the Spaniards are*

The British Library, London, UK / Bridgeman Images

portrayed at the bottom. Within a week of this meeting, Cortés imprisoned Moctezuma in his own palaces with the Tlaxcalans' help. Moctezuma the prisoner appears in the upper right of the image as an old, weak ruler whose sun has set.

DISCUSSION QUESTIONS

1. In what ways do the artist's depictions of Cortés and Moctezuma differ? What do the depictions share?

2. Why do you think the artist chose to depict Moctezuma in Tlaxcalan dress? How was this choice related to the artist's audience and the message he sought to convey?

3. What are the possible strengths of a visual source like this for historians? What are the possible weaknesses?

3. Defending Indigenous Humanity

Bartolomé de Las Casas, *In Defense of the Indians* (c. 1548–1550)

Indigenous peoples in the Americas suffered heavily under Spanish colonization. Millions died as the result of war and disease, and many who survived were used as forced labor. The fate of indigenous Americans did not go unnoticed in Europe, where the ethical and legal basis of their harsh treatment became the subject of significant debate. Charles V, king of Spain and the Holy Roman Emperor, added fuel to the fire. In 1550, he ordered a panel of lawyers and theologians at the University of Valladolid to evaluate the positions of two prominent opposing voices on the issue, Juan Ginés de Sepúlveda (1490–1573) and Bartolomé de Las Casas (1474–1566). Drawing heavily on Aristotle's notion that hierarchy was natural, Sepúlveda argued that the Spanish had the right to enslave indigenous Americans because they were an inferior and less civilized people. Las Casas, whose response is excerpted below, rejected Sepúlveda's position, based in part on his own experience living in Spanish America. Here he witnessed firsthand the devastating human impact of colonization and was ultimately swayed by the local Dominican monks' campaign against the mistreatment of Indians. He joined the Dominican order and thereafter was a vocal advocate for indigenous Americans until his death in 1566. Although the Valladolid panel did not declare a winner, in practice Las Casas's views were drowned out by Sepúlveda and other advocates of slavery and conquest.

As a result of the points we have proved and made clear, the distinction the Philosopher [Aristotle] makes between the two above-mentioned kinds of barbarian is evident. For those he deals with in the first book of the *Politics*, and whom we have just discussed, are barbarians without qualification, in the proper and strict sense of the word, that is, dull witted and lacking in the reasoning powers necessary for self-government. They are without laws, without king, etc. For this reason they are by nature unfitted for rule.

However, he admits, and proves, that the barbarians he deals with in the third book of the same work have a lawful, just, and natural government. Even though they lack the

From *In Defense of the Indians*, trans. Stafford Poole (DeKalb: Northern Illinois University Press, 1974), 41–46.

art and use of writing, they are not wanting in the capacity and skill to rule and govern themselves, both publicly and privately. Thus they have kingdoms, communities, and cities that they govern wisely according to their laws and customs. Thus their government is legitimate and natural, even though it has some resemblance to tyranny. From these statements we have no choice but to conclude that the rulers of such nations enjoy the use of reason and that their people and the inhabitants of their provinces do not lack peace and justice. Otherwise they could not be established or preserved as political entities for long. This is made clear by the Philosopher and Augustine. Therefore not all barbarians are irrational or natural slaves or unfit for government. Some barbarians, then, in accord with justice and nature, have kingdoms, royal dignities, jurisdiction, and good laws, and there is among them lawful government.

Now if we shall have shown that among our Indians of the western and southern shores (granting that we call them barbarians and that they are barbarians) there are important kingdoms, large numbers of people who live settled lives in a society, great cities, kings, judges and laws, persons who engage in commerce, buying, selling, lending, and the other contracts of the law of nations, will it not stand proved that the Reverend Doctor Sepúlveda has spoken wrongly and viciously against peoples like these, either out of malice or ignorance of Aristotle's teaching, and, therefore, has falsely and perhaps irreparably slandered them before the entire world? From the fact that the Indians are barbarians it does not necessarily follow that they are incapable of government and have to be ruled by others, except to be taught about the Catholic faith and to be admitted to the holy sacraments. They are not ignorant, inhuman, or bestial. Rather, long before they had heard the word Spaniard they had properly organized states, wisely ordered by excellent laws, religion, and custom. They cultivated friendship and, bound together in common fellowship, lived in populous cities in which they wisely administered the affairs of both peace and war justly and equitably, truly governed by laws that at very many points surpass ours, and could have won the admiration of the sages of Athens. . . .

Now if they are to be subjugated by war because they are ignorant of polished literature, let Sepúlveda hear Trogus Pompey:

> Nor could the Spaniards submit to the yoke of a conquered province until Caesar Augustus, after he had conquered the world, turned his victorious armies against them and organized that barbaric and wild people as a province, once he had led them by law to a more civilized way of life.

Now see how he called the Spanish people barbaric and wild. I would like to hear Sepúlveda, in his cleverness, answer this question: Does he think that the war of the Romans against the Spanish was justified in order to free them from barbarism? And this question also: Did the Spanish wage an unjust war when they vigorously defended themselves against them?

Next, I call the Spaniards who plunder that unhappy people torturers. Do you think that the Romans, once they had subjugated the wild and barbaric peoples of Spain, could with secure right divide all of you among themselves, handing over so many head of both males and females as allotments to individuals? And do you then conclude that the Romans could have stripped your rulers of their authority and consigned all of you, after you had been deprived of your liberty, to wretched labors, especially in searching for gold and silver lodes and mining and refining the metals? And if the Romans finally did that, . . . [would you not judge] that you also have the right to defend your freedom, indeed your very life, by war? Sepúlveda, would you have permitted Saint James to evangelize your own people of Córdoba in that way? For God's sake and man's faith in him, is this the way to impose the yoke of Christ on Christian men? Is this the way to remove wild barbarism from the minds of barbarians? Is it not, rather, to act like thieves, cutthroats, and cruel plunderers and to drive the gentlest of people headlong into despair? The Indian race is not that barbaric, nor are they dull witted or stupid, but they are easy to teach and very talented in learning all the liberal arts, and very ready to accept, honor, and observe the Christian religion and correct their sins (as experience has taught) once priests have introduced them to the sacred mysteries and taught them the word of God. They have been endowed with excellent conduct, and before the coming of the Spaniards, as we have said, they had political states that were well founded on beneficial laws.

Now if Sepúlveda had wanted, as a serious man should, to know the full truth before he sat down to write with his mind corrupted by the lies of tyrants, he should have consulted the honest religious who have lived among those peoples for many years and know their endowments of character and industry, as well as the progress they have made in religion and morality. . . .

From this it is clear that the basis for Sepúlveda's teaching that these people are uncivilized and ignorant is worse than false. Yet even if we were to grant that this race has no keenness of mind or artistic ability, certainly they are not, in consequence, obliged to submit themselves to those who are more intelligent and to adopt their ways, so that, if they refuse, they may be subdued by having war waged against them and be enslaved, as happens today. For men are obliged by the natural law to do many things they cannot be forced to do against their will. We are bound by the natural law to embrace virtue and imitate the uprightness of good men. No one, however, is punished for being bad unless he is guilty of rebellion. Where the Catholic faith has been preached in a Christian manner and as it ought to be, all men are bound by the natural law to accept it, yet no one is forced to accept the faith of Christ. No one is punished because he is sunk in vice, unless he is rebellious or harms the property and persons of others. No one is forced to embrace virtue and show himself as a good man. . . .

. . . Therefore, not even a truly wise man may force an ignorant barbarian to submit to him, especially by yielding his liberty, without doing him an injustice. This the poor Indians suffer, with extreme injustice, against all the laws of God and of men and against the law of nature itself.

DISCUSSION QUESTIONS

1. Why does Las Casas reject Sepúlveda's argument? What is the basis of his reasoning?

2. How does Las Casas depict indigenous American civilization? What attributes does he highlight, and why?

3. Why does Las Casas cite the example of Rome's conquest of Spain under Caesar Augustus to support his point?

4. Despite Las Casas's vigorous defense of the Indians, what prejudices and assumptions of his own did he bring to bear in this work?

4. Scripture and Salvation

Martin Luther, *Freedom of a Christian* (1520)

German monk Martin Luther's attempt to reform the Catholic Church from within developed into a new branch of Christianity known as Protestantism. After his excommunication by Pope Leo X in 1520, Luther published several treatises that attacked church authority, clerical celibacy, and the sacraments while illuminating his evangelical theology. He set forth the guiding principles of his beliefs with particular clarity in Freedom of a Christian. Although originally written in Latin and addressed to the pope, the tract was soon translated into German and widely circulated among Luther's ever-growing number of followers. In the excerpt that follows, Luther defined what became a central tenet of the reform movement: faith in Christ and his promise of salvation is all that a Christian needs to be saved from sin.

Many people have considered Christian faith an easy thing, and not a few have given it a place among the virtues. They do this because they have not experienced it and have never tasted the great strength there is in faith. It is impossible to write well about it or to understand what has been written about it unless one has at one time or another experienced the courage which faith gives a man when trials oppress him. But he who has had even a faint taste of it can never write, speak, meditate, or hear enough concerning it. It is a living "spring of water welling up to eternal life," as Christ calls it in John 4 [:14].

As for me, although I have no wealth of faith to boast of and know how scant my supply is, I nevertheless hope that I have attained to a little faith, even though I have been assailed by great and various temptations; and I hope that I can discuss it, if not more elegantly, certainly more to the point, than those literalists and subtile disputants have previously done, who have not even understood what they have written. . . .

First, let us consider the inner man to see how a righteous, free, and pious Christian, that is, a spiritual, new, and inner man, becomes what he is. It is evident that no external thing has any influence in producing Christian righteousness or freedom. . . . It does not help the soul if the body is adorned with the sacred robes of priests or dwells in sacred places or is occupied with sacred duties or prays, fasts, abstains from certain kinds of food, or does any work that can be done by the body and in the body. . . .

One thing, and only one thing, is necessary for Christian life, righteousness, and freedom. That one thing is the most holy Word of God, the gospel of Christ, as Christ says, John 11 [:25], "I am the resurrection and the life; he who believes in me, though he die, yet shall he live"; and John 8 [:36], "So if the Son makes you free, you will be free indeed"; and Matt. 4 [:4], "Man shall not live by bread alone, but by every word that proceeds from the mouth of God." Let us then consider it certain and firmly established that the soul can do without anything except the Word of God and that where the Word of God is missing there is no help at all for the soul. If it has the Word of God it is rich and

From Martin Luther, *Christian Liberty*, ed. Harold J. Grimm (Philadelphia: Fortress Press, 1957), 6–10.

lacks nothing since it is the Word of life, truth, light, peace, righteousness, salvation, joy, liberty, wisdom, power, grace, glory, and of every incalculable blessing. . . .

You may ask, "What then is the Word of God, and how shall it be used, since there are so many words of God?" I answer: The Apostle explains this in Romans 1. The Word is the gospel of God concerning his Son, who was made flesh, suffered, rose from the dead, and was glorified through the Spirit who sanctifies. To preach Christ means to feed the soul, make it righteous, set it free, and save it, provided it believes the preaching. Faith alone is the saving and efficacious use of the Word of God. . . . Therefore it is clear that, as the soul needs only the Word of God for its life and righteousness, so it is justified by faith alone and not any works. . . .

When you have learned this you will know that you need Christ, who suffered and rose again for you so that, if you believe in him, you may through this faith become a new man in so far as your sins are forgiven and you are justified by the merits of another, namely, of Christ alone. . . .

DISCUSSION QUESTIONS

1. According to Luther, what is faith, and where does it come from?

2. How can an individual Christian become a "new man" through such faith?

3. By defining faith alone as essential to salvation, in what ways does Luther undermine basic Catholic teachings?

4. What authority does Luther draw on to defend his point of view? What does this reveal about the basis of his theology?

5. Reforming Christianity

SOURCES IN CONVERSATION | John Calvin, *Ordinances for the Regulation of Churches* (1547) and *Registers of Consistory of Geneva* (1542–1543)

In 1533–1534, while studying in Paris at the same time as Ignatius of Loyola (1491–1556), Frenchman John Calvin (1509–1564) became a convert to the reform movement. Fleeing the dangers of Paris, Calvin settled in Geneva, where he remained for the majority of his life, intent upon transforming it into his vision of a godly city. Geneva soon became a haven for reformers and a training ground for preachers. Theologically, Calvin embraced Luther's

John Calvin, *Ordinances for the Regulation of Churches* (1547), in Merry Wiesner-Hanks, ed., *Religious Transformations in the Early Modern World* (Boston: Bedford/St.Martins, 2009), 77–78, and *From Registers of the Consistory of Geneva in the Time of Calvin,* Volume 1, 1542–1544, ed. Robert M. Kingdon, trans. M. Wallace McDonald (Grand Rapids, MI: William B. Eerdmans, 2002), 13, 155, 161–62, 252.

doctrine that people cannot earn their salvation, and he then took it further. He argued that God had ordained every person to salvation or damnation before the beginning of time (predestination); only God's chosen "elect" would be saved. For Calvin, a righteous life might be a sign that the person had been chosen for salvation. With this goal in mind, in Geneva Calvin and his officials set up a strict system of moral and religious discipline, issuing ordinances such as the ones excerpted below to regulate public and family life. A group of pastors and laymen, known as the consistory, was established to investigate and discipline improper conduct and belief. People from all walks of life were called before consistorial officials to account for alleged infractions. Written notes were taken at such sessions in real time and were then later revised into official minutes — these minutes have survived in abundance. While one step removed from the encounters they describe, the selections here provide a view of how Calvin's vision played out in the lives of ordinary people.

Ordinances for the Regulation of Churches (1547)

Blasphemy

Whoever shall have blasphemed, swearing by the body or by the blood of our Lord, or in similar manner, he shall be made to kiss the earth for the first offence; for the second to pay 5 sous,[1] and for the third 6 sous, and for the last offence be put in the pillory for one hour.

Drunkenness

1. That no one shall invite another to drink under penalty of 3 sous.
2. That taverns shall be closed during the sermon, under penalty that the tavern-keeper shall pay 3 sous, and whoever may be found therein shall pay the same amount.
3. If any one be found intoxicated he shall pay for the first offence 3 sous and shall be remanded to the consistory; for the second offence he shall be held to pay the same sum of 6 sous, and for the third 10 sous and be put in orison.

Songs and Dances

If any one sing immoral, dissolute or outrageous songs, or dance the *virollet* or other dance, he shall be put in prison for three days and then sent to the consistory.

Usury

That no one shall take upon interest or profit more than five percent, upon penalty of confiscation of the principal and of being condemned to make restitution as the case may demand.

---

[1]**sou:** A small coin.

Games

That no one shall play at any dissolute game or at any game whatsoever it may be, neither for gold nor silver nor for any excessive stake, upon penalty of 5 sous and forfeiture of stake played for. . . .

Concerning the Celebration of the Marriage

That the parties at the time when they are to be married shall go modestly to the church, without drummers and minstrels, preserving an order and gravity becoming to Christians; and this before the last stroke of the bell, in order that the marriage blessing may be given before the sermon. If they are negligent and come too late they shall be sent away.

Registers of Constitory of Geneva (1542–1543)

Thursday, March 2, 1542

Pernete, wife of Master Robert the pack-saddler.

Asked about the discipline and fashion of living in her household according to the Word of God, about songs, sermons and her faith and her servants and maids. And she gave a sound explanation of her faith and creed. The consistory gave her proper remonstrances to buy a Bible to put before her people to read instead of game boards, cards, songs, and to eschew all dice.

Tevenete, wife of Master Jaques Emyn, pack-saddler.

She was sufficiently admonished, First given proper admonitions concerning attendance at sermons, her faith, the manner of living in religion and her foreign guests. And she could not say her creed, at least the confession. She was admonished that within a month she should learn to render a better account of her creed and that she buy a Bible to show to the guests in her house. Also that she have good servants and maids and that God not be blasphemed or offended in her house.

Thursday, December 14, 1542

Mychie, daughter of Gallatin, from Peney.

Answers that she does not want her promised husband because he has nothing and it is better that she be with her father than elsewhere in difficulty. And that she swore faith to him and does not want him to be her husband for the reason above, and that she has not been debauched.

Jehan Jallio, promised husband of the said Mychie, on the said marriage. Answers no, because the girl does not want it. And if it pleases the Council he is ready to marry her if she wants it, and it is not his fault, and he has done nothing to make her refuse him.

The said Michie recalled. Answers when she swore faith to him he had plenty of goods, and no one tried to prevent her from doing this. Says that if she gives him her goods he will waste them, and she would not know what to do with him. Remanded to respond whether she wants it or not on leaving here, and if not that she be kept in this city until tomorrow. Asked for a term to respond and have counsel from her mother and her friends, since it pleases the Seigneurie, and to marry him next Tuesday, and they agreed to this.

Thursday, December 21, 1542

Françoys Comparet.

Because of games. Answers that he goes to the sermon when he can and sometimes with friends to drink, and yesterday they drank a pot of wine together with good company. And answers nine sous for three, and he was not there, and he lost three sous per man. And that he was at the sermon Sunday and . . .[2] preached. Said the prayer and the confession. Remonstrances just as to the other, and let him abstain from the next Communion.

François Comparet the younger, brother of the aforesaid François, in the bakery. Goes to the sermon on Sundays when he can, and they bake every day at seven o'clock in their shop and go to the market to supply the shop. And said the prayer in Latin. And it is only about six months ago that he came to this city. Wat at the vespers sermon Sunday.

Camparet's widow,[3] mother of the two named above, because she does not discipline her children, who are badly taught in all good morals. Answers that other young boys lead them astray and ruin them, and they are good children and obedient, and they were not at the scandal that was made thus, and she does not know what it is. And goes willingly to the sermons when she can, and above all on Sundays. The younger son does not come to Communion. The consistory advises that she watch out from now on, that she teach her children and frequent the sermons and the catechism on Sundays; otherwise the Council will see to her. And that the children frequent the sermons.

Thursday, May 10, 1543

Donne Aymaz Charletaz, daughter of D[omaine] d'Arloz.

Because of usury, and that she is a rebel against the Seigneurie. Begged mercy of God and the Seigneurie. Answers that she was ill and did not lend at interest and gave her money to the merchants to use and they give her what they choose, because she has nothing to live on otherwise and has no other lands or goods. And that no one asks her anything or complains of her, and she has been a widow 40 years, and then she had 300 écus and now does not have 300 florins. And she submits herself to prison if she has ever spoken against the Gospel, and she left the neighborhood of Faucigny to come here to the Gospel.

DISCUSSION QUESTIONS

1. What type of behaviors do the Ordinances prohibit? What do these prohibitions reveal about Calvin's vision for an ideal Christian society?

---

[2]Name omitted.
[3]Jaquema, widow of Claude Comparet.

2. What evidence do the consistory records offer on how Calvin's vision was translated into practice in Geneva? What specific offenses did the consistory focus on, and why?

3. What forms of discipline did the consistory impose for these offenses? What functions do you think their admonitions and instructions served in the community as a whole?

6. Responding to Reformation

St. Ignatius of Loyola, *A New Kind of Catholicism*
(1546, 1549, 1553)

The interests of Ignatius of Loyola (1491–1556), born of a Spanish noble family, centered more on chivalry than religion before his serious injury at the Battle of Pamplona in 1520. While recovering, he experienced a conversion when he began reading the only books available to him, The Golden Legend *(about saints' lives) and the* Life of Christ. *After begging and spending time at the monastery of Montserrat, he began work on* The Spiritual Exercises, *a manual of discernment for the pilgrim journeying to God. After studying at the University of Paris, Ignatius, Francis Xavier (1506–1552), and other friends made vows of chastity and poverty, determining to travel to Jerusalem. When this became impossible, they went to Italy. The Society of Jesus (the Jesuits), founded by Ignatius and his early companions, was officially recognized by Pope Paul III in 1540 as a new order directly under the papacy. Its spirituality would be expressed most prominently through teaching and missionary work. The following letters of Ignatius reveal a new form of Catholic spiritual expression that was active and apostolic in its orientation. It was less a "response" to Protestantism than a model for Catholic life and work. Along with the works of other early Jesuits, it embodied a new spirit that so many had sought but not found in the late medieval church.*

Conduct at Trent: On Helping Others, 1546

Our main aim [to God's greater glory] during this undertaking at Trent is to put into practice (as a group that lives together in one appropriate place) preaching, confessions and readings, teaching children, giving good example, visiting the poor in the hospitals, exhorting those around us, each of us according to the different talents he may happen to have, urging on as many as possible to greater piety and prayer. . . .

In their preaching they should not refer to points of conflict between Protestants and Catholics, but simply exhort all to upright conduct and to ecclesiastical practice, urging everyone to full self-knowledge and to greater knowledge and love of their Creator and Lord, with frequent allusions to the Council. At the end of each session, they should (as has been mentioned) lead prayers for the Council.

From Joseph A. Munitiz and Philip Endean, eds. and trans., *Saint Ignatius of Loyola, Personal Writings: Reminiscences, Spiritual Diary, Select Letters, Including the Text of The Spiritual Exercises* (New York: Penguin Books, 1996), 165, 166, 230, 233–34, 257, 259, 262–63.

They should do the same with readings as with sermons, trying their best to influence people with greater love of their Creator and Lord as they explain the meaning of what is read; similarly, they should lead their hearers to pray for the Council. . . .

They should spend some time, as convenient, in the elementary teaching of youngsters, depending on the means and disposition of all involved, and with more or less explanation according to the capacity of the pupils. . . . Let them visit the alms-houses once or twice a day, at times that are convenient for the patients' health, hearing confessions and consoling the poor, if possible taking them something, and urging them to the sort of prayers mentioned above for confession. If there are three of ours in Trent, each should visit the poor at least once every four days.

When they are urging people in their dealings with them to go to confession and communion, to say mass frequently, to undertake the Spiritual Exercises and other good works, they should also be urging them to pray for the Council.

It was said that there are advantages in being slow to speak and measured in one's statements when doctrinal definitions are involved. The opposite is true when one is urging people to look to their spiritual progress. Then one should be eloquent and ready to talk, full of sympathy and affection.

Spreading God's Word in a German University, 1549

The aim that they should have above all before their eyes is that intended by the Supreme Pontiff who has sent them: to help the University of Ingolstadt, and as far as is possible the whole of Germany, in all that concerns purity of faith, obedience to the Church, and firmness and soundness of doctrine and upright living. . . .

They must be very competent in them, and teach solid doctrine without many technical terms (which are unpopular), especially if these are hard to understand. The lectures should be learned yet clear, sustained in argument yet not long-winded, and delivered with attention to style. . . . Besides these academic lectures, it seems opportune on feast days to hold sermons on Bible readings, more calculated to move hearts and form consciences than to produce learned minds. . . . They should make efforts to attract their students into a friendship of spiritual quality, and if possible towards confession and making the Spiritual Exercises, even in the full form, if they seem suitable to join the Society. . . .

On occasion they should give time to works of mercy of a more visible character, such as in hospitals and prisons and helping other kinds of poor; such works arouse a "sweet fragrance" in the Lord. Opportunity may also arise to act as peacemakers in quarrels and to teach basic Christian doctrine to the uneducated. Taking account of local conditions and the persons concerned, prudence will dictate whether they should act themselves or through others.

They should make efforts to make friends with the leaders of their opponents, as also with those who are most influential among the heretics or those who are suspected of it yet seem not absolutely immovable. They must try to bring them back from their error by sensitive skill and signs of love. . . . All must try to have at their finger-tips the main points concerning dogmas of faith that are subjects of controversy with heretics, especially at the time and place when they are present, and with those persons with whom they are dealing. Thus they will be able, whenever opportunity arises, to put forward and defend the Catholic truth, to refute errors and to strengthen the doubtful and wavering, whether by lectures and sermons or in the confessional and in conversations. . . .

It will be helpful to lead people, as far as possible, to open themselves to God's grace, exhorting them to a desire for salvation, to prayer, to alms, and to everything that conduces to receiving grace or increasing it. . . .

Let [the duke] understand also what glory it will mean for him if he is the first to introduce into Germany seminaries in the form of such colleges, to foster sound doctrine and religion.

The Final Word on Obedience, 1553, to the Brothers in Portugal

To form an idea of the exceptional intrinsic value of this obedience in the eyes of God Our Lord, one should weigh both the worth of the noble sacrifice offered, involving the highest human power, and the completeness of the self-offering undertaken, as one strips oneself of self, becoming a "living victim" pleasing to the Divine Majesty. Another indication is the intensity of the difficulty experienced as one conquers self for love of God, opposing the natural human inclination felt by us all to follow our own opinions. . . .

Let us be unpretentious and let us be gentle! God Our Lord will grant the grace to enable you, gently and lovingly, to maintain constantly the offering you have made to Him. . . .

All that has been said does not exclude your bringing before your superiors a contrary opinion that may have occurred to you, once you have prayed about the matter and you feel that it would be proper and in accord with your respect for God to do so. . . . Such is the model on which divine Providence "gently disposes all things," so that the lower via the middle, and the middle via the higher, are led to their final ends. . . . The same can be seen upon the earth with respect to all secular constitutions that are duly established, and with respect to the ecclesiastical hierarchy, which is subordinated to you in virtue of holy obedience to select among the many routes open to you that which will bring you back to Portugal as soon and as safely as possible. So I order you in the name of Christ Our Lord to do this, even if it will be so as to return soon to India. . . . Firstly, you are well aware how important for the upkeep and advancement of Christianity in those lands, as also in Guinea and Brazil, is the good order that the King of Portugal can grant from his kingdom. When a prince of such Christian desires and holy intentions as is the King of Portugal receives information from someone of your experience about the state of affairs in those parts, you can imagine what influence this will have on him to do much more in the service of God Our Lord and for the good of those countries that you will describe to him. . . .

You are also aware how important it is for the good of the Indies that the persons sent there should be suitable for the aim that one is pursuing in those and in other lands. . . . Quite apart from all these reasons, which apply to furthering the good of India, it seems to me that you would fire the King's enthusiasm for the Ethiopian project, which has been planned for so many years without anything effective having been seen. Similarly, with regard to the Congo and Brazil, you could give no small help from Portugal, which you cannot do from India as there are not the same commercial relations. If people in India consider that your presence is important given your post, you can continue to act as superior no less from Portugal than from Japan or China, and probably much better. Just as you have gone away on other occasions for longer periods, do the same now.

DISCUSSION QUESTIONS

1. What does the Catholic life mean to Ignatius?

2. What advice does Ignatius offer about dealing with the problem of heresy?

3. What role will Jesuits play throughout Europe and the rest of the world according to Ignatius's instructions?

4. How does Ignatius think political leaders can be enlisted to support the aims of the Catholic reform movement?

COMPARATIVE QUESTIONS

1. How do Bernal Díaz del Castillo, the *Lienzo de Tlaxcala*, and Bartolomé de Las Casas portray indigenous peoples? Can you trust these portraits? What do they reveal about the ways in which Europeans and indigenous peoples viewed themselves?

2. According to Las Casas, indigenous Americans were not "barbarians" because they had many marks of "civilization," including cities and self-sustaining governments. What evidence can you find in Díaz to support this view?

3. What similarities do you see among Luther's, Calvin's, and Ignatius's models of Christian life? Where do they diverge?

4. How do you think Las Casas might have responded to Ignatius's advice to Jesuit missionaries in Portugal? What does this suggest about the role of Catholic Christianity in European colonization?

CHAPTER 15

Wars of Religion and Clash of Worldviews
1560–1648

For kings, nobles, and ordinary folk alike, the late sixteenth through mid-seventeenth centuries were a time of turmoil and change, as the following documents illustrate. Religious wars galvanized much of Europe during this period, fueled by both ecclesiastical and lay leaders' attempts to maintain the commonly held idea that political and social stability depended on religious conformity. With the escalation of violence, however, some people came to question — and in some cases openly criticize — conventional views about the basic order of governance. They argued successfully that peace would come only if state interests took precedence over religious ones (Documents 1 to 3). Some governments attempted to harness these changes to better understand and help their struggling populations (Document 4). Europeans' views of the earth and the heavens also expanded in response to the rise of new scientific methods and discoveries (Document 5), while, at the same time, the lure of traditional beliefs remained strong within communities struggling to make sense of the upheavals occurring around them (Document 6).

1. Legislating Tolerance
Henry IV, *Edict of Nantes* (1598)

The promulgation of the Edict of Nantes in 1598 by King Henry IV (r. 1589–1610) marked the end of the French Wars of Religion by recognizing French Protestants as a legally protected religious minority. Drawing largely on earlier edicts of pacification, the Edict of Nantes was composed of ninety-two general articles, fifty-six secret articles, and two royal warrants. The two series of articles represented the edict proper and were registered by the highest courts of law in the realm (parlements). The following excerpts from the general

Modernized English text adapted from Edmund Everard, *The Great Pressures and Grievances of the Protestants in France* (London, 1681), 1–5, 10, 14, 16.

articles reveal the triumph of political concerns over religious conformity on the one hand and the limitations of religious tolerance in early modern France on the other.

Henry, by the grace of God, King of France, and Navarre, to all present, and to come, greeting. Among the infinite mercies that it has pleased God to bestow upon us, that most signal and remarkable is, his having given us power and strength not to yield to the dreadful troubles, confusions, and disorders, which were found at our coming to this kingdom, divided into so many parties and factions, that the most legitimate was almost the least, enabling us with constancy in such manner to oppose the storm, as in the end to surmount it, now reaching a part of safety and repose for this state. . . . For the general difference among our good subjects, and the particular evils of the soundest parts of the state, we judged might be easily cured, after the principal cause (the continuation of civil war) was taken away. In which having, by the blessing of God, well and happily succeeded, all hostility and wars through the kingdom being now ceased, we hope that we will succeed equally well in other matters remaining to be settled, and that by this means we shall arrive at the establishment of a good peace, with tranquility and rest. . . . Among our said affairs . . . one of the principal has been the complaints we have received from many of our Catholic provinces and cities, that the exercise of the Catholic religion was not universally re-established, as is provided by edicts or statutes heretofore made for the pacification of the troubles arising from religion; as well as the supplications and remonstrances which have been made to us by our subjects of the Reformed religion, regarding both the non-fulfillment of what has been granted by the said former laws, and that which they desired to be added for the exercise of their religion, the liberty of their consciences and the security of their persons and fortunes; presuming to have just reasons for desiring some enlargement of articles, as not being without great apprehensions, because their ruin has been the principal pretext and original foundation of the late wars, troubles, and commotions. Now not to burden us with too much business at once, as also that the fury of war was not compatible with the establishment of laws, however good they might be, we have hitherto deferred from time to time giving remedy herein. But now that it has pleased God to give us a beginning of enjoying some rest, we think we cannot employ ourself better than to apply to that which may tend to the glory and service of His holy name, and to provide that He may be adored and prayed unto by all our subjects: and if it has not yet pleased Him to permit it to be in one and the same form of religion, that it may at the least be with one and the same intention, and with such rules that may prevent among them all troubles and tumults. . . . For this cause, we have upon the whole judged it necessary to give to all our said subjects one general law, clear, pure, and absolute, by which they shall be regulated in all differences which have heretofore risen among them, or may hereafter rise, wherewith the one and other may be contented, being framed according as the time requires: and having had no other regard in this deliberation than solely the zeal we have to the service of God, praying that He would from this time forward render to all our subjects a durable and established peace. . . . We have by this edict or statute perpetual and irrevocable said, declared, and ordained, saying, declaring, and ordaining;

That the memory of all things passed on the one part and the other, since the beginning of the month of March 1585 until our coming to the crown, and also during the other preceding troubles, and the occasion of the same, shall remain extinguished and suppressed, as things that had never been. . . .

We prohibit to all our subjects of whatever state and condition they be, to renew the memory thereof, to attack, resent, injure, or provoke one another by reproaches for what is past, under any pretext or cause whatsoever, by disputing, contesting, quarrelling, reviling, or offending by factious words; but to contain themselves, and live peaceably together as brethren, friends, and fellow-citizens, upon penalty for acting to the contrary, to be punished for breakers of peace, and disturbers of the public quiet.

We ordain, that the Catholic religion shall be restored and re-established in all places, and quarters of this kingdom and country under our obedience, and where the exercise of the same has been interrupted, to be there again, peaceably and freely exercised without any trouble or impediment. . . .

And not to leave any occasion of trouble and difference among our subjects, we have permitted and do permit to those of the Reformed religion, to live and dwell in all the cities and places of this our kingdom and countries under our obedience, without being inquired after, vexed, molested, or compelled to do any thing in religion, contrary to their conscience. . . .

We permit also to those of the said religion to hold, and continue the exercise of the same in all the cities and places under our obedience, where it was by them established and made public at several different times, in the year 1586, and in 1597.

In like manner the said exercise may be established, and re-established in all the cities and places where it has been established or ought to be by the Statute of Pacification, made in the year 1577 . . .

We prohibit most expressly to all those of the said religion, to hold any exercise of it . . . except in places permitted and granted in the present edict. As also not to exercise the said religion in our court, nor in our territories and countries beyond the mountains, nor in our city of Paris, nor within five leagues of the said city. . . .

We prohibit all preachers, readers, and others who speak in public, to use any words, discourse, or propositions tending to excite the people to sedition; and we enjoin them to contain and comport themselves modestly, and to say nothing which shall not be for the instruction and edification of the listeners, and maintaining the peace and tranquility established by us in our said kingdom. . . .

They [French Protestants] shall also be obliged to keep and observe the festivals of the Catholic Church, and shall not on the same days work, sell, or keep open shop, nor likewise the artisans shall not work out of their shops, in their chambers or houses privately on the said festivals, and other days forbidden, of any trade, the noise whereof may be heard outside by those that pass by, or by the neighbors. . . .

We ordain, that there shall not be made any difference or distinction upon the account of the said religion, in receiving scholars to be instructed in the universities, colleges, or schools, nor of the sick or poor into hospitals, sick houses or public almshouses. . . .

We will and ordain, that all those of the Reformed religion, and others who have followed their party, of whatever state, quality or condition they be, shall be obliged and constrained by all due and reasonable ways, and under the penalties contained in the said edict or statute relating thereunto, to pay tithes to the curates, and other ecclesiastics, and to all others to whom they shall appertain. . . .

To the end to re-unite so much the better the minds and good will of our subjects, as is our intention, and to take away all complaints for the future; we declare all those who make or shall make profession of the said Reformed religion, to be capable of holding and exercising all estates, dignities, offices, and public charges whatsoever. . . .

We declare all sentences, judgments, procedures, seizures, sales, and decrees made and given against those of the Reformed religion, as well living as dead, from the death of the deceased King Henry the Second our most honored Lord and father in law, upon the occasion of the said religion, tumults and troubles since happening, as also the execution of the same judgments and decrees, from henceforward canceled, revoked, and annulled. . . .

Those also of the said religion shall depart and desist henceforward from all practices, negotiations, and intelligences, as well within or without our kingdom; and the said assemblies and councils established within the provinces, shall readily separate, and also all the leagues and associations made or to be made under any pretext, to the prejudice of our present edict, shall be cancelled and annulled, . . . prohibiting most expressly to all our subjects to make henceforth any assessments or levies of money, fortifications, enrollments of men, congregations and assemblies of other than such as are permitted by our present edict, and without arms. . . .

We give in command to the people of our said courts of parlement, chambers of our courts, and courts of our aids, bailiffs, chief-justices, provosts and other of our justices and officers to whom it appertains, and to their lieutenants, that they cause to be read, published, and registered this present edict and ordinance in their courts and jurisdictions, and the same keep punctually, and the contents of the same to cause to be enjoined and used fully and peaceably to all those to whom it shall belong, ceasing and making to cease all troubles and obstructions to the contrary, for such is our pleasure: and in witness hereof we have signed these presents with our own hand; and to the end to make it a thing firm and stable for ever, we have caused to put and endorse our seal to the same. Given at *Nantes* in the month of April in the year of Grace 1598, and of our reign the ninth.

Signed

HENRY

DISCUSSION QUESTIONS

1. What are the edict's principal objectives?

2. In what ways does the edict balance the demands of both French Catholics and Protestants?

3. What limits does the edict place on Protestants' religious rights?

4. Did Henry IV regard this edict as a permanent solution to the religious divisions in the realm? Why or why not?

4. Codifying Poverty

City of Norwich, *Poor Rolls* (1570)

During this time of religious warfare and social strife, a combination of population growth and monetary inflation further added to the sufferings of everyday people. In the second half of the sixteenth century, England's population alone grew by 70 percent. Coupled with rising food prices and a weak economy, the number of impoverished people skyrocketed. King Henry VIII's break from the Catholic Church and establishment of the Church of England meant the end of traditional sources of Catholic charity. During the reign of Elizabeth I (r. 1558–1603), both Parliament and local communities stepped in to fill the void, working to codify and centralize poor relief in new ways. With a population of approximately ten thousand, the city of Norwich was a pioneer on this front. In 1570, city leaders conducted a detailed census of the poor in order to determine the scope of poverty in the city as well as who was receiving relief at the time. The resulting document included hundreds of entries, encompassing close to three thousand local men, women, and children. The excerpts below are typical of the document as a whole. Census takers categorized the poor based on their place of residence, age, gender, and ability and/or willingness to work. As part of a broader trend of codifying the poor, the census divides the poor into three distinct groups: people worthy of alms because they were unable to work due to age or infirmity, people who allegedly could work but chose not to do so ("indifferent"), and the working poor. Although the results of the census prompted the city to double the number of people receiving aid, many were left to fend for themselves, a struggle that captures the difficulties faced by everyday people during a time of great change.

These be the names of the poor within the said City [of Norwich in the parish of St. Peter's of Southgate] as they were viewed in the year of our Lord God 1570.

Richard Rich of the age of 35 years, a husbandman who works with Mrs. Cantrell and does not stay with his wife (except at times) and helps her little. And Margaret his wife of the age of 40 years she spins white warp [wool yarn] and Joan her daughter, of the age of 12 years, that also spins the same. And Simon her son of the age of 8 years who goes to school. And Alice and Faith the eldest of the age of 8 years and the other of the age of 3 years, and have dwelt here 2 years since Whitsuntide. . . .

No alms and very poor. Able to work. To go away.

Peter Browne (porter) a cobbler of the age of 50 years and has little work. And Agnes his wife of the age of 52 years that does not work, but has been sick since Christmas but when in good health she spins white warp having three daughters, the one of the age of 18 years, and the other of the age of 14 years, and the other of the age of 13 years, who all spin when they can get it, but now they are without work: they have dwelt here these 20 years, and they have one daughter Elizabeth who is idle and sent from service with William Naught of Thorp, where she dwelt three quarters of a year.

4 pennies a week and very poor. Able to work.

Modernized English text adapted from E. M. Leonard, *The Early History of English Poor Relief* (Cambridge: Cambridge University Press, 1900), 308–10.

Rafe Claxton, boot wright, is abroad at work, and comfort his wife to his power, and is of the age of 43 years, and Anne his wife that is of the age of 27 years, and two sons; the eldest of the age of 4 years; she [the wife] spins white warp and he has dwelt here ever and now she is pregnant. . . .	4 pennies a week. Indifferent.
Thomas Matheu laborer, who is gone from his wife being of the age of 40 years, from whom she has no help, and Margaret his wife of the age of 32 years, and has no children, she spins white warp, and has dwelt here (ever) and knows not where her husband is.	No alms. Very poor.
William Brydges of the age of 40 years (a laborer) and Joan his wife, of the age of 23 years, she spins white warp, having one son and one daughter: the eldest of the age of 8 years, and they keep together and have dwelt here eight years.	No alms. Very poor. Able to work.
Also there is Thomas Gared and his wife but they live by their labor.	Indifferent.
Thomas Wylson, of the age of 30 years a basket maker, and Katherine his wife of the age of 25 years who makes buttons having two daughters the eldest of the age of 5 years, they have dwelt here ever.	Indifferent. No alms.
Myhell Coke, of the age of 40 years a laborer and his wife, of the age of 50 years, they live together, and have dwelt here about three years.	Indifferent. No alms.
Nycholas Fyld of the age of 30 years sometimes a painter, and Rose his wife of the age of 30 years who spins white warp having two sons, the eldest of the age of 6 years, and have dwelt there ever.	Very poor. No alms.

DISCUSSION QUESTIONS

1. What details do each of these entries have in common? What does this suggest about broader efforts to codify poor relief at the time?

2. Based on these excerpts, what factors do you think contributed to rising poverty rates in England?

3. What kind of work did the people included in the census do, and what does this reveal about the English economy in the late sixteenth century?

4. What does the census suggest about the family structure among the poor at the time?

5. The Scientific Challenge

Galileo, *Letter to the Grand Duchess Christina* (1615)

Italian born and educated, Galileo Galilei (1564–1642) was among the most illustrious proponents of the new science in the seventeenth century. Early in his studies, he embraced the theory held by Nicolaus Copernicus (1473–1543) that the sun, not the Earth, was at the center of the universe. Having improved on the newly invented telescope in 1609, Galileo was able to substantiate the heliocentric view that the earth revolved around the sun through

From *Discoveries and Opinions of Galileo*, trans. Stillman Drake (New York: Doubleday, 1957), 175–86.

his observations of the moon and planets. Because Galileo's work challenged both traditional scientific and religious views, it sparked considerable controversy. In the letter excerpted here, written in 1615 to Grand Duchess Christina of Tuscany, an important Catholic patron of learning, Galileo defends the validity of his findings while striving to separate matters of religious faith from the study of natural phenomena.

Galileo Galilei to The Most Serene Grand Duchess Mother

Some years ago, as Your Serene Highness well knows, I discovered in the heavens many things that had not been seen before our own age. The novelty of these things, as well as some consequences which followed from them in contradiction to the physical notions commonly held among academic philosophers, stirred up against me no small number of professors — as if I had placed these things in the sky with my own hands in order to upset nature and overturn the sciences. . . .

Well, the passage of time has revealed to everyone the truths that I previously set forth. . . . But some, besides allegiance to their original error, possess I know not what fanciful interest in remaining hostile not so much toward the things in question as toward their discoverer. No longer being able to deny them, these men now take refuge in obstinate silence, but being more than ever exasperated by that which has pacified and quieted other men, they divert their thoughts to other fancies and seek new ways to damage me. . . .

Persisting in their original resolve to destroy me and everything mine by any means they can think of, these men are aware of my views in astronomy and philosophy. They know that as to the arrangement of the parts of the universe, I hold the sun to be situated motionless in the center of the revolution of the celestial orbs while the earth rotates on its axis and revolves about the sun. . . .

Now as to the false aspersions which they so unjustly seek to cast upon me, I have thought it necessary to justify myself in the eyes of all men, whose judgment in matters of religion and of reputation I must hold in great esteem. I shall therefore discourse of the particulars which these men produce to make this opinion detested and to have it condemned not merely as false but as heretical. To this end they make a shield of their hypocritical zeal for religion. They go about invoking the Bible, which they would have minister to their deceitful purposes. Contrary to the sense of the Bible and the intention of the holy Fathers, if I am not mistaken, they would extend such authorities until even in purely physical matters — where faith is not involved — they would have us altogether abandon reason and the evidence of our senses in favor of some biblical passage, though under the surface meaning of its words this passage may contain a different sense. . . .

The reason produced for condemning the opinion that the earth moves and the sun stands still is that in many places in the Bible one may read that the sun moves and the earth stands still. Since the Bible cannot err, it follows as a necessary consequence that anyone takes an erroneous and heretical position who maintains that the sun is inherently motionless and the earth movable.

With regard to this argument, I think in the first place that it is very pious to say and prudent to affirm that the holy Bible can never speak untruth — whenever its true meaning is understood. But I believe nobody will deny that it is often very abstruse, and may say things which are quite different from what its bare words signify. Hence in expounding the Bible if one were always to confine oneself to the unadorned grammatical meaning, one might fall into error. Not only contradictions and propositions far from true might thus be made to appear in the Bible, but even grave heresies and follies. Thus it would be necessary to assign to God feet, hands, and eyes, as well as corporeal and human affections, such as anger, repentance, hatred, and sometimes even the forgetting of things past and ignorance of those to come. These propositions uttered by the Holy Ghost were set down in that manner by the sacred scribes in order to accommodate them to the capacities of the common people, who are rude and unlearned. For the sake of those who deserve to be separated from the herd, it is necessary that wise expositors should produce the true senses of such passages, together with the special reasons for which they were set down in these words. This doctrine is so widespread and so definite with all theologians that it would be superfluous to adduce evidence for it.

Hence I think that I may reasonably conclude that whenever the Bible has occasion to speak of any physical conclusion (especially those which are very abstruse and hard to understand), the rule has been observed of avoiding confusion in the minds of the common people which would render them contumacious toward the higher mysteries. Now the Bible, merely to condescend to popular capacity, has not hesitated to obscure some very important pronouncements, attributing to God himself some qualities extremely remote from (and even contrary to) His essence. Who, then, would positively declare that this principle has been set aside, and the Bible has confined itself rigorously to the bare and restricted sense of its words, when speaking but casually of the earth, of water, of the sun, or of any other created thing? Especially in view of the fact that these things in no way concern the primary purpose of the sacred writings, which is the service of God and the salvation of souls — matters infinitely beyond the comprehension of the common people.

This being granted, I think that in discussions of physical problems we ought to begin not from the authority of scriptural passages, but from sense-experiences and necessary demonstrations; for the holy Bible and the phenomena of nature proceed alike from the divine Word, the former as the dictate of the Holy Ghost and the latter as the observant executrix of God's commands. It is necessary for the Bible, in order to be accommodated to the understanding of every man, to speak many things which appear to differ from the absolute truth so far as the bare meaning of the words is concerned. But Nature, on the other hand, is inexorable and immutable; she never transgresses the laws imposed upon her, or cares a whit whether her abstruse reasons and methods of operations are understandable to men. For that reason it appears that nothing physical which sense-experience sets before our eyes, or which necessary demonstrations prove to us, ought to be called in question (much less condemned) upon the testimony of biblical passages which may have some different meaning beneath their words. For the Bible is not chained in every expression to conditions as strict as those which govern all physical effects; nor is God any less excellently revealed in Nature's actions than in the sacred statements of the Bible. . . .

From this I do not mean to infer that we need not have an extraordinary esteem for the passages of holy Scripture. On the contrary, having arrived at any certainties in physics, we ought to utilize these as the most appropriate aids in the true exposition of the

Bible and in the investigation of those meanings which are necessarily contained therein, for these must be concordant with demonstrated truths. I should judge that the authority of the Bible was designed to persuade men of those articles and propositions which, surpassing all human reasoning, could not be made credible by science, or by any other means than through the very mouth of the Holy Spirit.

Yet even in those propositions which are not matters of faith, this authority ought to be preferred over that of all human writings which are supported only by bare assertions or probable arguments, and not set forth in a demonstrative way. This I hold to be necessary and proper to the same extent that divine wisdom surpasses all human judgment and conjecture.

But I do not feel obliged to believe that that same God who has endowed us with senses, reason, and intellect has intended to forego their use and by some other means to give us knowledge which we can attain by them. He would not require us to deny sense and reason in physical matters which are set before our eyes and minds by direct experience or necessary demonstrations. This must be especially true in those sciences of which but the faintest trace (and that consisting of conclusions) is to be found in the Bible. Of astronomy, for instance, so little is found that none of the planets except Venus are so much as mentioned, and this only once or twice under the name of "Lucifer." If the sacred scribes had had any intention of teaching people certain arrangements and motions of the heavenly bodies, or had they wished us to derive such knowledge from the Bible, then in my opinion they would not have spoken of these matters so sparingly in comparison with the infinite number of admirable conclusions which are demonstrated in that science. . . .

From these things it follows as a necessary consequence that, since the Holy Ghost did not intend to teach us whether heaven moves or stands still, whether its shape is spherical or like a discus or extended in a plane, nor whether the earth is located at its center or off to one side, then so much the less was it intended to settle for us any other conclusion of the same kind. And the motion or rest of the earth and the sun is so closely linked with the things just named, that without a determination of the one, neither side can be taken in the other matters. Now if the Holy Spirit has purposely neglected to teach us propositions of this sort as irrelevant to the highest goal (that is, to our salvation), how can anyone affirm that it is obligatory to take sides on them, and that one belief is required by faith, while the other side is erroneous? Can an opinion be heretical and yet have no concern with the salvation of souls? Can the Holy Ghost be asserted not to have intended teaching us something that does concern our salvation? I would say here something that was heard from an ecclesiastic of the most eminent degree: "That the intention of the Holy Ghost is to teach us how one goes to heaven, not how heaven goes." . . .

From this it is seen that the interpretation which we impose upon passages of Scripture would be false whenever it disagreed with demonstrated truths. And therefore we should seek the incontrovertible sense of the Bible with the assistance of demonstrated truth, and not in any way try to force the hand of Nature or deny experiences and rigorous proofs in accordance with the mere sound of words that may appeal to our frailty. . . .

To that end they would forbid him the use of reason, divine gift of Providence, and would abuse the just authority of holy Scripture — which, in the general opinion of theologians, can never oppose manifest experiences and necessary demonstrations when rightly understood and applied. If I am correct, it will stand them in no stead to go running to the Bible to cover up their inability to understand (let alone resolve) their opponents' arguments.

DISCUSSION QUESTIONS

1. What do you think was Galileo's goal in writing this letter to the grand duchess?

2. What is the basis of the attacks against Galileo by his critics?

3. According to Galileo, what role should the Bible play in scientific inquiry?

4. How does this document lend support to historians who have credited Galileo for helping to popularize the principles and methods of the new science?

6. The Persecution of Witches

SOURCES IN CONVERSATION | *The Witch of Newbury* (1643) and *The Trial of Suzanne Gaudry* (1652)

Even as the new science gained support, most Europeans continued to believe in the supernatural. This belief found violent expression in a wave of witchcraft persecutions across Europe between 1560 and 1640. Older, poorer women often living on the margins of society were typical targets, and they were subjected to both formal trials and summary executions as these documents attest. The first is the cover page of a pamphlet published in England in 1643 about an event that became notorious at the time. With the English civil war in full swing, a group of parliamentary forces passing through the town of Newbury spotted a woman walking in a river with a plank. From their vantage point, she appeared to be dancing on the water's surface with no aid, a sure sign she was under the devil's influence, symbolized here by the two ravens hovering above. After she came to shore, the soldiers brought her to their commanders. When they asked her who she was and she refused to answer, they decided to execute her on the spot. The selections from the trial records of Suzanne Gaudry included below likewise attest to the predominant notion that the witches were not only agents of the devil but also most likely to be women. Although both sources originated at a time when the number of witch hunts and persecutions were in decline, they highlight the persistence of a deeply felt fear among many people regarding the presence of diabolical forces in everyday life.

From Alan C. Kors and Edward Peters, eds., *Witchcraft in Europe, 1100–1700: A Documentary History* (Philadelphia: University of Pennsylvania Press, 1972), 266–75.

Private Collection / Bridgeman Images

At Ronchain, 28 May, 1652. . . . Interrogation of Suzanne Gaudry, prisoner at the court of Rieux. Questioned about her age, her place of origin, her mother and father.

— Said that she is named Suzanne Gaudry, daughter of Jean Gaudry and Marguerite Gerné, both natives of Rieux, but that she is from Esgavans, near Odenarde, where her family had taken refuge because of the wars, that she was born the day that they made bonfires for the Peace between France and Spain, without being able otherwise to say her age.

Asked why she has been taken here.

— Answers that it is for the salvation of her soul.

— Says that she was frightened of being taken prisoner for the crime of witchcraft.

Asked for how long she has been in the service of the devil.

— Says that about twenty-five or twenty-six years ago she was his lover, that he called himself Petit-Grignon, that he would wear black breeches, that he gave her the name Magin, that she gave him a pin with which he gave her his mark on the left shoulder, that he had a little flat hat; said also that he had his way with her two or three times only.

Asked how many times she has been at the nocturnal dance.

— Answers that she has been there about a dozen times, having first of all renounced God, Lent, and baptism; that the site of the dance was at the little marsh of Rieux, understanding that there were diverse dances. The first time, she did not recognize anyone there, because she was half blind. The other times, she saw and recognized there Noelle and Pasquette Gerné, Noelle the wife of Nochin Quinchou and the other of Paul Doris, the widow Marie Nourette, not having recognized others because the young people went with the young people and the old people with the old. [. . .]

Interrogated on how and in what way they danced.

— Says that they dance in an ordinary way, that there was a guitarist and some whistlers who appeared to be men she did not know; which lasted about an hour, and then everyone collapsed from exhaustion.

Inquired what happened after the dance.

— Says that they formed a circle, that there was a king with a long black beard dressed in black, with a red hat, who made everyone do his bidding, and that after the dance he made a . . . [the word is missing in the text], and then everyone disappeared. . . .

Questioned if she has abused the Holy Communion.

— Says no, never, and that she has always swallowed it. Then says that her lover asked her for it several times, but that she did not want to give it to him.

After several admonitions were sent to her, she has signed this

Mark

X

Suzanne Gaudry

Second Interrogation, May 29, 1652, in the Presence of the Afore-Mentioned

This prisoner, being brought back into the chamber, was informed about the facts and the charges and asked if what she declared and confessed yesterday is true.

— Answers that if it is in order to put her in prison it is not true; then after having remained silent said that it is true.

Asked what is her lover's name and what name has he given himself.

— Said that his name is Grinniou and that he calls himself Magnin.

Asked where he found her the first time and what he did to her.

— Answers that it was in her lodgings, that he had a hide, little black breeches, and a little flat hat; that he asked her for a pin, which she gave to him, with which he made his mark on her left shoulder. Said also that at the time she took him oil in a bottle and that she had thoughts of love.

Asked how long she has been in subjugation to the devil.

— Says that it has been about twenty-five or twenty-six years, that her lover also then made her renounce God, Lent, and baptism, that he has known her carnally three or four times, and that he has given her satisfaction. And on the subject of his having asked her if she wasn't afraid of having a baby, says that she did not have that thought.

Asked how many times she found herself at the nocturnal dance and carol and who she recognized there.

— Answers that she was there eleven or twelve times, that she went there on foot with her lover, where the third time she saw and recognized Pasquette and Noelle Gerné, and Marie Homitte, to whom she never spoke, for the reason that they did not speak to each other. And that the sabbat took place at the little meadow. . . .

Asked what occurred at the dance and afterwards.

— Says that right after the dance they put themselves in order and approached the chief figure, who had a long black beard, dressed also in black, with a red hat, at which point they were given some powder, to do with it what they wanted; but that she did not want to take any.

Charged with having taken some and with having used it evilly.

— Says, after having insisted that she did not want to take any, that she took some, and that her lover advised her to do evil with it; but that she did not want to do it.

Asked if, not obeying his orders, she was beaten or threatened by him, and what did she do with this powder.

— Answers that never was she beaten; she invoked the name of the Virgin [and answered] that she threw away the powder that she had, not having wanted to do any evil with it.

Pressed to say what she did with this powder. Did she not fear her lover too much to have thrown it away?

— Says, after having been pressed on this question, that she made the herbs in her garden die at the end of the summer, five to six years ago, by means of the powder, which she threw there because she did not know what to do with it. [. . .]

Charged once more with having performed some malefice with this powder, pressed to tell the truth.

— Answers that she never made any person or beast die; then later said that she made Philippe Cornié's red horse die, about two or three years ago, by means of the powder, which she placed where he had to pass, in the street close to her home.

Asked why she did that and if she had had any difficulty with him.

— Says that she had had some difficulty with his wife, because her cow had eaten the leeks. [. . .]

After having been admonished to think of her conscience, was returned to prison after having signed this

Mark

X

Suzanne Gaudry

Deliberation of the Court of Mons — June 3, 1652

The under-signed advocates of the Court of Mons have seen these interrogations and answers. They say that the aforementioned Suzanne Gaudry confesses that she is a witch, that she has given herself to the devil, that she has renounced God, Lent, and baptism, that she has been marked on the shoulder, that she has cohabited with him and that she has been to the dances, confessing only to have cast a spell upon and caused to die a beast of Philippe Cornié; but there is no evidence for this, excepting a prior statement. For this reason, before going further, it will be necessary to become acquainted with, to examine and to probe the mark, and to hear Philippe Cornié on the death of the horse and on when and in what way he died. . . .

Deliberation of the Court of Mons — June 13, 1652

[The Court] has reviewed the current criminal trial of Suzanne Gaudry, and with it the trial of Antoinette Lescouffre, also a prisoner of the same office.

It appeared [to the Court] that the office should have the places probed where the prisoners say that they have received the mark of the devil, and after that, they must be interrogated and examined seriously on their confessions and denials, this having to be done, in order to regulate all this definitively. . . .

Deliberation of the Court of Mons — June 22, 1652

The trials of Antoinette Lescouffre and Suzanne Gaudry having been described to the undersigned, advocates of the Court of Mons, and [the Court] having been told orally that the peasants taking them to prison had persuaded them to confess in order to avoid imprisonment, and that they would be let go, by virtue of which it could appear that the confessions were not so spontaneous:

They are of the opinion that the office, in its duty, would do well, following the two preceding resolutions, to have the places of the marks that they have taught us about probed, and if it is found that these are ordinary marks of the devil, one can proceed to their examination; then next to the first confessions, and if they deny [these], one can proceed to the torture, given that they issue from bewitched relatives, that at all times they have been suspect, that they fled to avoid the crime [that is to say, prosecution for the crime of witchcraft], and that by their confessions they have confirmed [their guilt], notwithstanding that they have wanted to revoke [their confessions] and vacillate. . . .

Third Interrogation, June 27, in the Presence of the Afore-Mentioned

This prisoner being led into the chamber, she was examined to know if things were not as she had said and confessed at the beginning of her imprisonment.

— Answers no, and that what she has said was done so by force.

Asked if she did not say to Jean Gradé that she would tell his uncle, the mayor, that he had better be careful . . . and that he was a Frank.

— Said that that is not true.

Pressed to say the truth, that otherwise she would be subjected to torture, having pointed out to her that her aunt was burned for this same subject.

— Answers that she is not a witch.

Interrogated as to how long she has been in subjection to the devil, and pressed that she was to renounce the devil and the one who misled her.

— Says that she is not a witch, that she has nothing to do with the devil thus that she did not want to renounce the devil, saying that he has not misled her, and upon inquisition of having confessed to being present at the carol, she insisted that although she had said that, it is not true, and that she is not a witch.

Charged with having confessed to having made a horse die by means of a powder that the devil had given her.

— Answers that she said it, but because she found herself during the inquisition pressed to say that she must have done some evil deed; and after several admonitions to tell the truth:

She was placed in the hands of the officer of the *haultes oeuvres* [the officer in charge of torture], throwing herself on her knees, struggling to cry, uttering several exclamations, without being able, nevertheless, she shed a tear. Saying at every moment that she is not a witch.

The Torture

On this same day, being at the place of torture.

This prisoner, before being strapped down, was admonished to maintain herself in her first confessions and to renounce her lover.

— Said that she denies everything she has said, and that she has no lover. Feeling herself being strapped down, says that she is not a witch, while struggling to cry.

Asked why she fled outside the village of Rieux.

— Says that she cannot say it, that God and the Virgin Mary forbid her to; that she is not a witch. And upon being asked why she confessed to being one, said that she was forced to say it.

Told that she was not forced, that on the contrary she declared herself to be a witch without any threat.

— Says that she confessed it and that she is not a witch, and being a little stretched [on the rack] screams ceaselessly that she is not a witch, invoking the name of Jesus and of Our Lady of Grace, not wanting to say any other thing.

Asked if she did not confess that she had been a witch for twenty-six years.

— Says that she said it, that she retracts it, crying Jésus-Maria, that she is not a witch.

Asked if she did not make Philippe Cornié's horse die, as she confessed.

— Answers no, crying Jésus-Maria, that she is not a witch.

The mark having been probed by the officer, in the presence of Doctor Bouchain, it was adjudged by the aforesaid doctor and officer truly to be the mark of the devil.

Being more tightly stretched upon the torture-rack, urged to maintain her confessions.

— Said that it was true that she is a witch and that she would maintain what she had said.

Asked how long she has been in subjugation to the devil.

— Answers that it was twenty years ago that the devil appeared to her, being in her lodgings in the form of a man dressed in a little cow-hide and black breeches.

Interrogated as to what her lover was called.

— Says that she said Petit-Grignon, then, being taken down [from the rack] says upon interrogation that she is not a witch and that she can say nothing.

Asked if her lover has had carnal copulation with her, and how many times.

— To that she did not answer anything; then, making believe that she was ill, not another word could be drawn from her.

As soon as she began to confess, she asked who was alongside of her, touching her, yet none of those present could see anyone there. And it was noticed that as soon as that was said, she no longer wanted to confess anything.

Which is why she was returned to prison.

Verdict

July 9, 1652   In the light of the interrogations, answers and investigations made into the charge against Suzanne Gaudry, coupled with her confessions, from which it would appear that she has always been ill-reputed for being stained with the crime of witchcraft, and seeing that she took flight and sought refuge in this city of Valenciennes, out of fear of being apprehended by the law for this matter; seeing how her close family were also stained with the same crime, and the perpetrators executed; seeing by her own confessions that she is said to have made a pact with the devil, received the mark from him, which in the report of *sieur* Michel de Roux was judged by the medical doctor of Ronchain and the officer of *haultes oeuvres* of Cambrai, after having proved it, to be not a natural mark but a mark of the devil, to which they have sworn with an oath; and that following this, she had renounced God, Lent, and baptism and had let herself be known carnally by him, in which she received satisfaction. Also, seeing that she is said to have been a part of nocturnal carols and dances. Which are crimes of divine lèse-majesty:

For expiation of which the advice of the under-signed is that the office of Rieux can legitimately condemn the aforesaid Suzanne Gaudry to death, tying her to a gallows, and strangling her to death, then burning her body and burying it there in the environs of the woods.

At Valenciennes, the 9th of July, 1652. To each [member of the Court] 4 *livres*, 16 *sous*. . . . And for the trip of the aforementioned Roux, including an escort of one soldier, 30 *livres*.

DISCUSSION QUESTIONS

1. According to the trial record, why was Suzanne Gaudry targeted for persecution? What does this reveal about contemporary beliefs in witches and their powers?

2. How would you characterize the legal procedures used in this trial? How might the procedures help to explain the widespread consistency in the content of confessions throughout the period of witchcraft persecutions?

2. Regime Change

SOURCES IN CONVERSATION | *The Trial of Charles I* and *The Confession of Richard Brandon the Hangman* (1649)

The seventeenth century was particularly turbulent in England, where Protestants, Catholics, royalists, and parliamentary supporters vied for power. The English king Charles I (r. 1625–1649) had long chafed under Parliament's demands for participation in government. Adamant in his belief in his divine right to rule, Charles worked to strengthen his grip over Parliament, setting the stage for war. As the conflict spilled from the halls of government onto the battlefield in 1642, each side accused the other of undermining the ancient legal rights of the people and the legal balance between the king and the two houses of Parliament enshrined in the English constitution. Parliamentary forces ultimately defeated the king's army, and Charles surrendered in 1646. Three years later, he was brought before a parliamentary high court for trial on the charge of treason. Below are extracts from the first three days of the proceedings when the king and his opponents each laid the foundations of their case. The proceedings culminated in Charles's condemnation and a death sentence. He was beheaded on January 30, 1649, as a huge crowed looked on. Richard Brandon claimed to have been Charles's executioner and published a short tract the same year lamenting his role in the king's death. Although Brandon was the Common Hangman of London at the time, whether he beheaded Charles I is questionable; his identity would have been concealed on the scaffold, and his confession was published after his death. Even so, the woodcut print included on the tract's title page offers an important contemporaneous view of the scene. When set against the backdrop of the civil war, the trial and execution raised a host of enduring questions regarding the nature of political authority.

Having again placed himself in his Chair, with his face towards the Court, silence being again ordered, the Lord President stood up, and said,

LORD PRESIDENT: Charles Stuart, king of England, the Commons of England assembled in Parliament being deeply sensible of the calamities that have been brought upon this nation, which is fixed upon you as the principal author of it, have resolved to make inquisition for blood; and according to that debt and duty they owe to justice, to God, the kingdom, and themselves, and according to the fundamental power that rests in themselves, they have resolved to bring you to Trial and Judgment; and for that purpose have constituted this High Court of Justice, before which they are brought.

This said, Mr. Cook, Solicitor for the Commonwealth standing within a bar on the right hand of the Prisoner, offered to speak; but the king having a staff in his hand, held it up, and laid it on the said Mr. Cook's shoulder two or three times, bidding him hold. Nevertheless, the Lord President ordering him to go on, he said,

MR. COOK: My lord, I am commanded to charge Charles Stuart King of England, in the name of the Commons of England, with Treason and High Misdemeanors; I desire the said Charge may be read.

From *State Trials: Political and Social*, vol. I, ed. H. L. Stephen (London: Duckworth and Co., 1899), 78–87, 89, 91–94.

The said Charge being delivered to the Clerk of the Court, the Lord President ordered it should be read; but the king bid him hold. Nevertheless, being commanded by the Lord President to read it, the Clerk begun, and the Prisoner sat down again in his chair, looking sometimes on the High Court, sometimes up to the Galleries; and having risen again, and turned about to behold the guards and spectators, sat down, looking very sternly, and with a countenance not at all moved, till these words, viz.: — "Charles Stuart to be a Tyrant and Traitor," etc. were read; at which he laughed, as he sat, in the face of the Court.

The Charge being read, the Lord President replied;

LORD PRESIDENT: Sir, You have now heard your Charge, containing such matter as appears in it; you find, that in the close of it, it is prayed to the Court, in the behalf of the commons of England, that you answer to your Charge. The Court expects your Answer.

KING: . . . Remember I am your king, your lawful king, and what sins you bring upon your heads, and the judgment of God upon this land; think well upon it, I say, think well upon it, before you go further from one sin to a greater; therefore let me know by what lawful authority I am seated here, and I shall not be unwilling to answer. In the mean time, I shall not betray my trust; I have a trust committed to me by God, by old and lawful descent; I will not betray it, to answer to a new unlawful authority; therefore resolve me that and you shall hear more of me.

LORD PRESIDENT: If you had been pleased to have observed what was hinted to you by the Court, at your first coming hither, you would have known by what authority; which authority requires you, in the name of the people of England, of which you are elected king, to answer them.

KING: No. Sir, I deny that.

LORD PRESIDENT: If you acknowledge not the authority of the Court, they must proceed.

KING: I do tell them so; England was never an elective kingdom, but an hereditary kingdom, for near these thousand years; therefore let me know by what authority I am called hither. I do stand more for the Liberty of my people, than any here that come to be my pretended Judges; and therefore let me know by what lawful authority I am seated here, and I will answer it; otherwise I will not answer it. . . .

LORD PRESIDENT: The Court expects you should give them a final Answer; their purpose is to adjourn to Monday next; if you do not satisfy yourself, though we do tell you our authority, we are satisfied with our authority, and it is upon God's authority and the kingdom's; and that peace you speak of will be kept in the doing of justice, and that is our present work. . . .

At the High Court of Justice sitting in Westminster Hall, Monday, January 22, 1649. . . .

LORD PRESIDENT: Sir, You may remember at the last Court you were told the occasion of your being brought hither, and you heard a Charge read against you, containing a Charge of High Treason and other high crimes against this realm of England: you heard likewise, that it was prayed in the behalf of the People, that you should give an Answer to that Charge, that thereupon such proceedings might be had, as should be agreeable to justice. You were then pleased to make some scruples concerning the authority of this Court, and knew not by what authority you were brought hither; you did divers times propound your questions, and were as often answered. That it was by authority of the Commons of England assembled in parliament, that did think fit to call you to account for those high and capital Misdemeanours wherewith you were then charged. Since that the Court hath taken into consideration what you then said; they are fully satisfied with their own authority, and they hold it fit you should stand satisfied with it too; and they do require it, that you do give a positive and particular Answer to this Charge that is exhibited against you; they do expect you should either confess or deny it; if you deny, it is offered in the behalf of the kingdom to be made good against you; their authority they do avow to the whole world, that the whole kingdom are to rest satisfied in, and you are to rest satisfied with it. And therefore you are to lose no more time, but to give a positive Answer thereunto.

KING: When I was here last, it is very true, I made that question; truly if it were only my own particular case, I would have satisfied myself with the protestation I made the last time I was here against the Legality of this Court, and that a king cannot be tried by any superior jurisdiction on earth; but it is not my case alone, it is the Freedom and the Liberty of the people of England; and do you pretend what you will, I stand more for their Liberties. For if power without law may make laws, may alter the fundamental laws of the kingdom, I do not know what subject he is in England, that can be sure of his life, or any thing that he calls his own: therefore when that I came here, I did expect particular reasons to know by what law, what authority you did proceed against me here. And therefore I am a little to seek what to say to you in this particular, because the affirmative is to be proved, the negative often is very hard to do: but since I cannot persuade you to do it, I shall tell you my reasons as short as I can — My Reasons why in conscience and the duty I owe to God first, and my people next, for the preservation of their lives, liberties, and estates I conceive I cannot answer this, till I be satisfied of the legality of it. All proceedings against any man whatsoever —

LORD PRESIDENT: Sir, I must interrupt you, which I would not do, but that what you do is not agreeable to the proceedings of any court of justice: You are about to enter into argument, and dispute concerning the Authority of this Court, before whom you appear as a Prisoner, and are charged as an high Delinquent: if you take upon you to dispute the Authority of the Court, we may not do it, nor will any court give way unto it: you are to submit unto it, you are to give a punctual and direct Answer, whether you will answer your charge or no, and what your Answer is.

KING: Sir, By your favour, I do not know the forms of law: I do know law and reason, though I am no lawyer professed; but I know as much law as any gentleman in England; and therefore (under favour) I do plead for the Liberties of the People of England more than you do: and therefore if I should impose a belief upon any man, without reasons given for it, it were unreasonable: but I must tell you, that that reason that I have, as thus informed, I cannot yield unto it.

LORD PRESIDENT: Sir, I must interrupt you, you may not be permitted; you speak of law and reason; it is fit there should be law and reason, and there is both against you. Sir, the Vote of the Commons of England assembled in parliament, it is the reason of the kingdom, and they are these that have given to that law, according to which you should have ruled and reigned. Sir, you are not to dispute our Authority, you are told it again by the Court. Sir, it will be taken notice of, that you stand in contempt of the Court, and your contempt will be recorded accordingly. . . .

At the High Court of Justice sitting in Westminster Hall, Tuesday, January 23, 1649. . . .

LORD PRESIDENT: Sir, you have heard what is moved by the Counsel on the behalf of the kingdom against you. . . . You were told, over and over again, That the Court did affirm their own jurisdiction; that it was not for you, nor any other man, to dispute the jurisdiction of the supreme and highest Authority of England, from which there is no appeal, and touching which there must be no dispute; yet you did persist in such carriage, as you gave no manner of obedience, nor did you acknowledge any authority in them, nor the High Court that constituted this Court of Justice. Sir, I must let you know from the Court, that they are very sensible of these delays of yours, and that they ought not, being thus authorised by the supreme Court of England, to be thus trifled withal; and that they might in justice, if they pleased, and according to the rules of justice, take advantage of these delays and proceed to pronounce judgment against you; yet nevertheless they are pleased to give direction, and on their behalfs I do require you, that you make a positive Answer unto this Charge that is against you, Sir, in plain terms, for Justice knows no respect of persons; you are to give your positive and final Answer in plain English, whether you be Guilty or Not Guilty of these Treasons laid to your charge.

The King, after a little pause, said,

KING: When I was here yesterday, I did desire to speak for the Liberties of the people of England; I was interrupted, I desire to know yet whether I may speak freely or not.

LORD PRESIDENT: Sir, you have had the Resolution of the Court upon the like question the last day, and you were told that having such a Charge of so high a nature against you, and your work was, that you ought to acknowledge the jurisdiction of the Court, and to answer to your Charge. Sir, if you answer to your Charge, which the Court gives you leave now to do, though they might have taken the advantage of your contempt; yet if you be able to answer to your Charge, when you have once answered, you shall be heard at large, make the best defence you can. . . .

KING: For the Charge, I value it not a rush; it is the Liberty of the People of England that I stand for. For me to acknowledge a new Court that I never heard of before, I that am your King, that should be an example to all the people of England for to uphold justice, to maintain the old laws: indeed I do not know how to do it. You spoke very well the first day that I came here (on Saturday) of the obligations that I had laid upon me by God, to the maintenance of the Liberties of my people; the same obligation you spake of, I do acknowledge to God that I owe to him, and to my people, to defend as much as in me lies the ancient laws of the kingdom: therefore, until that I may know that this is not against the fundamental Laws of the kingdom, by your favour I can put in no particular Charge. If you will give me time, I will shew you my Reasons why I cannot do it, and this —

Here, being interrupted, he said,

By your favor, you ought not to interrupt me: How I came here, I know not; there's no law for it to make your king your prisoner. . . .

Here the Lord President said, Sir, you must know the pleasure of the Court.

KING: By your favour, sir.

LORD PRESIDENT: Nay, sir, by your favour, you may not be permitted to fall into those discourses; you appear as a Delinquent, you have not acknowledged the authority of the Court, the Court craves it not of you; but once more they command you to give your positive Answer. — Clerk, do your duty.

KING: Duty, Sir!

The Clerk reads.

"Charles Stuart, king of England, you are accused in behalf of the commons of England of divers Crimes and Treasons, which Charge hath been read unto you: the Court now requires you to give your positive and final Answer, by way of confession or denial of the Charge."

KING: Sir, I say again to you, so that I might give satisfaction to the people of England of the clearness of my proceeding, not by way of Answer, not in this way, but to satisfy them that I have done nothing against that trust that has been committed to me, I would do it; but to acknowledge a new Court, against their Privileges, to alter the fundamental laws of the kingdom — sir, you must excuse me.

LORD PRESIDENT: Sir, this is the third time that you have publicly disowned this Court, and put an affront upon it. How far you have preserved the privileges of the people, your actions have spoke it; but truly, Sir, men's intentions ought to be known by their actions; you have written your meaning in bloody characters throughout the whole kingdom. But, Sir, you understand the pleasure of the Court. — Clerk, Record the Default. — And, Gentlemen, you that took charge of the Prisoner, take him back again.

Universal History Archive / Universal Images Group / REX / Shutterstock

DISCUSSION QUESTIONS

1. According to the prosecution, why did Parliament have both a duty and a right to bring charges against the king?

2. What does the high court's argument suggest about its understanding of the role of Parliament in governance and its relationship to the monarchy?

3. In what way does the woodcut's depiction of the public nature of Charles's execution visually reinforce this understanding?

4. In his defense, why does the king refuse to acknowledge the court's authority to bring charges against him? In doing so, what did he reveal about his views on the basis of royal authority?

3. Civil War and Social Contract

Thomas Hobbes, *Leviathan* (1651)

Thomas Hobbes (1588–1679), an English philosopher with close aristocratic and royalist ties, viewed England's troubles as an indictment of traditional political thinking. According to Hobbes, in their natural state humans were violent and prone to war. Absolute authority was the only way to counter this threat to social order. Whether this authority rested in a king or a parliament was immaterial to Hobbes; what mattered was that it gained its power from a social contract, or "covenant," between ruler and ruled. Individuals agreed to relinquish their right to govern themselves to an absolute ruler in exchange for collective peace and defense. Hobbes published his views in 1651 in his book Leviathan, *most of which he wrote during the final stage of the English civil war while living in exile in France, where he was the tutor of the future king Charles II. The excerpt that follows speaks not only to Hobbes's understanding of human nature, absolute authority, and the social contract but also to the relationship among them.*

Of the Natural Condition of Mankind as Concerning Their Felicity and Misery

Nature hath made men so equal in the faculties of body and mind as that, though there be found one man sometimes manifestly stronger in body or of quicker mind than another, yet when all is reckoned together the difference between man and man is not so considerable as that one man can thereupon claim to himself any benefit to which another may not pretend as well as he.

From this equality of ability ariseth equality of hope in the attaining of our ends. And therefore if any two men desire the same thing, which nevertheless they cannot both enjoy, they become enemies; and in the way to their end (which is principally their own

From Thomas Hobbes, *Leviathan*, Renascence Editions, at www.luminarium.org/renascence-editions/hobbes/leviathan.html.

conservation, and sometimes their delectation only) endeavor to destroy or subdue one another. And from hence it comes to pass that where an invader hath no more to fear than another man's single power, if one plant, sow, build, or possess a convenient seat, others may probably be expected to come prepared with forces united to dispossess and deprive him, not only of the fruit of his labor, but also of his life or liberty. And the invader again is in the like danger of another. . . .

. . . [M]en have no pleasure (but on the contrary a great deal of grief) in keeping company where there is no power able to overawe them all. For every man looketh that his companion should value him at the same rate he sets upon himself, and upon all signs of contempt or undervaluing naturally endeavors, as far as he dares (which amongst them that have no common power to keep them in quiet is far enough to make them destroy each other), to extort a greater value from his contemners, by damage; and from others, by the example. So that in the nature of man, we find three principal causes of quarrel. First, competition; secondly, diffidence; thirdly, glory. The first maketh men invade for gain; the second, for safety; and the third, for reputation. The first use violence, to make themselves masters of other men's persons, wives, children, and cattle; the second, to defend them; the third, for trifles, as a word, a smile, a different opinion, and any other sign of undervalue, either direct in their persons or by reflection in their kindred, their friends, their nation, their profession, or their name. Hereby it is manifest that during the time men live without a common power to keep them all in awe, they are in that condition which is called war; and such a war as is of every man against every man. For war consisteth not in battle only, or the act of fighting, but in a tract of time, wherein the will to contend by battle is sufficiently known: and therefore the notion of time is to be considered in the nature of war, as it is in the nature of weather. For as the nature of foul weather lieth not in a shower or two of rain, but in an inclination thereto of many days together: so the nature of war consisteth not in actual fighting, but in the known disposition thereto during all the time there is no assurance to the contrary. All other time is peace.

Whatsoever therefore is consequent to a time of war, where every man is enemy to every man, the same consequent to the time wherein men live without other security than what their own strength and their own invention shall furnish them withal. In such condition there is no place for industry, because the fruit thereof is uncertain: and consequently no culture of the earth; no navigation, nor use of the commodities that may be imported by sea; no commodious building; no instruments of moving and removing such things as require much force; no knowledge of the face of the earth; no account of time; no arts; no letters; no society; and which is worst of all, continual fear, and danger of violent death; and the life of man, solitary, poor, nasty, brutish, and short. . . .

Of the Causes, Generation, and Definition of a Commonwealth

The final cause, end, or design of men (who naturally love liberty, and dominion over others) in the introduction of that restraint upon themselves, in which we see them live in Commonwealths, is the foresight of their own preservation, and of a more contented life thereby; that is to say, of getting themselves out from that miserable condition of war which is necessarily consequent, as hath been shown, to the natural passions of men when there is no visible power to keep them in awe, and tie them by fear of punishment to the performance of their covenants. . . .

The only way to erect such a common power, as may be able to defend them from the invasion of foreigners, and the injuries of one another, and thereby to secure them in such sort as that by their own industry and by the fruits of the earth they may nourish themselves and live contentedly, is to confer all their power and strength upon one man, or upon one assembly of men, that may reduce all their wills, by plurality of voices, unto one will: which is as much as to say, to appoint one man, or assembly of men, to bear their person; and every one to own and acknowledge himself to be author of whatsoever he that so beareth their person shall act, or cause to be acted, in those things which concern the common peace and safety; and therein to submit their wills, every one to his will, and their judgments to his judgment. This is more than consent, or concord; it is a real unity of them all in one and the same person, made by covenant of every man with every man, in such manner as if every man should say to every man: I authorize and give up my right of governing myself to this man, or to this assembly of men, on this condition; that thou give up, thy right to him, and authorize all his actions in like manner. This done, the multitude so united in one person is called a COMMONWEALTH; in Latin, CIVITAS. This is the generation of that great LEVIATHAN, or rather, to speak more reverently, of that mortal god to which we owe, under the immortal God, our peace and defense. For by this authority, given him by every particular man in the Commonwealth, he hath the use of so much power and strength conferred on him that, by terror thereof, he is enabled to form the wills of them all, to peace at home, and mutual aid against their enemies abroad. And in him consisteth the essence of the Commonwealth; which, to define it, is: one person, of whose acts a great multitude, by mutual covenants one with another, have made themselves every one the author, to the end he may use the strength and means of them all as he shall think expedient for their peace and common defense. . . .

Of the Rights of Sovereigns by Institution

A Commonwealth is said to be instituted when a multitude of men do agree, and covenant, every one with every one, that to whatsoever man, or assembly of men, shall be given by the major part the right to present the person of them all, that is to say, to be their representative; every one, as well he that voted for it as he that voted against it, shall authorize all the actions and judgments of that man, or assembly of men, in the same manner as if they were his own, to the end to live peaceably amongst themselves, and be protected against other men.

From this institution of a Commonwealth are derived all the rights and faculties of him, or them, on whom the sovereign power is conferred by the consent of the people assembled.

First, because they covenant, it is to be understood they are not obliged by former covenant to anything repugnant hereunto. And consequently they that have already instituted a Commonwealth, being thereby bound by covenant to own the actions and judgments of one, cannot lawfully make a new covenant amongst themselves to be obedient to any other, in anything whatsoever, without his permission. And therefore, they that are subjects to a monarch cannot without his leave cast off monarchy and return to the confusion of a disunited multitude; nor transfer their person from him that beareth it

I now wished for the last friend, death, to relieve me; but soon, to my grief, two of the white men offered me eatables; and on my refusing to eat, one of them held me fast by the hands, and laid me across, I think, the windlass, and tied my feet, while the other flogged me severely. I had never experienced anything of this kind before; and although not being used to the water, I naturally feared that element the first time I saw it, yet, nevertheless could I have got over the nettings, I would have jumped over the side, but I could not; and, besides, the crew used to watch us very closely who were not chained down to the decks, least we should leap into the water; and I have seen some of these poor African prisoners most severely cut for attempting to do so, and hourly whipped for not eating. This indeed was often the case with myself. In a little time after, amongst the poor chained men I found some of my own nation, which in a small degree gave ease to my mind; I inquired of these what was to be done with us? They gave me to understand we were to be carried to these white people's country to work for them. I then was a little revived, and thought if it were no worse than working, my situation was not so desperate: but still I feared I should be put to death, the white people looked and acted, as I thought, in so savage a manner; for I had never seen among my people such instances of brutal cruelty; and this not only shewn towards us blacks but also to some of the whites themselves. One white man in particular I saw, when we were permitted to be on deck, flogged so unmercifully with a large rope near the foremast that he died in consequence of it; and they tossed him over the side as they would have done a brute. This made me fear these people the more; and I expected nothing less than to be treated in the same manner. . . .

At last, when the ship we were in had got in all her cargo, they made ready with many fearful noises, and we were all put under deck so that we could not see how they managed the vessel. But this disappointment was the last of my sorrow. The stench of the hold, while we were on the coast, was so intolerably loathsome, that it was dangerous to remain there for any time, and some of us had been permitted to stay on the deck for the fresh air; but now that the whole ship's cargo were confined together, it became absolutely pestilential. The closeness of the place, and the heat of the climate, added to the number in the ship, which was so crowded, that each had scarcely room to turn himself, almost suffocated us. This produced copious perspirations, so that the air soon became unfit for respiration, from a variety of loathsome smells, and brought on a sickness among the slaves, of which many died, thus falling victims to the improvident avarice, as I may call it, of their purchasers. This deplorable situation was again aggravated by the galling of the chains, now become insupportable; and the filth of the necessary tubs, into which the children often fell, and were almost suffocated. The shrieks of the women, and the groans of the dying, rendered the whole a scene of horror almost inconceivable. Happily, perhaps, for myself, I was soon reduced so low here that it was thought necessary to keep me almost always on deck; and from my extreme youth, I was not put in fetters. In this situation I expected every hour to share the fate of my companions, some of whom were almost daily brought upon deck at the point of death, which I began to hope would soon put an end to my miseries. . . .

At last we came in sight of the island of Barbados, at which the whites on board gave a great shout, and made many signs of joy to us. We did not know what to think of this; but as the vessel drew nearer, we plainly saw the harbor and other ships of different kinds and sizes; and we soon anchored amongst them off Bridgetown. Many merchants and planters now came on board, though it was in the evening. They put us in separate parcels, and examined us attentively. They also made us jump, and pointed to the land, signifying we were to go there. . . . We were not many days in the merchant's custody before we were sold after their usual manner, which is this: On a signal given, (as the beat of a drum) the buyers rush at once into the yard where the slaves are confined, and make choice of that parcel they like best. The noise and clamor with which this is attended and the eagerness visible in the countenances of the buyers, serve not a little to increase the apprehensions of the terrified Africans, who may well be supposed to consider them as the ministers of that destruction to which they think themselves devoted. In this manner, without scruple, are relations and friends separated, most of them never to see each other again. I remember in the vessel in which I was brought over, in the men's apartment, there were several brothers, who, in the sale, were sold in different lots; and it was very moving on this occasion to see and hear their cries at parting. O, ye nominal Christians! might not an African ask you, learned you this from your God who says unto you, Do unto all men as you would men should do unto you?

DISCUSSION QUESTIONS

1. What are Equiano's impressions of the white men on the ship and their treatment of the slaves? How does this treatment reflect the slave traders' primary concerns?

2. What message do you think Equiano sought to convey to his readers? Based on this message, to whom do you think his book especially appealed?

3. What do the last lines of this excerpt suggest about the connection between Equiano and the abolitionists' use of Christianity in their arguments against slavery?

2. A "Sober and Wholesome Drink"

SOURCES IN CONVERSATION | *A Brief Description of the Excellent Vertues of That Sober and Wholesome Drink, Called Coffee* (1674) and *The Coffee House Mob* (1710)

The expansion of the slave trade in the late seventeenth and eighteenth centuries was directly linked to Europeans' appetite for the commodities the labor of enslaved people produced, including coffee. With the drink came the rise of a new type of gathering place, the coffeehouse. In 1652, a Greek merchant who had learned to make coffee while working in a Turkish trading port opened the first coffeehouse in western Europe in London. Long a tradition in the Islamic world, the number of coffeehouses in London — and eventually all over Europe — exploded when western European trading nations moved into the business of coffee production. Coffeehouses became places for men to meet for company and conversation, often with a political bent. The broadsheet transcribed here illuminates the origins of European coffeehouse culture as merchants sought to entice customers to partake in the

Transcription of original, as reproduced in Markman Ellis, ed., *Eighteenth-Century Coffee-House Culture*, vol. 1, *Restoration Satire* (London: Pickering & Chatto, 2006), 129.

sociability of the coffeehouse. Composed of two poems, the broadsheet was printed in 1674, most likely as an advertisement for coffee, coffeehouses, and the retail coffee business of Paul Greenwood situated in the heart of London's textile district. The first poem contrasts the detrimental effects of alcohol with the "sober and merry" effects of coffee. The second describes the rules of behavior coffeehouse patrons were expected to follow. Scholars have suggested that, despite its slightly satirical tone, the poem is an accurate portrayal of the regulations governing coffeehouses. However, the engraving "The Coffee House Mob" indicates that these regulations may not always have been followed. It shows men in a coffeehouse drinking coffee, reading newspapers, and violently arguing—one patron even splashes his coffee into the face of another! For opponents of coffeehouse culture, including Edward Ward, the author of the book in which the engraving appeared, the coffeehouse fostered uncivil and even seditious behavior, not reasoned discussion.

A Brief Description of the Excellent Vertues of that Sober and Wholesome Drink, called Coffee, and its incomparable effects in preventing or curing most diseases incident to humane bodies (London, printed for Paul Greenwood . . . who selleth the best Arabian Coffee-Powder and Chocolate, made in Cake or in Roll, after the Spanish Fashion, &c., 1674).[1]

When the sweet Poison of the Treacherous Grape,
Had Acted on the world a General Rape;
Drowning our very Reason and our Souls
In such deep Seas of large o'reflowing Bowls,
That New Philosophers Swore they could feel
The Earth to Stagger, as her Sons did Reel:
When Foggy Ale, leavying up mighty Trains
Of muddy Vapors, had besieg'd our Brains;
And Drink, Rebellion, and Religion too,
Made Men so Mad, they knew not what to do;
Then Heaven in Pity, to Effect our Cure,
And stop the Ragings of that Calenture,
First sent amongst us this All-*healing-Berry*,
At once to make us both *Sober* and *Merry*.
　　Arabian coffee, a Rich Cordial
To Purse and Person Beneficial,
Which of so many Vertues doth partake
Its Country's called *Felix* for its sake.[2]
From the Rich Chambers of the Rising Sun,

---

[1]**Chocolate, made in Cake or in Roll, after the Spanish Fashion:** chocolate is made from the fermented, roasted, and ground beans of the cocoa tree (*Theobroma cacao*). Imported from Spanish America, chocolate was sold as a bitter paste made up into small cylindrical cakes or rolls, which were used in the preparation of hot drinks with the addition of water, sugar, and sometimes eggs. Only in the nineteenth century was eating chocolate developed.
[2]**Country's called Felix:** Arabia Felix (Arabia the happy), the name of one of three zones of the Arabian peninsula in classical geography, roughly corresponding to modern Yemen.

. . .

COFFEE arrives, that Grave and wholesome Liquor,
That heals the Stomack, makes the Genius quicker,
Relieves the Memory, Revives the Sad,
And cheers the Spirits, without making Mad;

. . .

Its constant Use the sullenest Griefs will Rout,
Remove the Dropsie, gives ease to the Gout,[3]

. . .

A Friendly Entercourse[4] it doth Maintain
Between the Heart, the Liver, and the Brain,

. . .

Nor have the LADIES reason to Complain,
As fumbling Doe-littles[5] are apt to Faign;
COFFEE's no Foe to their obliging Trade,
By it Men rather are more active made;
'Tis stronger Drink, and base adulterate Wine;
Enfeebles Vigor, and makes Nature Pine;
Loaden with which, th' Impotent Sott is Led
Like a Sowe'd Hogshead to a Misses Bed;[6]
But this Rare Settle-Brain prevents those Harms,[7]
Conquers Old Sherry, and brisk Claret Charms.
Sack, I defie thee with an open Throat,
Whilst Truly COFFEE is my Antedote

. . .

The RULES and ORDERS of the COFFEE-HOUSE.[8]
Enter Sirs Freely, But first if you please,

---

[3]**Dropsie . . . Gout**: dropsy, a morbid condition characterized by the accumulation of watery fluid in the serous cavities; gout, a disease characterized by the painful inflammation of the smaller joints (*Oxford English Dictionary*).
[4]**Entercourse**: intercourse, communication between something, here the heart, liver, and brain.
[5]**fumbling Doe-littles**: one who does little, a lazy person (*OED*).
[6]**th' Impotent . . . to a Misses Bed**: a complicated disparagement: a sot is one who dulls or stupefies himself with drink, here to the state of impotence, who must be induced to visit a young woman's bed, like a pickled or soused pig's head (an unwieldy and unrewarding dish).
[7]**Settle-Brain**: something that calms the brain (*OED*).
[8]**The RULES . . . COFFEE-HOUSE**: an ironic title for a satire on coffee-house sociability. "Rules and Orders" is a commonplace phrase in legal discourse, signifying the administrative regulations of certain judicial institutions, especially courts of law, or the body of rules followed by an assembly.

Peruse our Civil-Orders,[9] which are these.
First, Gentry, Tradesmen, all are welcome hither,
And may without Affront sit down Together:
Pre-eminence of Place, none here should Mind,[10]
But take the next fit Seat that he can find:
Nor need any, if Finer Persons come,
Rise up for to assigne to them his Room;
To limit Mens Expense, we think not fair,
But let him forfeit Twelve-pence that shall Swear:
He that shall any Quarrel begin,
Shall give each Man a Dish t' Atone the Sin;
And so shall He, whose Complements extend
So far to drink in COFFEE to his Friend;
Let Noise of loud Disputes be quite forborn,
No Maudlin Lovers[11] here in Corners Mourn,
But all be Brisk, and Talk, but not too much
On Sacred things, Let none presume to touch,
Nor Profane Scripture, or sawcily wrong
Affairs of State[12] with an Irreverent Tongue:
Let Mirth be Innocent, an each Man see,
That all his Jests without Reflection be;
To keep the House more Quiet, and from Blame,
We Banish hence Cards, Dice, and every Game:
Nor can allow of Wagers, that Exceed
Five shillings, which oft-times much Trouble Breed;
Let all that's lost, or forfeited be spent
In such Good Liquor as the House doth Vent,
And Customers endeavor to their Powers,
For to observe still seasonable Howers.
Lastly, let each Man what he calls for Pay,
And so you're welcome to come every Day.

---

[9]**Civil-Orders**: the civil laws. A term in legal debate current in the period.

[10]**Pre-eminence of Place, none here should Mind**: seats around the table in the coffee room were not organized hierarchically, referring to the custom in coffee-houses, that each man should take the next free seat around the table.

[11]**Maudlin Lovers**: men who discuss their illicit gallantries and amors in a mawkish or sentimental manner, one of the ordeals of the coffee-house.

[12]**Affairs of State**: transactions concerning the state or nation, politics. The coffee-houses had come to be emblematic locations for debate on public affairs by those outside the court and ministry, where it was still assumed that ordinary people did not need to know about the state and its affairs.

Engraving by Edward Ward, from "Vulgus Britannicus," 1710 / Private Collection / Bridgeman Images

DISCUSSION QUESTIONS

1. What does the imprint of the broadsheet, which lists where and by whom the poem was printed, suggest about changing consumption patterns at the time and their links to Europe's growing worldwide economic connections?

2. According to the first poem, what were the medicinal effects of coffee? How might these effects have contributed to coffeehouses' growing popularity?

3. Based on the "Rules and Orders," what type of people frequented early coffeehouses? How would you describe their social interactions there?

4. Describe the scene in the engraving *The Coffee House Mob*. Based on this scene, why do you think coffeehouse rules legislated against swearing, disputes, and noise in coffeehouses?

3. A Domestic Drink

Richard Collins, *A Family at Tea* (c. 1726)

Rowdy or not, coffeehouses became a permanent fixture in seventeenth-century masculine public life. By contrast, tea, originally an exclusive import from China and later a product of British East India Company trade and of the plantation economy, was integrated into

Painting by Richard Collins, c. 1727 / Victoria and Albert Museum, London, UK / DEA Picture Library / AGE Fotostock

Acknowledg...

TEXT CREDITS
Bracketed num...

Chapter 1
  [1.1] *Epic of...*
tion by N. K. S...
1960, 1964, and...
  [1.2] *The Co...*
to the Old Test...
Princeton Univ...
conveyed throu...
  [1.3] *Hymn t...*
Kingdom, pp. 9...
permission of t...
  [1.4] *Egyptia...*
ume 2, *The Nev...*
fornia. Reprint...
  [1.5] *The "1...*
ed., *Ancient Ne...*
© 1950, 1955, ...
Princeton Univ...

Chapter 2
  [2.1] *Inscripti...*
ern Texts Relati...
renewed 1978 b...
Press; permissic...
  [2.6] Xenoph...
and the Trustee...
Volume 183, tr...
published 1925...
Library® is a regi...

Chapter 3
  [3.5] *Property...*
and Historical L...
Matthew Dillon...
Taylor & Francis...
  [3.6] *Euphilet...*
and Other Trials...
Hackett Publishi...
  [3.6b] *House...*
Slope of Areopa...
"Women and H...
Antiquity, edited...
by permission of...
  [3.7] Excerpt...
Lysistrata, ed. an...
sion of Liverpoo...

women's private domestic domains. Not only was tea a luxury item during this time, but the way of serving and drinking it also came to be seen as a hallmark of female refinement. The conversation piece, a type of portrait painting that became fashionable in the 1720s and early 1730s in England, illuminates the link between women, femininity, and tea forged during this time. Rather than portraying its subjects in formal or idealized settings, conversation pieces shifted attention to men, women, and children engaged in simple pleasures inside the home, including the drinking of tea. The subject matter of A Family at Tea *by Richard Collins is typical of the genre. It depicts a well-off family seated around a tea table and prominently displays their expensive silver and porcelain tea equipage: a sugar dish, a tea canister, sugar tongs, a hot-water jug, a spoon boat with teaspoons, a slop bowl, and a teapot. The composition of the painting highlights the manner in which the family consumes their tea, with the woman placed prominently alongside the tea table to showcase her role as beacon of civility, high social standing, and domestic calm.*

DISCUSSION QUESTIONS

1. Note the variation in the positions of the three figures, including the direction of their gazes. In what ways do these differences visually emphasize the woman's place of importance within the tableaux?

2. While in practice children were excluded from tea parties, they were frequently included in conversation piece paintings such as Rollins's. What role might the child play in the composition of the painting and the message the artist sought to convey?

3. Based on this painting, what type of life did tea and tea drinking embody during this period?

4. Westernizing Russian Culture

Peter I, *Decrees and Statutes* (1701–1723)

During the eighteenth century, European states turned much of their attention to the political and military scene burgeoning within Europe, vying to keep one step ahead of their rivals. Russian tsar Peter I (r. 1689–1725) was especially successful at this game, transforming Russia into a formidable European power with all the trappings of an absolutist state, including a strong army and centralized bureaucracy. After spending time abroad, notably in England and the Dutch Republic, Peter came to admire western European technology, commerce, and customs and worked relentlessly to refashion Russia accordingly. For him, Westernization was more than an act of admiration; it provided him with powerful tools for enhancing Russia's status on the European stage. Below are several decrees and a statute he issued seeking to reform various aspects of Russian life and society, all with the aim of bringing them more in line with western European models.

From *A Source Book for Russian History from Early Times to 1917,* vol. 2, ed. George Vernadsky (New Haven, CT: Yale University Press, 1972), 347, 357–58, and Eugene Schuyler, *Peter the Great: Emperor of Russia* (New York: Charles Scribner's Sons, 1884), 140–41.

Chapter 4

[4.1] *The Campaigns of Alexander the Great* (Fourth Century B.C.E.): From Arrian, *The Campaigns of Alexander,* trans. Aubrey de Sélincourt, revised with an introduction and notes by J. R. Hamilton (Penguin Classics, 1958; revised edition, 1971). Copyright © The Estate of Aubrey de Sélincourt, 1958. Introduction and notes copyright © J. R. Hamilton, 1971. Reproduced by permission of Penguin Books Ltd. and David Higham Associates Ltd.

[4.2] Zeno, Egyptian Official, *Records* (259–250 B.C.E.): Reprinted by permission of the publishers and the Trustees of the Loeb Classical Library from *Select Papyri: Volume I,* Loeb Classical Library Volume 266, translated by A. S. Hunt and C. C. Edgar. Cambridge, Mass.: Harvard University Press. First published 1932. Loeb Classical Library® is a registered trademark of the President and Fellows of Harvard College.

[4.3] *Funerary Inscriptions and Epitaphs* (Fifth–First Centuries B.C.E.): From Mary R. Lefkowitz and Maureen B. Fant, eds., *Women's Life in Greece and Rome,* 2nd ed, epitaphs #36, 37, 38, 42, 254, 275, 333, 363, 376, and 379. Copyright © 1982, 1992 M. B. Fant and M. R. Lefkowitz. Reprinted with the permission of The Johns Hopkins University Press and Bristol Classical Press, an imprint of Bloomsbury Publishing Plc.

[4.6] Marcus Vitruvius Pollio, *Archimedes' "Eureka!" Moment* (c. 30–20 B.C.E.): From *Vitruvius: Ten Books on Architecture,* edited by Ingrid D. Rowland and Thomas Noble, translated by Ingrid D. Rowland. Copyright © Cambridge University Press 1999. Reprinted with the permission of Cambridge University Press.

Chapter 5

[5.1] *The Twelve Tables* (451–449 B.C.E.): Excerpted from Allan Chester Johnson, Paul Robinson Coleman-Norton, and Frank Card Bourne, *Ancient Roman Statutes: A Translation with Introduction, Commentary, Glossary, and Index,* pp. 9–17. Copyright © 1961. Courtesy of the University of Texas Press.

[5.3] *Roman Women Demonstrate against the Oppian Law* (195 B.C.E.): Reprinted by permission of the publishers and the Trustees of the Loeb Classical Library from *Livy: Volume IX,* Loeb Classical Library 295, translated by Evan T. Sage, Cambridge, Mass.: Harvard University Press. First published 1935. Loeb Classical Library® is a registered trademark of the President and Fellows of Harvard College.

[5.4] Cicero, *In Defense of Archias* (62 B.C.E.): From *Ancient Rome: An Anthology of Sources,* edited and translated by Christopher Francese and R. Scott Smith. Copyright © 2014 by Hackett Publishing. Reprinted by permission of Hackett Publishing Company, Inc. All rights reserved.

Chapter 6

[6.1] Virgil, *The Aeneid* (First Century B.C.E.): From "Book Six: The Kingdom of the Dead," from *Virgil: The Aeneid* by Virgil, translated by Robert Fagles. Copyright © 2006 by Robert Fagles. Used by permission of Viking Books, an imprint of Penguin Publishing Group, a division of Penguin Random House LLC. All rights reserved. Any third-party use of this material, outside of this publication, is prohibited. Interested parties must apply directly to Penguin Random House LLC for permission.

[6.2] *Notices and Graffiti Describe Life in Pompeii* (First Century C.E.): From *Roman Civilization: Selected Readings,* Vol. 2: *The Empire,* Third Edition, edited by Naphtali Lewis and Meyer Reinhold. Copyright © 1990 by Columbia University Press. Reprinted by permission of Columbia University Press.

[6.5] *The Martyrdom of Saints Perpetua and Felicitas* (203 C.E.): From Herbert Musurillo, trans., *The Acts of the Christian Martyrs* (Oxford University Press, 1972). Copyright © 1972. By permission of Oxford University Press.

Chapter 7

[7.2] Augustine of Hippo, *Confessions* (c. 397 C.E.): From *Confessions* by Saint Augustine, translated with an introduction by R. S. Pine-Coffin (Penguin Classics, 1961). Copyright © R. S. Pine-Coffin, 1961. Reproduced by permission of Penguin Books Ltd. (UK).

[7.3] Benedict of Nursia, *The Rule of Saint Benedict* (c. 540 C.E.): From *RB 1980: The Rule of St. Benedict, in Latin and English with Notes*, ed. Timothy Fry. Copyright © 1981 by Order of Saint Benedict, Inc. Published by Liturgical Press, Collegeville, Minnesota. Reprinted by permission.

[7.5] *The Burgundian Code* (c. 475–525 C.E.): From *The Burgundian Code*, translated by Katherine Fischer Drew. Copyright © 1972 by the University of Pennsylvania Press. Reprinted by permission of the University of Pennsylvania Press.

Chapter 8

[8.1] Qur'an, *Suras 1 (the Fatihah), 53:1–18 (the Star), 98 (the Testament)* (c. 610–632): From *Approaching the Qur'an: The Early Revelations*, introduced and translated by Michael Sells (Ashland, OR: White Cloud Press, 1999). Copyright © 1999. Reprinted by permission of the publisher.

[8.4] *The Life of Lady Balthild, Queen of the Franks* (Late Seventh Century): From *Late Merovingian France: History and Hagiography, 640–720*, edited by Paul Fouracre and Richard A. Gerberding. Copyright © 1996 Manchester University Press. Reprinted by permission of Manchester University Press; permission conveyed through Copyright Clearance Center, Inc.

Chapter 9

[9.2] Liutprand of Cremona, *Report to Otto I* (968): From *The Works of Liudprand of Cremona*, translated by F. A. Wright. Copyright 1930, G. Routledge & Sons, Ltd. Reproduced by permission of Taylor & Francis Books UK.

[9.3] Ahmad al-Ya'qūbī, *Kitāb al-buldā* (Ninth Century): From Bernard Lewis, ed. and trans., *Islam from the Prophet Muhammad to the Capture of Constantinople*, vol. 2 (New York: Walker & Co., 1974). Copyright © 1974. Reprinted by permission of Oxford University Press.

Chapter 10

[10.1] *Commenda Contracts* (Eleventh–Twelfth Centuries): From *Medieval Trade in the Mediterranean World:* Number LII of the *Records of Civilization, Sources and Studies*, edited by Austin P. Evans and translated by Robert S. Lopez and Irving W. Raymond. Copyright © 1961 by Columbia University Press. Reprinted by permission of Columbia University Press.

[10.2] *Henry IV: Letter to Gregory VII* (1076): From *The Correspondence of Pope Gregory VII*, translated by Ephraim Emerton. Copyright 1932, © 1990 by Columbia University Press. Reprinted by permission of Columbia University Press.

[10.2b] *Gregory VII: Excommunication of Henry IV:* From *Imperial Lives and Letters of the Eleventh Century*, translated by Theodor E. Mommsen and Karl F. Morrison and edited by Robert L. Benson. Copyright © 1962 by Columbia University Press. Reprinted by permission of the publisher and Karl Morrison.

[10.4] Ibn al-Athīr, *A Muslim Perspective* (1097–1099): From Ibn al-Athīr, *The Chronicle of Ibn al-Athīr for the Crusading Period from al-Kamil fi'l-Ta'rikh*, part 1, translated by D. S. Richard. Copyright © 2006 Ashgate Publishing. Reproduced by permission of Taylor & Francis Books UK.

[10.5] *The Anglo-Saxon Chronicle* (1085–1086): Excerpted from pp. 161–65 in *The Anglo-Saxon Chronicle*, translated by Dorothy Whitelock. Copyright © 1961. Republished by permission of Rutgers University Press; permission conveyed through Copyright Clearance Center, Inc.

Chapter 11

[11.1] Peter Abelard, *The Story of My Misfortunes* (c. 1132): From *The Letters of Abelard and Heloise*, translated by Betty Radice, revised by M. T. Clanchy (Penguin Classics, 1974, 2003). Copyright © Betty Radice, 1974. Reproduced by permission of Penguin Books Ltd.

[11.2] *Students at Oxford Write to Their Parents for Money:* From *Lost Letters of Medieval Life: English Society, 1200–1250,* edited and translated by Martha Carlin and David Crouch. Copyright © 2013 by the University of Pennsylvania Press. Reprinted by permission of the University of Pennsylvania Press.

[11.3] Chrétien de Troyes, *Lancelot: The Knight of the Cart* (c. 1170s): From *Lancelot: The Knight of the Cart* by Chrétien de Troyes, edited and translated by Burton Raffel. Copyright © 1997 by Yale University. Reprinted by permission of Yale University Press.

[11.5] From *Clare's Testament*: From *Francis and Clare: The Complete Works,* from the Classics of Western Spirituality Series, translated by Regis J. Armstrong, O.F.M. CAP, and Ignatius C. Brady, O.F.M. Copyright © 1982 by Paulist Press, Inc., New York; Mahwah, NJ. Republished with permission of Paulist Press; permission conveyed through Copyright Clearance Center, Inc.

Chapter 12

[12.2] Hadewijch of Brabant, *Letters and Poems*: From *Medieval Women Writers,* edited by Katharina M. Wilson. Copyright © 1984 by the University of Georgia Press. Reprinted by permission of the University of Georgia Press.

[12.4] Dante Alighieri, *Divine Comedy* (1313–1321): Canto II, from *The Inferno of Dante: A New Verse Translation* by Robert Pinsky. Translation copyright © 1994 by Robert Pinsky. Reprinted by permission of Farrar, Straus and Giroux.

[12.5] King Philip IV of France, *General Assembly of Paris,* 1303. From *Medieval Europe,* edited by Julius Kirshner and Karl F. Morrison. University of Chicago Press. Copyright © 1986 by the University of Chicago. Reprinted by permission.

Chapter 13

[13.1] *The Black Death* (Fourteenth Century): From *The Black Death,* edited and translated by Rosemary Horrox. Copyright © 1994. Reprinted by permission of Manchester University Press; permission conveyed through Copyright Clearance Center, Inc.

[13.2] *Jean Froissart on the Jacquerie* (1358): From Froissart, *Chronicles,* edited and translated by Geoffrey Brereton (Penguin Classics 1976; revised 1978), 151–55. Translation copyright © Geoffrey Brereton, 1968. Reproduced by permission of Penguin Books Ltd.

[13.3] Geoffrey Chaucer, *The Pardoner's Prologue* (1387–1400): From *The Canterbury Tales,* translated by Nevill Coghill. Translation copyright © 1951, 1958, 1960, 1975, 1977 by Nevill Coghill. Used by permission of Penguin Classics, an imprint of Penguin Publishing Group, a division of Penguin Random House LLC. All rights reserved. Any third-party use of this material, outside of this publication, is prohibited. Interested parties must apply directly to Penguin Random House LLC for permission.

[13.5] Giovanni Rucellai, "*A Merchant's Praise of Florence*": From Stefano Ugo Baldassarri and Arielle Saiber, eds., *Images of Quattrocento Florence: Selected Writings in Literature, History, and Art.* Copyright © 2000 by Yale University. Reprinted by permission of Yale University Press.

[13.6] Alessandra, *Letters from a Widow and Matriarch of a Great Family* (1450–1465): From Eric Cochrane and Julius Kirshner, eds., *University of Chicago Readings in Western Civilization,* Vol. 5: *The Renaissance.* University of Chicago Press. Copyright © 1986 by the University of Chicago. Reprinted by permission.

[13.7] Bartolommeo Faxzio, *On Famous Men* (1456): From *Northern Renaissance Art, 1400–1600: Sources and Documents,* 1st ed., edited by Wolfgang Stechow. Copyright © 1966 by Prentice-Hall, Inc. Reprinted by permission of Pearson Education, Inc., New York, New York.

Chapter 14

[14.3] Bartolomé de Las Casas, *In Defense of the Indians* (c. 1548–1550): From *In Defense of the Indians,* translated by Stafford Poole. Copyright © 1974 by Northern Illinois University Press. Used with the permission of Northern Illinois University Press.

[14.5] *Genevan Consistory Records:* Excerpt from *Registers of the Consistory of Geneva in the Time of Calvin,* Volume 1, *1542–1544,* ed. Thomas A. Lambert and Isabella M. Watt, trans. M. Wallace McDonald, pp. 13, 155, 161–62, 252. Copyright © 2002. Reprinted by permission of the publisher.

[14.6] St. Ignatius of Loyola, *A New Kind of Catholicism* (1546, 1549, 1553): From Saint Ignatius of Loyola, *Personal Writings: Reminiscences, Spiritual Diary, Select Letters, Including the Text of The Spiritual Exercises* (New York: Penguin Classics, 1996), edited and translated by Joseph A. Munitiz and Philip Endean. Translation, introductions, and notes copyright © Joseph A. Munitiz and Philip Endean, 1996. Reproduced by permission of Penguin Books Ltd.

Chapter 15

[15.3] *Apology of the Bohemian Estates* (May 25, 1618): From *The Thirty Years War: A Documentary History,* edited and translated by Tryntje Helfferich. Copyright © 2009 by Hackett Publishing Company, Inc. Reprinted by permission of Hackett Publishing Company, Inc. All rights reserved.

[15.5] Galileo, *Letter to the Grand Duchess Christina* (1615): From *Discoveries and Opinions of Galileo* by Galileo, trans. Stillman Drake. Translation copyright © 1957 by Stillman Drake. Used by permission of Doubleday, an imprint of the Knopf Doubleday Publishing Group, a division of Penguin Random House LLC. All rights reserved. Any third-party use of this material, outside of this publication, is prohibited. Interested parties must apply directly to Penguin Random House LLC for permission.

[15.6] *The Trial of Suzanne Gaudry* (1652): From Alan C. Kors and Edward Peters, eds., *Witchcraft in Europe, 1100–1700: A Documentary History.* Copyright © 1972. Reprinted with the permission of the University of Pennsylvania Press.

Chapter 16

[16.5] Ludwig Fabritius, *The Revolt of Stenka Razin* (1670): From Anthony Glenn Cross, ed., *Russia under Western Eyes, 1517–1825* (New York: St. Martin's Press, 1971). Copyright © 1971. Reprinted by permission of Anthony Glenn Cross.

Chapter 17

[17.2] A *Brief Description of the Excellent Vertues of That Sober and Wholesome Drink, Called Coffee* (1674): From *Eighteenth-Century Coffee-House Culture,* vol. 1: *Restoration Satire,* edited by Markman Ellis. Copyright © 2006, Pickering & Chatto. Reproduced by permission of Taylor & Francis Books UK.

[17.4] Peter I, *Decrees:* From *A Source Book for Russian History from Early Times to 1917,* vol. 2, edited by George Vernadsky. Copyright © 1972 by Yale University. Reprinted by permission of Yale University Press.